Regulation Theory and Australian Capitalism

Studies in Social and Global Justice

Series Editors:

Ben Holland, Lecturer in International Relations, The University of Nottingham

Tony Burns, Associate Professor, The University of Nottingham

As transnational interactions become more prevalent and complex in our interconnected world, so do the questions of social justice that have often featured in political discourse. From new debates in human rights and global ethics to changing patterns of resistance and precarity in the global economy, via an interrogation of the impact of climate change, *Studies in Social and Global Justice* publishes books that grapple with a broad array of critical issues faced in the world today.

Labour and Transnational Action in Times of Crisis, edited by Andreas Bieler, Roland Erne, Darragh Golden, Idar Helle, Knut Kjeldstadli, Tiago Matos and Sabina Stan

A Human Right to Culture and Identity: The Ambivalence of Group Rights, by Janne Mende

Exploitation: From Practice to Theory, edited by Monique Deveaux and Vida Panitch

Social Institutions and the Politics of Recognition: From Hegel to the Present, by Anthony Burns (forthcoming)

Regulation Theory and Australian Capitalism, by Brett Heino

Regulation Theory and Australian Capitalism

Rethinking Social Justice and Labour Law

Brett Heino

ROWMAN &
LITTLEFIELD
INTERNATIONAL
London • New York

Published by Rowman & Littlefield International Ltd
Unit A, Whitacre Mews, 26–34 Stannary Street, London SE11 4AB
www.rowmaninternational.com

Rowman & Littlefield International Ltd is an affiliate of Rowman & Littlefield
4501 Forbes Boulevard, Suite 200, Lanham, Maryland 20706, USA
With additional offices in Boulder, New York, Toronto (Canada), and Plymouth (UK)
www.rowman.com

British Library Cataloguing in Publication Data
A catalogue record for this book is available from the British Library

ISBN: HB 978-1-7866-0355-5

Library of Congress Cataloging-in-Publication Data
Names: Heino, Brett, author.
Title: Regulation theory and Australian capitalism : rethinking social justice and labour law / Brett Heino.
Description: Lanham, Maryland : Rowman & Littlefield International, 2017. | Series: Studies in social and global justice | Includes bibliographical references and index.
Identifiers: LCCN 2017040649 (print) | LCCN 2017041120 (ebook) | ISBN 9781786603579 (Electronic) | ISBN 9781786603555 (cloth : alk. paper)
Subjects: LCSH: Labor laws and legislation—Australia. | Social Justice—Australia. | Social justice. | Labor laws and legislation.
Classification: LCC KU1224 (ebook) | LCC KU1224 .H45 2017 (print) | DDC 344.9401—dc23
LC record available at https://lccn.loc.gov/2017040649

The paper used in this publication meets the minimum requirements of American National Standard for Information Sciences—Permanence of Paper for Printed Library Materials, ANSI/NISO Z39.48–1992.

Printed in the United States of America

Contents

Acknowledgements

This book would not have been possible without the help I have received from many quarters. I am deeply indebted to Associate Professor Andrew Frazer, whose encyclopaedic mind, ability to recall the most amazing range of facts and high standards have been invaluable in guiding my research and writing. I am equally grateful to Associate Professor Di Kelly, who supported the development of my ideas and bolstered my morale with her confidence in my overall vision.

I owe thanks to the many people who have helped me in conducting archive research. In particular, I would like to thank the staffs of the Noel Butlin Archives Centre, the State Library of New South Wales, the Fair Work Commission Library and the University of Wollongong Library.

I would also like to express my gratitude to my colleagues in the University of Wollongong School of Law, especially Yvonne Apolo, whose insights helped me identify and correct flaws and who provided valuable feedback in the development of my concepts. Thanks are also due to Dr. James Dahlstrom and Dr. Luke Gliganic, who were fellow travellers on this road.

Lastly, chief thanks belong to my wife and soulmate, Erin. It isn't too much to say that without her this book would not have happened.

Chapter 1

Introducing Labour Law

> The ever-changing forces of society incessantly mould and transform the law and yet it pretends to stand aloof and prides itself on its immutability in a tumultuous world. While it seems to be a spectator of the great social drama, serene and imperturbable, it suffers all the agonies and fights all the struggles of an actor in the play.[1]

There are a few components of a capitalist society that penetrate as deeply and profoundly into the lives of the people as law. Capitalism is legalised to a degree that is historically unprecedented. The very form of bourgeois law is premised on its universality and abstraction, a reality grasped by Kahn-Freund. In a society where everyone is considered an abstract, de-classed juridical citizen, law becomes the medium through which these citizens relate to each other and to the state. Within this pervasive and immensely powerful social force, labour law forms an especially crucial segment. The fact that within capitalism labour assumes a generalised commodity form means that the sale and purchase of labour power, together with the conditions on which it is exploited, becomes an explicitly legal matter. The resultant body of labour law is a most complex amalgam, with the law of 'things', namely property and contract law, attempting to commodify and regulate a living, breathing and thinking subject, the proletarian. This domain of law is an object of class struggle in its own right, as labour and capital attempt to impress their own competing political economies on the legal form.

Given this significance of labour law, the dramatic changes in the labour law regimes of many Western states since the 1980s are a matter of tremendous importance, particularly for the working class. This process of legal evolution has been a phenomenon with deep ramifications for social justice. The dissolution of productive industry, the fragmentation of employment categories, the rise of profound employment precarity and an increasingly hostile legal environment for trade unionism have been powerful impulses in the creation of key social justice issues, including income inequality, the rise of a new working underclass, entrenched unemployment and the marginalisation of organised labour.

Despite its importance, however, the nature of labour law change remains poorly theorised. The disciplines of labour law and industrial relations are largely beholden to an empiricist method, with the result that they are usually unable to explain why labour law has changed in the way it has, or elucidate the abstract functions it fulfils within different models of development. By contrast, the considerable body of political-economic work dealing with the evolution of capitalism in Western states over the past several decades typically pays scant attention to the issue of law beyond the descriptive account that neo-liberalism has been associated with legal change. This myopia is often a function of a lack of a sophisticated theory of law as a *specific form* of capitalist social relations. The role of labour law in helping constitute the process of capitalist crisis and transformation is elided in such accounts, with the result that the capacity of social justice activists to understand, let alone combat, these forces is severely limited.

It is in to this lacuna that this book steps. Combining the methodology and concepts of the Parisian Regulation Approach (PRA) with a Marxist jurisprudence I have constructed, this book seeks to create a model of labour law change that is both theoretically rigorous and empirically sensitive. In order to develop this model in its finest granularity, I have operationalised it in this book by a detailed study of Australian labour law from the end of World War II through the present day. In particular, I deploy the PRA to periodise Australian capitalism in this period into two models of development, which are historically specific crystallisations of capitalist social relations unifying an industrial paradigm, accumulation regime and mode of regulation. Within these models of development, and within the capitalist mode of production more generally, I argue that law is best conceived as a *juridic form* of capitalist production relations, rather than as a fundamentally a-capitalist institution determined by an economic base. Such a construction allows us to appreciate that law not only performs certain functions within a model of development, but also helps constitute its fabric, and is thus a legitimate arena of action for social justice advocates in and of itself.

Throughout this book I seek to restore to the study of labour law the engine of capitalist social relations and their evolution through class struggle. By the end, I will have shown that labour law 'suffers all the agonies and fights all the struggles of an actor in the play',[2] precisely because it *is* an actor in the capitalist ensemble. The waxing and waning of the class struggle, together with the historically variant character of capitalism's crisis tendencies, ensures that demands are made of the legal form that consistently threaten its integrity and mould its contours. Given its historically novel labour law system, these processes can be seen in particularly sharp relief in Australia. Indeed, there are few better examples of the intimate link between labour law and capitalist coherence, crisis and transformation. In particular, I will elucidate how labour law simultaneously helps constitute the coherence of particular models of development while at the same time contributing towards the particular crisis tendencies of those models. This is demonstrated through a rigorous hierarchy of abstraction, beginning with the most abstract roots of law in capitalist social relations, proceeding through a general history of labour law evolution in Australia using a regulationist periodisation schema, to specific case studies centred on the metals, food processing and retail sectors.

It is vital to note at the beginning that, although the model of labour law change is operationalised by application to the Australian context, it is of far broader compass, and can be employed in the study of labour law in other advanced capitalist economies. The over-arching Australian narrative matches, in broad outline, the experiences of other Western countries like the United States, the United Kingdom, New Zealand, Germany and Sweden. Although each state has its own distinct matrix of economic, political and cultural forces and institutions, many of the same legal themes can be found across all. This book thus represents more than a localised study of Australian capitalism; instead, it highlights the key role of labour law within the models of development that have characterised advanced capitalist states since World War II, and demonstrates the rich potential for legal analysis from within the regulationist project. In so doing, it integrates the economic, political and legal/state dimensions of capitalist transformation in a much deeper, more organic fashion than is currently the case in mainstream legal and political economic scholarship.

STRUCTURE OF THE BOOK

My departure point is chapter 2, where the PRA is introduced and analysed. This chapter explores the historical origins of the approach, as well as elucidating some of its key concepts, including 'industrial paradigm', 'accumulation regime', 'mode of regulation' and 'model of development'. I argue that a model of development, the most embracing regulationist concept, is ideally placed to deliver the PRA's promise of a sophisticated intermediate-level account of capitalist development and crisis, cognisant of the abstract, long-run tendencies of capitalism identified by Marx yet able to account for stabilising forces in the short to medium term. The criticisms of the approach are discussed and addressed. The most serious of these, namely an increasingly eclectic theoretical framework cut free from its Marxist foundations and an inadequate treatment of the state and law, are given special attention. Through a reconnection with its Marxist heritage and an acknowledgement of capital as having juridic, as well as economic, forms, these challenges can be met.

The conception of capitalism as having a multifaceted economic and juridical existence is the platform for chapter 3. The chapter begins by tracing the treatment of law in the works of Marx and Engels. Although they never focused on law in a systematic way, their best accounts of it demonstrate that they regarded law as a strange creature, whose form and content is structured by capitalist relations of production and exchange, and the class struggle underpinning them. Building upon the work of scholars such as Pashukanis, Fine, and Kay and Mott, I argue that the most basic cell of the legal form, the owner of private property, is common to all societies, capitalist or pre-capitalist, with large-scale commodity exchange. However, it is only with the development of capitalist production relations that there emerges the specifically bourgeois legal form, an axiomatic system of abstract, universal and formal norms regulating juridically equal citizen-subjects. Most importantly, the commodification of labour-power ensures that law becomes a proper object of class struggle in its own right, as the competing political economies of labour and capital attempt to impress themselves on the legal form. As a result of this process, the fabric of the legal form, woven out of abstract equality and the de-classed juridical citizen, can become rent and torn, unable to contain the *collective* interests of workers. Proletarian struggle can force the state to plug these gaps with administrative solutions, producing institutions and practices which take as their reference point collective subjects such as industrial organisations, and whose subject matter is often specific. I argue law and administration form two poles of a law-administration continuum, whose exact configuration is intimately tied to a model of development. In particular, the method in which the latter handles and orders the contradictions of capitalism, derives coherence and embeds or excludes working-class power to varying degrees fixes the nexus point of this continuum.

Chapter 4 takes the theoretical union of the PRA and Marxist legal theory established in the preceding chapters and applies them, both broadly and to the Australian context more specifically. I periodise post–World War II Australian capitalism into two distinct models of development, separated by a period of profound crisis and institutional searching: antipodean Fordism, stretching from 1945 to the early 1970s; and liberal-productivism, which had begun to cohere in the late 1980s and early 1990s and remains on foot today. I elucidate the way in which each model of development handles the abstract crisis tendencies of capitalism, orders different institutional forms, achieves coherence and carries latent within it fresh seeds of crisis. In these processes, labour law is absolutely central. I argue that both antipodean Fordism and liberal-productivism are characterised by unique labour law regimes that not only perform certain abstract functions within their models of development but also in fact help constitute their physiology. Labour law features here not as a passive reflection of an economic base, but as a specific juridic form of capital that imparts its own logic and crisis tendencies within a model of development.

Chapters 5 and 6 provide the concrete legal history necessary to flesh out the abstract framework of labour law produced in chapter 4. In both chapters I explore labour law change over four key themes: wage fixation, forms of employment/flexibility, collectivism/individualism together with the scale of industrial relations and the broader legal matrix. Certain key years are selected as part of a 'slice' approach and are analysed according to the state of labour law vis-à-vis these themes. Each period represents a crucial point in the process of political-economic transformation. Chapter 5 focuses on the nature of the antipodean Fordist labour law regime, both *en régulation* and in crisis. I will demonstrate that it helped constitute and maintain the coherence of antipodean Fordism, but at the cost of generating its own crisis tendencies. Chapter 6, by contrast, traces the development of the liberal-productivist labour law regime, which emerged out of a long and often contradictory process of institutional searching in the 1980s. Although pregnant with its own contradictions, it provisionally answered the dysfunctionalities of its antipodean Fordist predecessor.

A series of case studies in chapters 7, 8 and 9 sharpen some of the key claims made in chapters 4, 5 and 6. In chapter 7, I trace the ascent and decline of the antipodean Fordist cycle of wage and conditions flow-on centred on the metal trades sector, one of the central dynamics of the antipodean Fordist wage-labour nexus. Labour law played an absolutely crucial role in constituting this cycle through institutionalising the metal awards at the apex of the award pyramid and facilitating flow-on between different sectors through 'comparative wage justice' claims. The growing dysfunctionality of this circuit proved to be one of the key levers of antipodean Fordist crisis in the 1970s and early 1980s. As the economic dynamism of the metals sector waned, its continued institutional role as a leader helped stoke large wage rounds that destabilised the wage structure and ate into the profit share of capital. The destruction of this cycle is a key moment in the formation of a liberal-productivist labour law regime, which instead separates the industrially strong from the weak and stymies industry-level bargaining. The Accord between the Australian Council of Trade Unions and the Labor government in the 1980s and the movement to enterprise bargaining in the early 1990s proved key forces in this process.

In chapter 8, the content of award restructuring and enterprise bargaining in the food processing sector is investigated. This sector has been selected for study precisely because it has been one of the most affected by liberal-productivist norms of precarity and international competition. After a more-or-less archetypical pattern of industrial regulation within antipodean Fordism, the industry was hit hard by forces fundamental to the new liberal-productivist model of development, including intensified international competition, rationalisation of production and the increasing domination of multinational corporations. In such an environment, award restructuring and enterprise bargaining effected profound change in the sector. Of particular importance is the extent to which both processes served to implant the precarity, intensified managerial prerogative and work reorganisation central to the liberal-productivist wage-labour nexus and industrial paradigm.

Chapter 9 explores much the same processes as chapter 8, but in the context of the New South Wales retail sector. Unlike the case of the food processing sector, retail proved a laggard when it came to crystallising an antipodean Fordist wage-labour nexus, particularly given that the working-time arrangements characterising the standard employment model were only achieved on the cusp of Fordist crisis. However, by dint of this fact and the broader economic restructuring of Australian capitalism, the retail sector precociously enshrined the liberal-productivist wage-labour nexus of increased precarity and intensification of labour stripped of the *quid pro quo* of job security, rising remuneration and internal labour markets of antipodean Fordism (making it a particularly important object of regulationist study). In the early to late 1980s, these impulses were refracted through the still-dominant award system, with the process of institutional searching generating a new quasi-administrative tribunal combining the juridical structure of arbitration with a corporatist practice. In the late 1980s, 1990s and 2000s, however, award restructuring, enterprise bargaining and statutory individual contracts effected much the same outcomes as in the food processing sector, namely, precarity, heightened managerial control over the labour process and deployment of labour, and increasingly fragmented and polarised wage and conditions outcomes. The fact that such similar outcomes and patterns emerge in two completely different industries strengthens the theory of transition forwarded in this book, demonstrating that liberal-productivist tendencies have taken hold of the workforce at large.

Finally, in chapter 10, I conclude by summarising my findings, discussing the usefulness of the approach I have taken (particularly in terms of its application to other political-economic contexts) and exploring some potential political implications.

Chapter 2

The Parisian Regulation Approach

If we take seriously the need to locate labour law within the broader spectrum of capitalist economic, social and political relations, then four broad areas of inquiry for a Marxist perspective are of signal importance. These are:

1. The operation of the circuit of capital, with particular emphasis upon the inherently contradictory and unstable process of accumulation this sets in train;
2. The form, functions and operation of the state in capitalist society;
3. The organisation of the capitalist labour process, particularly how it is arranged to beget surplus value; and, most importantly,
4. The role of law in the constitution, regulation and maintenance of capitalist society, both in terms of its content and the specificity of the legal form.

It is important to note that these distinctions are to an extent arbitrary and a product of the balkanisation of economics, politics and law that evolved throughout the late nineteenth and twentieth centuries. This was not always so. Indeed, the early proponents of classical jurisprudence were in many cases the same pioneers of classical political economy, such as Smith, Hegel and Rousseau.

A reification of the disciplinary boundaries arising around these themes is also antithetical to a genuinely Marxist analysis of law. As Lebowitz states of Marx's methodology, 'Firstly, it is an emphasis on the "whole." Marx's goal was to understand bourgeois society as a totality, as an inter-connected whole'.[1] Lukács goes even further, elucidating the core of the revolutionary method Marx pioneered: 'The category of totality, the all-pervasive supremacy of the whole over the parts is the essence of the method which Marx took over from Hegel and brilliantly transformed into the foundations of a wholly new science'.[2]

The Marxist political economy that underlies this book thus demands an integration of capital, the state, the labour process and law as analytic categories. These must not be thought of as internally coherent and externally delimited fields, but as complex and ultimately interdependent structures, part of a basket of invariant features of the capitalist mode of production. It is in addressing this need for explanatory coherence that the Parisian Regulation Approach (PRA) proves its utility.

The PRA goes further than most alternative approaches (though not far enough, as we shall see) in theorising the interconnections between these four areas to provide a wide-ranging account of how the circuit of capital, particular state forms, a dominant labour process model and forms of regulation including law combine to produce and reproduce distinctive capitalist social formations.

Given the centrality of law to this book, the entire following chapter will be dedicated to unfolding the form and function of law, particularly labour law, in a capitalist society. The current chapter will focus on introducing, analysing and interrogating the PRA. In keeping with the need to move along the hierarchy of the abstract to the concrete, and in so doing generating conclusions of *both* theoretical rigour *and* empirical sensitivity, it is necessary to first outline the basic ontological and methodological parameters of the Marxist political economy on which the PRA has historically been grounded. I will then explicate the concepts used by regulationists to explain the articulations between capital, the state and the labour process. With this understanding in hand, I will then broaden the focus to both tackle criticisms of the PRA and indicate necessary theoretical additions to buttress the utility of the approach.

THE POLITICAL ECONOMY OF CAPITALISM

The PRA was founded on an essentially Marxist political economy. Thus, in the study of capitalist social formations, a theoretically informed regulationist analysis must begin with the contradictions inherent in the capitalist mode of production.

Before further analysis, it is necessary to put in hand a working, albeit incomplete, definition of capitalism. The capitalist mode of production is characterised by a basket of invariant core elements, in the absence of which it would be incorrect to speak of a capitalist society. Following Marx's method of logical abstraction, Neilson states: 'As a rational abstraction, private ownership, wage dependence, and the market define key institutions and norms that govern core capitalist production relations. In turn, these relations can be expressed as the exploitative capital-wage-labor relation, plus competition-based market coordination of production'.[3] I will have occasion to add to this definition later in the chapter, but it will suffice for now as the basis for deeper exploration.

Like preceding class societies (such as those founded on the slave or feudal modes of production), capitalism is based on exploitative class relations characterised by differential ownership of the surplus that human labour produces once a certain level of economic and social development is attained. Capitalism, however, is governed by a radically different modality of both producing and appropriating this surplus. Unlike, say, feudal peasants, who effectively possessed their own means of production, the capitalist labour process is premised upon the private ownership of these means of production by a class minority, the bourgeoisie. In turn, the majority of the population has no access to the means of production except through the medium of wage-labour. This makes for a system that formally demands both the present and continued compulsion of an essentially propertyless, wage-earning class (the proletariat), to sell their labour power in exchange for money and an inability of that class to reproduce itself except through purchasing commodities in the marketplace.

These requirements are intimately related to the method by which surplus labour is obtained and the form it takes. Feudal and slave exploitation was direct and specific, premised upon an explicit union of economic and political/legal coercion.[4] At the height of feudalism, the feudal lord extracted primarily surplus *goods*, which in turn was dependent upon the military strength they could muster under their banner; the moments of economic and extra-economic coercion constituted a unity.[5] Mature capitalism, by contrast, is historically unique, in that these moments are formally distinct (rooted in the divorce of the proletariat from the means of production) while the appropriation of surplus *value* (the difference between what workers are paid by employers and the value which they produce for them)[6] is mediated through a formally free contract operating in a labour market. This separation of economic and extra-economic coercion forms the basis of the distinction between the economic and political spheres that arises under capitalism and is the basis of the alienated, formally neutral, capitalist state.[7]

Marx identifies this unique mode of production as erected on the fundamentally contradictory character of the commodity as a (dis-)unity of use value and exchange value.[8] This tension, which underwrites real and fictitious commodities (e.g. labour) alike,[9] manifests itself in different forms at various stages in the circuit of capital, as it transitions between money, fixed capital and commodities. Jessop and Sum observe the full play of this process:

> The commodity is both an exchange value and a use value; the worker is both an abstract unit of labour power replaceable by other such units (or, indeed, other factors of production) and a concrete individual with specific skills, knowledge

> and creativity; the wage is both a cost of production and a source of demand; money functions both as an international currency and as national money; productive capital is both abstract value in motion (notably in the form of realized profits available for reinvestment) and a concrete stock of time-and-place-specific assets in the course of being valorized; and so forth.[10]

Given the contradictory character of the commodity (particularly in an economy of generalised commodity production) and the power asymmetry between workers and capital, this characterisation of the paradoxical nature of the circuit of capital is no surprise. These contradictions are exacerbated by various other tendencies that bedevil the capitalist mode of production. Key among these is the corrosive competition between many separate, atomised capitals competing for surplus value in a market founded on highly interdependent but privately made economic decisions. In such a fragmented system, what is best for collective capital, such as a high level of working-class consumption, often grates against the interests of individual capitalists, who will often attempt to limit their outlay in wages. Another tendency is that towards over-accumulation, whereby too much capital is available for profitable investment, such that profitability falls (either relatively or in absolute terms).[11] Yet, given the desire to maximise surplus value appropriation and outcompete other units of capital, the fundamental drive of individual capitalists, as well as the system as a whole, is to accumulate, to continually produce on an expanded scale.[12] Coeval with this drive to accumulate is the tendency towards ever greater concentration and centralisation of capital (larger units of productive capital under the control of fewer capitalists, respectively). These processes aid various capitals to rationalise production, provide insulation from competition, vest a greater ability to monopolise resources and mobilise a counter to Marx's much-debated observation of the tendency of the rate of profit to fall.[13] These crisis tendencies, which will be discussed in greater detail where they are relevant in the following chapters, are just that – tendencies, in the face of which counter-tendencies can be mobilised.[14] They do not operate as iron historical laws beyond the tautological point that among capitalist society's aforementioned invariant features is private ownership, creation of surplus value by wage-labour and competition.

Most important for our discussion here is the fact that the class distinctions and class struggles that both constitute and are reproduced by capitalism throw the sustainability of the circuit of capital into constant peril. Lebowitz crucially notes that the fundamental labour-capital divide in a capitalist society leads to two disparate and competing political economies, with the capitalist's valourisation and profit creation objectives grating against the proletariat's desire for the full product of its labour and the fulfilment of concrete needs.[15]

Taking all these tendencies into account, it is clear that the circuit of capital is wrought with structural contradictions which render continued capital accumulation in the long term not only difficult but inherently improbable. The result, as Marx and Engels vividly described, is that 'modern bourgeois society with its relations of production, of exchange and of property, a society that has conjured up such gigantic means of production and of exchange, is like a sorcerer, who is no longer able to control the powers of the nether world whom he has called up by his spells'.[16]

Given the fact that, despite a litany of failed experiments and horrendous creations, the sorcerer remains at work, the question posed by Boyer becomes both obvious and logically necessary in understanding the evolution of capitalist social formations: 'If one accepts Marx's intuitions regarding capitalism, the central question then takes the form of a paradox: how can such a contradictory process succeed over a long period of time'.[17]

The dominant economic paradigm of our time, neoclassicism, and its political stablemate, neo-liberalism, are particularly ill-suited to answering this question. Geared towards a highly abstract, vacuous conception of general equilibrium and a methodological individualism based on a transhistorical *homo economicus*, mainstream economics is incapable of explaining crisis as anything other than a temporary aberration resulting from market imperfections; the work of irrational consumers, workers or interest groups (such as trade unions or the state) with a vested interest in blocking market mechanisms.[18] The history of capitalism, littered as it is with crisis, breakdown and 'crippled monstrosities',[19] simply cannot be explained by reference to neoclassical theory. By extension, its future is also beyond the ability of the neoclassical school to chart.

It was partly in response to both the theoretical poverty of neoclassicism and the fossilisation of post–World War II orthodox Marxism that the PRA first stepped onto the scene.[20]

ENTER THE REGULATIONISTS

The Parisian school is dominant within the broader regulationist project and 'enjoys the greatest international impact'.[21] Notable scholars who kick-started the approach, including Michel Aglietta, Robert Boyer and Alain Lipietz, were heavily influenced by Althusserian structuralism, even if they rejected its problematic construction of reproduction as quasi-automatic and its piecemeal treatment of contradiction.[22] Neilson continues: 'Central to the appeal of Althusser's French Regulation School (FRS) "rebel sons" was the implicit promise of a mid-range theory of capitalist development that could complement Marx's long-range account'.[23]

The focus on generating an intermediate account of capitalist development entailed a development of concepts and methods to achieve four primary goals:

1. 'Describe the institutions and practices of capitalism';
2. 'Explain the various crisis tendencies of modern capitalism and/or likely sources of crisis resolution';
3. 'Analyse different stages . . . of capitalism and compare accumulation regimes and modes of regulation in a given period of capitalist development'; and
4. 'Examine the social embedding and social regularization of economic institutions and conduct'.[24]

Implicit in these questions is both an historical and logical acknowledgement that, despite the crisis tendencies of capitalism, strong accumulation and stability can be achieved in the short to medium term. The thirty-year post–World War II Fordist boom (the elucidation of which is the subject of chapter 4) presented the first regulationists with a reality that defied explanation in orthodox Marxist terms.[25] The boom had been an epoch of unrivalled growth and stability in the West, with increased production, productivity improvements and high-profit margins being complemented by full employment, rising real incomes and a redistributive welfare state. Mainstream economics, dominated by Keynesianism, spoke of the demise of the traditional business cycle and the crises of overproduction Marxism holds dear.[26] Although the early regulationists witnessed the demise of this system and the emergence of crisis in the 1970s, they nevertheless had to grapple with the reality that capitalism could be comparatively stable and prosperous for a period of time. This situation highlighted the need for an intermediate account of capitalist development that, while employing a Marxist methodology and cognisant of Marx's long-run observations, was able to account for stabilising forces in the short to medium term.

The answer, for the Parisians, lay in the notion of regulation. Capital accumulation could be guided and regularised through a contingent, historically variant combination of economic and extra-economic factors in a distinctive institutional matrix, handling, to varying degrees, the different crisis tendencies of capitalist social relations. Aglietta, one of the leading pioneers of the school, eloquently states:

> To speak of the regulation of a mode of production is to try to formulate in general laws the ways in which the determinant structure of society is reproduced. . . . *[A] theory of social regulation is a complete alternative to the theory of general equilibrium*. . . . The study of capitalist regulation, therefore, cannot be the investigation of abstract economic laws. It is the study of the

> transformation of social relations as it creates new forms that are both economic and noneconomic, that are organized in structures and themselves reproduce a determinant structure, the mode of production (my emphasis).[27]

This definition pays clear homage to the structural Marxist roots of the PRA and is echoed by Lipietz, who, recognising the dialectical link between regulation and crisis, notes that the former describes a situation where there is a temporary, relative primacy of unity over struggle in a deeply contradictory society.[28] Neilson adds that 'regulation politically modifies the economic process to temporarily stabilize, or contain, the contradictory core of capitalism'.[29] While there is a certain danger, latent in this statement, in seeing capitalism as a fundamentally economic concern regulated by an autonomous realm of politics (a danger that will be explored later), the acknowledgement that capitalism must be regulated if it is to succeed through time is well made.

A critical precondition of the attempt to create a mid-range account of capitalist development shaped through regulation is a theory that is armed with a range of concepts of varying compass occupying different locations on the plane from abstract to concrete. This is certainly evident in the spiralling method of analysis advocated by the regulationists, which employs a *dialectical* movement along the plane from abstract-simple to concrete-complex.[30] Aglietta describes this spiral thus:

> It follows that concepts are not introduced once and for all at a single level of abstraction. They are transformed by the characteristic interplay which constitutes the passage from the abstract to the concrete and enables the concrete to be absorbed within theory. Theory, for its part, is never final and complete, it is always in the process of development.[31]

In generating these spiralling, intermediate-level accounts of the trajectory of capitalist development, it follows that the PRA must be equipped with concepts of a lower level of abstraction that, while taking their methodological lead from Marx, must nevertheless be more concrete and historically sensitive in their operation. Broadly speaking, four such concepts are apparent within the school. They are:

- Industrial paradigm;
- Accumulation regime;
- Mode of regulation; and
- Model of development.

These four concepts traverse the analytical categories of capital, the state, the labour process and law that were introduced at the beginning of this chapter. The conceptual breadth and the opportunity for careful, incremental movement along the plane from abstract to concrete which these concepts open is what vests the Parisian school with its exceptional ability to combine theoretical rigour with empirical sensitivity. These notions thus require further unpacking and articulation as distinct moments of that hierarchy.

Industrial Paradigm

Absolutely central to the early work of Aglietta and Lipietz is a dominant 'industrial paradigm' or labour process model. The organisation of the labour process, particularly the manner in which it produces surplus value for the capitalist, has a powerful influence on the architecture of a capitalist society, a reality that Lukács grasped when he stated that the organisation of the factory 'contained in concentrated form the whole structure of capitalist society'.[32] In this light, it is somewhat surprising that an industrial paradigm does not generally assume the status of a discrete concept in later regulationist work,[33] although there are promising signs of a renewed emphasis on the labour process.[34]

Generally speaking, early regulationist labour process analysis was closely related to Braverman's influential account.[35] Aglietta thus neatly describes how:

> Capitalist production is the unity of a labour process and a process of valorization, in which the valorization is dominant. . . . On the one hand, we have defined the wage relation, the appropriation of labour-power as a commodity, as *the* fundamental relation of production. On the other hand, we said that capitalist relations of production present a dual character of antagonism and cooperation. In showing how the labour process is transformed under the impulse of the struggle for surplus-value, we must acquit a task that is essential for the transition from the abstract to the concrete in any theory of accumulation: namely to demonstrate that the transformation of the labour process creates relationships within production that adapt the cooperation of labour-power to the domination of the wage relation.[36]

The particular nexus point between valourisation and production, together with the state of technology, results in an industrial paradigm, which can be thought of as a dominant model of labour process organisation, governing the social and technical division of labour, such as mass production on semi-automatic production lines.[37] This does not necessarily imply that all branches of the economy are organised according to the same principles; it is enough that the leading sectors (the role of which will be explored in later chapters) revolve around them.[38]

Accumulation Regime

Boyer describes an accumulation regime as 'a set of regularities that ensure the general and relatively coherent progress of capital accumulation'.[39] It is a structure of economic and social patterns governing the composition of social demand corresponding to productive capacity, the time horizons of capital valourisation and the distribution of value within and between classes.[40] Such a regime is necessary in the attempt to contain capitalism's contradictions. Of particular importance is the reality that within capitalist social formations the factors that favour profitability in the sphere of production are the same factors which impinge upon the realisation of surplus value in the sphere of circulation.[41] In a very general sense, a viable accumulation regime must then articulate production and consumption at the macro-level in a stable, reproducible fashion.[42] I thus argue that we can essentially conceive of this structure of production and consumption as a concrete arrangement of the economic forms of capital, of the circuit of capital as an *economic process* (conceptually distinct, that is, from its juridic forms).

In Volume II of *Capital*, Marx identified the difficulties facing the achievement of such stability, due in part to the restricted nature of working-class purchasing power and the disjunction between the two great departments of the economy (namely, Department I, producing means of production, and Department II, producing means of consumption).[43] Unless surplus value were reduced to nought, workers could never have the purchasing power to procure all they had made, while the interlocking demand of capitalists in one department for the products of the other was beset by a host of temporal irregularities and discontinuities.[44]

Aglietta, using Marx's reproduction schemas, demonstrated how an accumulation regime could help combat this tendency towards instability by the development of particular linkages between the two departments.[45] Specifically, he developed a notion of *extensive* versus *intensive* accumulation. While the former revolved around transformations of the labour process narrowly construed, the latter involves a simultaneous development of both the labour process and the proletariat's conditions of existence through a commodification of individual consumption.[46] Put another way, extensive accumulation (which characterised capitalism in America and other capitalist countries up to the 1920s) was, in the face of continued petty-bourgeois production of working-class subsistence goods and the poverty of the proletariat, dependent primarily on increasing the scale of production in Department I, resulting in recurrent obstacles to the pace of accumulation.[47] Intensive accumulation, through extending the field of capitalist production to the very necessities of life, permitted a more organic series of linkages between the two departments, allowing the creation of a social consumption norm and a more rapid and regular increase in the rate of accumulation.[48] Intensive accumulation thus denotes more than the link between rapid technological change and surplus value; it is a specific mechanism by which social reproduction is mediated.[49]

This outwardly simple typology of regimes of accumulation has become increasingly nuanced and complicated, particularly as the school has expanded its ambit of study beyond advanced industrialised economies. Boyer in particular notes the profusion of regimes of accumulation in the developing world, including those of pre-industrial, rentier and inward-looking industrialising states.[50]

Mode of Regulation

An accumulation regime cannot in isolation secure the continued reproduction of capital. For this, it requires an attendant mode of regulation, which Jessop and Sum have described as an 'emergent ensemble of norms, institutions, organizational forms, social networks and patterns of conduct that can temporarily stabilize an accumulation regime'.[51] Typically, this includes coherent and compatible structures of wage relations, state forms, enterprise forms and linkages, money and (arguably) international relations.[52] A functioning mode of regulation both channels the crisis tendencies of a particular capitalist society through institutional pathways and modifies the behaviour of actors (both individual and collective) to accord with the rhythms of the accumulation regime. In containing, ameliorating or deferring the contradictions of an accumulation regime, a mode of regulation can ensure a period of relative stability and growth in capital accumulation.[53] Alternatively, to the extent that modes of regulation contain certain capitalist contradictions at the expense of others and shape economic and social relations in a path-dependent manner, they routinely undermine the very source of their success and become barriers to new modalities of capitalist growth.[54] Moreover, if we move beyond a reductionist conception of capitalism as a purely economic concern, and instead perceive capitalist social relations as assuming both economic *and* extra-economic forms, then it follows that a political handling of capitalism's contradictions does not dispel them; they merely assume a different form.

In the same manner in which I conceived of an accumulation regime as a concrete arrangement of capital's economic forms, a mode of regulation can equally be regarded as a concrete hierarchy of capital's juridic forms, the extra-economic struts that allow capital to move through its circuit. The abstract state and legal forms, as root juridic forms, are absolutely key in constituting the particular structural forms making up a mode of regulation. This conception best captures the reality that capital has a juridic, as well as economic, existence. Elam hits upon this truth when he states of the regulation approach:

> The result of this marriage between Marxist political economy and institutionalist tradition is a conceptualization of qualitative change within capitalism which posits the existence of not one, but *two*, fundamental dynamics forcing change. Two dynamics growing out of the same discordant soil of capitalist social relations. One giving rise to specific *regimes of accumulation*, the other to particular *modes of regulation*.[55]

Elam's conception is correct and dovetails with my view that accumulation regimes and modes of regulation, as concrete orders of economic and juridic forms, respectively, cannot be viewed as 'macro' or 'meso' vis-à-vis each other.[56] As will be demonstrated in the next chapter, this construction is necessary if a fruitful union between the PRA and a sophisticated Marxist theory of law is to be achieved.

Model of Development

A model of development is the most embracing regulationist concept. Neilson describes a model of development as 'a stable regime of accumulation or virtuous cycle of production, investment, and consumption engineered by the stabilizing regulation of unstable tendencies of the capitalist mode of production'.[57] Boyer and Saillard proffer a somewhat more dynamic definition that recognises the dialectical unfolding of regulation and crisis, describing a 'mode' of development as 'the way in which an accumulation regime and a type of *régulation* stabilize themselves over the long term and how they enter into a period of crisis and then renew themselves'.[58] Lipietz's conception is perhaps the most embracing, defining a model of development as *a coherent combination of an industrial paradigm, accumulation regime and mode of regulation.*[59]

I find this definition of Lipietz's the most holistic and most useful, particularly as it conceives of a structured totality of economic, political and social forms (thus allowing the PRA to escape a perceived economistic bias). Given this, it is odd that his concept has not really achieved broader traction. In chapter 4, when I come to define antipodean Fordism and liberal-productivism as models of development, it is *specifically* in the sense indicated by Lipietz. It will also be argued there that the model of development concept can be pitched at varying levels of abstraction, depending upon the generality or specificity accorded to the model.

With this basket of concepts (summarised in Table 2.1 at the end of this chapter) and a spiralling method of theory construction, the PRA is ideally placed to deliver theoretically sophisticated yet empirically rigorous mid-range accounts of the development of capitalist societies, accounts that both recognise the presence of entrenched structures while affirming the role of human agency.

CRITICISMS

The school has, nevertheless, faced a host of criticisms and critiques. Of chief importance here are those targeted at the regulationist theoretical matrix and methodology. These must be addressed if the utility of the approach is to be maintained.

Lack of Commitment to a Marxist Political Economy

The most serious matter with which I am concerned is the weakening relationship with Marxism which the school currently exhibits.

I have already noted the influence of Althusserian structuralism upon the early regulationists. The key innovation of structural Marxism was that it opened new pathways to conceptualising relations between the economic, political and social moments of capitalism in a way that avoided the crude 'base-superstructure' dichotomy of orthodox Marxism (deformed as it was by Stalinism).[60] A strict observance of this latter framework led in no small part to the 'fossilisation' of post–World War II orthodox Marxism as both an academic discipline and political programme. It also hampered efforts to develop an organically Marxist conception of the law.[61]

Structuralism was explicitly concerned with how the economic, political and social spheres combine to produce and reproduce capitalism. Although they sought to analyse and problematise this process of reproduction more intimately, the continuities between structuralists and the early regulationists are manifest in the latter's desire to understand and articulate, in a non-reductionist manner, both the economic and extra-economic aspects of a capitalist society.

Over time, however, the distinctly Marxist provenance and calling of the approach has been neglected. A case in point was the divisions that emerged in the 1980s over the standing of the labour theory of value. Although Aglietta based his influential book *A Theory of Capitalist Regulation: The US Experience* on a fundamentally Marxist labour theory of value, he abandoned it in later work. Some key thinkers, such as Boyer and Mistral, do not specify their conception of value theory,[62] while others, such as Lipietz, continue to take the labour theory of value as an analytical concept seriously.[63]

The divergence within the Parisian school regarding the status of Marx's theory of value is symptomatic of a broader movement away from an explicitly Marxist political economy. It is no accident that in a recent regulationist compendium, *Régulation Theory: The State of the Art,* Keynes, Kalecki and Kaldor feature as heavily as Marx. Out of some forty-two chapters, only one is reserved for an explicit treatment of the influence of Marx, both historically and in terms of the current research agenda, and that is as much concerned with distancing the school from its Marxist roots as with embracing them.[64]

Neilson attributes the sources of this estrangement to a 'focus on national difference, linked with a de-emphasis of the Fordist model of development and the absence altogether of a model of development in the analysis of the contemporary era'.[65] He cites as a key example the efforts of regulationist doyen Robert Boyer to seek rapprochement with other heterodox currents, such as the Varieties of Capitalism school, which are not necessarily theoretically commensurable.[66] The corrosive effect of such theoretical eclecticism is a danger that has already been recognised, one that stymies the approach in delivering on its initial promise of a powerful mid-range Marxist analysis of capitalist development.[67] The result is that the PRA is increasingly at odds with its Marxist heritage.

The two key issues seem to be a lack of commitment to a holistic theory of the dynamics of the capitalist mode of production and a growing confusion as to the relationship of regulationist concepts to concrete history. On the first score, whereas early regulationist work located its mid-range analysis explicitly within Marx's conception of the capitalist mode of production, and the more general, abstract trends he identified therein, later work left these links unstated, neglected and undermined by increasing eclecticism. In the absence of these links, the PRA loses what had made it so attractive in the first place – the promise of reconciling an intermediate account of capitalism with the more long-run tendencies identified by Marx.

Secondly, the power of the PRA to make wide-ranging accounts of the transformation of advanced capitalist countries has been impaired by the increasingly narrow vistas of several of its key notions, most particularly 'Fordism'. In sophisticated PRA analysis, Fordism (as a model of development) is the result of a dialectical pattern of theorising and historical study derived from Marx. When pitched at its highest operational level of abstraction, Fordism is an ideal-type which, in the manner of Marx, 'brings out and fixes the common element'.[68] The ideal-typical model of development does not describe the concrete experience of any particular society in the absence of sensitisation to specific national contexts. Rather, as Treuren notes, it forms a vital intermediate link in the movement from abstract to concrete.[69] It enters into a dialectical relationship with concrete existence in which the model identifies causal relationships while empirical study comments on the adequacy of the theoretical construct.[70]

If, however, the model is confused for an exact account of the experience of any one society, it rapidly loses its explanatory potential; more and more caveats and qualifications have to be added in the face of the infinitely diverse historical experience, ultimately resulting in the model imploding. On this basis, Boyer could state 'Fordism, when defined by a conjunction of three properties, was a feature found only in a few countries at best'.[71] Boyer's confusion represents both a strong tendency towards empiricism and the abdication of the hierarchy of abstraction, whereby the explanatory power of grand theory is foregone for an ever-increasing profusion of more descriptive models.

The relevance of these developments to this book is that I concur with Neilson that the regulationist research programme must be placed back on course to deliver on its promise of a mid-range Marxist account of the dynamics and trajectories of capitalist social formations. This involves both re-establishing the links between the PRA and the deep-seated tendencies of the capitalist mode of production and the reaffirmation of the utility of the ideal-type as a means of identifying causal relationships and broad structures. Happily, this task has already begun, and this project is firmly located within this movement.[72]

Criticism from within Marxism

The PRA has also come in for criticism from within Marxism, being subjected to sustained critique by scholars including John Holloway, Werner Bonefeld, Simon Clarke, Peter Kennedy, Robert Brenner, Mark Glick and Stavros Mavroudeas. Their critiques cover a lot of ground, ranging from attacks on the theory and methodology of the PRA to the political ramifications of its prescriptions. While not discounting the significance of the latter, what concerns us here are those criticisms targeted at the former.

The main criticisms of the PRA on these theoretical and methodological scores can be summarised as:

- a reification of capitalist social production relations;
- a functionalist and undialectical separation of capitalist structures and class struggle;
- weak mid-range theorising leading to the creation of historically vacuous models of real epochs within capitalism; and
- a poor treatment of the state.

These are serious charges, which must be addressed if the contention of this book, that the PRA is a most useful vehicle for reconciling theory and practice in accounting for labour law change, is to be justified.

The first and second accusations are best answered as a couplet, for the latter is the logical outcome of the former. By a reification of capitalist social relations, critics seem to mean that regulationists subscribe to a view of capitalism as dominated by a set of self-contained and self-sufficient objective laws, a structuralist view devoid of the motive force of class struggle.[73] Kennedy states this view powerfully in his attack on Hirsch's work: 'He commences with the erroneous idea that somehow the objective laws of value exist in a perpetually crisis ridden state *separately* from social relations of production. The law of value, according to this regulationist view, becomes little more than a sealed and timeless movement'.[74]

If it is true that regulationists reify tendencies within capitalism to abstract historical laws, then it follows that class struggle is, as Bonefeld describes, 'seen as either accelerating or retarding the definite course of the law-determined path of development but it is incapable of challenging it'.[75] The supposed result is that the PRA reproduces the bourgeois fetishism of conceptually segregating laws and real-life human struggle and generates 'a picture which seals the appearance of bourgeois society rather than prising it open'.[76]

The first criticism is comparatively easy to deal with. The concept of a reification of capitalist social relations appears to be confused with the regulationist positing of an invariant core of relations that sits at the heart of capitalism. Regulationism, like any Marxist political economy approach worth its salt, is not suggesting that capitalist social relations are somehow eternal, immutable or mechanistically derived from the abstract advance of productive forces.[77] Indeed, Marx was explicitly concerned with understanding how different relations hold under different modes of production. This does not mean, however, that Marx neglected to study the laws and tendencies that characterised the capitalist mode of production; conversely, such an inquiry was the business of a great deal of his life. As I outlined at the beginning of the chapter, the capitalist mode of production is characterised by a basket of invariant features, in the absence of which it would be improper to talk of 'capitalism'.

To run with Kennedy's example, let us take the laws of value, principally the labour theory of value. Of course, he is correct to state that it is impossible to separate an eternal, objective law of value from the social relations of production.[78] Fine notes astutely that, for Marx, 'value, money and capital are not things but economic expressions of definite productive relations'.[79] Marx states explicitly of commodities in Volume I of *Capital* that 'their objective character as values is therefore *purely social*' (my emphasis).[80] The full operation of the law of value presupposes a society of generalised commodity production, which in turn is prefaced on the compulsion of the majority of people to sell their labour-power.

It is in this sense that the generalised value relation faces humankind as a 'law', as an abstraction that subjugates real people. This is a phenomenon with its roots deeply within capitalist social relations which, although it will necessarily manifest itself in different ways, can be thought of as flowing from the invariant features of a capitalist society. In other words, the basic properties that make a capitalist society what it is will generate a universalised value relation. If describing this reality constitutes a reification of the law of value, then we can equally say that any notion of a distinctive capitalist mode of production is also a reification. Faced with the corruption of that model, we would eventually be led to a structureless conception of political economy in which the capitalist epoch would lose all specificity. Such a development would of course kill a Marxist inquiry and runs counter to the essence of Marx's life work.

Accepting that a capitalist society will exhibit certain tendencies on account of it being capitalist, however, is not the same as suggesting that structure is an empty bucket within which an un-related class struggle is contained. One of Marx's central preoccupations was in explaining why the social relations of production, which is the very matter of class struggle, manifest themselves in certain economic and political forms.[81] Within its own purview, regulationists critiqued structural Marxism's unsophisticated portrayal of the maintenance and reproduction of structures. Jessop and Sum note that:

> the Parisians criticized the Althusserian view that structures somehow maintain themselves quasi-automatically, independently of effective social agency, and with no significant transformations. Rejecting the emphasis on structural unity typical of Althusser's concern with reproduction, regulation theorists stressed the 'unity of unity and struggle in regulation'.[82]

This can be seen most clearly in the regulationist treatment of 'institutionalised class compromises', particularly in the work of Delorme and Andre.[83] Here, the focus is on how class struggle directly stimulates institutional development and how the resulting institutions play a key role in canalising such struggle in a manageable fashion, a theme we shall explore in detail in chapters 5 and 6. Class struggle and institutions are, in this conception, intricately linked, and indeed represent the unity of structure and struggle. The same unity underpins Jessop's contention that the structure/struggle duality is a false one, which can only be properly articulated 'by *dialectically relativizing* (as opposed to *mechanically relating*) both analytical categories'.[84]

To say that regulationist analysis disarticulates the two thus seems off the mark. The claim that it does is based on a reluctance to label the features and structures of a capitalist society, which, although not the intention of critics such as Holloway and Bonefield, is itself part of a broader trend to empiricism in the social sciences under the impact of post-structuralism. The result is a voluntarist, structureless conception of capitalism that abdicates the need to theorise and identify the invariant features of capitalism and their concrete manifestations.

The contention that the PRA produces inadequate mid-range theory and/or vacuous historical models is not one I intend to dwell on. Suffice it to say that critics on both fronts misunderstand the nature of the process of abstraction engaged in by sophisticated regulationist work, and the status of the resulting ideal-type models of development. As I have outlined earlier, these ideal-typical models follow Marx's lead in his description of modes of production, which 'brings out and fixes the common element' but apprehends 'no real historical stage'.[85] The ideal-typical model of development, although it does outline an historical epoch, does not describe the concrete experience of any particular society. Vidal is completely correct when he states that 'to expect a sort of narrow technical precision out of the broad conceptual architecture of Fordism/postfordism would be to misunderstand this framework'.[86] Rather, it forms a vital intermediate link in the movement from abstract to concrete. It enters into a dialectical relationship with concrete existence in which the model identifies causal relationships while empirical study comments on the adequacy of the theoretical construct.[87] This is exactly the kind of process upheld by Mavroudeas as the correct Marxist one, so it is difficult to see on what grounds he dismisses the PRA as eclectic and historicist in this regard.[88] Criticisms like Salvati's, that the PRA is 'neither theory nor history', are therefore very wide of the mark.[89]

Ultimately, however, the reader will be best placed to judge if the PRA constructs employed in this book have produced vacuous and/or inadequate models, or are instead valuable focusing devices illuminating the evolution of Australian capitalism.

Treatment of the State and Juridic Forms

The last criticism of import to deal with here is the claim that the PRA does not have a coherent theory of the state. This one is critical to address, as this book proceeds on the assumption that the state and law are related juridic forms of capitalist social relations. Meeting this challenge also involves elucidating my own conception of the state and law as juridic forms. Given the fact that both are intimately involved in the construction of law deployed in the following chapter, it is best to deal with this basket of issues separately.

Specifically, some allege that its theory of the state is either underdeveloped or borrowed from other disciplines,[90] while other critics accuse it of a narrow, functionalist account of state action.[91] While there is some truth to these criticisms, sophisticated regulationist analyses can overcome both of them.

The claim that the PRA renders functionalist and economistic accounts of the state can be dealt with fairly quickly. It is fair to say that simplistic regulationist accounts (which ironically are often constructed by the critics of regulationism, who then caricature them)[92] have a proclivity towards both functionalism and economism. On the first score of functionalism, it seems that the tendency to slip into it is a danger inherent in the objects of regulationist research. Given that the PRA is geared towards understanding how capitalism can be made stable within certain limits, it is easy to assume not only that the state performs certain functions, but that it actually has the capacity to do so. As regarding the charge of economism, it is true that much regulationist work (particularly the more recent) is economically dense and displays an inordinate preoccupation with econometrics. The fact that many practitioners of regulation theory, past and present, were economists no doubt contributes here. It is equally true that there lurks within the PRA a more insidious form of economism, which Jessop and Sum describe as regarding 'the state and civil society as largely external to the economy. Thus it overlooks how the latter is deeply penetrated by extra-economic forces and relations'.[93] It would not be unfair to state that this is an issue which has dogged Marxist work ever since Marx and Engels outlined their method, exacerbated by the unfortunate base-superstructure metaphor of *Contribution to the Critique of Political Economy*.[94] My view is that the claim that the regulationist treatment of the state tends towards economism is a function more of an ever-present tendency within Marxist political economy than any peculiarity of the Parisian school's theoretical orientation and/or methodology.

Moreover, these issues are not insurmountable from within a regulationist paradigm. The PRA is predicated on acknowledging and understanding the intertwining and co-evolution of the economic and extra-economic moments of capitalism, the state included. The Althusserian structuralism which initially grounded the PRA was explicitly premised upon a rejection of economism. This goes much further than Neilson's aforementioned description of capitalism being 'politically modified' in the interests of capital's stability and sustainability.[95] The issue with Neilson's statement is that it appears to reify an image of a fundamentally capitalist 'economy' distinct from the political sphere of the state and civil society whose form is merely contingent and capacities only functional. In doing so, he risks hypostasising the economism which structural Marxism sought to combat.

Rather than conceiving capitalism as a fundamentally economic system paired with contingent or epiphenomenal political forms, it is far better to remain true to the spirit of Marx's analysis and comprehend capitalism as a totality. This is what structural Marxism attempted to do; however, it tended to too rigidly enforce its distinction between economics, politics and ideology, regarding them as separate regions rather than many-sided manifestations of the same relations of production.[96]

The way to retain the structural Marxist emphasis on the role of the state without necessarily relegating it to a self-enclosed political sphere is to recognise that capitalist production relations assume both economic *and* juridic forms, a reality we saw Elam grasp earlier.[97] Marx's method in *Capital* was not that of base and superstructure, but instead analysing why the social relations of production (the innermost social 'content') necessarily expressed itself in certain forms, such as value and money.[98] Although Marx was primarily concerned with tracing the economic forms of capitalist society, Fine notes that this focus has been confused as concept, giving 'rise to the impression that the economic expression of relations of production is their only expression'.[99] As Marsden states eloquently:

> The state is not 'above' society, as 'base-superstructure' suggests. Rather civil society and political state are twin illusions atop a substratum: capital. This civil society/political state couplet corresponds to the twin forms of capital, economic

> and juridic, fused as private property. There are not 'economic' relations here and 'legal' relations there. There is one network of relations of production with juridic and economic forms.[100]

In their economic forms, capitalist production relations, by separating workers from their means of production and marketising the commodities needed for their subsistence, generate a commodity fetishism, whereby the social relations between people are distorted into the economic relations between things.[101] However, the existence of general commodity production/exchange and private property presupposes, and is partly constituted by, parallel juridic forms. Property rights, particularly capitalist notions of absolute property ownership, are almost invariably legal from their beginning; indeed, to speak of 'rights' is difficult without recourse to law.[102] As Marx noted, the enormous expansion of commodity relations entailed by capital requires mutual recognition of proprietary right on the part of commodity buyers and sellers;[103] the violence and robbery that characterised feudal society, for example, would not be commensurable with the day-to-day conduct of a market system. This mutual recognition of right and abstract equality is the simplest incarnation of the legal form (whose contours I will trace in much greater detail in the following chapter).

In the transition to a capitalist society, the separation of the economic and extra-economic moments of coercion, alongside the roots of abstract equality between commodity producers/owners, generates an additional juridic form, that of the alienated, national state. The disintegration of the organic community of feudalism and the atomisation of civil society is matched by the development of a formally equal political community. Raised above civil society, Marx notes that 'the political state, in relation to civil society, is just as spiritual as is heaven in relation to earth'.[104]

These juridic forms are every bit as inscribed in, and derived from, capitalist production relations as economic forms. It is thus better to conceptualise them as Taiwo does, as part of the essence of the capitalist mode of production, in the absence of which it would be incorrect to speak of a capitalist society.[105] Or, to return to the beginning of the chapter, the working definition of capitalism I used identified private ownership, wage dependence and the market as the key institutions which express both an exploitative wage-labour relationship and competition-based private coordination of production, the core social relations of capitalism. The admission of the state and law as juridic forms of capital means that we can add both to the invariant features of the capitalist mode of production. In other words, a stateless, lawless society would not, over the long run, be a capitalist one.

Despite the fact that this theory of juridic forms has historically been counterposed to the Althusserian notion of separate economic, political and ideological 'regions',[106] there is nothing in it that would make it incompatible with the PRA. In particular, Jessop draws attention to the existence of strong extant linkages in the work of scholars such as Hirsch and Esser,[107] who combine the concepts of the PRA with the insights of the state derivation debate of the 1970s and 1980s. In such analyses, although the form of the state is implanted in capitalist social relations, this form, like all others, is so thoroughly underwritten by contradictions that there is no certainty it can perform the functions required of it.[108] To ascertain if it does, the more intermediate regulationist notion of a mode of regulation comes into its own. If the particular state under analysis coheres with an underlying accumulation regime, and fits into the constellation of other institutional forms, such as the wage-labour nexus, money and enterprise relations, then we can say that it more or less executes its historically conditioned variety of functions.

This approach characterises the best work on the state from a regulationist perspective.[109] The variety and sophistication of this work also puts paid to the claim that the PRA has an unoriginal account of the state and affirms its potential for theoretically rigorous yet historically sensitive accounts of the functions, capacities and historical trajectories of capitalist states.

CONCLUSIONS

I began this chapter by noting that a book which seeks to truly ground an analysis of workplace law within a critical political economy must work at the intersections of capital, the state, the capitalist labour process/industrial relations and the law. I also noted how such distinctions are in a sense arbitrary, and these categories are instead intimately related through their status as invariant features of the capitalist mode of production.

I have demonstrated how the PRA analytically unites these moments of a capitalist society using a variety of sophisticated concepts that together form a distinct hierarchy on the plane from abstract to concrete. Building upon the long-term tendencies that Marx identifies, the regulationists proffer a dynamic mid-range account of the development of capitalist societies, particularly in their economic and political facets. The regulationist notion of a model of development uniting a dominant industrial paradigm, mode of regulation and an accumulation regime traverses the categories of capital, the state, the labour process/industrial relations and law and, in doing so, offers a wide-ranging account that allows us to understand the interpenetration of economic and extra-economic forces in a capitalist society and their evolution through time and space. Importantly, a perceived weakness in treating the state and, by extension, law was resolved by explicitly including both of these in the bundle of invariant features of a capitalist society. Capitalist production relations have juridic, as well as economic, forms. It thus does not pay to see the law and the state as secondarily derived from an economic base; they are simply different forms of capital's existence, in the absence of which the resulting society would be something other than capitalist. Making this strong claim, implicit in better regulationist work, does no damage to a PRA analysis when it is acknowledged that the form's functionality is always in question; conversely, it helps purge it of a claimed economistic bias. It does, however, require the regulationist project to cease its drift into eclecticism and reconnect with its roots in Marxism.

Table 2.1. Regulationist concepts

Concept	*Definition*	*Examples*
Industrial paradigm	• dominant method of organising the labour process. • governs social and technical division of labour. • not necessary that all labour processes are organised on these lines; enough that certain lead sectors are.	• mass-production on semi-automatic production lines, governed by logic of Taylorism.
Accumulation regime	• macro-level articulation of production and consumption reproducible through time. • governs relationship between Departments I and II. • can broadly be conceived as a concrete arrangement of capitalism's economic forms.	• extensive accumulation, where capitalist production in Department I sits alongside petty-bourgeois production in Department II. • intensive accumulation, where capitalist production in Department I is matched by commodification of working-class consumption goods.
Mode of regulation	• ensemble of structural forms stabilising and guiding an accumulation regime. • forms include wage-labour nexus, particular form of the state, enterprise forms and competition, and money form. • can broadly be conceived as a concrete arrangement of capitalism's juridic forms.	• mode centred on Keynesian Welfare National State. • neo-liberal mode of regulation.
Model of development	• coherent combination of an industrial paradigm, accumulation regime and mode of regulation.	• Fordism • Liberal-productivism

Chapter 3

The Legal Form, Labour Law and the Law-Administration Continuum

In the previous chapter, I demonstrated how the PRA's concepts and methodology broach capital, the state, the labour process and law as analytic categories. Given the centrality of law to this book, this chapter will be concerned primarily with developing a theoretically rigorous account of the form and function of law generally, and labour law more specifically. This task requires placing law within a precisely defined hierarchy of abstraction, rooted in Marxist political economy. This must explicate the abstract place of law within the capitalist mode of production at the same time that it tackles legal change at the concrete level. Only by integrating both can we arrive at an understanding of law that is theoretically lucid yet empirically accurate. Through generating ideal-typical models periodising capitalism into distinctive epochs, the Parisian Regulation Approach (PRA) is ideally placed to serve as the mid-wife of this process of unifying the abstract and the concrete. Taking the PRA as the point of articulation between the two levels, this chapter will construct a coherent hierarchy of abstraction that retains the theoretical incisiveness of Marxism while exploring the impact of history on the legal form.

In chapter 2 I identified the law, along with the state, as juridic forms of capital that are part of the basket of invariant features characterising the capitalist mode of production. Given that to many Marxists this would appear a bold claim, it is necessary to first explore something of the history of legal analysis from within a Marxist political economy. Only once we have canvassed the best of such work can we lay a solid foundation at the abstract level saying what the legal form is, how it is actualised at the concrete level and how it is reproduced over time.

MARXISM AND THE LAW

Considering the fact that law is a highly visible and potent presence in both public and private life, it is somewhat surprising that Marxist analyses specifically grappling with the law are, with several very notable exceptions, uncommon. Given that 'Marx's goal was to understand bourgeois society as a totality, as an inter-connected whole',[1] this legal lacuna seems, at first instance, to be inexplicable. It becomes more understandable, though no less inadequate, in light of the fact that many Marxist scholars have historically tended to subsume law within an epiphenomenal 'superstructure' determined by an economic 'base'. While establishing a vision of a totality, this species of determinism leaves little space for a specific understanding of the *form* of law. It is to these shortcomings Collins (a staunch critic) refers when he states: 'The paucity of Marxist jurisprudence until modern times is probably largely a result of the materialist emphasis of Marxism. Since the primary focus rests on the economy and the corresponding power relations within a society, law is treated as a peripheral concern'.[2]

Undoubtedly there is a certain truth to this contention, especially insofar as it describes the Stalinist, economistic vision of Marxism that came to dominate the politics of mainstream Communist parties in the decades bracketing World War II. However, it must be qualified in two ways. Firstly, one must be very cautious not to confuse the traditional focus and emphases of any theory with the actual explanatory possibilities opened by it. Marxism's historical neglect of the law as an object of study must be distinguished from the opportunities for legal analysis from within that theoretical framework. Relatedly, as we shall see in this chapter, this neglect is by no means absolute; there is indeed a body of Marxist work explicitly concerned with elucidating the place of law within capitalism.

By way of grounding, it is worth briefly surveying the contributions of Marx and Engels on law. While it is true that neither ever developed a detailed and consistent theory of law, they nevertheless had more to say of it than is commonly supposed.[3] It is apparent that their approach (particularly Marx's) was a dynamic one, characterised by intellectual evolution and the discarding of concepts no longer deemed useful. Fine notes how 'Marx's point of departure was classical jurisprudence and his journey away from it was accomplished only in stages, without a preconceived destination'.[4] More specifically, this point of departure was Hegelianism, the influence of which informed Marx's initial idealist notion of law. On this score, the essence of law was Reason's achievement of a positive, impersonal existence free of particularistic interests, a view that led to Marx describing a nation's statute book as 'a bible of freedom'.[5]

Marx and Engels' movement towards their historical materialist method necessitated the abandonment of this conception, and a recognition that the law must be approached from the class perspective they had developed for political economy.[6] This appreciation opened up two potential conceptions of law: as an element in a reactive superstructure which is ultimately determined by an economic base; or as a social institution with its roots deeply embedded within, and constitutive of, capitalist relations of production and exchange. The tension between the two was never fully resolved in their writings, but, as indicated in the previous chapter's discussion of juridic forms, the latter represents a most fruitful line of enquiry that remains true to the tenets of historical materialism while avoiding an instrumentalist view of law as unproblematically functioning in the interest of capital.

A prime example of this more sophisticated treatment of law can be found in Marx's treatment of commodity ownership and exchange in Volume I of *Capital*. Marx acknowledged that commodities cannot walk to market and exchange themselves.[7] He continues:

> In order that these objects may enter into relation with each other as commodities, their guardians must place themselves in relation to one another as persons whose will resides in those objects, and must behave in such a way that each does not appropriate the commodity of the other, and alienate his own, except through an act to which both parties consent. The guardians must therefore recognize each other as owners of private property. The content of this juridical relation (or relation of two wills) is itself determined by the economic relation.[8]

Despite seeming on the surface to suggest some type of economic determinism (depending upon the exact meaning given to the term 'economic' in this context), the practical effect of this statement is in fact quite the opposite. As Von Arx states of this passage, 'By asserting that exchange requires mutual recognition of private property rights, Marx clearly acknowledges that *the legal relation between subjects is intrinsic to the value relation*' (my emphasis).[9] The association of commodities with some minimum notion of juridical equality preventing theft was developed further by Engels, who stated that law, while manifesting the general economic expression, must nevertheless be 'coherently unified . . . and free from glaring internal inconsistencies'.[10] Such notions are the fertile ground out of which a theory of law as a juridic form of capital can grow.

Alongside this admittedly inchoate understanding of law as deeply embedded in capitalist production and exchange relations, there is another important insight Marx and Engels give us on law: that it is *not* simply a tool functioning in the interests of the capitalist class. This can be seen most clearly in Marx and Engels's treatment of the Ten Hours statute fought for by the British proletariat in the middle decades of the nineteenth century.[11] For Marx, this legislation represented the concrete manifestation of working-class power crystallised in the political arena, the first time that 'the political economy of the middle class succumbed to the political economy of the working class'.[12]

By uniting as a class, workers were capable of introducing laws that, in terms of content, both represented and facilitated their class interests. The struggle to force such change was a genuine political movement of the class 'with the object of enforcing its interests in a general form, in a form possessing general, socially coercive force'.[13] In this conception, law, far from being immune to the class struggle, is instead a focal point for it, and it is exactly over the content of labour law that we can expect the greatest contestation.

From this very brief sketch, we can discern two central points for our analysis: firstly, that law is a strange creature whose basic form is structured by the capitalist relations of production and exchange of which it is part; and secondly, that class struggle can play a formative role in determining the exact shape and content of law. The famous dictum 'between equal rights, force decides'[14] is of signal importance in understanding the practical struggles over law that occurs within the framework of capitalist social relations. These two points are, moreover, intertwined: form is meaningless except through its material iterations, while the salience of using distinctions between different kinds of struggle is predicated upon an understanding that capital has a multifaceted economic and juridical existence.

For all the promising hints within Marx and Engels' work, however, it remains the case that law never truly interested them in its own right.[15] We must thus consult scholars who, while taking their conceptual and methodological lead from Marx, explore these questions of legal form and the class struggle surrounding it in much greater detail.

LEGAL FORM

In both the preceding and current chapter, repeated reference has been made to law as a juridic form of capital. Before further developing this notion, it is necessary to ascertain just what a 'form' is. Fine proffers a useful definition, using the 'form-content' couplet:

> The imagery which informs *Capital* . . . is not that of base and superstructure, but rather of 'form' and 'content' . . . starting with economic forms, e.g. value, price, money, capital, interest, profit, etc – analysing the specific relations of production which lie hidden beneath these forms, and then explaining 'synthetically' why these relations of production necessarily express themselves in this economic way.[16]

Fine and Saad-Filho note of *Capital* that the 'divorce between reality (or content or essence) and the way it appears (or form) is a central aspect of Marx's (dialectical) thought'.[17] So, simply enough, the form of a thing is its external appearance, the structure it presents to the perceiver. Within this world of perception it is easy enough, beneath the endless diversity of material existence, to perceive regularities which might be thought of as 'master forms'. Amid the countless iterations of money, wage-labour, laws and states, for example, a commonality can be observed which allows us to speak of each in abstract terms, as modes of appearance in a capitalist society. What Marx did was to disassemble mainly economic forms and demonstrate why capitalist production relations generate these appearances. His method, while starting from the real world, thus avoided the pitfalls of crude empiricism in mistaking appearance for reality.[18]

Law forms a more-or-less distinctive entity in the life of a capitalist society. Kay and Mott incisively characterise this form, stating, 'Law is not a set of coercive rules, but a tangible expression of a social form with a predetermined historical content, namely the commodity nature of the products of labour under a regime of absolute property'.[19] Poulantzas notes that the developed legal form is defined by abstract, universal and formal norms that together comprise an axiomatic system.[20] In a mature capitalist society, it regulates areas of social life as diverse as employment, commerce, administration and the family, and it does so with a peculiar set of institutions, modes of operation and norms. Indeed, to meaningfully speak of law necessitates conceptually distinguishing these institutions and norms from other, non-legal, ones.

Historically, however, Marxist work has been little concerned with why law is such a pronounced feature of capitalism, and, more deeply, why relationships should take a legal form at all. Evgeny Pashukanis, a leading Soviet jurist in the 1920s and early 1930s, posed the problem of a Marxist account not sensitive to the specificity of the legal form:

> All we get is a theory which explains the emergence of legal regulation from the material needs of society. . . . Instead of being able to avail ourselves of an abundance of internal structures and interconnections of the juridical, we are forced to make do with bare outlines, only approximately indicated. These outlines are so blurred that the borderline between the sphere of the juridical and adjacent spheres is completely obliterated.[21]

We must thus construct such an account of the legal form, drawing carefully from the work of scholars such as Pashukanis, Fine, and Kay and Mott, who concern themselves with this question of form.

In the previous chapter I noted the distinction between use-value and exchange-value which characterises the commodity form. This distinction is also what actually constitutes the commodity; if it meets no concrete need it is worthless, while if it is not produced for exchange it is not a commodity. A commodity, therefore, fulfils its life mission only if it is traded on the market, either in kind for another commodity or for money. As indicated in the statement by Marx earlier, this in turn requires that the owners of those commodities be able to relate to one another *as fellow owners*.[22] In other words, alongside the economic relation between the objects being traded, there is a 'relation of two wills'[23] whereby owners recognise each other as such and formally respect their right of ownership.[24] In this recognition lies the cell of the legal form, the owner of private property,[25] and the understanding that law 'is inseparably linked with private property and production for exchange – in other words with commodity production'.[26]

Like the relationship between commodities being expressed at a certain stage of development through the universal equivalent of money, so too does this juridic relation achieve a form independent of the respective parties.[27] A section of society becomes vested with overseeing, guaranteeing and codifying this relationship; the law courts and judges thus emerge on the historical scene.[28] All pre-capitalist societies which engage in an appreciable measure of commodity exchange exhibit these kinds of institutions and personnel, and it is telling (as Pashukanis presciently observed) that the most highly developed systems were in formations like the Roman Empire.[29] Indeed, the reappearance of Roman contract jurisprudence from the 1100s coincided with the onset of a long decay in European feudalism, partly due to the influence of rising merchant and commercial classes re-establishing wide-scale commodity exchange.[30]

The commodity form therefore requires the most basic cell of the legal form, owner of private property, and all societies, capitalist or pre-capitalist, with large-scale commodity exchange will be marked by it. While some Marxist critics would decry this as deriving forms from exchange, rather than production relations (and so running against the grain of Marx's emphasis on the determining role of the latter), this criticism is misplaced on two counts. Firstly, it *is* appropriate to direct attention to the influence of exchange when talking of commodities and the legal form, as it is precisely exchange that partially constitutes that form.[31] To be exchanged is part of the essence of a commodity, and whatever the production relations underlying them, it must still go through a process of purchase and sale. Secondly, the positing of a bare legal form consonant with the commodity form is not to suggest this form is immutable and unchanging, nor that the difference between the law of pre-capitalist and capitalist societies is one of degree and not kind.[32] Such an understanding runs counter to the dialectical relationship between the two elucidated by Marx.

Instead, form and content represent a dialectically intertwined unity. While the exchange of commodities provides a most basic, abstract legal form, the content of this form (namely, the social relations of production) determines its exact shape and development. This is a reality Marx demonstrated in relation to the commodity form. The development from simple to expanded commodity production is not merely emptying and filling a static form with new content, but is a simultaneous alteration of that form.[33] The union of economic and extra-economic coercion in pre-capitalist societies, along with the particularistic nature of property,[34] ensures that the boundaries between law and other forms of social power (such as religion and direct force) are ambiguous and the reach of the law circumscribed.[35] Legal authority in a feudal society, for example, was often vested in manorial courts, where the dispenser of justice and the economic exploiter was often the same person, while feudal law recognised all manner of estate, guild and military distinction. The notion of impersonal law binding all members of society as juridically equal citizens, which capitalist society would come to know as the rule of law, would have been thoroughly foreign in such societies.[36]

It is only with the development of capitalist production relations that the specifically bourgeois legal form, an axiomatic system of abstract, universal and formal norms regulating juridically equal citizens, emerges.[37] This is so for several reasons. Firstly, the conceptual separation of economic and political exploitation, together with the divorce of the producers from the means of production, opens the space for the abstract, alienated capitalist state.[38] Although not reducible to each other, the law and the state are related forms, and the development of the latter takes the former to a new plane. The state now 'introduces clarity and stability into the structure of law',[39] and vests law with the formal equality which was only latent in it before.

More significant for our purposes is the universality of commodity production and exchange and the commodification of labour power that occurs under capitalism. The fact that the vast majority of capitalist production is for sale, rather than immediate use, intensifies greatly the legal form, allowing it to penetrate every pore of social life.[40] Capitalism is legalised to a degree unknown in other class societies.[41] Even more importantly, the fact that labour generally now takes the commodity form means that the sale and purchase of labour power becomes an explicitly legal matter. Unlike the feudal lord or slave owner, the capitalist's extraction of surplus value is mediated through a free contract in a labour market. As the capitalist is appropriating not fixed sums of labour, but instead *the capacity to labour*, this appropriation cannot be once-and-for-all, but must be repeated on an episodic basis. It is at this nexus that we identify that unique body of law regulating the terms and conditions of the alienation of labour-power: labour law. Labour law is a most complex amalgam, with the law of 'things' and exchange relations, namely property and contract law, attempting to incorporate and regulate a living, breathing and thinking subject, the proletarian. The result, Kay and Mott most incisively observe, is that 'labour law is the most complex and equivocal of the laws of property for fundamental reasons. . . . The buying and selling of labour-power summarises the contradictions of capitalist society in a single moment'.[42]

Formal equality with unequal content, an alienation of capacities in fact with a disavowal of it in contract, equivalent exchange being transformed into its polar opposite – these are the contradictions with which the employment contract, one of the planks of labour law, is riven. These contradictions are inevitable and will endure for as long as the capitalist legal form predominates. It is worth reiterating here what was said in the previous chapter: law and the state are juridic forms integral to the capitalist mode of production. A society that is lawless and stateless would not, in the long run, be a capitalist one.[43]

LEGAL FORM AND ADMINISTRATION

Although the preceding discussion has been abstract, it has been necessary insofar as we now understand what is distinctive about the capitalist legal form and the specific problems with which labour law must grapple. In particular, it is clear that the latter 'is shot through with all the tensions of capitalist social relations'.[44] Along with the general mediating function of law between juridically equal subjects, labour law is specifically concerned with ensuring the continued commodification of labour-power.[45] This process is not, however, given or uncontested. In the previous chapter it was argued that the workings of capitalist class relations generate two disparate and competing bourgeois and proletarian political economies.[46] The objects that were the matter of the simple commodity exchange/legal form couplet could not make demands of that form. The exchange of human labour-power for wages, however, is inseparable from the people supplying that labour. Workers are capable of mobilising as a class and attempting to impose their own political economy on the legal form, which not only suffuses it with new content, but alters the form itself. I have previously noted that 'the integration of a collective historical subject (the proletariat) into the legal process ensures the law itself becomes an arena of class struggle in which the competing political economies of labour and capital struggle for the higher ground'.[47]

As the proletariat moves through class struggle and the development of social labour advances, it can struggle for new laws and new legal institutions. In the process, the tension between a legal form revolving around juridically equal, de-classed citizen-subjects and the reality of inequality and exploitation is sharply foregrounded. One of the state's primary functions is to facilitate the continued commodification of labour-power.[48] A theoretical commitment to the purity of the legal form does not trouble the minds of state personnel when they are seeking to reproduce labour. Although it must continue to abstract and formalise working-class power, the state nevertheless receives and acts upon the impulses of the working class in struggle. What it then does depends on a variety of factors, including the balance of class forces, the particular epoch of capitalism and the structure and path dependence of extant institutional structures (in short, depending upon the kinds of forces the PRA best captures). If the working class, either singly or in combination with other classes, is able to apply a critical mass of economic and/or political pressure, the state is often forced to develop techniques of *administration*, whereby the spot-fires of proletarian activism are dampened by recourse to new tribunals, bureaucracies and procedures.[49] Whereas the abstract legal form aspires to universality and equality between de-classed juridical equals, administration plugs the gaps created when this form can no longer contain the *collective* interests of workers.[50] As a result of contestation, institutions whose subject matter is the specific, and whose subjects are often industrial organisations representing labour and capital collectively, are created.

Such institutions represent a modification of the legal form, rather than its destruction. On the one hand, they are material codifications of working-class power, of its ability to rise above the appearance of formal equality and demand action on the basis of material inequality. On the other, administration responds to this pressure in ways that exhaust their subversive potential. Kay and Mott claim that administrative structures represent 'working-class power *post-festum*; working-class political victories captured and formalised at their moment of triumph'.[51] Neocleous adds that state administration:

> appropriates and nullifies the struggle of the working class; as such they are the fossilised remnants of class struggle; they are the subsumption of struggle – working-class struggle abolished and preserved. Born of the struggle of the working class, these structures are then left with the task of administering that same class, a task performed in relation to *both collective organisations of the working class and its decomposed elements, known as 'citizens'* (my emphasis).[52]

The corrosiveness of the legal form,[53] its useful capacity to interpellate people as individualised citizens[54] and the inability of the state to depart from a notion of juridical equality mean that administrative institutions, although a counter to holes in the abstract legal form, nevertheless are legal in terms of their constitution and modes of operation. Indeed, they are normally bound to the formal legal system through the vehicle of judicial review under the separation of powers doctrine. On these bases, Kay and Mott note that law and administration are not separate phenomena, but are instead points on a law-administration continuum.[55] Using the example of administrative law, they demonstrate the interpenetration of the two forms: 'Administration is law in the sense that it creates law, is subject to law, and acts through legal forms; and the law affecting administration . . . is probably the greater part of all law today'.[56]

As will be demonstrated in this book, the unique Australian system of compulsory conciliation and arbitration is an example of state administration *par excellence*. The system will be elucidated in much greater detail in chapters 4–9, but it suffices here to understand it as a set of quasi-judicial arbitral tribunals that could compulsorily determine disputes between employers and unions, with the resulting determinations called 'awards'. A response to the devastating Great Strikes of the 1890s, the structure came about through the political mobilisation of the working class in the form of the Australian Labor Party, allied with middle-class liberals.[57] In terms of the props given to trade union recognition and input into the process of determining disputes, arbitration was, at the time, a definite historical advance for the proletariat. However, from its inception the system was highly legalised (both in terms of operation and personnel), time-consuming and directed union attention away from the building of strong rank-and-file organisation. Moreover, arbitration quickly proved itself amenable to capital, with a series of decisions in the late 1920s and early 1930s enforcing real wage reductions and increased working hours.[58]

The history of the arbitration system reveals the dynamic nature of the law-administration continuum. Unlike Kay and Mott, who seem to suggest that the development of the continuum effaces once-and-for-all the distinctiveness of its two constituent features, I have argued that the nexus point between law and administration is moveable.[59] That is, depending upon the nature of the class struggle and the fortunes of its respective parties, a labour law regime can be more heavily reliant upon those branches of law closest to the abstract legal form (such as the common law of contract and property) or can have a greater reliance on administrative structures, such as quasi-judicial arbitral tribunals. Given the fact that administration is spawned by the state responding to working-class pressure and is an answer to the gaps created by the abstract legal form, it is likely to be the stronger current when the proletariat has a critical mass of strength, is integrated in some way within the state apparatus and is committed to the administrative structures thus created. Conversely, when the working class is in retreat, the state is less impelled to generate administrative responses to its struggle. In such an environment, the traditional forms of law tend to reassert themselves, particularly if the climate is one of increased commodification and the expansion of the competition principle.[60] Given its abstraction, assumption of juridical equality between unequal subjects and its individualising effect, the abstract legal form is the form in which capital has always operated most comfortably (as shall be seen in chapter 6 in the context of common law industrial torts).

Of course, what the proletariat and capital are struggling over is, within the broad parameters of the capitalist mode of production, time and place specific. Alongside the understanding that the working class develops a political economy of its own, intertwined with but distinct from that of capital's, the manifold crisis tendencies of capitalism are handled differently and to varying degrees in different historical epochs. For example, capitalists seeking to boost their profit by cutting labour costs simultaneously reduce the purchasing power of their workers, jeopardising the realisation of surplus value in the marketplace. Jessop, building upon Althusser, notes how capitalist contradictions are internally variegated, such that different poles of each contradiction assume varying weight in different historical conjunctures.[61] In this realisation lies the secret; the labour law regime is constantly evolving, with the nexus point between law and administration shifting as the class struggle itself ebbs and flows. The fact that this struggle is itself not static, but also ebbs and flows, revolving around one set of contradictions before turning to others, means that the form and content of labour law will vary between different periods. It is at this point that we can introduce the PRA.

THE PARISIAN REGULATION APPROACH AND LEGAL ANALYSIS

We have seen how the PRA combines a number of concepts along the plane from abstract to concrete to render an understanding of distinct models of development, which represent a coherent and compatible combination of an accumulation regime, mode of regulation and industrial paradigm. Of particular significance for the study of labour law is the mode of regulation. In chapter 2, I noted that a mode of regulation more or less represented a stable, historically conditioned arrangement of capital's juridic forms, revolving around four chief institutional forms which must be guaranteed by the state, often through the vehicle of law. Among these four forms, two are of critical importance for our analysis, namely, state forms and the wage-labour nexus.[62] The contention made previously, that law and the state are related juridic forms of capital, informs my reading of what exactly is entailed by the term 'state forms'. Located at a lower level of abstraction, 'state forms' as part of a mode of regulation refers to the historically conditioned manifestations of the legal and state forms. Labour law forms a distinct subset within this structure. It also serves a key role in constituting the wage-labour nexus, what Boyer describes as the process of socialisation of productive activity within capitalism.[63] He goes on to state that its specific form is 'defined by the set of *legal* and institutional conditions that govern the use of wage-earning labour as the workers' mode of existence' (my emphasis).[64] Labour law is thus a crucial component in the constitution of a mode of regulation, particularly so regarding the two key institutional forms identified.

The models of development of which modes of regulation are part have their own distinct mechanisms of coherence and trajectories of crisis. They handle the contradictions of capitalism differentially, embed or exclude working-class power to varying degrees, and, given the evolving political economy of both labour and capital, impart their own hue to the class struggle. It will be recalled that these are the same features which determine the balance point in the law-administration continuum. There is thus an intimate connection between the two, such that we can say *that models of development are tied to distinctive arrangements of this continuum*.

The aforementioned dynamism of the processes of law and administration is itself tied to the fortunes of the model of development of which it is part. As seen in chapter 2, the latter represent broadly coherent formations in which the crisis tendencies of capital are contained, managed and/or deferred. While the contradictions of capital, and the class struggle that generates them, ensure that the basis of such coherence is temporary and inevitably undermined, continuity and stability prevail over the short to medium term. By contrast, crisis disrupts extant institutions and norms, typically resulting in periods of experimentation and 'institutional searching', whereby new structures are sought which can restabilise and renew capital accumulation.[65] The same process holds for the law-administration continuum and is the subject of extensive discussion in chapters 5 and 6. The particular balance between law and administration, and the institutions which express it, will be generally stable, albeit evolving, in periods *en régulation*. However, this arrangement can never absolve the fundamentally contradictory character of the wage-labour/capital relationship. To the extent that it solves some problems of labour commodification, it opens others, a reality strongly expressed in times of crisis. It is at these junctures, when capital accumulation breaks down and support for previously functional institutions wanes, that opportunities for remaking the continuum are strongest. A theoretically rigorous understanding of the evolution of labour law is thus impossible without an adequate account of capitalist periodisation, and it is precisely in the latter task that the PRA outperforms competing approaches.

It is worth noting at this point that specific regulationist studies of labour law are uncommon (law generally, still less). This is not necessarily because regulationists deny causal power to the law. Indeed, Boyer has opined that 'laws, regulations, and rules imposed or confirmed by the state often play an essential role in spreading, *and sometimes even originating*, essential institutional forms' (my emphasis).[66] He also notes that law plays a key role in mediating between the system-level needs of an accumulation regime and individual decision-making, through exercising a combination of coercion and symbolism.[67] However, what is lacking in such a perspective is an understanding of law as a juridic form of capital, as a necessary and embedded feature of capitalism. Studies of labour law tend to be in discussions of broader compass, and commonly analyse it in terms of the instrumental purposes it serves.[68] Law doesn't feature here as a specific, form-determined battleground, but as just one of so many forms of regulation and control in a capitalist society. The warning of Pashukanis against conceiving law in these terms springs to mind.[69]

As canvassed in chapter 2, this historical shortcoming presents no great difficulty. The PRA is perfectly capable of accommodating a theory of juridic forms, provided the mode of regulation concept is not conceived as a 'meso'-level bundle of institutions designed to *externally* control a capitalist economy, but is instead a hierarchy of forms no less rooted in capitalist social relations. With this union, a powerful synthetic theory emerges, one capable of unifying the abstract and the concrete in the study of labour law.

Moreover, the comparative neglect of labour law from a PRA perspective is ameliorated somewhat by the fact that the past two decades have seen a broader resurgence in work exploring the articulations between law and the economy. Perspectives include the law and economics literature, Varieties of Capitalism, Legal Origins, Critical Legal Studies, the 'New Institutionalism', institutional complementarity and the Labour Market Regulation Approach.[70] Certain of these approaches, notably the law and economics literature, are thoroughly incompatible with a PRA perspective, rooted as it is in a neoclassical conception of rational actors and efficiency.[71] I have elsewhere criticised others, such as the Varieties of Capitalism and Legal Origins, for being markedly inferior to the PRA in terms of explaining legal development.[72] None of these traditions start from a rigorous Marxist political economy, revealed by the fact that notions like 'endogenity' and 'complementarity' start from a conceptual separation of law and economics, as opposed to conceiving them as different forms of capital. For all that, however, much of this work paints a rich empirical picture of the developments taking hold of labour law at the concrete level. Where relevant, and with a retooling to fit a regulation perspective, such work can help illuminate the legal changes which PRA scholars have generally eschewed to analyse.

CONCLUSIONS

In this chapter I have constructed a rigorous hierarchy of abstraction accounting for the place of law within the capitalist mode of production generally, and within models of development more concretely. The most abstract legal form is a necessary correlate to the commodity form, which explains its roots in pre-capitalist societies. However, the development of capitalist production relations sees both a quantitative extension and qualitative deepening of this form. The advent of the state as a related juridic form, the generalisation of commodity production and exchange, and the commodification of labour power exert a fundamentally transformative influence. The lattermost in particular is crucial; by commodifying labour-power, and thus extending the legal form over it, capitalism integrates a thinking and active collective subject, the proletariat, into the legal process.

Labour law features most prominently in this process, as it is the area of law most intimately related to the class struggle, defining as it does the terms and conditions upon which labour-power can be employed and exploited by capitalists. By unifying as a class, the proletariat is capable of forcing its own political economy onto the legal form, which the state registers through acts of administration. These are ad hoc responses to working-class power that plug the gaps opened in the abstract legal form with specific institutions that address workers and their organisations at the same time that they extinguish the subversive potential of their struggle. Within the framework of a capitalist society, administration can thus never liberate the working class; it can only alter the terms on which it is exploited.

The structure of a law-administration continuum, and the balance between its two poles, is an explicitly historical product. Labour law forms a key part of a mode of regulation and is especially significant regarding state forms and the codification of the wage-labour nexus. Given the contribution of a mode of regulation to a stable model of development, it is clear that particular arrangements of this continuum are in part constitutive of the latter. To the extent that models of development work out the many contradictions of capital to varying degrees, are premised upon a particular modality of accumulation and extant institutions and channel the class struggle in different fashions, the regimes of labour law corresponding with them will be unique. When, however, crisis undermines the stability of a model of development, its labour law regime will be called into question. At such historical junctures, the nexus point between law and administration proves fluid and can, depending upon the balance of social forces, be shifted. In chapters 5 and 6 I will elucidate the relationship between the evolution of post–World War II Australian capitalism and regimes of labour law, focusing particularly upon the reformulation of the law-administration continuum.

Chapter 4

Antipodean Fordism and Liberal-Productivism in Australia

In chapter 2 I outlined the concepts and methodology underpinning a regulationist perspective. In particular, I noted that a coherent combination of an industrial paradigm, accumulation regime and mode of regulation can constitute a model of development, a stable instantiation of the capitalist mode of production. Understanding the ascendency of certain models, their ensuing crisis and the rise of new models is a most useful means by which capitalism can be periodised into distinct epochs.

Here, I elucidate the two models of development which have defined post–World War II Australian capitalism: *antipodean Fordism* and *liberal-productivism in Australia*. These are derived from the more abstract regulationist ideal-types, *Fordism* and *liberal-productivism*, which have broadly characterised the nature of capitalism in advanced capitalist countries. The former, however, have been sensitised to the Australian context and exhibit distinctive industrial paradigms, accumulation regimes and modes of regulation, which in concert establish unique modalities of coherence and distinctive trajectories of crisis. These models are therefore pitched at a lower level of abstraction and do, *contra* the ideal-types, concretely describe the experience of a specific society.

This reality informs the second task of this chapter, which is to indicate in an abstract way the place of labour law within these two models. The picture presented is somewhat one-sided, in that I am here more concerned with how the labour law regime gives effect to the functional requirements of a model of development; that is, what abstract conditions does a model of development require to successfully reproduce, and how does labour law contribute to that process? The results of this analysis specify the kind of functions a labour law regime will be called upon to perform and its resultant basic characteristics, as well as the particular configuration of the law-administration continuum it manifests. However, echoing Jessop, the fact that particular functions are expected of a form is no indication it can actually perform accordingly.[1] If this chapter concentrates more on the political economic framework within which labour law operates, this is not to suggest that the latter plays no role in constituting that framework. The conception of law as a juridic form of capital does not admit of conceiving law in these terms. The following two chapters will explore in a more detailed and dynamic sense the internal structure of the labour law regime, and how it shaped the fortunes of both models of development.

Before this closer investigation, however, I must first outline the ideal-typical models of development from which the Australian variants are derived.

FORDISM AS AN IDEAL-TYPE

The construction for which the PRA is most well known is Fordism. The term has, within a regulationist perspective, been used variously to describe an industrial paradigm, an accumulation regime and a mode of regulation.[2] This is not to mention the confusion added by use outside of a regulationist paradigm.[3] I stated in chapter 2 that it was specifically as a model of development that I deployed Fordism. It is thus necessary to unfold it precisely.

Lipietz is the scholar who has most consistently and rigorously described Fordism as a model of development. According to him, Fordism combined:

- a Taylorist, mechanised labour process paradigm within large, multi-department firms;
- an autocentric mass production/mass consumption intensive accumulation regime synthesising full employment with rising productivity and real wages; and
- a mode of regulation involving a Keynesian Welfare National State (KWNS) that guaranteed effective demand through protective social legislation and the generalisation of mass consumption norms.[4]

Each of these structures had their roots in the late nineteenth and early twentieth centuries. However, it was only after World War II – which simultaneously soaked up Depression-era unemployment, intensified industrial production, resulted in a massive devalourisation of capital and forged a new international hierarchy – that these elements could cohere into the Fordist model of development in Western states.

As was indicated in the previous chapter, the contradictions of capitalism are not expressed uniformly, or assume the same significance, in different historical conjunctures. Althusser notes that within given social orders, certain contradictions appear as primary, others secondary.[5] Moreover, each contradiction has opposite poles, tension points pulling in opposite directions.[6] On this basis, Jessop states that

> a given stage or variety of capitalism would differ in terms of the weights attributed to different contradictions and dilemmas (hierarchisation), the importance accorded to their different aspects (prioritisation), the role of different spaces, places, and scales in these regards (spatialisation), and the temporal patterns of their treatment (temporalisation).[7]

Fordism was indelibly marked by the ruination of the Great Depression out of which it emerged. The causes of this economic catastrophe were complex, but a yawning disproportion between Departments I and II, and relative overproduction compared to the restricted purchasing power of the working class, were root problems.[8] It is thus unsurprising that various regulationists have remarked that the wage-labour nexus, the set of legal and institutional conditions governing the terms of wage-labour, was the site of dominant contradiction in the Fordist model of development.[9] To prevent a recurrence of the species of crisis seen in the Great Depression, the working class had to be subsumed within the developing Taylorist, mechanised industrial paradigm and guaranteed the purchasing power to absorb the mass of commodities emanating therefrom. The keys to both were the repositioning of wages as a source of domestic demand (rather than simply a cost of production) and the encouragement of moderate unionism, which obtained increased wages for workers at the cost of deeper real subordination to managerial prerogative in the organisation of the labour process.[10]

With this understanding, we can schematically describe the dynamic of Fordism *en régulation*. The application of Taylorist, mass production principles in the labour process resulted in substantial productivity gains for capitalists.[11] In exchange for accepting the enhanced managerial prerogative and labour intensification consequent upon this development, workers were given liberal rights to organise and assured employment security and a growth in their real wages in line with productivity improvements.[12] The resultant increased purchasing power in the proletariat's hands allowed it to consume a greater proportion of the goods and services it created, ensuring both high utilisation of capital capacity and further opportunities for capitalists to expand the scale of production.[13] This demand thus begets further productivity improvements, beginning the cycle afresh. To fortify and guarantee this process, the KWNS adopts policies designed to maintain full employment, smooth the business cycle and support the stability of demand by ensuring those temporarily out of work or not a part of the labour force can nevertheless consume.[14] This in turn presupposes both the capacity and willingness of the state to directly involve itself in the circuit of capital.

This 'virtuous' cycle served to offset and/or defer the crisis tendencies of capitalism, albeit in a provisional and ultimately self-defeating way. Vidal notes that

> a rise in the technical composition of capital was offset by a continuous rise in productivity generated by intensive growth, underconsumptionism offset by rising real wages and overproduction moderated through nationally bound, oligopolistic competition, again with balanced growth via standardized mass production and institutional supports for mass consumption.[15]

This ability to ameliorate some of capitalism's most powerful crisis tendencies is the key to understanding the physiology of the post–World War II boom, extending up until the early 1970s. Kettell describes this period as

> the greatest economic boom in the history of world capitalism. Between 1950 and 1973 the growth of output and fixed capital investment in 'advanced' capitalist economies reached virtually double the levels attained during the previous golden age of capitalism from 1870 to 1913, while the global market experienced an almost continuous expansion as industrialization spread further into 'developing' nations. These factors enabled major capitalist economies to enjoy a heady mix of high profit margins, annual wage increases, moderate inflation, and relatively low levels of unemployment.[16]

Faulkner adds, 'High growth rates, rapidly rising living standards, a business cycle whose occasional slowdowns were so slight as to be barely noticeable – these things made it appear to many that capitalism had solved its problems and could now deliver endless and increasing prosperity for all'.[17] Countries as varied as the USA, France, West Germany and, as we shall see, Australia, experienced a Fordist boom, albeit to varying degrees and with distinct institutional twists.[18]

ANTIPODEAN FORDISM

Australia most certainly shared in the post–World War II boom. Between the years 1950 and 1969, the Australian economy grew at the very impressive average of over 5 per cent per annum.[19] The pattern from the late 1940s through the early 1970s was one of high and sustained growth, free from the perturbations in growth rates that characterised the 1920s and 1930s.[20] Labour productivity grew vigorously in the 1950s, with a veritable surge of 2.75 per cent average annual growth between 1964–1965 and 1973–1974.[21] This tremendous growth was reflected in the fact that the growth of gross domestic product (GDP) per worker waxed in the 1950s and 1960s.[22] As would be anticipated in a Fordist society, this productivity growth was articulated to real wage improvements: real wage growth in the 1950s, 1960s and early 1970s averaged 2–3 per cent per annum.[23] Effective and durable full employment was attained, with the unemployment rate rarely exceeding 2 per cent between 1945 and the early 1970s.[24] The growth of investment in fixed capital, both in trend terms and as a percentage of GDP, reached new highs.[25] Most significantly for capitalists, the basic indicators of the robustness of capital accumulation were healthy; the average rate of profit achieved during the boom is higher than at any subsequent point.[26] The same can be said for the rate of surplus value.[27]

That broadly similar results were achieved in countries identified by regulationists as Fordist makes a *prima facie* case for saying that Australia too experienced a Fordist phase. There are certainly a considerable number of scholars who have explicitly made that claim, although the exact meaning they ascribe to the term Fordism is subject to the ambiguities I noted earlier.[28] Additionally, there is the work of those such as Lloyd and Broomhill who, although they have coined their own terms, draw heavily from regulationist concepts and recognise something distinctive about Australian capitalism during the long boom.[29]

The analysis embarked on here uses the ideal-typical model of Fordism elucidated earlier as a focusing device, an abstract outline of causal relationships to guide investigation into the structure of post–World War II Australian political economy. The pattern of economic growth, the nature of macroeconomic indicators, the roles and functions of the state and, most importantly here, the success of labour law and industrial relations institutions in codifying the requisite wage-labour nexus entitle us to call Australian society between 1945 and the early 1970s a Fordist one. However, it will be recalled that in chapter 2 I noted that Fordism as an ideal-type captures the dynamic of an epoch of capitalism without describing the concrete experience of any one society. For the model to fulfil its analytical potential, it must be sensitised to particular concrete contexts. If this process of sensitisation is ignored, important features of national difference are elided and the experiences of the country closest to the ideal-type (in the case of Fordism, the USA) tend to be reified. Treuren highlights the dangers in so applying the Fordist concept to Australia: 'Simply reading off the results of French or US regulationist research, and importing into the Australian context is methodologically inappropriate, and will provide misleading results'.[30]

The proper method of placing the Fordist concept into a dialectical relationship with the Australian experience of the post–War boom reveals a model of development that, while recognisably Fordist, modifies some of its key constituent components. Broadly, this Australian incarnation of Fordism combined:

- an industrial paradigm based on mass production but marked by an incomplete incorporation of Taylorist forms of work control and organisation;
- an intensive accumulation regime of mass production and mass consumption which *was not autarkic*; that is, it was premised upon the ability of the

export-oriented farming and mining sectors to underwrite high levels of industrial protection; and

- a mode of regulation that precociously enshrined the Fordist wage-labour nexus in the arbitration system. This mode, although guaranteed by the KWNS, was characterised by the unification of that state's economic and social objectives/functions.

I have dubbed this model of development *antipodean Fordism* (a term coined by Rolfe who, however, uses it as a vague cultural construct).[31] It builds upon the features of the 'Australian mode of development' Treuren hinted at while more clearly systematising it in line with discrete PRA concepts.[32]

With this cursory definition in hand, we can now move to a closer investigation of the convergences and differences between the abstract Fordist model of development and antipodean Fordism. This is best done by exploring the latter's constituent industrial paradigm, accumulation regime and mode of regulation.

Industrial Paradigm

The dominant Fordist industrial paradigm is summarised pithily by Lipietz, who describes it as 'Taylorism plus mechanization'.[33] It combined a Taylorist structure of job organisation, culture and control with mechanised, supply-driven mass production deriving economies of scale from the employment of rigid, specialised machinery.[34] As mentioned in chapter 2, this is not to suggest that all work has to be organised on these principles; indeed, the success of the latter was often reflected by a growth in those sectors not then amenable to them. It is enough that certain 'lead sectors', industries in which outcomes disproportionately affect industrial, economic and social outcomes in other industries, employ them.[35] The above-average productivity growth and resultant wage increase obtaining in Fordist lead sectors, like the automobile and whitegoods manufacturing industries, can then, with appropriately supportive institutions, spill over into the workforce at large.

It is clear that the industrial paradigm of antipodean Fordism fulfilled the mechanised mass productionist side of the abstract model. World War II had fuelled a tremendous increase in the scale and diversity of the manufacturing sector. The most pronounced growth was in relatively capital-intensive industries, such as metals, chemicals/petrochemicals and electrical goods, which were able to exploit a growing domestic market to reap economies of scale through the employment of machinery and advanced manufacturing techniques.[36] True, widespread mass production thus took off, and Australians were soon consuming a wide variety of mass produced goods.

While antipodean Fordism demonstrably took a mass productionist industrial paradigm as the source of manufacturing dynamism, it didn't, however, integrate Taylorist forms of work organisation to the extent the abstract model would suggest. This claim can be considerably sharpened if a nuanced approach to Taylorism is adopted.

To provide a complete overview of Taylorism (or 'scientific management' as it became popularised) is beyond the ambit of this work. Indeed, a whole book could be devoted simply to unfolding the different, and in many instances competing, definitions of Taylorism. For the purposes of this chapter, I will advance a two-pronged definition of scientific management: firstly, as a general ideology of labour process control; and secondly as a concrete set of practices and techniques (such as the creation of a planning department to specify jobs and control the production process, time and motion studies, and incentive payment systems related to effort norms) adopted by management.[37]

As an ideology of industrial organisation, Taylorism is best conceived as the divorce of the conception and execution elements that together unify the labour process.[38] The former becomes the preserve of management, which arrogates to itself the knowledge and control once exercised by the skilled craftsperson. Simultaneously, this separation of functions was to run parallel to a cultural revolution which was deliberately targeted at the destruction of worker sub-cultures of collectivism and their substitution by a unified culture of shared interests between labour and capital.[39] Allied to systems of machinery, scientific management apprehended at this level is a key moment in capital gaining real, as opposed to formal, control of the labour process.

Considered in this broad sense, there is no denying the influence of Taylorism in the Australian context. Australian capitalists routinely looked to their overseas counterparts in America and Britain for what was perceived to be the 'latest' in managerial practices and strategy, a process that intensified after World War II.[40] The formation of groups such as the Australian Institute of Management represented a determined effort on the part of sections of capital to train and support a new managerial class, schooled in the techniques and culture of Taylorism.[41] Moreover, Taksa notes that scientific management had profound cultural and ideological implications in Australia that went well beyond the extent of its technical application, most notably education reform and the cult of 'Americanisation'.[42]

The question of how pervasive Taylorism as shop-floor practice was in Australia, however, is the source of some debate. It is clear that both capital and the state made intensive efforts to implant Taylorist forms of work organisation; indeed, as we shall see in chapter 7 with the metal trades, the arbitration system itself was sometimes a vehicle for their imposition. Moreover, the dominant narrative among the union movement, particularly the peak Australian Council of Trade Unions (ACTU), is certainly that these forms were the prevailing logic of the labour process during the era according with antipodean Fordism.[43] Empirical research by Wright, however, suggests that the actual adoption of Taylorist work practices in this period was somewhat less widespread than its ideology. He states that 'Taylorist practices were used by only a minority of Australian firms and tended to be concentrated in particular industries'.[44] Unsurprisingly, these industries were concentrated in the manufacturing sector, where the production of physical goods generally allowed for a more thorough division of labour and an ability to more accurately measure productivity, both on a collective and individual basis.

Outside of manufacturing, the spread of Taylorism as a suite of shop-floor routines appears limited. Despite the best efforts of capital and the state, for example, the building industry proved less amenable to Taylorist techniques than was hoped and expected.[45] Even within manufacturing, the diffusion of Taylorism was retarded in some cases by the nature of the production process itself, particularly insofar that the state of technology did not yet allow for a rigid application of Taylorist principles. Wright notes that 'in particular, detailed work measurement was less practical in highly capital intensive industries or those whose products were produced over longer periods of time'.[46]

As was often the case in the United Kingdom, the adoption of Taylorist techniques could also be stymied by trade union resistance. Powerful metal unions such as the Amalgamated Engineering Union were particularly opposed, as evidenced by their struggle against the imposition of pay incentive schemes.[47] In the face of such hostility, some employers in the metal trades took discretion as the better of valour and backed down.

A somewhat piecemeal and incomplete circulation of Taylorist work practices should not be taken, however, as a refutation of both its material and symbolic importance during the era of antipodean Fordism. As Wright himself acknowledges, 'The decades of the 1950s and 1960s then were boom years for the application of Taylorist techniques in Australian industry'.[48] To the extent that Taylorist practices were imposed, they tended to be concentrated in the manufacturing sector, the engine of intensive accumulation. Moreover, even in the absence of strictly defined and identifiable work practices, the ideology of Taylorism informed the radical separation of conception and execution that underlay the mass-production oriented industrial paradigm of antipodean Fordism.

Accumulation Regime

The accumulation regime of antipodean Fordism was unmistakably intensive in character; that is, it involved an effort on the part of capital to raise the share of relative surplus value through a commodification of the proletariat's means of consumption and, in so doing, created an organic series of linkages between Department I and II in the production (and reproduction) process.[49]

More simply, this intensive accumulation regime unified mass production with mass consumption. The post–War decades saw profligate advertising, easy access to banking capital, and comparatively high wages create a market for the vehicles, white goods, televisions and other appliances which mass production and a diversified manufacturing sector could now proffer at an affordable price for the working class. Suburbanisation, and the concomitant rise in home ownership levels to record highs, was also a key element of this mass consumption paradigm; indeed, Rolfe describes it as 'the focal point of antipodean Fordism'.[50] Broadly, Walsh notes how 'new houses, cars, clothing and consumer durables all provided an expanding market for the producers of the Fordist bloc'.[51] The net effect was to provide the skeleton of the virtuous circle described earlier.

As the abstract model of Fordism suggests, the engine of this regime was the manufacturing sector. Balnave and Patmore state that 'the average annual rate of growth for manufacturing output, employment and productivity between 1945–1950 and 1967–1968 was 6.1 per cent, 2 per cent and 4.1 per cent'.[52] The Australian Bureau of Statistics adds:

> Growth of manufacturing output per employee from Federation to World War II had varied from 1.0 to 1.3% per annum (excluding the years of the Great Depression). During the 1950s and 60s, however, growth rose dramatically to an average of 4.3% per annum. Over this period *the expansion of manufacturing productivity per annum was 11% higher than in the agricultural sector and almost double that of the economy as a whole* (my emphasis).[53]

The fact that manufacturing outperformed agriculture (the traditional bastion of the Australian economy and its historical means of insertion into the international economy) specifically, and the economy generally, *prima facie* justifies calling it the leading sector. In chapter 7 we will see how the metals sector assumed a particularly important lead sector role, acting as the primary site upon which the gains of intensive accumulation were institutionally levered.

However, despite these similarities between the accumulation regime of the abstract model and antipodean Fordism, the latter was distinct in a highly significant way. Unlike the ideal-typical construction, this accumulation regime was *not autarkic*; that is, it was unable to form a self-sufficient system. It was heavily dependent upon the export of primary commodities (such as agricultural and mineral products), the success of which provided the material basis of the highly protective tariff system which allowed Australian manufacturing to fuel intensive accumulation.[54]

This introduced a latent yet fundamental fracture point into antipodean Fordism, cleaving a line between export-oriented, 'competitive' primary production and the largely inward-looking, 'uncompetitive' manufacturing sector. The ability of antipodean Fordism to accumulate intensively was predicated in part upon the subordination of pastoral and mining capital to industrial capital, largely through the former paying higher prices for labour and capital inputs.[55] While the former (particularly the farming sector) were co-opted into the system somewhat through the liberal imposition of tariffs on imported products, the increase in mining and energy exports in the late 1960s and early 1970s exposed, through a species of the 'Dutch Disease', this fragility of the accumulation regime of antipodean Fordism.[56]

Mode of Regulation

In many ways, the mode of regulation that ensured the coherence of the post-war long boom was the archetypal Fordist exemplar. As Lloyd notes, key features of his 'labourist-protectionism' model (which he plots as beginning in the early 1900s), such as the historic class compromise between capital and labour and the institutions created to crystallise and channel it, only became widespread in other industrial countries from the 1940s.[57] In a more explicitly regulationist fashion, Grieg adds: 'The Australian federal state was well placed to perform a central role in the advent of Fordism, as many of the institutions established in the infancy of Federation coincided with the requirements of Fordist growth'.[58] He adds, 'If the experience of the US during the 1930s can be described as a Fordist regime of accumulation in search of a mode of regulation, then *the Australian experience appears as a mode of regulation waiting for a Fordist regime of accumulation*' (my emphasis).[59]

This reality should not be taken to suggest that Australia represented a 'proto-Fordist' society. Fordism constructed as a model of development denotes not the history of disparate institutions (the mistake Lloyd makes), but the coherence of the structured whole; a requisite mode of regulation revolving around the KWNS could not be construed as an element of Fordism if it did not articulate with a regime of intensive accumulation. What the presence of certain precocious institutions did mean, however, was an ability to rapidly assume a Fordist trajectory once a critical mass of industrialisation had been achieved thanks to World War II.

Where the Australian mode of regulation was truly Fordist *par excellence* was in its unique system of compulsory conciliation and arbitration. A much deeper exploration of this structure will be made in the subsequent chapters. Suffice it to say here that the arbitration framework proved exceedingly adept at effecting outcomes necessary for the Fordist model of development, particularly insofar as it institutionally entrenched the Fordist wage-labour nexus. As this touches directly on the labour law regime, further discussion will be reserved for the following section.

More broadly, other aspects of the ideal-typical Fordist mode of regulation were also present. The Commonwealth Bank of Australia and, from 1960 onward, the Reserve Bank of Australia, executed the functions of a central bank and lender of last resort, one of the key responses to the crisis of extensive accumulation in the 1930s. Both oversaw a tightly managed national currency (pegged to the British pound sterling until 1971) subject to strict exchange and capital controls, which aided in the effort to shield domestic institutions from the vagaries of the international economy. The state was unmistakably Keynesian in its approach to macroeconomic management and actively used the budget as a counter-cyclical tool.[60] The domestic economy was dominated by a comparatively small number of large firms, particularly in the mining and manufacturing sectors,[61] with the latter selling its wares to a predominantly closed, national market.[62] Oligopolistic competition between such large, often vertically integrated firms was the norm.[63] In these respects, the Australian mode of regulation during the long boom period closely resembled the ideal-typical Fordist model.

This mode did, however, possess features which represented a unique antipodean twist to the abstract structures and tendencies of Fordism. For the purposes of this book, the most significant were certain characteristics of the KWNS, most notably the mechanisms through which it performed its redistributive capacities.

Ironically, the arbitration system, which I regarded earlier as a precociously Fordist institution, was also the vehicle of considerable divergence from the ideal-typical Fordist model of development. This paradox stems not so much from the structure or function of the arbitral tribunals themselves, but rather from their articulation with the wider institutional ensemble of the state. Broadly, whereas the ideal-typical model of the KWNS (and the experience of many European countries) envisages a comprehensive system of social support married to a large public sector as the instruments of government welfare, the Australian state used the arbitration system as a vehicle to deliver social and economic policy. As shall be outlined in chapter 5, from the landmark *Harvester* decision in 1907, the arbitration system took as a foundational concept the 'basic wage', a wage minimum deemed necessary to support the male worker, his wife and three children in 'frugal comfort'.[64] The provision of a substantial arbitral safety net, combined with industry protection and a selective inward migration scheme, rendered possible a rather 'minimalist and residual state welfare system'.[65]

The uniqueness of the Australian state in this regard has been well captured by Castles, who coined a new term to describe it – the 'wage earners' welfare state'.[66] He states of it:

> The simplest way of locating the essential difference between Australia and most other nations is to say that, in Australia, wages policy, in large part, substituted

> for social policy, with the functional identity between the two being denoted by the peculiar (in terms of capitalistic criteria) importation into Antipodean wage-setting mechanisms of such concepts as the 'fair wage'.[67]

Although the Australian KWNS performed the functions necessary to Fordism, it delivered these policy goals through an institutional configuration which was thoroughly novel. As we shall see later, this idiosyncratic imbrication of the wage-labour nexus and the form of the Australian KWNS had profound ramifications for the structure of antipodean Fordism, particularly insofar as it planted within it the seeds of its own unique crisis tendencies.

ANTIPODEAN FORDISM AND LABOUR LAW

With an understanding of antipodean Fordism now in hand, we can move to an abstract consideration of the regime of labour law that characterised it. As was previously stated, elements of the mode of regulation corresponding with antipodean Fordism predated the structured coherence of the whole; certainly this was the case with the system of compulsory conciliation and arbitration. But Fordism as a concept denotes the congruity of the whole, a totality that emerged only under the impulses of the crisis of the Depression and World War II. It is to this era that my analysis of labour law applies.

We have established that the circuit of capital is wrought by contradictions which, although all broadly derived from capitalist social relations, are nonetheless variegated and fluid through time. The Fordist model of development, partly as a response to the crisis dynamics of the Depression and partly as an effort to formalise labour-power within the context of growing union strength, crystallised the wage-labour nexus as its primary contradiction.

It will be recalled that the key to this nexus is the exchange of employment security, liberal rights to unionise and growing real wages for labour intensification and the acceptance of managerial prerogative in the labour process. These are processes which go to the heart of labour-power as a commodity, determining the terms and conditions upon which labour-power will be exploited by capital. Chapter 3 demonstrated that this process of commodification was an inherently legal process, with labour law playing this function in concrete societies through particular arrangements of the law-administration continuum. We can thus say that the antipodean Fordist wage-labour nexus both presupposed and reproduced a distinctive labour law regime.

So what are the basic legal premises of the antipodean Fordist wage-labour nexus? I argue that for this nexus to function, a set of distinct legal and institutional conditions was required, namely those that allowed for the diffusion of wage increases from high-productivity 'lead sectors'; permitted collective and 'connective' bargaining; encouraged the organisation of labour; and developed a notion of the 'standard', full-time employment contract.

These functional requirements undergirded the key features of this regime, namely a permissive attitude towards organised labour, bargaining between capital and labour at a broad occupational and/or industry level, a series of institutions which diffused wage gains from leading sectors and the growth of administrative fixes to heightened worker power. With this abstract understanding in hand, a sketch can be made of the broad brush form and content of labour law during the period of antipodean Fordist functionality.

As identified earlier, one of the key features rendering antipodean Fordism distinctive is the unique system of compulsory arbitration. This structure proved exceedingly adept at meeting one of the key requirements of the Fordist model of development, namely, ensuring the stability of effective demand, and with it the stability of Fordist intensive accumulation, through the creation of a coherent and relatively homogenous wage structure.[68] This coherence was ensured by institutions linking high-productivity lead sectors with the economy and labour force at large. In Australia, the arbitration system was better placed to deliver these outcomes than in other Fordist countries, largely through the pyramidal structure of the award system.[69]

Cochrane observes the process at play in the post–World War II years, with militant unions in the metal trades, mining and stevedoring applying 'plant by plant duress' to individual employers; concessions, once granted, could 'flow-on' to other sectors of the economy.[70] As we shall see in great detail in chapter 7, this was particularly the case with the metals industry, an archetypal Fordist lead sector. Well into the late 1960s/early 1970s, the Metal Trades Award was at the apex of the award system, with tribunal decisions about wage margins for skill being founded upon it. Respondents to other federal awards would then have their own award varied accordingly, while state tribunals would generally follow the lead of their federal counterpart.

This tendency for the Fordist wage-labour nexus to take root in the Australian arbitration system was further expedited by the notion of 'comparative wage justice', which enshrined the view that equal work should be equally recompensed regardless of industrial location.[71] When combined with the dynamic of the metals sector and the carefully established relationships of relativities and differentials between various awards in the structure, comparative wage justice ensured the flow-on of national wage cases to the workforce at large. As shall be demonstrated in chapter 5, such an ideology was a powerful force of the wage homogeneity characteristic of the Fordist model of development.

Arbitration was also instrumental in the deployment of another key element of the Fordist wage-labour nexus, namely the creation of the category of the full-time, ongoing employee working a delimited range of ordinary hours and enjoying a basket of legally enforceable entitlements and protections, so-called standard employment. Bosch has described this relationship as:

> 'stable, socially protected, dependent, full-time job . . . the basic conditions of which (working time, pay, social transfers) are regulated to a minimum level by collective labour and/or social security law' (Bosch 1986: 165). The full-time nature of the job, its stability, and the social standards linked with permanent full-time work are the key elements in this definition.[72]

The standard employment model, together with the internal labour markets with which they were intimately associated, accorded with the industrial paradigm of Fordism, with security of employment part of the *quid pro quo* for managerial prerogative and labour intensification. Moreover, it buttressed the ability of workers to take a share in the large productivity increases that helped power Fordism, maintaining the high levels of endogenous demand it required.[73] Within the fabric of antipodean Fordism, it fell to the arbitral tribunals to codify this model. In the following chapter I will investigate the mechanics of this process, but it suffices here to note that it was only by the mid-twentieth century, and particularly after World War II, that standard employment came to define the working arrangements of the greater part of the Australian working class.[74] This is perfectly commensurate with the periodisation forwarded in this book.

Another element of antipodean Fordism that directly shaped the modality of labour law was its aforementioned unification of the economic and social policy goals of the Australian KWNS. This tended to both support and place pressure on the antipodean Fordist model of development in two distinct ways. Firstly, the dissemination of 'occupational welfare benefits'[75] through the award system produced and reproduced the relatively homogenous, compressed wage structure typical of Fordism. Secondly, however, the fact that the mode of regulation peculiar to antipodean Fordism largely subsumed the economic and social functions of the KWNS into the quasi-judicial system of wage regulation heightened the fundamentally contradictory nature of labour law remarked upon previously. That antipodean Fordism combined this contradictory structure with broader social and economic imperatives could not help but exacerbate this tension, particularly insofar as it encouraged an intimate identity of economic and social performance with the regulation of the labour market. This was a tendency that pronounced itself strongly in the crisis of antipodean Fordism from the mid-1970s onwards, where the source of malaise was often located in the award system and trade union militancy.

Labour law under antipodean Fordism was premised upon moderate trade unionism, the encouragement of which was one of the purposes of the original Conciliation and Arbitration Act 1904 (Cth). The arbitration system itself can be viewed as an institutionalised class compromise between labour and capital, one that fixed a pronounced institutional role for labour within the fabric of labour law. Indeed, it had been observed that 'without unions, it is hard to conceive how arbitration could be worked'.[76] This integration of labour demands a particular arrangement of the law-administration continuum, including a whole suite of administrative concepts and institutions which take as their subjects the *collective* organs of labour and capital. The arbitral tribunals and trade unions related to each other as part of an administrative totality; the former 'registered' trade unions, in the process recognising them as the legitimate representatives of the working class at the same time as conferring a host of benefits and costs. Unions, in turn, made the system effective, policing awards, bringing actions and enforcing discipline over their members. Arbitration required unionism (of a moderate stripe), and unionism came to rely heavily upon arbitration. The administrative forms that constituted and mediated their interactions represented in themselves the essential character of administration; dealing with labour and capital as collective entities, responding at times in an ad hoc fashion to the spot-fires of proletarian activism, yet always striving to abstract the latter into an impersonal and formalistic process. The following chapter will explore the historical unfolding of this process in a more rigorous and detailed fashion.

In short, the features of the labour law regime appropriate to antipodean Fordism reflected and crystallised its unique structuring of capitalism's contradictions, most particularly its construction of the wage-labour nexus, and was premised upon a highly distinctive law-administration continuum, the heart of which was the arbitration system. The crisis of antipodean Fordism from the mid-1970s onwards was simultaneously the crisis of this order of labour law.

FORDIST CRISIS

For Fordist countries generally, crisis broke out in the early 1970s. De Vroey notes how this crisis exhibited distinctive domestic and international characteristics:

> On one hand, most of the advanced capitalist countries experience a parallel dysfunction of intensive accumulation though each has a specific character. On the other hand, on the international scene, we notice a weakening of the American hegemony, shifts in the hierarchical structure among national economies, and disruptions in the international monetary system.[77]

More specifically, Fordism began to come apart under the weight of several notable crisis tendencies. The most important of these were the exhaustion of the productivity-realising potential of mechanised Taylorism in lead sectors, the resistance of empowered workers to intensified exploitation and job fragmentation, the internationalisation of production and resultant ebbing of state power over an enclosed national space and the dismemberment of the post–War Bretton Woods financial framework.[78] The result was burgeoning inflation and the re-emergence of mass unemployment combined with slowing economic growth, the infamous 'stagflation'.

That Australian capitalism fell into crisis at this time is indisputable. The Australian Treasury's figures demonstrate that average GDP growth decreased from 5.3 per cent in the 1960s to 3.4 per cent in the 1970s and 1980s, while per capita GDP over the same period decreased from 3.2 per cent to 1.8 per cent and 1.9 per cent, respectively.[79] Inflation increased alarmingly, rising from an average of 2.5 per cent in the 1960s to a whopping 10.4 per cent in the 1970s, and remaining high at 8.1 per cent in the 1980s.[80] Unemployment rose from around 2 per cent in the late 1960s and early 1970s to 6 per cent by the end of the decade, spiking at 10 per cent in 1983 and 11 per cent in 1993.[81] After a large increase brought about by a wages explosion in 1974–1975, real wage levels remained more or less stagnant for the next twenty years,[82] while the wages share of GDP (which had peaked in 1974–1975 and jumped again in 1979–1982) entered a period of retreat throughout the majority of the 1980s.[83] Productivity growth stagnated,[84] while the value of private equipment investment and gross fixed capital formation as a percentage of GDP generally declined after the early 1970s, bottoming out in the recession of the early 1990s.[85] Finally, O'Hara notes that two key indicators of capitalist health, the rate of profit and the rate of surplus value, took a hit: the former fell from an annual average of 5.5 per cent from 1960–1969 to 3.3 per cent in 1970–1979 and 3.0 per cent in 1980–1989; the latter dropped by almost a third, from 15.0 per cent in 1960–1969 to 10.1 per cent in 1970–1989.[86]

Although the domestic and international angles of this crisis of antipodean Fordism were intimately related, it is salutary to treat them separately for purposes of analytical clarity. Beginning with the former, this crisis was first and foremost a crisis of the wage-labour relationship, particularly in its manifestation in the dominant industrial paradigm and its fixture as a precociously institutionalised nexus in the mode of regulation.

Although the actual diffusion of Taylorist work practices was uneven, and subject in some instances to strong union resistance, Taylorism began to encounter both technical and ideological limits by the late 1960s.[87] Technical barriers to a mass production–based industrial paradigm derived largely from the stagnation of productivity growth that could be achieved by further intensification and routinisation of the labour process.[88] Beyond a certain point, efforts to this end tended to provoke worker resistance, which manifested itself in both an individual, inchoate way (seen through high absenteeism, rapid employee turnover, poor quality work, sabotage, etc.) and in an organised fashion (such as strikes).

This phenomenon was no stranger in the Australian context. Broomhill notes how 'manufacturing industry, the engine of post-war growth, began to stumble as labour productivity levels fell from an average of 3.4 per cent between 1960–1973, to 2.3 per cent between 1973–1999 and then to 1.2 per cent between 1979–1993'.[89] Growing labour turnover and absenteeism led to the so-called blue-collar blues in the leading metals sector.[90] One research group added that 'during this period absenteeism, labour turnover and industrial disputation reached record levels. . . . Workers were sick of alienating and inhuman production lines, filthy factories and low wages, they voted with their feet, followed the highest pay and stayed away from work often'.[91]

Productivity improvement was the engine of the virtuous circle of manufacturing underlying antipodean Fordism. Its stumbling undermined intensive accumulation in that it distorted the articulation of mass production and mass consumption with the continued valourisation of capital. Lipietz adroitly summarises this contradiction:

> Capital can only remain profitable on two conditions: unless increased productivity in the producer-goods sector offsets the rising technical composition of capital, the proportion of immobilized assets will become dangerously high; and unless increased productivity in the consumer-goods sector balances the rise in mass purchasing-power, the share of wages in total value-added will climb to the detriment of profit.[92]

The last point is particularly significant. If wage rises outstrip productivity growth, the foundation of intensive accumulation is fractured; where wages and productivity once grew synergistically, wage growth now becomes directly competitive with profits in a zero-sum game.

The irony of Fordism is that, in crystallising the wage-labour nexus as the key site of contradiction and the lever of intensive accumulation, it was hamstrung in addressing the productivity challenge and the dysfunctions of the accumulation regime. The need to maintain effective demand among the working class, the co-opting of trade unions within the fabric of Fordism and, in the Australian context, the centrality of unions to the operation of the labour law regime all institutionally entrenched trade unionism. This phenomenon ensured that, while productivity stagnated, wage demands did not, particularly when accompanied by a wave of militancy among union rank-and-file members, who engaged in wildcat stoppages to extract over-award payments. In consequence, wage claims, which until 1973 had roughly been in line with productivity gains, started to outstrip them.[93] The 1974–1975 wage explosion discussed earlier had seen the wages share of GDP climb to 62.4 per cent, the highest ever figure for which statistics are available.[94] This heightening of the real value of labour power spiked the long-run tendency of the rate of profit to fall, which was in turn reflected in the share of profit in the national income; after peaking at approximately 17 per cent around 1968–1969, the profit share declined rapidly, shrinking to just over 13 per cent by the mid-1970s (at factor cost).[95]

These domestic developments were reinforced by the international dimensions of Fordist crisis. Mass production began to become spatially disaggregated as multinational corporations relocated labour-intensive manufacturing to low-wage, newly industrialising countries in Southeast Asia. Declining manufacturing competitiveness against these countries was exacerbated by the growing importance of mineral and energy exports, which led to something of a resources boom during the late 1960s and early 1970s, and early 1980s.[96] This development produced a form of 'Dutch Disease', whereby progressive increases in the exchange rate on the back of the strength of commodity exports erode the competitive position of manufacturing. Paradoxically, at the same time the strength of farming exports was being undermined by technological advances in the farming sectors of most other industrialised countries in concert with increased agricultural protectionism.[97] In such a context, the latent divide between export-oriented mining and agricultural capital and inward-looking manufacturing capital became explicit. The heavy tariff wall protecting Australian manufacturing came to be regarded as no longer feasible. It is in this light that the Whitlam government's 1973 decision to introduce a blanket 25 per cent cut in tariffs must be read. Such a policy, however, fundamentally revealed the cleaving point of the intensive accumulation regime of antipodean Fordism; not being autarkic, its dynamic could be maintained only so long as wide-ranging industrial protection was viable, both economically and politically. The collapse of this consensus and the growth of competition from low-wage jurisdictions resulted in the essential collapse of Australian manufacturing, a development we shall explore in greater detail in chapters 7 and 8.

The loss of manufacturing jobs in Australia went hand in hand with the growth of typically low-productivity/low-wage sectors, such as hospitality and retail, along with the expansion of the services sector generally.[98] The growing importance of information and communication technologies (ICTs) also served to overcome some of the barriers Taylorism had experienced in Australia, both within and between different sectors. Technological change associated with ICTs tended to intensify and deepen the reach of Taylorism within manufacturing, particularly sectors such as metals and automobiles.[99] Moreover, the new technologies (especially the computer) allowed the diffusion of Taylorism to industries which had previously remained relatively immune because of technical limitations, such as retail, warehousing, fast food and health care.[100] The decline in the pre-eminence of manufacturing, associated with the diffusion of Taylorist forms of work control into the services sector, fractures the functional unity between lead sector productivity gains and general wage improvements for the proletariat (particularly insofar as the hitherto lead sector is no longer so).

So, how did the crisis of antipodean Fordism in the 1970s and 1980s impact upon the regime of labour law appropriate to it? It is best to answer this question at this point in terms of the forces this crisis unleashed and their ramifications for the legal system. A key issue for capital that had to be tackled was the large wage-rounds consequent upon the institutionalised position of labour and the hierarchical award structure. The pattern of flow-on from certain key awards, most particularly the Metal Trades and Metal Industry Awards, and the ideology of comparative wage justice that lubricated it, ate into the profit share of national income once productivity growth began to stagnate and the metal trades sector lost steam. This led to capital seeking ways to sever the institutionalised links binding the workforce together, so that the gains of the industrially strong could be quarantined from the weak.

The spatial disaggregation of the mass production paradigm, the diffusion of ICT technologies into the labour process of tertiary sector jobs and the general decline of manufacturing also challenged the norms with which labour law was used to dealing, particularly the view of the typical worker as a male, unionised, manual employee. The increasing corrosiveness of competition from low-wage countries, together with the capacity of ICTs in more perfectly fragmenting and aligning labour-power with increasingly volatile market conditions, undermined the standard employment model and encouraged the growth of precarious employment forms, forms characterised by a 'lack of protective regulation, short or uncertain duration, lack of "standard" employment benefits, and ambiguous or unprotected legal status'.[101] As shall be seen in the following chapters, awards in the 1960s, 1970s and 1980s were complex and involved documents, based around standard, full-time employment and often equipped with a host of qualitative and quantitative controls over part-time and casual labour. The impulses towards precarisation thus tended to grate against the award system at the same time as they found expression within it.

The unique structure of the Australian KWNS also contributed towards the unfolding of Fordist crisis as a *distinctly legal* process. Indeed, the decline of antipodean Fordism was in many cases seen as a *prima facie* crisis of labour law and industrial relations institutions. The aforementioned unification of economic and social goals within the arbitration system heightened the tendency to identify industrial relations outcomes as a proxy for the economy at large. The perception of an 'industrial relations problem', together with a reputation for industrial strife (not wholly deserved),[102] created the view that industrial law would have to be reformed if the conditions for economic growth were to be restored. Indeed, this view was, in a highly fetishised way, at least partly true; the limits of antipodean Fordism were in part constituted by the rise of union militancy and an inability to contain proletarian struggle within Fordist institutions.

The crisis also directly informed the transformation of labour law instruments and institutions through the process of 'institutional searching', whereby the state, capital and labour are engaged in a contradictory and contested process of institutional experimentation to negotiate an escape from crisis and a return to growth and stability. These efforts were neither homogenous nor always coherent. In some cases, recourse was made to an *intensification and deepening of the institutions of antipodean Fordism itself.* For example, the Prices and Income Accord between the Australian Council of Trade Unions and the Hawke Labor government (which we shall explore in great detail in chapter 6) reinvigorated the federal Arbitration Commission, placing it firmly in charge of national wage-setting. On the other hand, certain developments represented a rejection of the tenets of antipodean Fordism and a new modality of ordering the social structure, including the recourse to common law torts against strike action and the adoption of restructuring and efficiency and structural efficiency principles by the Commission in the late 1980s. Both movements necessarily assumed a legal form (being partly legal in origin), pulling the labour law regime in different directions.

Given the precocious nature of the wage-labour nexus and its entrenchment in antipodean Fordism's mode of regulation, this period of transition was bound to be difficult, prolonged and contested. This reality, however, forebodes both the means and ends of the process, each of which are profoundly important for the modality of labour law. Firstly, the strength and institutional insertion of trade unionism within antipodean Fordism suggests that change was likely to be incremental and conducive towards corporatist political arrangements. Secondly, the intractable nature of the obstacles besetting the Fordist wage-labour nexus suggests that new sites of contradiction will assume importance in the effort to escape crisis. Given the fact that this wage-labour nexus assumed in Australia a unique legal form in the shape of the arbitration system, this phenomenon unleashed a motive force that pushed the balance point of the law-administration continuum towards its former pole. That is, as the law of labour lost the wider economic and social influence it once wielded as part of the arbitration structure, it would tend to become less functionally differentiated vis-à-vis other bodies and institutions of law, and become more heavily 'juridified', that is, subsumed to the logic of the abstract legal form at the expense of administration. This tendency was invigorated by the increased valency of market forces under neo-liberalism and the declining power of organised labour (which had the effect of reducing the pressure on the state to formalise labour-power through administrative firefighting). These two lattermost tendencies will be discussed in greater detail later.

With an understanding of the forces unleashed by the crisis of antipodean Fordism, and the legal implications of them, I can now turn to a consideration of the form and function of labour law within the successor model of development: liberal-productivism.

LIBERAL-PRODUCTIVISM AS AN IDEAL-TYPE

The worldwide decline of Fordism forced regulationists to consider what would come after. Was a successor model of development in evidence? If so, what did it look like, how did it solve Fordist crisis and would it enable a return to durable economic growth and stability? These investigations informed the debates on 'post-Fordism' in the 1980s and 1990s. I do not intend to recapitulate the often-vitriolic debates that have surrounded this notion. Suffice it to say here that, from the late 1980s and early 1990s onwards, a recognisable, more-or-less coherent post-Fordist model of development *did* emerge, answering, in a provisional fashion, the crisis of Fordism.

As with Fordism, the scholar who has most closely theorised this post-Fordist epoch in line with the model of development concept is Lipietz. He has dubbed the model that has become dominant liberal-productivism, a term that makes explicit the fact that the post-Fordist model of development did not simply invert the characteristics of Fordism, but crystallised and ordered the contradictions of capitalism in distinct ways. According to him, it combines:

- an intensification and deepening of Taylorism into the tertiary sector, together with the rise of 'lean' production;
- an intensive accumulation regime that disassociates wages and productivity (and is thus debt-fuelled); and
- a neo-liberal mode of regulation in an increasingly complex global division of labour.[103]

Each of these structures had their roots in the development of Fordism's crisis tendencies. However, they only began to cohere into something resembling a cogent model of development from the late 1980s through early 1990s.

Bearing in mind the discussion earlier about the nature of capitalism's contradictions, their division into dominant and secondary poles and the uneven nature of their historical manifestation, what can be said about the ordering of these contradictions within the fabric of liberal-productivism? Unlike Fordism, which crystallised the wage-labour nexus as the site of dominant contradiction in response to the ruinous underconsumption of the Great Depression, liberal-productivism was born of a crisis rooted at least partially in the power of organised labour and the grating of national state boundaries against growing transnational capital. Of particular note in the latter regard is the spatial and temporal disaggregation of liberal-productivism's dominant industrial paradigm. Whereas Fordism enshrined a mass-productionist labour process model which was nationally organised and executed, liberal-productivism reformulates the social division of labour on an increasingly global scale. Unlike previous configurations of the global social division of labour, liberal-productivism has segmented the production process of manufactured goods and distributed the resulting atoms in spatially uneven ways. The typical example is of a globally organised production chain in which high-end research and development, marketing and financial arrangements are concentrated in the previous hubs of Fordism, while labour-intensive manufacturing is relocated to low-wage, newly industrialising zones such as China and Southeast Asia. This has led to a certain degree of deindustrialisation in the former countries and a commensurate growth in the tertiary sector.[104] In such an environment, the competition principle, both between firms and between countries, requires an open field of action if capitalists are to exploit the global production system to their advantage. This in turn has seen competition within liberal-productivism assume the place once occupied by the wage-labour nexus within Fordism,[105] a reformulation with profound influences for labour law.

Additionally, the centrality of the competition principle in a new global division of labour necessarily entails an inversion of the wage-labour nexus, whereby the wage is reconstructed as a cost of international production, rather than source of domestic demand.[106] This places downwards pressure on wages, encourages the intensification of Taylorism and lean production within the labour process and dovetails with the growth of low-paying, low-productivity service sector jobs mentioned earlier. These developments undermine the domestically focused virtuous circle of manufacturing that had fuelled the intensive accumulation regime of Fordism. The question then becomes how intensive accumulation is maintained within liberal-productivism and what its version of a virtuous circle looks like.

Broadly, the application of intensified Taylorism and lean production within both the manufacturing and service sectors has the effect not only of raising productivity but of deepening managerial control of the labour process even further.[107] Companies are thus able to appropriate a greater share of surplus value, resulting in extremely high profit shares of national income (and concomitantly low labour shares) even in the midst of profit rates below that achieved during Fordist coherence.[108] In the midst of a continued tendency towards global overproduction, finance often proves the more attractive investment for these profits, and it is finance capital which provides the engine of the accumulation regime.[109] This remains intensive in character, in that it is premised upon a commodification of the proletariat's means of subsistence and an articulation of mass production and consumption. However, as mentioned earlier, intensive accumulation is now based on a disassociation of wages and productivity, and is globally configured (such that even if Fordist institutions had remained on foot, the gains of its accumulation regime could not be contained within the nation state).

Cheap credit emanating from the financial system covers the gap between worker demand and worker purchasing power expressed in hard money.[110] This cheap credit, a function of the financialisation of capital investment and the hypermobile, international capital flows it begets, now provides the motive force of intensive accumulation.

A neo-liberal mode of regulation is both constitutive of and constituted by these developments. Neo-liberalism is a multifaceted and value-laden concept, but it can in regulationist terms be described as a mode of regulation that supports the accumulation regime of liberal-productivism. Broadly speaking, the KWNS (which was crippled by heavy fiscal burdens and a corroded ability to control a bounded economic and political space) is replaced by a Schumpeterian Workfare Postnational Regime (SWPR).[111] This performs a variety of functions, including the recasting of labour as a commodity like any other, the subordination of social policy to the increasingly de-regulated labour market and reducing fetters on the free movement of commodities and capital across an increasingly connected yet variegated global space.[112] These developments represent a huge expansion of the frontiers of the commodity form, a qualitative and quantitative extension with profound influences for labour law.

Like Fordism, liberal-productivism bears within itself the seeds of crisis, derived from the abstract crisis tendencies of capitalism yet given a distinct character. Of particular note is the lack of a distinctive scale of primary regulation (the space occupied by the national state within Fordism), the centrality of debt as the motive force of intensive accumulation, the mountain of fictitious financial capital which can never be validated by the real economy and the still-depressed state of the rate of profit.[113] The global financial crisis of 2008 arguably represents the beginning of a period of terminal decline for liberal-productivism. However, these are questions for the future and do not weigh upon the discussion of labour law here. I can thus move to an investigation of the relationship between liberal-productivism in Australia and the ideal-type.

LIBERAL-PRODUCTIVISM IN AUSTRALIA

There is certainly a *prima facie* case that a liberal-productivist model has taken hold in Australia since the early 1990s. Indeed, more so than other advanced capitalist nations, Australia has, in macroeconomic terms, benefitted from the coherence of this model. After the doldrums of the early 1990s recession, average GDP growth recovered to 4.5 per cent in the second half of the 1990s (3.2 per cent in per capita terms).[114] Over the period of 1995–2005, the average rate of GDP growth weighed in at 3.5 per cent, while another measure recorded growth of 3 per cent between 2000 and 2010 (both considerably superior to the commensurate Organisation for Economic Co-operation and Development, or OECD, figures of 2.5 per cent and 1.9 per cent).[115] Productivity generally, and labour productivity specifically, surged in the 1990s, averaging 3.9 per cent average annual growth from 1994/94 to 1998/99.[116] Real wage growth, which had remained stagnant between 1975 and the early 1990s, resumed from the mid-1990s and has outperformed many other OECD nations,[117] but has, in accordance with liberal-productivist ideal-type, not been able to arrest a declining wage share of national income, and started to lag behind productivity gains from 2000 onwards.[118] This growth, moreover, has been achieved despite the fact that the Australian manufacturing sector has contracted sharply, going from accounting for nearly 30 per cent of GDP in the late 1950s and early 1960s to a paltry 6.2 per cent in early 2015.[119] As anticipated in the abstract model, this dissolution has been accompanied by exponentially increased levels of personal debt.[120]

We are thus in a position to make the claim that Australia is in a liberal-productivist phase. The constituent features of this model of development continue to demonstrate unique structures and mechanisms of coherence. However, given the fact that liberal-productivism is characterised by a corrosive global logic that undermines the ability of individual states to remain outside it, and has achieved purest expression in liberal-market economies such as Australia, the US and the UK, fewer divergences from the abstract model are encountered.

Industrial Paradigm

The dominant model of labour-process organisation in Australia matches almost exactly that of the ideal-type. The diffusion of ICTs, changed managerial practices, a shift from supply to demand-driven production and the development of economies of scope have cohered as a system of lean production, which subsumes both the manufacturing and services sectors within its logic.[121] As indicated earlier, this has allowed the extension of Taylorism deep into the service sector, particularly insofar as computer technologies allowed the measurement and routinisation of work that 'mechanical' Taylorism found difficult to penetrate. In chapter 9 I will elucidate the impact of this development for retail workers, most specifically the link between the new industrial paradigm and precarious employment forms.

Accumulation Regime

In a conceptual sense, the accumulation regime of liberal-productivism in Australia closely accords with that of the ideal-typical model. The fracturing of the virtuous circle of domestic manufacturing destroyed the engine of growth which had powered antipodean Fordism. An alternative basis of intensive accumulation was found in the shape of debt-financed consumption, which allowed consumption levels to remain high even in the face of the growing disassociation between productivity growth and real wages.

However, the accumulation regime of Australian liberal-productivism is also characterised by significant continuities with its predecessor, continuities which made the process of transition less radical than was the case with, say, the USA. Unlike the latter, the accumulation regime of antipodean Fordism was never self-sufficient. Rather, the viability of its virtuous cycle of manufacturing was underwritten by the stability of agricultural and mining commodity exports. Today, Australia depends as heavily as ever on commodity exports, particularly from the mining sector. The unprecedented level of demand for coal and metals consequent upon the industrialisation of China led both to massive investment in the development of Australia's vast mineral resources and burgeoning commodity prices on world markets. The resultant upsurge in Australia's terms of trade (which peaked in the middle of 2011 and has declined substantially since) is probably the single greatest factor in Australia's superior economic performance compared to other OECD nations.[122] However, given the fact that mining is highly capital-intensive, it employs a comparatively small number of workers.[123] The currency appreciation brought about on the back of strong commodity exports has had a deleterious effect on the competitiveness and viability of Australian manufacturing, which, even at its May 2015 nadir, still employs four times as many workers as the mining sector.[124] As shall be seen in chapters 7 and 8, this exacerbation of the long-term decline of manufacturing, together with the broader economic volatility associated with an increased dependence upon commodity exports, eroded the standard employment model at its very heart.

Mode of Regulation

The aforementioned features of the neo-liberal mode of regulation have largely taken hold in Australia. The most important of these is the inversion of the wage-labour nexus from a source of domestic demand to a cost of international production. This required a frontal assault on the institutionalised crystallisation of this nexus in its Fordist form, the arbitration system. This is of such importance to the labour law regime that it is discussed in the following section.

Also of key importance is the effective dissolution of many of the key functions of the KWNS and its replacement by the SWPR. In practical terms, the movement towards the SWPR involved an intensified commodification of social life through the marketisation of goods and services previously rendered by the state (such as education, health and public utilities), a general state aversion towards explicit intervention in the economy and, most importantly for our purposes, an abandonment of the principle of full employment. The latter development is of particular significance in that the crisis of the antipodean Fordist wage-labour nexus was understood by some, in a highly fetishised manner, as the issue of industrial relations in a climate of full employment.[125]

Lastly, and in line with the SWPR's ethos of bolstering economic competitiveness through exposure to international competition, Australian liberal-productivism has effected a transformation in the regime of industrial protection. After peaking in the late 1970s and early 1980s, levels of protection entered a period of sustained reductions. Whereas in 1978–1979 the average tariff plus primage on all dutiable goods was 31.3 per cent, in 2004–2005 the figure stood at only 9.5 per cent.[126] Leigh states more broadly that 'from 1970 to 2001, the average level of industry assistance fell from over thirty percent to under five percent'.[127] This reduction has both constituted and been constituted by the fracturing of the base of antipodean Fordist accumulation; the phasing out of tariffs as a long-term response to the crisis of Fordism both removed the domestic engine of intensive accumulation and, in so doing, exposed the vulnerability of the manufacturing sector.

LIBERAL-PRODUCTIVISM AND LABOUR LAW

The general characteristics, or 'essences', of the liberal-productivist regime of Australian labour law include hostility to trade unions, a destruction of the conciliation and arbitration system, a severing of the institutional links homogenising the wage structure and associating productivity and wage growth, intensified juridification and the erosion of the standard employment model and the profusion of precarious forms of employment.

The single most important distinction between antipodean Fordism and liberal-productivism vis-à-vis labour law is the latter's inversion and reordering of the contradictory wage-labour nexus. The precocious institutionalisation of the Fordist wage-labour nexus in the form of the arbitration system, together with the bundle of functions this particular institution played in antipodean Fordism *en régulation*, meant that a cogent liberal-productivist system could be rolled out only after a multi-pronged attack had rolled back arbitration. This attack has both displaced the arbitral tribunals from their traditional functions and usurped their centrality within the fabric of Australian industrial relations.

As has been outlined, the dysfunctionality of the antipodean Fordist wage-labour nexus largely derived from the power and privileged institutional position accorded to organised labour (especially insofar as it allowed the industrially strong to universalise their gains through the award framework). In answer, wage bargaining within liberal-productivism is fragmented and generally decentralised. In particular, I will demonstrate in chapter 7 how the pyramidal structure of the award system, spearheaded by the Metal Trades and Metal Industry Awards, was broken by the Accord in the 1980s and 'enterprise bargaining' in the 1990s. Metal trades margins cases and comparative wage justice claims no longer exist to homogenise the wage structure and act as a transmission belt linking the strong and the weak.

Awards more generally have been recast as 'safety nets', providing minimum wages and conditions which can only be improved upon through enterprise bargaining. The rise of enterprise bargaining in both federal and state jurisdictions from the early 1990s onwards has been of immense importance to the rise of a cogent liberal-productivist labour law regime. Indeed, enterprise bargaining is the node at which many of the essences of legal change have been realised. Increasingly strict statutory control has seen the process pitched at the workplace and/or firm level, increasing resource demands upon unions while intensifying the atomisation of the proletariat into competing units agglomerated around 'their' separate capitals.

While the form of bargaining thus hinders the proletariat in making common cause, the content of these agreements has often dovetailed with the lean production/neo-Taylorist industrial paradigm and the displacement of the standard employment model. The general pattern of enterprise agreements has been that they trade headline wage increases for a thoroughgoing enhancement of the real subordination of labour. Workers have been subjected to a radical increase in both functional and numerical flexibility; that is, they have had to accept management's right to deploy them across a broader range of functions with ever greater control over when and in what numbers. Enterprise agreements have also typically restricted union input into key management decisions such as manning and the control over part-time and casual labour. In chapters 7, 8 and 9, it will be demonstrated that this is a development which holds in both the manufacturing and retail sectors.

The tendency of enterprise agreements to reduce or dispose of qualitative and quantitative controls over part-time, casual and contract labour is representative of a broader truth. The standard employment model, so significant to the antipodean Fordist wage-labour nexus, has been fundamentally usurped by a host of precarious forms, characterised above by a 'lack of protective regulation, short or uncertain duration, lack of "standard" employment benefits, and ambiguous or unprotected legal status'.[128] In 2004, some 34.4 per cent of the workforce fell outside the standard employment model,[129] while in

2013 nearly one-quarter of employees were casual.[130] The profusion of such employment forms has stymied working-class power in a variety of ways, not least the fact that such employees are less likely to be union members[131] and are less likely to resist the exercise of managerial prerogative precisely because of the insecurity of their position.

The disempowerment of workers under the impact of precarisation has had its mirror at the macro-level, with the power of the trade union movement at an historic nadir. Union density, which had peaked at two-thirds of the workforce in the early 1950s, has been in free-fall since the early 1990s, and in August 2014 only 15 per cent of employees were union members in their main job.[132] Organisational weakness has both constituted and been constituted by a movement to legally hamstring the ability of trade unions to make common cause, itself a result of the inversion of the antipodean Fordist wage-labour nexus. The dysfunction of the latter manifested itself in a wave of industrial militancy in the late 1960s and early 1970s, which often pressed against and outside the established legal and administrative channels. The threat this posed to the continued valourisation of capital, and the related strain this placed on the state's ability to formalise labour-power, necessitated mechanisms by which the unification and solidarity of the proletariat (a development that Fordism continually tends toward)[133] could be disrupted. This tendency was the driving force behind a legal climate that became increasingly hostile towards trade unionism, firstly by breaking the most militant sections of organised labour (such as the de-registration of the powerful Builder's Labourers Federation in 1986),[134] and then through gradually severing the institutionalised links between trade unionism and the conduct of industrial relations. The tight embrace between the arbitral tribunals and unions has been replaced by an arm's length relationship, one in which the state finds it easier to legislate against union interests. This has informed a myriad of legal prohibitions against concerted union action, with laws against secondary boycotts, solidarity strikes and industrial action outside of designated bargaining periods disrupting the expression of common working-class interests.

We saw in chapter 3 that a labour law regime is both predicated upon and tends to reproduce a certain arrangement of the law-administration continuum. The decline of proletarian power that has been a feature of liberal-productivism is itself a force that impinges upon this regime. The erosion of trade union power and the fragmentation of the proletariat reduces the ability of the working class to force the state to generate administrative solutions to the class struggle; administrative fixes which take as their subjects the collective organs of labour give way to an increasing penetration of the legal form narrowly construed, the form in which capital has always operated most comfortably. In the Australian experience of liberal-productivism, this reality has seen a continual state retreat from direct administrative regulation of the labour market, partly substituted by an increasing juridifcation of work relations that constructs the labour-capital relationship in the fetishised image of abstract, de-classed juridical equals engaged in mutually beneficial exchange. Juridification, which I construct as the subsumption of administrative fixes beneath the abstract legal form, is, on this score, merely the concrete expression of the reduced need of the state to spawn institutional fixes to proletarian struggle. The combined effect of juridification in supplanting arbitration, weakening administration's collective subjects and re-asserting the 'purer' legal form has resulted in the lengthy experiment with statutory individual contracts, the channelling of industrial disputes through the regular court system or a weakened tribunal, the recrudescence of common law industrial torts and the usurping of the constitutional basis for federal industrial regulation. These will be the focus of deeper investigation in chapter 6.

As was the case with antipodean Fordism, the regime of labour law appropriate to liberal-productivism reflects and crystallises its unique structuring of capitalism's crisis tendencies. Although it comes with a host of its own unique twists to these abstract tendencies and is inherently unstable given its international configuration and debt-financed accumulation regime, it does answer the crisis of the antipodean Fordist wage-labour nexus. This was achieved through shattering the law-administration continuum, and its nexus point in the arbitration system, and the erection of a new order of labour law fixed in a transformed continuum and predicated on working-class weakness.

CONCLUSIONS

In this chapter I have demonstrated that post–World War II Australian capitalism can be usefully periodised using the regulationist concepts of Fordism and liberal-productivism. A process of sensitisation to the Australian context reveals two distinct models of development, separated by a period of profound crisis and institutional searching: antipodean Fordism, stretching from 1945 to the early 1970s; and liberal-productivism in Australia, which had begun to cohere in the late 1980s and early 1990s and remains on foot today. These clearly share in the dynamic and hierarchisation of crisis tendencies of their ideal-types but are often unique in how the key abstract functions are performed. This is particularly true of antipodean Fordism, given that its central scale of economic and political regulation was the nation-state (unlike liberal-productivism, which is premised on an explicitly global production system).

In Table 4.1, I have summarised the key similarities and differences between the ideal-types and antipodean Fordism/liberal-productivism in Australia across their respective industrial paradigms, accumulation regimes and modes of regulation.

Table 4.1. Ideal-types and Australian instantiations

	Industrial paradigm	*Accumulation regime*	*Mode of regulation*
Ideal-typical Fordism	• based on unification of Taylorism and mechanisation in lead sectors. • tailored to mass production; economies of scale.	• autocentric mass production/mass consumption intensive accumulation regime. • productivity and wages linked.	• KWNS guaranteed effective demand through protective social legislation and the generalisation of mass consumption norms. • wage-labour nexus site of primary contradiction.
Antipodean Fordism	• based on mass production but marked by an incomplete incorporation of Taylorist forms of work control and organisation.	• intensive accumulation regime based on mass production/mass consumption. • however, regime not autarkic. • depends upon primary commodity exports to underwrite industrial protection.	• Fordist wage-labour nexus preciously institutionalised in arbitration system. • KWNS economic and social objectives/functions unified.
Ideal-typical liberal-productivism	• intensification and deepening of Taylorism into the tertiary sector. • rise of 'lean' production; economies of scope.	• intensive accumulation, still based on mass production/mass consumption but globally configured. • disassociation of wages and productivity; regime debt-fuelled.	• SWPR oversees neo-liberal of regulation. • labour recast as a commodity like any other; subordination of social policy to increasingly free labour market; reduced fetters on the free movement of commodities and capital. • competition site of primary contradiction; Fordist wage-labour nexus inverted.
Liberal-productivism in Australia	• dominant model of labour process organisation closely matches ideal-type.	• intensive accumulation regime closely matching ideal-type. • significant continuities with forebear.	• mode of regulation closely matches ideal-type. • Fordist wage-labour nexus destroyed.

Chapter 5

Evolution and Crisis of the Antipodean Fordist Labour Law Regime

In the preceding chapter, I outlined the abstract tendencies and characteristics of the labour law regimes of antipodean Fordism and liberal-productivism. I noted that the picture was somewhat one-sided, focusing more upon the conditions that must be fulfilled for both models of development to reproduce themselves and the place of labour law in constituting those conditions. It established the functions of law within these models of development, the requisite structure of the law-administration continuum and regions of change. The *actual legal history* of these processes, however, was only cursorily indicated.

Chapters 5 and 6 provide this concrete legal history. I begin by noting that the transition between antipodean Fordism and liberal-productivism saw labour law transform along a number of broad fronts. The dimensions I am focusing on can be described thematically as:

- **Wage fixation** – how wages and conditions for workers are determined, the instruments that control them and the motive force of the system;
- **Forms of employment/flexibility** – the legal categories defining work relationships, the relationship between 'standard' employment and more precarious forms and the ability of management to deploy labour and organise the labour process as it sees fit;
- **Collectivism/individualism and the scale of industrial relations** – the degree to which the industrial relations system takes collective entities of capital and labour or individual workers and corporations as its subject, who controls the creation, content and enforcement of the rules of the employment relationship, and the predominant spatial scale at which this relation is expressed; and
- **The legal matrix** – how the labour law regime is embedded within the broader legal framework, particularly regarding the former's constitutional basis.

To highlight best the fundamental characteristics of the antipodean Fordist and liberal-productivist labour law regimes, a 'slice' approach is employed. Certain key years are selected as a snapshot and are analysed according to the state of labour law vis-à-vis the four themes identified. Each period represents a crucial point in the process of political-economic transformation. The year 1964 is the departure point, a time when antipodean Fordism was at its height. From there I move to 1975, by which time the antipodean Fordist boom had ended and serious symptoms of crisis were becoming manifest. The year 1982 marks a time of institutional exhaustion, where the final iteration of the post-war cycle of metal trade flow-on revealed the intractable nature of Fordist crisis. This period of profound and insoluble crisis is the end point of the current analysis. In chapter 6, I will pick up the threads in the late 1980s, when some of the constituent legal elements of liberal-productivism were coming into existence.

Together with the framework established in chapter 4, this analysis allows us to come to an account of labour law change that is theoretically rigorous yet empirically rich. As shall be seen, the nature and timing of the transformations taking place is completely in keeping with the periodisation schema forwarded in this book and reflects the fundamental soundness of the theory advanced.

1964 – HEIGHT OF ANTIPODEAN FORDISM

The starting point of my analysis is the year 1964, the high watermark of the antipodean Fordist model of development. At this point in time, the institutions of the antipodean Fordist mode of regulation cohered fully with the intensive accumulation regime and Taylorised, mass-production–based industrial paradigm.

In terms of the key themes elucidated earlier, the antipodean Fordist labour law regime exhibited a coherent and self-reinforcing character. Wage fixation, particularly regarding marginal payments for skill, revolved around the manufacturing sector generally, and the metal trades industries specifically. Gains won in the latter, crystallised in the leading Metal Trades Award, generally diffused throughout the workforce at large, producing the relatively homogenous wage structure described in the previous chapter and a 'standardised award structure'.[1] In turn, this structure was premised upon the dominance of standard, full-time employment for male workers, with the male fitter employed in blue-collar industries generally taken as the regulatory yardstick by arbitral tribunals. The labour law regime itself was highly collectivist, with organised labour deeply imbricated in the workings of the arbitration system and awards, the latter of which provided detailed and comprehensive rules governing the employment relationship. Lastly, the unique legal matrix surrounding the labour law regime helped shape the architecture of the system, particularly concerning the overlapping jurisdictions of the federal and state governments. Together, these structures constituted a cogent whole, channelling class conflict through institutionalised pathways and moderating certain crisis, albeit at the expense of setting others in motion.

Wage Fixation

The fundamental concepts of wage fixation in 1964 had been in evidence since the beginnings of the compulsory arbitration system. In the famous *Harvester* case, Justice Higgins had established a two-tiered structure, composed of a 'basic wage' (that ideally supported all working men and their families in 'frugal comfort') and a system of marginal payments for skill.[2] Whereas the former was based upon the needs of an unskilled labourer, the latter represented an increment paid for 'those who have acquired a skilled handicraft'.[3] Margins were defined more exhaustively in a 1954 case as 'minimum amounts awarded above the basic wage to particular classifications of employees for the features attaching to their work which justify payments above the basic wage'.[4]

By 1964, this dual-wage remained on foot, albeit with significant modifications since *Harvester*. Whereas the initial determination of a basic wage was on a needs basis, the Great Depression had infused it with a more economistic logic, with the capacity of industry to pay becoming a key concern.[5] Moreover, the attempt to maintain the value of the basic wage through automatic quarterly adjustments (indexed to prices), introduced in 1922, had been abandoned in 1953 (again, largely on the grounds that this principle was inconsistent with the capacity of the economy to pay).[6] The combined result of both developments was a substantial increase in the size and scope of basic wage cases. Faced with a basic wage that would not maintain purchasing power automatically, unions resorted to launching claims more frequently, with basic wage cases generally conducted annually from 1956 onwards.

Capacity to pay had also come to feature prominently in the fixation of margins. As will be seen in chapter 7, from 1947 onwards the metal trades sector was increasingly institutionalised at the apex of the award structure, a Fordist lead sector *par excellence*. The fixation of margins there tended to 'flow-on' to other awards, while the capacity of the metal trades and of the national economy was largely taken as synonymous.

Equally important as the macro-level methods of basic wage and margins fixation were inter-award relationships, regulated by the notion of 'comparative wage justice'. This concept had a long pedigree in the landscape of Australian industrial regulation. Its core is that 'employees doing the same work for different employers or in different industries should by and large receive the same amount of pay irrespective of the capacity of their employer or industry'.[7] Such a system requires certain benchmark occupations to which most others can be compared. From the 1920s, the fitter was increasingly taken as the measuring rod by which other blue-collar occupations were judged,[8] a reflection both of the fact that fitters were found throughout the industrial structure and played a significant role in the growing manufacturing sector. Combined with the dominance of the metal trades in the post–World War II award framework, the general engineering fitter within the Metal Trades Award occupied a special place in the architecture of Australian wage fixation, providing the nexus point between the metals awards and most others in the structure.

Comparative wage justice has also been used to describe the preservation of historical inter-award relativities.[9] The practice of using benchmark occupations, combined with the historically occupational-based structure of Australian trade unionism, established a complex web of intra- and inter-award relativities, with certain awards sharing 'historical nexus' with others. How these differentials arose was less important than the fact that once on foot, they were jealously guarded by unions.[10] A change in the pay rates of one classification produced pressures for the changes in others in the name of maintaining wage relativities.

The sensitivity of unions to intra- and inter-award relativities, together with a willingness to take action to maintain them, was such as to force a *de facto* acknowledgement on the part of the arbitral tribunals of the role of comparative wage justice in ensuring industrial order. A federal tribunal judge, Raymond Kelly, commented in 1942 that 'it will of course be conceded by employers and employees alike that in default of the adoption of, and adherence to the principle of comparative wage justice, nothing but chaos would result in the field of minimum wage fixation. *No basis could be laid without this "cornerstone of industrial regulation" for industrial contentment in the community*' (my emphasis).[11]

Kelly's statement reveals much more than it means to. It was made at a time when the immense stresses of World War II were forging the critical industrial mass that could found the antipodean Fordist model of development. It is remarkably prescient in understanding how central comparative wage justice became to the post-War Australian wage structure.

We are now in a position to describe the means by which wages were set for the majority of the workforce during the height of antipodean Fordism. From 1956 onwards, more-or-less annual basic wage cases took as their reference point national economy capacity. The union movement appeared quicker on the draw in developing a cogent and sophisticated model of wage-fixation before the tribunal, particularly after future Prime Minister Bob

Hawke became the Australian Council of Trade Unions (ACTU) advocate in 1959. From 1961 to 1964, its 'prices plus productivity' formula of adjusting the basic wage for both price increases *and* productivity improvements was the officially accepted model employed by the federal Commission.[12] Importantly, in the latter year, the employers' proposal for a 'total wage', a fundamental reformulation of the basic structure of Australian wage fixation, was rejected out of hand.

When adjustments were made to the basic wage and margins, it was technically only the Metal Trades Award that was being varied, with other awards moving in line when the unions responsible for them applied to the Commission. The metals sector was a Fordist lead sector *par excellence*, providing the motive force by which the institutional structure turned. The typical antipodean Fordist wage cycle it dominated can be described thus. Militant metal unions, such as the Amalgamated Engineering Union, were adroit in applying industrial pressure in a comparatively small number of large, well-organised 'hot shops' over issues of margins, conditions and over-award payments.[13] The threat, efficacy and results of such industrial action then informed national-level basic wage and margins cases, which proved more likely to grant substantial increases when so pressured.[14] The paramountcy of the Metal Trades Award, together with the complex web of relativities and nexus between awards, ensured that the Commission's decisions eventually flowed-on to the most workers. Stewart described this reality as "the shunter's law" or the law of transmitted shock. An upward pressure is generated in one section or location in the economy and rapidly moves with a series of successive thrusts, through other sections or territories, until its momentum comes to rest'.[15]

This phenomenon is key to a Fordist model of development, the 'connective' bargaining identified by Boyer, that links the gains of employees in lead sectors with the workforce at large,[16] producing the relatively homogenous wage structure noted in the previous chapter and buttressing the contention that the arbitration system precociously enshrined the Fordist wage-labour nexus.

At this point of maximum Fordist functionality, however, there were already indications of potential crisis tendencies. Firstly, the two-tier basic wage/margin structure was becoming increasingly unwieldy, with separate benches having to be constituted to hear claims that from 1965 were heard concurrently anyway.[17] As national economic capacity came to underpin both components of the formal wage, employers came to resent the process of dual determination, regarding it as an opportunity for unions to 'double-dip'.[18] The entrenchment of the Metal Trades Award as an institutionalised pace-setter depended in part on the dynamism of the metals sector. As shall be seen in chapter 7, if this dynamism waned, the relatively larger wage gains in other sectors would tend to encourage wage rounds as metals workers sought to catch-up. This potential was exacerbated by the pervasive ideology of comparative wage justice which, in a situation of high inflation and industrial instability, could lead to wage 'leap-frogging', the stoking of a wage-price spiral and, most significantly for capitalists, an erosion of the profit share of national income. Moreover, full employment strengthened the union hand in extracting over-award payments, which risked larger and larger segments of total wage rises occurring outside the purview of the Commission.[19]

In 1964, however, these threats were largely latent, kept in check by the coherence of antipodean Fordism.

Employment Forms/Flexibility

Absolutely central to the Fordist wage-labour nexus was the provision of employment security and a basket of rights and entitlements in exchange for the intensification of labour and Taylorist work practices, the standard employment model described in chapter 4.

By 1964, standard employment was firmly established as 'the crucial pivot in the development of labour regulation, social welfare policy and trade union action',[20] having assumed a more-or-less cogent shape in the post–World War II period. Part of the basket of rights, both in Australia and in other Fordist countries, was the prescription of regular, so-called ordinary, working hours. In Australia, the specific form this assumed was the forty-hour workweek spread over five days. For many Australian workers, this was won off the back of a massive wave of industrial action following the end of World War II. Reduced working hours were seen as an essential component of the post-War order, and were reflected by the universal support the forty-hour campaign commanded among the union movement.[21] After some groups of workers achieved a forty-hour workweek during the conflict, a general test case was convened before the federal tribunal. Under pressure from a massive, contemporaneous dispute in the metals sector, the Commission acquiesced to union demands and, on 8 September 1947, granted the forty-hour workweek, with the other state tribunals following its lead.[22] Although the various commissions did not state that this had to be worked over five days, unions sought to ensure that it did, proving willing to apply industrial pressure to this end.[23] The success of unions in this regard is evidenced by Jones's observation that 'since the adoption of the 40-hour week, there has been general acceptance that ordinary hours of work should be within a five-day week, except for retail and similar trades rendering service direct to the public'.[24]

The development of a forty-hour, five-day ordinary working week was one of the primary hallmarks of the entrenchment of the standard employment model. By 1964, other rights and entitlements consonant with the model had also been achieved. For example, test cases before the federal Commission increased paid annual leave to two weeks in 1945, three weeks in 1963 and would soon (in 1973–1974) be set at the still-prevailing standard of four weeks.[25] The majority of the states provided for long-service leave in the 1950s, with the federal tribunal following suit in 1964,[26] a development reinforcing the notion of lifetime employment significant to the workings of the antipodean Fordist wage-labour nexus.

The entrenchment of the standard employment model was also effected by the imposition of strict award controls over the use of other forms of labour. The link between the former and full-time employment was particularly strong in Australia, with the result that unions took active steps to protect its position vis-à-vis other employment categories. Provision for part-time workers within awards was very limited, with unions typically intensely suspicious of its capacity to supplant full-time employment. Casual employees had a greater standing in the award system; indeed, O'Donnell argues that 'the category of casual employment in Australia is largely the creation of the award system rather than the common law'.[27] However, as chapters 8 and 9 will demonstrate, this form was tightly hemmed in by a variety of qualitative and quantitative measures, including proportions clauses regulating the ratio of casual to full-time staff and/or the share of casual hours in total hours worked.

These developments, together with the plentiful supply of full-time jobs in a strongly growing economy, ensured the dominance of the standard employment model during the period of antipodean Fordist functionality. However, as was the case with the system of wage fixation, this state of affairs came with its own inbuilt crisis tendencies. The development of a basket of standard hours and conditions had to be won through struggle. In a demonstration of the contradiction between the interests of collective capital and individual capitalists, employers and their organisations typically begrudged each and every concession to labour, despite the fact they ultimately benefited from the resultant coherence of the Fordist wage-labour nexus. In other words, the momentum that propelled this model forward was premised on working-class strength. Moreover, the dominance of the standard employment model went hand in hand with full employment. The two exhibited a mutually reinforcing character; full employment enabled unions to leverage the benefits of standard employment, while standard employment tended to buttress the strength of organised labour.[28]

Full employment would prove to be one of the key levers of the crisis of antipodean Fordism, abrading the ability of the arbitration system to keep union power within the boundaries set by valourisation imperatives. To the extent of their interrelationship, standard employment contributed to this reality.

Collectivism/Individualism and the Scale of Industrial Relations

In chapter 3 I elucidated the basic distinction between law and administration. Whereas the former is centred on the de-classed juridic citizen-subject, administration fills the gaps class struggle rends in this structure by taking as its reference point the organised collectives of labour and capital. There are few better concrete examples of this theoretical point than the nature of the Australian arbitration system in 1964. In this period, the labour law regime was highly collectivist, as it had been ever since the steady expansion of federal and state awards in the 1920s progressively crowded out (but did not extinguish) the common-law contractual system. Indeed, one of the stated purposes of the original Conciliation and Arbitration Act was 'to facilitate and encourage the organization of representative bodies of employers and of employees',[29] while we have already noted the statement of Justice Higgins that 'without unions, it is hard to conceive how arbitration could be worked'.[30]

This centrality was reflected in a number of ways. Firstly, after becoming a 'registered' organisation, a host of benefits accrued to a trade union. Most importantly, it could initiate proceedings unilaterally in the Commission. This guaranteed juridical recognition of trade unions tended to prevent employers from refusing to recognise or treat with them.[31] Registration also conferred other benefits, such as the guarantee of a union monopoly over a certain group of workers (both in terms of representation and, in some instances, membership), the attainment of corporate status, the ability to be party to awards and the protection of trade union officials and members from certain acts of discrimination by employers.

The collectivism of the regime was also reflected in the fact that the respondents to awards were unions, and *ipso facto* those eligible to be members, as opposed to individual workers. It was the union, rather than individual workers, who had standing to appear before the Commission.[32] It is telling that, formally speaking, non-unionists were not parties to an award.[33] The understanding which buttressed this particular structure was that trade unions were the legitimate representatives of workers, including employees who weren't members and were working in non-union shops. Unions were empowered to act on their behalf, even if the workers caught up in resultant disputes were happy with their terms and conditions of employment.[34]

The period of antipodean Fordist functionality had seen this system reinforced, particularly through cementing the ability of unions to maintain *de facto* monopolies of labour through strengthened preference provisions. From the beginnings of the arbitration system it was within the power of both the federal and state tribunals to award preference to unionists. This power, however, was tightly regulated and actual use was comparatively rare.[35] The aforementioned upsurge in industrial action in the immediate post–World War II period, however, led to a rethink. As part of a basket of amendments enacted in 1947, the federal tribunal was given a much wider power to enact preference clauses in awards.[36] Although the High Court read the provision in a narrow way, so preventing absolute preference to unionists,[37] it was nevertheless an attempt on the part of what was probably the most left-wing federal Labor government to further integrate unionism with the award system.[38]

The 1947 amendments are also an instructive example of administration as practice as well as structure. A concern that excessive legalism in the conduct of conciliation and arbitration stoked industrial disruption encouraged the Chifley government to appoint a host of 'lay' commissioners.[39] These need not have come from a legal background and enjoyed wide powers to make awards and settle disputes, except where these touched on wages and hours. Frazer notes that 'it was expected that they would operate *as administrative bodies rather than legal tribunals*, exercising their powers with discretion to prevent impending disputes before they arose' (my emphasis).[40] Such a system was predicated on an understanding and acknowledgement of union power and the willingness of workers to resort to the strike weapon. Scholars have noted the recourse to more administrative or 'accommodative' attitudes and practices on the part of the Commission during periods of intense class struggle and heightened worker power,[41] an implicit acknowledgement of the movement towards administration during the antipodean Fordist period.

Despite the collectivism of the labour law regime, however, the species of collectivism that it encouraged was of a moderate, bureaucratic nature. Peetz has described how so-called arbitral unionism was often more concerned with organisational efficiency before the tribunals than the building of an activist, self-reliant rank and file.[42] Moreover, part of the historic mission of compulsory arbitration, as Justice Higgins saw it, was to ameliorate 'the rude and barbarous processes of strike and lockout. Reason is to displace force; the might of the State is to enforce peace between industrial combatants'.[43]

By 1964, the initial prohibitions on strikes and lockouts provided for in the original Conciliation and Arbitration Act had long been repealed, but their disciplinary function had been assumed by so-called bans clauses, provisions inserted in awards that typically prohibited conduct such as bans, limitations or restrictions upon the performance of work. Once ascertained, breaches of bans clauses could be punished by injunctions and/or fines. While reflecting the collectivist nature of the Australian labour law system (through making bans clauses binding on unions rather than individual employees), these penal provisions exploited this collectivism to ensure both union moderation and centralised union control over militant rank-and-file members. After the 1956 *Boilermakers* case,[44] which saw the arbitral and judicial functions of the federal tribunal separated between the re-dubbed Commonwealth Conciliation and Arbitration Commission and a new Industrial Court, respectively, the latter was charged with the machinery of enforcing penal provisions. The Court existed as an element of the formal judicial system, bound by the application of rigid juridical formula, an ideological affinity with the employers, a preference for lawyers and barristers over trade union secretaries and a profound aversion to the more pragmatic approach of the arbitral tribunals.[45] In short, it was an example of the nature of law counter-posed to administration. Unsurprisingly, it proved itself a safe pair of hands for business, freely granting injunctions for breaches of bans clauses; non-complying unions faced fines for contempt. From 1961 onwards in particular, the use of these provisions by employers to discipline militant unions, especially in the metal trades, escalated,[46] and foreboded a showdown between metal unions and the employers, the latter of whom would be supported by the state. In 1964, however, metal union leaders were not at this point, and bans clauses were effective enough at moderating industrial behaviour (or at least making militant unions pay a premium for their activities).

As would be anticipated by the model of the antipodean Fordist labour process, the collectivism of the regime was also generally barred entry to the inner sanctum of control over the labour process. The federal tribunal was empowered to hear and determine disputes only insofar as they revolved around 'matters pertaining to the relations of employers and employees',[47] the definition of which fell to the High Court. Stating the case in 1972, Justice Stephen noted 'the subject of demands by either party which are, for example, of a political or social *or managerial* nature will not be industrial matters' (my emphasis).[48] The period of antipodean Fordist functionality, therefore, saw the domain of managerial prerogative more or less armoured against the intrusion of trade unions into the control and organisation of the labour process (excepting the aforementioned award controls on the use and deployment of precarious labour).

With this understanding in hand, I can move to a consideration of the scale of industrial relations during this period of antipodean Fordist functionality. As can be gathered from the discussion on wage fixation previously, the Commonwealth tribunal was coming to exercise a growing dominance over industrial regulation generally, with the state equivalents increasingly following its lead. Given the centrality of the KWNS to the fabric of Fordism generally, this increasing development of the federal level as the primary scale of industrial relations is unsurprising. However, the unique institutional fabric of the arbitration system ensured that the way in which this increasing centralisation came about was novel.

As will be discussed in the following section, the Constitution vests the federal parliament with the ability to legislate 'conciliation and arbitration for the prevention and settlement of industrial disputes extending beyond the limits of any one State'.[49] The early history of arbitration saw this power read narrowly, with the High Court maintaining that federal awards could not have common rule effect (unlike their state equivalents).[50] In other words, awards could only be made in the resolution of inter-state disputes between identifiable parties.

By the period of antipodean Fordist functionality, however, this situation had changed, in practice if not necessarily in the letter of the law. Firstly, the High Court had validated the union tactic of creating 'paper disputes' (by serving logs of claims on employers in more than one state), by which they could enliven the federal jurisdiction.[51] Secondly, the High Court had also given as expanded meaning to section 109 of the Constitution,[52] which guarantees the paramountcy of laws of the Commonwealth over individual states in the event of inconsistency. Lastly, as the sphere of economic activity increasingly took on a national, as opposed to strictly state-based, character, the field of federal regulation naturally tended to grow.[53] Within this framework, the federal tribunal gradually came to influence state bodies more than they influenced it; from the 1950s in particular, the latter came to generally follow the lead of the former in matters such as basic wage determination and in fields where the Commonwealth was dominant.[54] Although not codified in the way it would be during the crisis of antipodean Fordism, by 1964 the federal tribunal exercised the kind of authority necessary to the maintenance of the national level as the primary scale of Fordist regulation.

Legal Matrix

Much of what is relevant about the broader legal matrix in the constitution of industrial regulation, particularly regarding the constitutional foundations of conciliation and arbitration, has been discussed earlier. Important to note here are two additional issues. Firstly, the limitations as to the extent of federal regulation extended to the nature of the industries under regulation. A dispute could only be handled under the arbitral power if it could be regarded as 'industrial'. The High Court came to regard industry as encompassing the production and/or distribution of tangible goods and commodities, as well as activities thought to be incidental or ancillary to it (such as banking and insurance).[55] This meant that considerable numbers of workers, such as teachers, firefighters and state health and welfare staff, remained outside federal jurisdiction. As well as impinging upon the ability of the federal Commission to control the aggregate movement of wages, it grated against the increasing spread of unionism into these white-collar occupations.

Secondly, the development of the machinery of arbitration and conciliation had in many ways submerged, although not extinguished, the significance of the common law as it applied to employment and industrial relations. Of particular note was the fact that the disciplining mechanisms used to rein in intransigent unions, such as bans clauses and union de-registration, operated through the arbitration system. Older means of employer redress, such as common law industrial torts, generally fell into desuetude. That is, the tools of union restraint were attached to a system that I have identified as an administrative response to class struggle, taking as its subjects the very bodies it was trying to keep in line. The supremacy of these forms over older common law remedies is evidence both of the relative dominance of administration over the 'pure' legal form within antipodean Fordism and the degree of consensus between labour and capital regarding arbitration's place as the central node of industrial relations.

1975 – END OF ANTIPODEAN FORDIST BOOM

By 1975, the scene had changed dramatically; the long boom had come to an end as antipodean Fordism lost coherence. The contradictions latent within the antipodean Fordist labour law regime had by now germinated and were rapidly coming into full bloom. In particular, the system of wage fixation had become deeply unstable and was increasingly outside the control of the federal tribunal, compromising the lynchpin role it exercised within the antipodean Fordist mode of regulation. The precocious institutionalisation of trade union power had also become dysfunctional, as waves of rank-and-file militancy broke over the walls of arbitration. Amid this turmoil can also be seen emerging the first attempts to address these crisis tendencies systematically. After a brief dalliance with the idea of supplementing arbitration with a system of collective bargaining in 1973, a system of wage indexation was officially adopted by the Commission in 1975. Such a development represented an attempt to resolve the contradictions of antipodean Fordism through the *intensification of its institutions*.

Wage Fixation

By 1975, huge changes had broken out all along the wage fixation front. Firstly, the two-part basic wage/margins structure had been superseded in 1967 by the so-called total wage, a single figure for award classifications into which both the basic wage and margins were collapsed. As mentioned earlier, employer groups first floated the idea before the federal tribunal in 1964. The Commission had rejected the application, noting that to do so was 'to abandon a concept which had been an integral part of Australian wage fixation for over fifty years', while adding that there was little more to the employers' proposal than 'greater tidiness'.[56]

However, union militancy in a situation of full employment had begun to tax the basic wage/margins structure, especially given the incidence of escalating over-award payments in key industries such as metals.[57] In particular, employers were coming to resent the centrality of the metals sector in the determination of marginal rates for the national wage structure.[58]

By 1966, the Commission had been convinced, approving of the total wage in principle and, consequent upon a work-value inquiry into the metal trades, deploying it in 1967. If, however, the goal was to disrupt the status of the metal trades as an institutionalised lead sector, the effort failed dismally. This brings us to the second major problem that had manifested itself by 1975: the increasing exhaustion of the metal trades as a lead sector. Given the deeper analysis in chapter 7, this issue can be presented rather schematically here. From the early 1970s in particular, it was becoming apparent that the aforementioned tension inherent in the position of the metal trades was manifesting itself. In particular, the place of the Metal Trades Award and its successor, the Metal Industry Award, at the apex of the award framework had generated a contradictory reality in which metal workers were increasingly disadvantaged *precisely because of this structure*. With the knowledge that any increase granted in metal awards would flow through to large sections of the workforce, minimum rates in these awards had tended to lose ground relative to other manufacturing awards, especially in the early 1970s.[59] This not only compelled metal workers to seek higher over-awards but also invited large 'catch-up' claims to match wage rises granted in other key sectors, such as transport and building.[60] Given the fact that the metal awards remained institutional leaders, even in the face of a loss of relative industrial significance, these catch-up claims then flowed-though to other industries on the basis of comparative wage justice claims. The result: large, 'leap-frogging' wage claims in the high-inflation environment of the early to mid-1970s, which made for industrial disruption and a fragile wage structure increasingly outside of the control of the federal tribunal.

The Commission's loss of control over the aggregate movement of wages, together with its often ad hoc and contradictory responses, constitutes a third major frontier of change. What Bramble posits as the start of the 'flood tide' of union militancy was the outcome of the 1967 work-value inquiry into the Metal Trades Award.[61] The Commission had become increasingly uneasy with the fact that this leading award was based upon a classification structure which was developed and valued when it was created in 1930. The concern of the Commission was that metal margins did not reflect the actual value of the work being performed.[62] Given the pronounced impact of new technologies on the content and range of jobs, and the use of the fitter as a yardstick for many awards, the Metal Trades Award was, according to the Commission, increasingly anachronistic as a pace-setter in its current form.

What was significant about the work-value inquiry, however, was not so much its findings as the aftermath. The Commission had granted comparatively generous marginal increases, but left it open to employers to 'absorb', or off-set, the rises out of existing over-award payments.[63] Moreover, as will be investigated further in chapter 7, the Commission explicitly sought to restrict the margins adjustments to the Metal Trades Award, an attempted usurpation of its place at the apex of the award framework. On both scores, the Commission failed dismally, with a huge upsurge of industrial action in the metals sector ensuring the defeat of absorption and paving the way for strong currents of flow-on.

This event marked an upswing in union militancy generally, a development greatly aided by unions breaking the shackles of the bans clauses. A massive strike in May 1969 essentially wrecked the penal provisions of the Conciliation and Arbitration Act.[64] The increasingly profligate use of such disciplining tools by employers, and the willingness of the Industrial Court to grant them, had pushed union tolerance to the edge. Although an amended framework of penal powers was developed in the aftermath, they fell into desuetude as their use became politically untenable in a context of union militancy and Commission reticence.[65]

The most important consequence of this new reality for wage fixation was the removal of legal-administrative impediments to union pay campaigns. Organised labour thus found it easier to extract higher over-award payments and/or secure 'consent' awards[66] through direct action. Employers generally caved along the front throughout the early 1970s, resulting in the real wage spike documented in the previous chapter, with workers receiving an increasingly large chunk of their wage rises outside of the purview of both state and federal tribunals. The percentage of wage increases stemming from national wage cases steadily declined from 52.6 per cent in 1969/1970 to a mere 19.1 per cent in 1973/1974.[67] That is, approximately 80 per cent of the wage increases obtained by workers in 1973/1974 were outside the Commission's main instrument of wage policy.

This fact was not lost on the Commission, a recognition that forced it to temporarily relinquish the system of principles developed throughout the 1960s (the administrative equivalent of legal precedent) and develop ad hoc accommodative responses that attempted to put out the spot-fires of proletarian struggle. It tacitly admitted as much in justifying the comparatively generous 6 per cent increase granted in the 1970 wage case, also foreshadowing restrictions on its scope to award future increases:

> If we are not *realistic in our attitude to wage fixation*, then those who look to the Commission as their main source of wage increases . . . will be treated inequitably while more and more of those who are strong enough to do so will seek increases in the field. . . . However, we wish to emphasise that the material before us . . . disclosed a state of affairs which if continued may inhibit the Commission in future national wage cases. This material shows *union pressure for wage increases outside the Commission* leading to concessions from employers, sometimes granted too easily, which favour the industrially strong (my emphasis).[68]

It will be noted that the Commission used the criterion of comparative wage justice as a justification for the increase granted. Indeed, throughout this period it had held the line on this principle as some unions sought to exploit the highly favourable economic conditions of the mid to late 1960s by introducing the profitability of individual firms as another basis upon which pay could be calculated.[69] The Commission reiterated the traditional view that capacity to pay, a central consideration in wage fixation, was to be assessed at the industry/macroeconomic level. This was thoroughly in keeping with the predominant spatial scales of industrial relations and the oligopolistic competition characterising antipodean Fordism. The Commission also argued that the system sought by the unions in these cases would disrupt the equalising role comparative wage justice played, as well as affirming the distribution of productivity gains to the workforce at a national level.[70]

However, as was foreshadowed earlier, the continued entrenchment of the comparative wage justice doctrine ensured accelerating wage rounds in the early to mid-1970s, particularly from 1973 to 1975 as inflation spiralled. In this latter period, average annual earnings increased by a massive 20.5 per cent,[71] constituting the real wage spike documented in chapter 4. Bentley states that as the resultant 'wage-price spiral was dealt with by trade unions (and employers) in an unplanned and decentralized manner, wage relativities were disturbed. These disturbances led to a process of wage-leapfrogging '.[72]

By the end of 1974, however, the deepening of the economic crisis, both globally and within Australia, had forced a rethink on the part of the state, capital and labour. The Whitlam Labor government grew perceptibly tired of union militancy and large wage claims.[73] It began to flirt with the idea of wage indexation, whereby wage increases granted by the Commission were limited to the rise in the Consumer Price Index. This would tend to reduce cost-push inflation, while the certainty in the level of wage rises would potentially limit ambit claims by unions.[74] Unions were generally supportive; right-wing unions welcomed the prospect of wage increases without strikes, while the union most likely to oppose indexation, the militant Amalgamated Metal Workers' Union (AMWU), was grappling with deepening economic problems in the metal sector.[75] For the movement generally, indexation seemed appealing as a means of locking-in the large real wage gains recently achieved.[76] Employers and the conservative parties were generally reluctant, but many of the former had come around to the idea that something needed to change.[77]

The ACTU and the Commonwealth proposed automatic wage indexation in the 1974 Wage Case. The Commission rejected it at this stage, citing among other things the need for unions to rein in wage claims outside of national wage cases.[78] Once the ACTU had reluctantly given such an undertaking, the Commission duly developed a set of wage-fixing principles centred on indexation in its 1975 national wage case. The essence of the system was that wage rises outside of indexation would be small and would not threaten the Commission's efforts to regulate aggregate wage outcomes.[79]

I am now in a position to describe the dysfunctional character of wage fixation and its role in constituting the crisis of antipodean Fordism in the early to mid-1970s. The advent of the total wage in 1967 had done very little to usurp the institutionalised position of the metals sector. However, the flagging dynamism of this sector, and manufacturing more broadly, saw workers in other industries pull ahead. Given the fact that many awards were tied to the Metal Trades and Metal Industry Awards, large catch-up campaigns by metal workers sparked comparative wage justice claims by other unions. In a context of high inflation, a destabilising process of wage leapfrogging ate into the profit share of national income and saw the Commission lose control of the aggregate movement in wages. This movement was greatly facilitated by the union victory over the penal powers in 1969. Employers found it harder to resist over-award demands, while the Commission and Industrial Court were shorn of a key tool used to discipline militant unions.

The confluence of these developments is key to understanding the Commission's decision, supported by the state and federal governments and the ACTU, to adopt a wage indexation system in April 1975. It represented a conscious effort to re-establish the Commission as the main source of wage increases and the arbiter of wage policy. That this was necessary was also a function of the limitations of the arbitral power, which rendered the Commission as the only real institutional means through which the federal state could exercise wage policy designed to address the economic crisis. Wage indexation was thus an explicit effort to address the crisis of antipodean Fordism through an intensification of its institutions. The arbitration system, a lynchpin of the antipodean Fordist mode of regulation, was seeing its authority augmented in an attempt to clamp down on the wage explosion that had largely come about outside its framework.

This was an effort fraught with danger. Deepening an antipodean Fordist institution risked magnifying its contradictions. Moreover, given the limitations inherent in the arbitral power of the Constitution, the Commission remained constrained in the ways it could intervene in the labour market. For wage indexation to be effective, a more-or-less durable consensus between the state, capital and labour was required. The support of the latter was especially critical; if unions rebelled, the system would be a dead-letter.

Forms of Employment/Flexibility

Unlike the case with wage fixation, the institutional arrangements surrounding the standard employment model remained essentially unchanged. Awards continued to encourage full-time employment, and the system of qualitative and quantitative checks on other forms, such as casual and part-time labour, remained in place.

However, beneath the surface of comparative institutional stasis, a major change was taking place in the composition of the workforce. From the early 1960s, women were entering the workforce in ever increasing numbers, being particularly concentrated in clerical and sales positions. Whereas in February 1968, 36.9 per cent of the female population aged fifteen and over were in the labour force, by November 1975 this had grown substantially to 43.7 per cent.[80] This growth was overwhelmingly in 'part-time' employment; indeed, Hancock shows that the number of women employed as part-time workers increased by 84 per cent between 1966 and 1975, compared to a 24 per cent increase in full-time female workers.[81]

Female workers not employed on a full-time basis were thus becoming an increasingly important segment of the workforce, a development that would grate against the award system's preference for, and defence of, the standard employment model.

Collectivism/Individualism and the Scale of Industrial Relations

The question of collectivism/individualism can be dispensed with easily enough. In chapter 4, it was argued that the crisis of antipodean Fordism was at least partially constituted by the very collectivism of the system, and the growing dysfunctionality in its articulation with the valourisation of capital. Certainly, trade union power was waxing in the early 1970s. After comparatively slow absolute growth in the 1960s (accompanied by a small but steady loss in density), union membership and density grew strongly in the early 1970s, even in traditionally poorly unionised white-collar sectors.[82] Industrial disputation sky-rocketed as workers increasingly resorted to direct action to get results. Whereas in 1963, some 581,568 working days were lost in industrial disputes, 1969 saw 1,957,957 days lost, while in 1974 (the peak of the early 1970s strike wave) an enormous 6,292,500 working days were forfeited to disputes.[83] The general upswell in class struggle also encouraged employers to come to closed-shop arrangements with unions perceived to be industrially moderate in sectors such as retail (more on which will be discussed in chapter 9), banking and administration, in the hopes of excluding militant competitors. Regardless of whether or not capital was successful in the latter regard, such agreements reinforced the institutional entrenchment of trade unionism within Australian industrial relations and buttressed the collectivist character of its labour law regime.

As regarding the scale of industrial relations, this burgeoning crisis period of antipodean Fordism saw a contradictory reality. The increasing significance of National Wage and margin cases in the 1960s had encouraged an increasing concentration of representation on the part of both capital and labour. The resource and research demands of wage cases facilitated the growth in ACTU power vis-à-vis affiliates. In the all-important metals sector, the immense AMWU had come into being in 1973, while the employers had created the Metal Trades Industry Association (MTIA). Workers and employers, therefore, were increasing the scale upon which they mobilised.

However, as can be gathered from the foregoing discussion of over-award campaigns and the marginalisation of national wage cases, increasing organisational centralisation was concomitant with the emergence of a *de facto* collective bargaining system, one that was most prevalent at the workplace, enterprise and, sometimes, industry levels. It made little sense for unions to go through the rigmarole of compulsory conciliation and arbitration for an uncertain outcome when the application of industrial pressure on employers could deliver better outcomes in a timely fashion.

The pervasiveness of union collective bargaining outside the bounds of the arbitration system had convinced many within both the industrial and political wings of the labour movement that the arbitration system was in need of a thorough overhaul. The ALP Industrial Relations Committee had in 1970 'recommended that tribunals should confine themselves to the fixation of minimum rates and conditions and expect that there will be bargaining for over-award payments and conditions. It also suggested that present bargaining procedures for over-award conditions should be regularized and formalized'.[84]

The recommendation was enshrined in the ALP's industrial relations platform unveiled in May 1971, which was 'based firmly on the principle of collective bargaining'.[85] The tabling in April 1973 of a bill to amend the Conciliation and Arbitration Act 1904 represented a wide-ranging reform package, including, among other things, a total abolition of the penal powers, granting of immunity from tort liability for unions and officials for acts related to an industrial matter and, most importantly, limiting the power of the Commission to refuse to certify 'collective agreements'. It was described by Minister for Labour Clyde Cameron as 'the first stage of a radical transformation of industrial relations in Australia'.[86] In the event, however, strong hostility from the business community and parliamentary conservatives, together with Senate obstructionism, ensured that the act that eventually passed was heavily diluted. In particular, a genuine collective bargaining system did not emerge, while immunity from tort actions was dropped and strike penalties retained.

Two key points are of note here. Firstly, the failure to grant unions immunity from actions in tort would come to bear dark fruit in the 1980s. Secondly, the conservative reaction to the original bill was due in no small part to the fear that collective bargaining in a context of union strength would amount to industrial duress untrammelled by arbitration. In 1970, the Minister for Labour Billy Snedden stated the conservative case quite candidly: 'The concern that I have about direct negotiation is the degree to which powerful unions in an industrial sense are able to use the threat of strike action to coerce employers to give wage increases beyond the capacity of the economy to pay and in advance of the development of productivity'.[87] From this perspective the arbitration system was perceived as a *defence against union militancy*, a view shared by some employers. The president of the Australian Capital Territory Employers Federation, for example, pleaded that 'the Government and Parliament need to strengthen authority to discourage strikes and *encourage conciliation and arbitration*' (my emphasis).[88]

This last statement is significant for our purposes in two ways. Firstly, it helps explain why the process of institutional searching for ways out of the developing crisis initially took the form of an intensification of antipodean Fordist institutions. If the arbitration system, rather than union militancy at the point of production, was identified as the core issue by a strategic majority of employers, it is hardly likely that the effort to recentralise control under its aegis would have succeeded. Secondly, it provides a stark point of contrast to the developing attitude of capital in the latter half of the 1980s and early 1990s, where the institutions of arbitration themselves were perceived to be the source of malaise. Capital would come to forget its own history when it championed the cause of collective, or 'enterprise', bargaining in these periods.

Legal Matrix

Broadly speaking, the constitutional basis upon which the arbitration system was erected remained unchanged. However, another head of power which the Commonwealth could use to legislate received a major boost in 1971 when the High Court significantly expanded the ambit of the corporations power.[89] This amplified power underwrote the Trade Practices Act 1974 (Cth), a statute that was initially concerned with mergers and acquisitions, restrictive trade practices and consumer protections. This piece of legislation would, however, become in the near future a potent weapon against militant unionism.

1982 – INSTITUTIONAL EXHAUSTION

The year 1982 represents the end point of the initial attempts to handle the crisis of antipodean Fordism through intensifying its institutions. The indexation system established in 1975 began to be abraded in the late 1970s and finally came unstuck in 1981. Its end was brought about by another large wage round, ostensibly based on work-value considerations but in essence simply another iteration of the post-war pattern of flow-on. Crucially, the system again reverted to a more de-centralised model, with the Commission's decision to abandon indexation based in no small part on the fact that employers were already conceding wage and conditions demands to unions at the enterprise and industry levels. Moreover, the conservative Fraser government's efforts to curb union power through a specialist body, the Industrial Relations Bureau (IRB), proved a dead letter.

Amid this stagnation, however, can be discerned the first developments that speak of a qualitatively different means of addressing crisis, means which cut across the grain of antipodean Fordism rather than buttressing it. Of special note was the development of tools to disrupt the unification of the proletariat, most notably through the emergence of statutory prohibitions on solidarity action, or 'secondary boycotts'. In outline, these can be considered 'proto' liberal-productivist impulses.

Wage Fixation

The wage indexation system established in 1975 operated effectively enough for several years, particularly when viewed from the perspective of capital and the state. Dabscheck notes that 'the commission was generally successful in ensuring that national wage cases were the major source of wage movements between 1975 and 1981'.[90] In particular, before December 1978, national wage cases accounted for well over 90 per cent of the movement in total wages.[91] If wage indexation was designed to reassert the Commission's control over aggregate wages, as is maintained here, then it must be regarded as a success, at least until 1979.

However, the fragility of the consensus underpinning indexation was glaringly revealed as the state and capital increasingly refused to hold up their end of the bargain in an arrangement still requiring union support. Among other things, the Fraser government repeatedly, and often successfully, petitioned the Commission to 'discount' wage rises based on the inflationary impact of some of their policies (such as raising the price of domestic oil to full import parity).[92] This discounting was tremendously frustrating to unions, who reasoned (legitimately) that the driving forces of inflation were non-wage factors.[93]

In the face of persistent discounting, and an economic upturn in the late 1970s and very early 1980s on the back of a minerals boom, some unions in construction, transport and metals attempted to get around the constraints of indexation by lodging 'work-value' cases, established exceptions to indexation guidelines based on the changing skill content of jobs. That unions in these industries were the spearhead was unsurprising – they were the same unions who in the early 1970s had been the most active in collective bargaining outside the arbitration system. Their activity informed the 1979 Biennial Congress of the ACTU, which carried a resolution that suggested collective bargaining and conciliation and arbitration were synonymous.[94]

Declining union commitment to indexation and the spread of work-value claims threw the whole system into jeopardy. The Commission correctly appraised the danger, noting that the future of the centralised system was in the hands of the participants themselves and that a general round of work-value cases was not compatible with indexation principles.[95] Moreover, it lamented that the government, through its insistent demands for discounting, was forcing it to choose between frustrating government policy or letting the 'fragile package' of indexation collapse.[96]

In the event, indexation did not survive. A wave of work-value cases originating among waterside, warehousing, road transport and metal workers had, by 1981, brought across-the-board increases (often around $8 a week) to approximately 80 per cent of the workforce.[97] Moreover, a 1981 consent award in the metals sector was the precursor to the general spread of the thirty-eight-hour workweek. Bramble's account clearly demonstrates that, in substance, the work-value round was little different to the processes of collective bargaining, backed by industrial action, that had produced the wage leap-frogging in the early 1970s.[98] Once on foot, the entrenched logic of comparative wage justice ensured the gains flowed-on. Quite simply, the event demonstrated the intractability of Fordist crisis.

Forms of Employment/Flexibility

The ongoing crisis of antipodean Fordism throughout the 1970s and early 1980s intensified and deepened the growing significance of employment forms outside the standard model. Hancock notes that between 1975 and 1984, part-time employment increased by a substantial 44 per cent, compared to the paltry 5 per cent increase recorded in full-time employment.[99] Whereas in 1966 only 10 per cent of the workforce worked part-time, by 1982 the figure had grown to 17 per cent.[100] Importantly, the crisis also had the effect of accelerating the growth of part-time employment among males,[101] foreshadowing the transformation from what was a highly gendered phenomenon into something of more general compass.

As will be demonstrated in the case study chapters, the successful union claim for a thirty-eight-hour working week in the early 1980s was accompanied by the demand for cost offsets, which often included either the introduction of part-time employment in awards or the relaxation of some of the controls, both qualitative and quantitative, on its use. These represented the first, very tentative and inchoate, steps towards a liberal-productivist wage-labour nexus based on precarity and increased managerial control over the engagement and control of labour-power as a commodity. Trade unions generally recognised the danger and attempted to maintain the strict award controls on part-time and casual work. Even in 1982, they had adequately held the line in this institutional regard.

Their stand was aided by the federal Commission, which agreed that part-time work should not be used to compromise the model of standard, full-time employment. In an important case involving the vehicle industry, employers cited the growth in part-time work, together with the recent provision for it in awards covering sectors as varied as insurance, banking and confectionary, as evidence that the Commission's presumption against part-time work should be voided.[102] The Commission response is telling: 'There has been no significant departure from the original concept that it must be shown to be desirable to meet the particular needs of the industry and that it would *not be detrimental to full time employment*' (my emphasis).[103] More thoroughgoing change in the institutional settings around non-standard employment forms and flexibility would have to wait until later on in the decade.

Collectivism/Individualism and the Scale of Industrial Relations

The fundamentally collectivist nature of the labour law regime and the award framework remained intact in 1982. As was the case in 1975, this collectivism was dysfunctional for capital, particularly insofar as union power remained entrenched. The wages explosion of the early 1980s was brought about by a large strike wave. While the strait-jacket of indexation had seen working days lost to industrial disputes reach a nadir of 1,654,800 in 1977, rounds of work-value cases beginning in 1978–1979 saw the rate pick up, reaching a peak of 4,192,200 days lost in 1981.[104] It was, in many ways, the re-emergence of the same crisis tendency that had manifested itself in 1975 – the system depended upon trade unions to function, but demanded they act in a way within the bounds of valourisation imperatives.

This re-emergence, however, was not for lack of the Fraser government trying to effect profound change which, although generally not realised, represented in essence a proto-liberal-productivist arrangement, particularly insofar as individual rights (historically marginal to the system) assumed a greater importance.

The government's reform program revolved around the creation of a body known as the Industrial Relations Bureau in 1977. The IRB was armed with a wide suite of powers well in excess of those it had inherited from its predecessor, the Arbitration Inspectorate. Of particular importance was the IRB's power to administer *individual* 'safeguards', namely the freedom of workers not to join a trade union on expanded conscientious grounds and a right not to be compelled to partake in industrial action.[105] Government MP John Martyr stated, 'The whole essence of the legislation before us is that it is *designed to protect the individual,* to protect his rights against arbitrary dismissal, to protect his rights against arbitrary action by union officials' (my emphasis).[106] This understanding sat uneasily with the administrative fabric of arbitration. The latter's primary function, the prevention and resolution of industrial disputes, took as its subject the collective organs of labour, while its administrative practice demanded a sensitivity to the industrial realities of the 1970s.

This tension was graphically demonstrated by the case of Barbara Biggs, a young woman employed as a tram conductor in the fiercely union Melbourne tramway system. She had obtained a certificate exempting her from union membership, but her employment by the Tramways Board was met by a strike of fellow employees 'in defence of the closed shop'.[107] It is worth quoting Mitchell at length about the subsequent events:

> At this point the Commission came into the dispute and subsequent events highlight *the clash between the traditional pragmatism of the Commission's dispute settling processes and the ideology of the individual rights legislation.* The Commission recommended the removal of Biggs from the roster and that she be offered alternative employment in exchange for a return to work. The Tramways Board refused to accede to this recommendation because it felt that such action on its part would involve a breach of the Act (my emphasis).[108]

The clash Mitchell observes assumes special importance in the context of this book. It represents an image of the law-administration continuum at a time of tension. The arbitration system was presented with a legislative agenda in which the collective subject was jostled by newly important *individual* subjects. The nexus point of the law-administration continuum was at stake, and the fact that Biggs discussed the dispute with the IRB and subsequently opted to take a position with another employer attests to the temporary victory of the established labour law institutions over the government's legislative baby.[109]

The case of Biggs was one of a number involving employees seeking to avoid union membership with the support of the IRB. All basically came unstuck in the face of unionists refusing to work with non-union labour.[110] Such failures, coupled with broader issues of maintaining adequate inspections and legal setbacks,[111] made the IRB a widely recognised failure. ALP Opposition Leader Bill Hayden's contention, that the IRB 'is useless and impotent',[112] was ultimately validated by its demise in 1983. For the moment, then, the administrative fabric of arbitration, and its crystallisation of a distinct form of the law-administration continuum, was maintained.

With this understanding in hand, I can now move on to a brief consideration of the scale of industrial relations. As was apparent from the foregoing discussion of wage fixation, the 1975–1982 period was characterised by efforts to intensify the federal arbitration commission as the lynchpin within antipodean Fordism. Outside of indexation, the Fraser government undertook other institutional reforms designed to buttress the position of the federal tribunal. For example, it legislated to provide greater consistency between the decisions of the Commission and its state counterparts.[113] Moreover, it attempted to develop a more co-ordinated approach between the Commonwealth and state governments regarding wage fixation, seeking agreement with the latter, for example, in enforcing its 1982 wage-freeze.[114] This effort at augmenting the centrality of the federal Commission was broadly successful, as Hancock notes: 'Since 1975, state tribunals have (with minor exceptions) conformed to the principles laid down in major decisions of the Arbitration Commission'.[115]

However, greater institutional coherence between the arms of federal and state arbitration meant little when unions broke the straitjacket of indexation and reverted to a system of *de facto* collective bargaining. Dabscheck pithily describes the result upon the destruction of indexation: 'After July 1981 Australia moved to a decentralised, unco-ordinated system of industrial relations regulation'.[116]

By 1982, therefore, Australian capitalism was in much the same intractably crisis-ridden state as it had been in 1975. The centrality of the Commission as the lynchpin in the antipodean Fordist mode of regulation had been breached by unions pressing against and outside the arbitration system. The Fraser government's 1982 wage freeze was a crude acknowledgement that its more sophisticated attempts at crisis resolution had failed. To fundamentally shift the ground, unions would either have to be *held* in line, or their integration into industrial relations fabric usurped. As I will demonstrate later, the achievement of the former during the rest of the 1980s paved the way for the latter in the 1990s.

Legal Matrix

While the constitutional basis of the arbitration system remained unchanged, change was in the offing. For some time members of the High Court had expressed dissatisfaction with the increasingly inadequate and complex definition of an industry for the purposes of ascertaining if an industrial dispute existed.[117] It deprived large groups of workers access to the federal system and was premised on a narrow, productivist reading of 'industry' increasingly at odds with the reality of an ever more intertwined economy. In the next chapter we will see major change on this front, particularly as the pressures of the Accord forced the opening of a wider conception while allowing for a more unified national system.

In other developments, the Trade Practices Act had, as foreshadowed above, been turned into a tool of union repression. A 1976 committee of review was tasked with exploring the application of the act 'to anticompetitive conduct by employees, and employee or employer organisations'.[118] It had the following to say about secondary boycotts: 'If an organisation or group of persons for its own reasons deliberately interferes with the competitive process, then the community is entitled to have those reasons scrutinised by a body independent of the persons engaged in the dispute. If that independent body finds those reasons inadequate, the community is entitled to require that the position be remedied'.[119]

Despite the fact that the committee made no recommendation as to whether the provisions should be inserted into the administrative fabric of the arbitration system or the more 'pure' legal form of the court system, the Fraser government opted for the latter course, duly introducing section 45D into the Trade Practices Act in June 1977. The section is highly complex but is broadly a very wide net designed to capture all manner of conduct in which 'persons' (most usually unions) disrupt one corporation's supply or acquisition of goods and services in an attempt to apply pressure on another. A member of the ALP opposition presciently grasped the implications, noting that what was termed 'secondary boycotts' by the government were really sympathy strikes, and what the government actually sought was to break the cycle whereby the *industrially strong helped the weak*.[120] That is, it was part of an effort to break the connective links binding the strong and the weak within antipodean Fordism under the aegis of the arbitration system.

Unsurprisingly, trade unions almost invariably lost their early battles with section 45D. The very first encounter, involving the Australasian Meat Industry Employees Union (AMIEU), saw the union injuncted from black-banning two abattoirs in an attempt to enforce compulsory unionism at a small butchery business.[121] Additional cases saw storehouse, meat and transport workers served with interlocutory injunctions under the legislation.[122] Full told, section 45D represented a determined effort on the part of employers and the conservative Fraser government to place sympathy strikes outside the administrative fabric of arbitration, where the resolution of disputes was paramount, and relocate it within the ordinary, and generally hostile, court system.

However, even at this stage, union power made capital somewhat gun-shy. Although section 82 of the act provides that the aggrieved party can reclaim damages, in 1982 no case had ever gone beyond the injunction phase. Employers were typically content to get the industrial action ended; pursuing further action for damages risked worsening it, as well as making it incumbent upon the business to prove loss. The latter course of action only became viable once the New Right ideology had congealed into a cogent and explicitly activist programme for utilising the legislation and court system to their advantage.

CONCLUSIONS

In this chapter I have provided the first half of the concrete legal history needed to flesh out the abstract framework developed in chapter 4. To demonstrate the soundness of the theory of transition forwarded there, the state of labour law has been described at certain key dates capturing the coherence and crisis of antipodean Fordism. I began in 1964, when antipodean Fordism was at its zenith. The unique structure of the law-administration continuum, in which the latter was dominant, was represented most perfectly in the arbitration system, which precociously institutionalised the antipodean Fordist wage labour nexus. In particular, compulsory arbitration at this time facilitated the pattern of flow-on from the industrially strong to the industrially weak, further developed and diffused standard employment, and strongly integrated organised labour into the fabric of the law and the state, all essential planes of coherence in antipodean Fordism.

By 1975, however, antipodean Fordism had entered a period of profound crisis, constituted in part by the same legal framework essential to its functionality. In particular, in a context of stagnating productivity and dynamism in lead sectors such as metals and rising inflation, the power of organised labour manifested itself in large, destabilising wage rounds which ate into the profits of capitalists. Early experiments in crisis management, such as wage indexation, proved exceedingly fragile, and by 1982 the institutional exhaustion of antipodean Fordism and its labour law regime had become apparent.

The stage was thus set for more radical changes in the second half of the 1980s, developments that would prove corrosive of antipodean Fordism's labour law regime and constitutive of a liberal-productivist successor.

Chapter 6

Formation and Ascendency of the Liberal-Productivist Labour Law Regime

In this chapter I continue to trace the concrete history of labour law change begun in chapter 5. From the intractably crisis-ridden and institutionally exhausted position of antipodean Fordism in 1982, major developments had occurred across our four themes. By 1989, some of the constituent legal elements of liberal-productivism were coming into existence, grating against the decaying yet still entrenched institutions of antipodean Fordism. Liberal-productivism had entered a stage of broad coherence by 1996, and by 2006 we can speak of the ascendency of a liberal-productivist labour law regime. This regime provisionally answers the crisis tendencies of its antipodean Fordist predecessor and helps maintain the coherence of liberal-productivism.

1989 – SEEDS OF LIBERAL-PRODUCTIVISM GERMINATING

Whereas 1982 had been the closing chapter of the post–World War II institutional status quo, by 1989 a deep process of institutional searching had led to profound changes in the fabric of industrial relations and labour law. Although some developments represented an extension of attempts at intensifying the institutions of antipodean Fordism, others indicated that the elements of a liberal-productivist model of development were coming into existence. This period is thus a crucial one, where the tension between the old and the new is at its height.

Substantial evolution had occurred across all the key themes in the period from 1982 to 1989. The majority of this change is bound up with a historic deal between the Australian Labor Party (ALP) and Australian Council of Trade Unions (ACTU), named 'the Accord'. It was struck in August 1982 and came into effect after the victory of the ALP, led by Bob Hawke, in the 1983 election. Over the course of its history, the Accord would be rewritten seven times, but in its original, 'Mark I' form, it was a comprehensive document that combined a return to wage indexation with a broad policy package providing for improvements in the social wage, tripartite institutions for industry planning and occupational health and safety, and a desired return to full employment. It was, in essence, corporatism established without the explicit cooperation of capital.[1]

There were other technological, economic, political and legal forces at play that bore upon the four themes. These will be discussed where they are relevant below. The primary vehicle of change, however, was the Accord, and it occupies a central place in the following analysis.

Wage Fixation

One of the Accord's primary impacts was the destruction of the post–World War II pattern of wage fixation centred on wage and conditions flow-on from the pace-setting metal trades. It required of the ACTU and its constituent unions an acceptance that the maintenance and improvement of living standards 'will require a suppression of sectional priorities and demands'.[2] Upon election, the Hawke government convened a National Economic Summit, bringing together representatives of the state, capital, organised labour and various community groups in an exercise of attempted crisis management. In light of that event, Hawke reiterated 'that if a centralised system of wage fixing is to work, there must be an abstention from sectional claims except in special and extraordinary circumstances'.[3]

The Accord and the Summit, therefore, evinced a desire to break the historical pattern of metal trade flow-on and the leap-frogging wage rounds of the mid-1970s and early 1980s. The institutional mechanisms to realise this goal were 'no-extra claims' provisions and a renovated system of wage indexation, whereby wages were moved in line with Consumer Price Index increases at six-monthly intervals. The former were designed to cut off sectional wage campaigns at their source. To be entitled to receive the wage increases awarded in national wage cases, trade unions were compelled to 'sign on' to the Accord principles, which included foregoing wage claims outside of indexation. Left-wing unions which proved reluctant to sign on (several of which feature in chapter 8) were excoriated by the Commission and denied the wage improvements given to other unions.[4] Regarding these unions, the ACTU was faced with a contradiction in reconciling its functions as the peak organ of labour solidarity and its newfound position in the Accord fabric as industrial disciplinarian. Faced with this paradoxical position, the ACTU leadership generally elected to perform the latter role.

In terms of re-establishing Commission control over the aggregate movement of wages, the Accord was very successful. Dabscheck notes:

'In June 1986 the commission reported that, between September 1983 and December 1985, 96 per cent of all award wage increases resulted from its decisions in national wage cases, and that it was unable to identify any sizeable movements in over-award pay in this period'.[5] By virtually eliminating over-award campaigns in the field, the Accord placed great strain on the unions who had the most to gain by them, such as the Amalgamated Metal Workers' Union (AMWU). This tendency was exacerbated by the fact that, despite the rhetoric of shared burden, the Accord was functioning as a massive exercise in income redistribution from wages to profit, producing the declining wage share of national income noted in chapter 4.

Amid the continued economic travails of the mid-1980s, full wage indexation came to be regarded as a source of problems rather a solution, and wage rises above certain minima needed to be justified by productivity and efficiency improvements. The development of the resultant 'restructuring and efficiency' and 'structural efficiency' principles (in 1987 and 1988, respectively) represented the first movements to a more decentralised system within the coordinated wages policy of the Accord framework. In following sections I will be more concerned with the ramifications of these principles for the structure and scope of industrial relations and the role of the Commission. Suffice it to say here both principles rejected a system of total wage indexation. The restructuring and efficiency principle provided for a flat $10 wage increase to all employees covered by awards, plus 'second-tier' increases of up to 4 per cent provided a range of productivity-directed, enterprise/workplace-based measures enunciated by the Commission were met.[6] The structural efficiency exercise saw a combination of flat and proportional increases consequent upon unions agreeing to the process of award restructuring and, later, upon the Commission ratifying an award restructuring package.[7] In both cases the Commission retained ultimate control over the wage fixation system but had changed the criteria for accessing it. These developments certainly presaged the turn to enterprise bargaining in the early 1990s and were indicative of a wage structure in which the needs of individual businesses were key. In this reality was implanted the dissolution of the homogenised wage structure of antipodean Fordism and its usurpation by the polarised, variegated wage system of liberal-productivism.

Forms of Employment/Flexibility

The 1980s proved an era that saw employment precarisation intensify, building upon the emergent tendencies of casualisation and part-time labour in the 1970s. The Australian Bureau of Statistics (ABS) recorded (using a measure that would have captured the majority of casual employment) that part-time employment had increased from 17.3 per cent of employed persons in December 1982 to 20.7 per cent of employed persons in December 1989.[8] Burgess and Campbell, using a more specific index, note that casual workers as a percentage of the workforce had increased from 15.8 per cent of employees in 1984 to 18.9 per cent in 1988.[9] As economy-wide figures, these measurements bespeak of a substantial increase in the incidence of forms of employment outside the standard model. At the sectoral level, the results demonstrate a highly uneven development of these forms, with certain sectors, particularly retail, community services and recreation/tourism, heavily dependent upon casualised and part-time labour, whereas other industries, such as manufacturing and transport, demonstrated much lower (but still rising) proportions of such workers.[10] At the same time, the use of contract labour, which was generally free of award coverage, proliferated.[11]

What is of significance here is the removal of legal impediments to this growing deployment of precarious labour. Here, the restructuring and efficiency and structural efficiency principles are of key importance. In discussing the context of the former, the Commission noted the stagnation of Australian manufacturing and the consensus among all parties of the need to promote improved efficiency and productivity.[12] Among other things, the Commission identified 'changed working patterns' as a potentially necessary result.[13] Consequently, a substantial number of second-tier agreements incorporated the use of part-time and casual labour, while others provided for the engagement of contract and off-site labour.[14] As will be seen in chapters 8 and 9 particularly, these agreements tended to loosen controls on part-time and casual labour, thus threatening the dominance of the standard model of employment.

The restructuring and efficiency exercise also provided a tremendous jolt to employer efforts to gain more control over the organisation of the labour process and the deployment of labour. A large number of agreements promoted multi-skilling and broad-banding, whereby workers were to be trained across a number of functions and certain narrow positions were to be collapsed into broader classifications.[15] More important were commitments to flexible staffing levels, a greater spread of hours, flexibility in scheduling breaks, Rostered Days Off and holidays, and changed overtime arrangements.[16] What Marx termed the 'porosity' of the working day was also reduced,[17] with strict controls on starting and finishing times and the explicit reduction in 'non-productive time' featuring in many agreements.[18]

The structural efficiency principle built upon the localised changes wrought by the restructuring and efficiency principle by systemic reform *at the award level*. In its August 1988 decision, the Commission explicitly stated that one of the fronts along which structural efficiency could proceed was 'ensuring that working patterns and arrangements *enhance flexibility and meet the competitive requirements of the industry*' (my emphasis).[19] A year later, the Commission indicated the kind of changes it was envisaging, including:

- flexibility in the arrangement of hours of work (including twelve-hour shifts and ordinary hours on any day of the week);
- greater flexibility in the taking of annual leave (with a view to maximising production);
- reviewing the role of part-time and casual employment; and
- changes in award provisions which restricted the right of employers to manage their business.[20]

Such changes were highly sought by employer groups, who 'stressed the need for these issues to be an integral part of the restructuring menu'.[21] Unions were compelled to sign on to the process, and saw their proposals scuttled if it did not accord with such principles (a fate that befell the Food Preservers' Union, explored in chapter 8).

In the late 1980s, therefore, the process of precarisation and flexibilisation, absolutely central to the development of a liberal-productivist wage-labour nexus and industrial paradigm, received institutional jolts from the Commission, supported, to varying degrees, by the Hawke Government, employers and the trade union movement. These developments sat uneasily with the continued presence of proportions clauses in both federal and state awards limiting casual and part-time labour and establishing a role for unions in its engagement, both of which would be the source of further conflict.

Collectivism/Individualism and the Scale of Industrial Relations

In this era, although the system remained fundamentally collectivist, movements were afoot concerning the scale at which collective arrangements operated. In 1985, a major report commissioned by the federal government into the Australian industrial relations system was handed down (the '*Hancock Report*').[22] Although the overall argument of the *Hancock Report* was for retention of the compulsory conciliation and arbitration system, it approved of existing provisions in the Conciliation and Arbitration Act (sections 115–117) relating to 'certified agreements' between parties given the force of awards, and argued for their strengthening.[23] These recommendation were taken up by the Hawke government in its 1988 Industrial Relations Act (Cth). Importantly, the act provided that, to the extent an agreement and the underlying award dealt with the same matters, the former prevailed.[24] It also sought to prevent these bargains becoming a method of wage flow-on, giving the Commission the power to refuse certification to agreements on public interest grounds and *prima facie* rejecting bargains where they were based on the terms of other agreements.[25] Additional provisions guarded against industrial agreements being used as a vehicle to force changes in awards.[26]

In chapter 4 I noted how a key feature of a liberal-productivist labour law regime is the decentralisation of bargaining in the context of union weakness.

At this particular historical juncture, however, movement on this front was stymied by the continued institutional entrenchment of the trade union movement through the Accord, a comparatively buoyant economy and the fear of some employers (most importantly the powerful Metal Trades Industry Association, or MTIA)[27] of a wages explosion in the manner of the mid-1970s and early 1980s. In the face of this array of forces, the desire of some employer organisations (notably the Business Council of Australia) for a system based on enterprise-level bargaining could not be realised.[28] The tension was reflected in the fact that the certified agreements provided for by the act were never particularly popular with employers or unions. It would take the economic recession of the early 1990s and the breakdown of union commitment to the Accord to clear the ground for the roll-out of a fundamentally more decentralised system.

Legal Matrix

The period from 1982 to 1989 saw considerable alterations in the legal framework surrounding the labour law regime which, unsurprisingly for this period, were paradoxical in character. On the one hand, as part of the broader intensification of the Commission as an antipodean Fordist institution, it benefited from an expansion of its jurisdiction consequent upon the enlarged meaning given to the term 'industrial dispute', upon which the Commission's powers of conciliation and arbitration depended. In the *Social Welfare Union* case, the High Court overturned the restrictive definition of 'industrial dispute' mentioned earlier, stating instead that the words 'have to be given their popular meaning – what they convey to the man in the street'. The fact that the Court's decision brought about a speedy expansion of federal authority in areas previously regulated by the states[29] is indicative of the thesis of intensification; the standing of the Commission as *the* macroeconomic lynchpin for industrial relations was enhanced, particularly insofar as important ACTU white-collar affiliates were no longer locked out of federal regulation.

The Accord process also informed other efforts to intensify the role of the Commission. We have seen how the federal tribunal was historically limited in its ability to deal with the full gamut of industrial disputes (including those involving managerial prerogative) by the requirement that the substance of the dispute be 'matters pertaining to the relations of employers and employees'. However, the Accord had pledged the government to 'support the establishment of rights for employees, through their unions, to be notified and consulted by employers about the proposed introduction of technological change'.[30] The government had also agreed to support the creation of redundancy protections for workers, including an obligation on employers to consult with unions in redundancy situations.[31] Both of these types of provisions, however, had usually been taken to be outside the jurisdiction of the Commission, or were at least in doubt.[32] Given the fact, noted in chapter 5, that the federal government could only effect such regulatory outcomes *through* the Commission, a broadened conception of matters pertaining to the employment relationship was required in order to deliver on these Accord promises.

Little more than a year after the *Social Welfare Union* case, the High Court ruled in a crucial decision that consultation with unions about technological change could be considered an industrial matter.[33] Armed with this broadened power, the Commission was able to hand down its landmark *Termination, Change & Redundancy* case, which allowed it to insert clauses in awards giving effect to the aforementioned Accord promises.[34] Like the broadening of the definition of 'industry', this is to be understood as an exercise in institutional intensification, augmenting and deepening the powers of the Commission so it could play the macroeconomic role required of it.

Against these developments, however, were others of an entirely different character and provenance that were corrosive of the established order. Perhaps of deepest significance here is the legal strategy of a bellicose section of capital, the so-called New Right, in a series of set-piece battles with militant unions, including the Australasian Meat Industry Employees Union (AMIEU) at the Mudginberri abattoir, the Federated Confectioners' Association (FCA) at Dollar Sweets and the Australian Federation of Air Pilots (AFAP). These disputes demonstrated the ability of employers to subvert the arbitration system through a two-pronged attack: exploiting the secondary boycott and fines provisions of the Trade Practices Act 1974; and making recourse to common law industrial torts such as the tort of nuisance and interference with contractual relations. In both cases disputes were basically removed from the administrative fabric of arbitration and funnelled into the regular court system, the domain of the legal form narrowly construed.

The Mudginberri dispute demonstrated how the 1977 trade practices amendments discussed in chapter 5 could be used to discipline labour *outside* of the traditional channels of conciliation and arbitration. In response to an AMIEU picket line designed to enforce a tally pay system, the abattoir owner successfully pursued the union for damages under section 82(1) of the act, with the Federal Court granting a crippling sum of $1,759,444.[35] Only *after* this critical damage had been inflicted was the Commission in a position to deliver a more permanent settlement, handing down a decision that validated the employer practice of seeking payment-by-result contracts with workers.[36] The Trade Practices Act 1974 had thus become a workable tool of union repression and offered a way for employers with the will and resources to avoid what the New Right regarded as the union-friendly arbitration system.

That avoidance of Commission oversight was the goal was even more vividly demonstrated by the actions against the FCA and AFAP. The former lost a pitched battle with the small confectionary manufacturer Dollar Sweets in 1985 over the refusal of certain employees to pledge adherence to the award and forego an FCA campaign for a shorter working week. Most significant here is the fact that the union was forced to lift the picket after the imposition of an interlocutory injunction by the Supreme Court of Victoria, based on actual and threatened torts of interference with contractual relations, intimidation, nuisance and wilful injury.[37] Subsequently, the FCA was forced to pay a hefty $175,000 in what was only the second case since the early 1970s where a company had pursued a damages claim after gaining interlocutory relief from the courts.[38] The Commission's role in the dispute was exceedingly minimal, limited to a recommendation to lift the pickets before the case was removed to the Supreme Court.[39]

The AFAP fared even worse, with pilots suffering a crushing defeat in 1989 in a showdown that revolved primarily around the government-owned Australian Airlines and the privately held Ansett. Upon application by the airlines, the Commission cancelled the awards covering the pilots. This, however, was not what mortally wounded the union. This blow was dealt when the AFAP was hit with a devastating suit for wrongfully interfering with contractual relations, interfering with trade or business by unlawful means and for conspiracy using unlawful means.[40] A cabal consisting of Prime Minister Hawke, the chairmen of Ansett and Australian Airlines and senior government ministers (with the support of the ACTU) explicitly constructed action using torts and the trade practices legislation as a means of defeating the pilots; if they intended to go outside the (Accord) system, then the state and capital would follow, so the reasoning went.[41]

These events are a window into a period where the centre of gravity in the law-administration continuum was shifting. The operation of the secondary boycott provisions of the Trade Practices Act and the re-emergence of archaic industrial torts were elements of the process of juridification described in chapter 3 and represented the diversion of matters usually determined by the Commission to common law courts. As was seen with the case of bans clauses, courts of ordinary standing were bound by the logics of the abstract rule of law, equality of juridical equals and the application of the law according to formalistic tests. They shared very little indeed with the historic mission of the Commission to reconcile the capitalist project of reproducing the commodity labour-power with the struggle of a vigorous proletariat.

Such tactics on the part of capital, however, were more than just opportunistic. They were elements of an inchoate liberal-productivism, capitalist answers to the unification of the labour force set in motion by Fordism. Moreover, Australian capitalism was becoming more competitive and more open to international competition at the same time as the field of commodification increased ever further (particularly as the Hawke government sought to rationalise and corporatise the public sector). These stimuli would tend to place a premium on the role of law as a medium of association between private property owners,[42] the role Pashukanis always perceived as its essence and driving force.[43] In terms of the law-administration continuum, it is 'law' which performs this function better, in that the concern of the working class to place limits on the exploitation of labour-power *as property* evident in administration is shorn away.

1996 – LIBERAL-PRODUCTIVISM COHERES

By 1996, the seeds of liberal-productivism which were germinating in 1989 were coming into full bloom. The 1980s had generally seen methods of crisis resolution which oscillated between intensification of antipodean Fordist institutions and the development of new liberal-productivist structures. The 1990s, however, would see the former, most particularly the federal Commission, become thoroughly degraded, occupying an increasingly marginalised place in the emergent model of development. Profound changes took place across our four themes. Of key importance were the rise of enterprise bargaining, the explosion in the incidence of precarious employment and the first full-blown statutory attempts to encourage an individualist employment relations taking as its subject the individual worker. Full told, these developments evinced the essential character of the liberal-productivist labour law regime outlined in chapter 4.

Wage Fixation

The enforced wage restraint of the Accord became increasingly untenable in the late 1980s, particularly given the comparatively buoyant labour market. The Accord saw the drop in the factor share of wages noted in chapter 4, while real award wages declined markedly.[44] For unions such as the AMWU, well-schooled in a tradition of over-award bargaining, a return to plant and enterprise-level agreements free from national wage guidelines was seductive. It dovetailed with the demands for enterprise bargaining emanating from some sections of the business community, most notably the Business Council of Australia. So far as it was concerned, most of the blame for Australia's poor economic performance was due to the structure and attitudes of trade unions and the existing legal-institutional framework.[45] Enterprise bargaining, from the perspective of this organ of capital, promised vastly increased productivity and flexibility.[46]

Enterprise bargaining had the virtue of being all things to all people. The confusion over just what enterprise bargaining actually entailed would prove the source of conflict between capital, labour and the state in the 1990s. However, by November 1990 the government, many unions and a strategic majority of employers agreed that movement to an enterprise bargaining system, however defined, was necessary.[47] In a submission to the April 1991 national wage case, the ACTU duly argued for the adoption of an enterprise bargaining principle, supported by the government and most employer groups.[48] In this claim they were supported by the majority of the states, some of which were beginning to experiment with enterprise bargaining systems of their own.

The response of the Commission is the institutional equivalent of Trotsky's observation of declining classes flaring 'with a bright although smoky light' before the march of history snuffs out their reason for being.[49] The Commission, taking its Accord role of macro-level wage regulator very seriously, noted the danger of outcomes deemed best at the enterprise level leading to excessive aggregate wage outcomes.[50] Moreover, the Commission was not duped by the language of novelty surrounding the current push to bargaining, opining that while the term may be new, 'the substance is not. . . . In its simplest form, enterprise bargaining explains much of the growth of overaward payments which has occurred since the 1940s'.[51] It summed up by saying that genuine enterprise bargaining required a whole new workplace culture and that 'the parties to industrial relations have still to develop the maturity necessary for the further shift of emphasis now proposed'.[52] The whole exercise led one major paper to state that 'the Industrial Relations Commission has moved aggressively to *protect and entrench its central role in national wage fixation*' (my emphasis).[53]

The response of the parties, particularly the ACTU and the government, demonstrated the fact that the Commission in its historic form was in the process of being sloughed off in the transition to liberal-productivism. ACTU Secretary Bill Kelty described the decision as 'vomit'.[54] He was supported, if in less strident terms, by the broader union movement, the Keating government and business groups.[55] In a portent of things to come, then-Opposition Industrial Relations spokesman, John Howard, stated that the Commission's rejection of enterprise bargaining evinced an 'almost insufferable paternalism'.[56]

In the event, the isolation of the Commission, together with the recalcitrance of the state, unions and employers in acting on its recommendations for more developed and coherent enterprise bargaining policies, forced its hand. Despite misgivings, the Commission duly adopted an enterprise bargaining principle in its October 1991 national wage case. It distinguished enterprise bargaining from the aforementioned structural efficiency exercise; whereas the latter was capped at a 2.5 per cent pay rise, the former was not.[57] Although agreements could sit alongside awards, they also had the potential to replace them, provided they did not involve a reduction in ordinary time earnings or a departure from Commission standards on matters such as hours of work, annual leave and long-service leave.[58] Lastly, and perhaps most tellingly, the Commission's preferred form of enterprise bargains was so-called section 115 agreements.[59] In 1991, the section was in a sense a micro-level historical snapshot of the transition between antipodean Fordism and liberal-productivism. On the one hand, it explicitly provided that bargains (known as certified agreements) could not be based on the terms of another certified agreement except in limited circumstances, while the legislation elsewhere provided that there could be no automatic flow-on from certified agreements to awards.[60] On the other, section 115 also maintained that the Commission had the power to refuse to certify agreements that were contrary to the public interest. In short, the Commission still held the kind of macroeconomic guardian role it exercised during the coherence and crisis of antipodean Fordism, but was expected to neuter the cycle of wage and conditions flow-on that had been one of its central dynamics.

Such a hybrid role could not be maintained for long and was reflected initially by the slow-uptake of certified agreements.[61] In the face of what was considered the conservatism of the Commission, the government passed the Industrial Relations Legislation Amendment Act 1992 (Cth), which removed the Commission's 'responsibility to examine enterprise agreements in the public interest'.[62] In its place was inserted a much narrower 'No-Disadvantage Test' (NDT) which sought merely to ensure that employees covered by agreements were not disadvantaged vis-à-vis the award. This was an historic departure from the Commission's traditional concern with moderating 'the outcomes of the industrial relations process by reference to the public interest'.[63]

The transformation of the Commission's role in wage fixation received a qualitatively new jolt from the passage of the Keating ALP government's Industrial Relations Reform Act 1993 (Cth), which sought to much more surely entrench enterprise bargaining as the primary lever of wage determination in Australia. The role of the Commission in this new model was substantially reduced, as Prime Minister Keating attests to in his description of the system:

> It is a model which places primary emphasis on bargaining at the workplace level within a framework of minimum standards provided by arbitral tribunals. It is a model under which compulsorily arbitrated awards and arbitrated wage increases would be there only as a safety net. . . . We would have an Industrial Relations Commission which helped employers and employees reach enterprise bargains, which kept the safety net in good repair . . . but which would rarely have to use its compulsory arbitral powers.[64]

In the following sections, I will explore the substantive implications of this shift in terms of the collectivism/individualism of the labour law regime and the content of awards and agreements. What is of interest here is the relationship of new methods of wage determination to the wage structure and the historical pattern of flow-on.

In chapter 4 it was explained that a relatively homogenous wage structure was an important structural feature of the antipodean Fordist model of development. By 1996, a yawning gulf had emerged between the wage outcomes of the considerable number of employees (some 35–40 per cent of total employees) who were reliant purely on awards and those who were bound by both awards and enterprise agreements (30–40 per cent of employees) or enterprise bargains alone (5–10 per cent of employees).[65] Whereas the former experienced an estimated average annual wage increase of 1.3 per cent, the latter two saw pay rises of between 4 per cent and 6 per cent.[66] Declining award coverage, together with generally small safety net adjustments, also ensured that award wage increases accounted for a decreasing share of average weekly ordinary time earnings.[67] Awards, which had previously been comprehensive instruments of wage and conditions control, were reduced to bare-bone minimums that left the workers reliant upon them increasingly worse off in relative terms. Claims for wages and conditions above it were considered the province of enterprise bargaining.

Even more importantly, enterprise agreements, generally revolving around the power dynamics, needs and nature of individual enterprises/workplaces, were a very poor vessel for the flow-on of wages and conditions from the industrially strong to the weak. The resource demands of negotiating many individual enterprise agreements, rather than campaigning over one award, made it difficult to coordinate action and translate the gains of some into gains for all. The Australian Chamber of Commerce and Industry came close to describing the reality of enterprise bargaining as it would develop. It asked that the Commission and the parties 'recognise the role of awards as a safety net, rather than for *example as a mechanism for flowing the results of enterprise bargaining to non-unionised and non-consenting employers*' (my emphasis).[68]

In chapter 7, it will be seen that unions, once they realised the danger, attempted to return to the industry-level bargaining once common in the award system through the tactic of 'pattern bargaining'. By 1996, this pressure was just beginning to manifest itself.

Forms of Employment/Flexibility

The recession of the early 1990s greatly intensified the growth of employment forms outside of the standard full-time model. The recession saw the loss of 127,900 full-time jobs go hand in and with a gain of 164,000 part-time jobs, while the proportion of employees working less than thirty-five hours a week increased from 21 per cent of the workforce in January 1990 to

24 per cent by December 1992.[69] Much of this growth was in the form of casual employment. Indeed, Burgess and Campbell note that the percentage of total employees who were casual increased from 19.4 per cent in 1990 to 26.3 per cent in 1996.[70] Importantly, although women as a whole remained over-represented in both part-time and casual employment, the growth in casual employment was proportionately faster among men.[71] There was also an age dimension to the growth of casual and part-time employment, with young men and women between ages fifteen and twenty-four (many of them students) being largely funnelled into part-time and casual positions as they entered the workforce in larger numbers.[72] Lastly, the expansion of these forms was, while still concentrated in certain industries such as retail and hospitality, a movement observed across all industry divisions.[73]

Whereas this process of precarisation had for the best part of the 1980s worked *through* the award system, the advent of enterprise bargaining saw precarity advance along a new front in the 1990s. In particular, enterprise bargains tended to fit a typical pattern: headline wage increases were obtained by trading away many of the conditions that constituted the standard employment model. The degradation of this model went much deeper than simply employing more casuals and/or part-timers. Indeed, bearing in mind the definition forwarded in chapter 4, precarity increasingly came to define the experience of full-time employees.

The assault on the standard employment model within agreements, explored in the case study chapters, broadly revolved around:

1. The removal of qualitative and quantitative controls on the deployment of part-time and casual employment; and
2. The increasing spread of ordinary working hours for all workers, including full-time employees, and concomitant reductions in penalty rates.

The process of trading-off conditions and controls in exchange for wage increases also extended to the organisation of the labour process. As shall be seen in great detail in relation to the food processing and retail industries, 'enterprise bargaining explicitly linked the provision of wage increases to changes in work arrangement'.[74] These included, but were not limited to:

- the introduction/deepening of performance benchmarks and productivity agreements;
- greater flexibility for management in rostering staff, with an emphasis on maintaining constant production at minimum possible cost;
- the broad-banding of classifications; and
- contracting out of certain functions which had historically been performed by employees of the enterprise.

For those left on awards, the same process of enforced precarity and flexibility ensued without the kind of wage improvements obtained through enterprise bargaining. The recasting of awards as a safety net tended to preclude them from providing the kind of comprehensive controls on precarious employment forms that they previously exhibited. This was made explicit by the Workplace Relations Act 1996 (Cth), which limited awards to twenty 'allowable' matters, which did not include proportions clauses governing the employment of different categories of workers, nor minimum or maximum hours of work for part-time employees.[75] Indeed, their inclusion in awards was prohibited. The processes of award restructuring set in motion by the structural efficiency principle in the late 1980s also flowered in the early 1990s and typically facilitated intensified managerial control over rostering, the allocation of labour to different functions and the organisation of the labour process generally.

These developments are, for our purposes, profound. Awards had been transformed from instruments crystallising the standard employment model and establishing more-or-less rigid controls on labour classifications and demarcations in the workplace to bare-boned minima that now placed no barrier to the further extension of precarity and flexibility into the heart of the employment relationship. This transition represents no less than a substantial codification of the liberal-productivist wage-labour nexus in the labour law regime.[76]

Collectivism/Individualism and the Scale of Industrial Relations

Whereas the fundamentally collectivist nature of labour regulation had largely survived the 1980s, the basket of reforms surrounding the introduction of enterprise bargaining took concrete steps towards severing the institutionalised link between trade unions and the labour law regime. Of paramount significance here is the Keating government's introduction of so-called enterprise flexibility agreements (EFAs). These essentially created a non-union bargaining stream, where employers could negotiate with their workers *without* trade union representation.

The stated rationale from the ALP government was that it facilitated the penetration of enterprise agreements to the non-union sector.[77] Unions, however, recognised the material and symbolic threat posed by EFAs. Tim Pallas, the ACTU Assistant Secretary, opined that employers could get the flexibility they desired from regular enterprise agreements; those that went for EFAs did so for 'ideological reasons'.[78] Their concern was heightened by the fact that some employers attempted to supplant union-negotiated agreements with EFAs.[79]

Although EFAs did not prove as popular with capital as one would have expected and had a comparatively low uptake,[80] a seismic symbolic shift had been effected, demonstrating that unions were not indispensable to the bargaining process. The conservative Howard government eagerly took the opportunity upon its election in 1996 to remove the institutional impediments to the union-excluding potential of EFAs, substituting a new form of certified agreement that did *not* give unions the right to be involved unless requested by members who were to be covered by it.[81]

The Howard government also took another, rather more direct, step to marginalise the role of unions within the system: outlawing the closed shop. Unlike the Conciliation and Arbitration Act 1904 and the Industrial Relations Act 1988, the new Workplace Relations Act 1996 did *not* have as one of its objects the facilitation and encouragement of representative organisations of workers and employers. Instead, it manifested for the first time at the federal level a negative freedom of association, that is, the freedom to not belong to a trade union.[82] A government member stated tellingly: 'It is a very important element of this legislation that *freedom of association be vested with the individual*, not with an organisation they are compelled to belong to so they can have a job in a particular workplace' (my emphasis).[83] Rimmer adds: 'Until the *Workplace Relations Act*, individual employees had to gain representation usually through the appropriate registered organisation if they wished to have locus standii before the Commission. The *Workplace Relations Act* has changed all that . . . the other objects make plain that the individual employee can have legal standing in this jurisdiction'.[84]

This concentration on the individual *as subject*, rather than the collective union subject, establishes a revealing point of difference with the aforementioned efforts of the Fraser government to make it easier for workers to avoid union membership. Whereas the latter took as its reference point the collective system, attempting to provide exemptions therefrom, the new legislation gave no conceptual pre-eminence to collective arrangements. To this end, the Commission was denied the power to insert preference clauses in federal awards, part of the Howard government's struggle to eradicate the closed shop.[85]

The Howard government also deployed a far more radical method of individualising industrial relationships: the introduction of statutory individual contracts known as Australian Workplace Agreements (AWAs). In this it was following the lead of some states, such as Western Australia and Queensland, which had developed their own individual contracting regimes in the early 1990s. AWAs were subject only to the weak NDT and were aggressively promoted by the government. Individual workers were legally free to nominate a 'bargaining agent', but unions did not possess automatic standing to participate in the process. Generally negotiated between single employees and bosses, AWAs were also perhaps the most de-centralised tools of industrial regulation yet devised in the liberal-productivist trajectory, and crucially appeared at a time of increasingly evident union weakness.

Perhaps the most important and telling element of the AWA reform bundle was the fact that the administration of AWAs was not placed within the purview of the Commission, but a new body called the Office of the Employment Advocate (OEA). Agreements were to be lodged with, and approved by, the OEA, and only in the event of uncertainty on its part could the agreement be referred to the Commission for determination. This process was nothing less than an explicit attempt to recast the law-administration continuum by marginalising the Commission, its dominant administrative form. Burdened (from the perspective of the state and capital) by its collectivist heritage and practice, the Commission was a poor vessel for the new species of individualism represented by AWAs. Instead, AWAs were guaranteed and aggressively promoted by their own, purpose-built institution, which took as its basic subject the individual worker contracting with the individual employer.[86]

The collectivism and centrality of the labour law regime was also breached by the nature of the 'safety net' established by the 1993 legislation. As discussed earlier, awards were recast as a floor of minimum rights and entitlements within the enterprise bargaining regime. Awards, the historically predominant instrument of collective labour law, guarded by particular unions and often covering a swathe of workplaces, were thus relegated to a lesser role within the fabric of the new system. By contrast, the scheme of statutory minima, including provisions relating to unfair dismissal, redundancy and equal pay, was conceived, and often enforced, as *individual* rights.[87] In a context of union strength, such a development might have been harmless. However, in the circumstances, it further attacked the representational monopoly Australian trade unions had typically possessed in the industrial relations system.

The last point of note to address here are the legislative fetters which were increasingly placed around the ability of unions to organise and struggle, particularly on an inter-union basis. While the 1993 statute did relocate the secondary boycott provisions of the Trade Practices Act 1974 into industrial legislation (and so within the purview of the Commission),[88] it nevertheless hemmed in the circumstances in which unions could strike. Ironically, the Keating government, in recognising the first *de jure* right to strike in Australian industrial history, simultaneously cramped the comparatively wide *de facto* ability of unions to engage in industrial action. Unions won a limited form of immunity from tort liability and Commission-imposed penalties in the case of strikes, but only if the action was deemed to be 'protected', which required, among other things, that it occurred within the bargaining period of an enterprise agreement.[89] Only when an agreement was in the negotiation phase did strike action enjoy immunity. Once an agreement had been struck, industrial action for the duration of the agreement was unprotected. Although the legislative green light to tort claims in these circumstances did not necessarily mean employers would take action, the threat was often enough, particularly given the regime of toughened penalties established for breaches during the currency of agreements.[90]

Howard's ascension to power in 1996 was marked by more stark anti-union measures. Section 170MM of the Workplace Relations Act 1996 explicitly provided that secondary boycotts could *not* be the subject of protected industrial action. The secondary boycott provisions were also reinserted into the Trade Practices Act 1974, which the conservative parties had always regarded as their natural home. Indeed, one government member revealingly stated: 'When we have restored those sections, they will eliminate the mindless, inane and insane strikes that we have seen around this country. . . . They will restore natural justice to the workplace'.[91] Ironically, the need to restore justice to the workplace did not save the requirement to bargain in good faith, introduced by the Keating government in 1993. Under the Coalition's new legislative scheme, 'there was no positive obligation on an employer to recognise a union that sought to negotiate a collective agreement on behalf of employees, and . . . no duty to bargain in good faith'.[92]

This last point is a particularly potent demonstration of the fundamental shift to a liberal-productivist model of development. We have seen that an integration of organised labour into the fabric of the arbitration system (realised in the privileged legal status of trade unions) was a defining characteristic of antipodean Fordism. By 1996, the scene had changed entirely. Now, the standing of unions was severely corroded, and employers who were so inclined had the legislative tools at their disposal to systematically expunge unions from the workplace through refusing to recognise them in the negotiation of agreements.

Legal Matrix

By the early 1990s, the limits of the arbitral power in supporting the reform agenda of the Keating government were becoming manifest. Informed by the radical de-regulation of the Victorian Employee Relations Act 1992 (Vic), Accord Mark VII included a commitment to a range of minimum employment standards that would apply to all employees; that is, they would have what amounted to common rule effect. To this end, some of the key protections embedded in the Industrial Relations Reform Act 1993, such as unfair dismissal, protections surrounding redundancy and equal pay for women, were enacted using the external affairs power of the Constitution.[93] In particular, reliance was placed upon Australia's ratification of a number of International Labour Organization Conventions. Additionally, the creation of EFAs relied for its validity not on the traditional arbitral power, but on the corporations power.[94] In the Industrial Relations Reform Act 1993, therefore, we have the first systemic effort on the part of any federal government to ground important segments of the labour law regime on something other than the traditional arbitral power.

Frazer has stated that, on this basis, 'the legislation was the most dramatic example of direct regulation by the Federal Parliament in the field of industrial relations since Federation'.[95] Unlike the arbitral power, both the corporations and external affairs powers are plenary powers. This means that in enacting industrial legislation on these grounds, the Commonwealth was not reliant upon the established channels of arbitration and the administrative subjects and practices it entailed. The recasting of the law-administration continuum noted throughout this section thus became immensely easier given that the legal fetters placed upon the state's statutory control of industrial relations were loosened. The 'purer' legal form was becoming easier to access at the same time that its administrative brethren was corroding.

The links binding the ALP to the union movement meant that the Keating government did not press this revolution as far as it could go. Indeed, the provisions enacted using the corporations and external powers were generally placed within the purview of the Commission. However, a precedent had been set, and when the Howard government constructed its AWAs on the basis of the corporations power, it exploited the potential to sideline arbitration and placed the administration of the programme with the OEA.

The re-assertion of the abstract legal form both informed and was constituted by the diversification of the constitutional bases of industrial regulation. However, in 1996 the arbitral power remained the most substantial of these and was central to the operation of the federal tribunal. It was not until 2005–2006 that Australian liberal-productivism purged itself of the arbitral power for good.

Almost as important in the reformulation of the law-administration continuum was a crucial 1995 High Court decision, which had brought a great deal of clarity into the relationship bonding law and administration together. It will be recalled from the previous chapter that the development of the arbitration system had largely submerged, but not extinguished, the traditional body of common law employment principles, most particularly the employment contract. The case revolved around the claim of two airport baggage handlers that an award clause providing for procedural fairness should be imported or implied into their contracts of employment.[96] The Court found that the award term could *not* be imported/implied into the award.[97] In other words, the employment contract and the award regime, although often intertwined, were conceptually distinct. To the extent that awards established some of the key terms and conditions of employment, it was unnecessary for the contract of employment to also provide for them.[98] However, we have seen that the comprehensiveness of this regime was failing. As administration continued to degrade, the regulatory vacuum could thus be captured by duties implied into the common law employment contract, duties which typically favoured employers.

2006 – ASCENDENCY OF LIBERAL-PRODUCTIVIST LABOUR LAW REGIME

On 27 March 2006, the Workplace Relations Amendment (Work Choices) Act 2005 (Cth) came into effect. The passage of this legislation was the apotheosis of the liberal-productivist labour law regime, which had deepened and rested on an increasingly sure institutional footing since 1996. Enterprise bargaining spread apace, while the role of unions in its conduct was reduced. The collectivism of the labour law regime continued to be corroded, especially after the passage of WorkChoices, which hampered the activities of organised labour, further degraded the status of awards and removed the NDT, the last vestige of the link between awards and other instruments. Concomitantly, the scope of individualisation was radically widened by the open legal and political facilitation and encouragement of AWAs. There was a continued diminution in the role of the Commission, a function of explicit legislative fetters, the development of competing institutions and the broader juridification of labour law as administration gave way to the legal form narrowly construed. Perhaps most importantly, the federal government at last succeeded in broadening its constitutional capacity to regulate industrial relations. A monumental High Court decision in 2006 sounded the death-knell of the arbitral power, the keystone upon which a good deal of the law-administration continuum peculiar to antipodean Fordism relied.

By 2006, therefore, the ascendancy of the liberal-productivist labour law regime had been achieved. It gave effect to the dynamics of coherence and balance of social forces constituting liberal-productivism in Australia, which were identified in chapter 4. The repeal of WorkChoices and its replacement by the Fair Work Act 2009 (Cth) (FWA) bears very little on this fundamental truth. Where differences are material they will be discussed, but the FWA is best conceived as a technical modulation of WorkChoices, concerned with calibrating liberal-productivist structures to the limits of political legitimacy.

Wage Fixation

The general pattern of wage and conditions fixation from 1996 onwards is one of decentralisation, fragmentation and increased polarity. The shift away from awards as the primary source of wage determination is captured nicely by the Australian Bureau of Statistics, which recorded methods of wage-setting between May 2000 and May 2010. In the former, 37 per cent of workers had their pay determined by enterprise agreements, 34 per cent by individual arrangements and 23 per cent by award alone.[99] By the latter, the respective figures were 43 per cent, 37 per cent and 15 per cent.[100] The gains in both collective and individual agreement coverage were thus almost totally at the expense of awards. Moreover, this contraction of awards in scope was matched by a diminution in their relevance to the quantum of average wage rises. For example, in May 2000, the average weekly total earnings of non-managerial award-only employees were equivalent to 68.4 per cent of the average for all non-managerial workers.[101] By August 2008, however, this had dropped to just 50.4 per cent.[102] Combined with further legislative undermining and the sidelining of the Commission, the award system had thus arrived at the point it was destined for within a liberal-productivist model of development. It was in many respects unrecognisable, a permeable floor of minimum rights and conditions, rather than a comprehensive, detailed framework of instruments which could be used to universalise the gains won by sections of organised labour.

The only way over and above the increasingly poor award wage floor was through enterprise bargaining or AWAs. WorkChoices succeeded in severing the main institutional link between these instruments and awards through abolishing the NDT (a development I will return to later). Rather tellingly for my analysis, one government member opined that only through removing this safeguard could agreements become full substitutes for awards.[103] Peetz and Preston conducted a most useful study comparing pay rates in AWAs and collective agreements in 2006, the first full year without the NDT. The results speak for themselves: employees on AWAs earned on average $2 less per hour than workers on collective agreements, while median AWA earnings in 2006 were $4 below the figure for collective agreements (a larger gap than had existed just two years before).[104] Importantly, the differences in earnings between workers on AWAs were pronounced, as they tended to capture both low-income workers, such as those in retail and hospitality, and high-income workers, such as miners.[105]

One can only wonder at the number of AWAs that would have failed the NDT had it been in place at this time. A disturbing insight is afforded following the reintroduction of a weak 'Fairness Test' in 2007 (the Howard government's response to the electoral damage threatened by public anger towards WorkChoices). Figures from the government's own Workplace Authority (a successor to the OEA) revealed that one in seven AWAs lodged failed the Fairness Test, usually through not compensating the removal of penalty rates with a higher hourly rate.[106]

Even after the Rudd government phased out AWAs (leaving alone generally less egregious unregistered individual contracts such as common law contracts) and replaced the Fairness Test with a more robust 'Better Off

Overall' test, the pay of non-managerial workers under 'individual arrangements' remained in 2012 $1.80 less per hour than those bound by a collective agreement.[107] The marginally higher average weekly total earnings of the former were bought by working, on average, an extra 2.4 hours a week.[108]

In short, since 1996 a three-part wage structure has crystallised, with an increasingly small group of award-dependent workers falling behind employees in individual arrangements, who themselves consistently earn less per hour than workers covered by collective agreements. The implications of this structure for inequality in earnings are best left to the government's own neo-liberal think tank, the Productivity Commission. This body has produced research conclusively demonstrating:

- labour income growth has been strongest in the top three income deciles;
- greater dispersion in earnings; and
- overall higher levels of labour income inequality.[109]

What we have here, therefore, is the fracturing of the relatively homogenous wage structure that characterised antipodean Fordism. While it would be exceedingly difficult to measure to what degree legal change 'caused' these developments, the question of causation is largely beside the point; whatever the source, transformations in the labour law regime were necessary for these wide degrees of inequality to result.

In chapter 7, I will explore in detail a striking example of the liberal-productivist assault upon wage equality: the struggle over pattern bargaining. Upon realising the danger posed by enterprise bargaining to the common weal of labour, unions such as the AMWU attempted to orchestrate industry-wide enterprise bargaining campaigns. In this effort, they were trying at least in part to re-establish the antipodean Fordist cycle of flow-on. As shall be seen, this endeavour, despite some promising early successes, ultimately came undone, stifled precisely because of newly developed statutory inhibitions that rendered such conduct illegal. Here, labour law achieved at last, and in totality, a purpose for which it had been pressed since at least the Accord years; a destruction of the links binding the industrially strong and weak, extinguishing the last remnants of the historical forces of flow-on.

Employment Forms/Flexibility

In the 1980s and 1990s the movement towards removing the formal barriers to the intensification of precarity had proceeded apace, most specifically the stripping of awards of qualitative and quantitative controls on the employment of casual, part-time and/or junior labour, culminating in the 1996 prohibition of such clauses being included in federal awards.[110] On an institutional front, therefore, there was little more to do regarding the accessibility of such forms for capital,[111] although the case study chapters will demonstrate a continued effort on the part of management to enhance their control over the deployment and conditions of precarious labour.

An issue that was still live at the time of WorkChoices, however, was the growing use of outsourcing strategies by increasingly lean firms, who sought to use labour hire companies and independent contractors to perform jobs historically done in-house at a lower cost and without the overheads associated with a direct employment relationship. There had been historical difficulties in measuring the incidence and trajectories of these particular forms. Nevertheless, a House of Representatives committee estimated that in 1998 independent contractors represented around 10 per cent of people in employment (a 15 per cent growth from 1978),[112] a figure that remained broadly constant through the 2000s.[113] The same committee found that in 2002, 3.9 per cent of all employees were labour hire workers, a large increase on the equivalent figure of 0.8 per cent in 1990.[114] Such developments were in themselves indicative of the decline of antipodean Fordism, evidencing the degradation of the internal labour markets and vertical company integration that characterised it.

As shall be seen in chapter 8 in the case of the food processing industry, both forms were valuable in capital's effort to break union power in the workplace and disempower employees, artificially dividing the workforce with complex tangles of legal relationships outside the traditional standard employment model. Given the evidence that outsourcing to contractors and labour hire companies did indeed effect these outcomes,[115] moves to reduce the controls on these kinds of arrangements could not help but exacerbate the deepening of flexibility and precarity at the heart of the liberal-productivist industrial paradigm and wage-labour nexus.

Such a deepening, however, was at the top of the Howard government's list of priorities. Historically, unfair contract provisions implanted in industrial legislation gave contractors ready access to the court system, allowing them to seek redress for 'unfair' or 'harsh' agreements.[116] The Howard government, however, had consistently formed the view 'that independent contracting arrangements should be regulated by commercial law, not workplace relations law',[117] an expression *par excellence* of my contention that capital prefers the legal form narrowly construed over administration in times of proletarian weakness.

The Coalition's efforts to realise their vision assumed a number of dimensions. Firstly, regulations enacted pursuant to WorkChoices rendered provisions in enterprise agreements or AWAs restricting or qualifying the engagement of independent contractors and/or labour hire workers as 'prohibited content'.[118] Secondly, a contemporaneous piece of legislation, the Independent Contractors Act 2006 (Cth), was passed, which essentially meant that 'henceforth subcontractors with grievances had access only to the much more expensive and time-consuming avenue of redress through commercial law'.[119] Again, the recourse to commercial law further strengthens my thesis of liberal-productivist reconstruction of the law-administration continuum in favour of the former pole.

As the case study chapters will demonstrate, both enterprise bargaining and AWAs in this period were subject to the forces of precarisation and heightened flexibility, which whittled away the basket of rights and entitlements attaching to the standard employment model. Of particular note is the damning evidence of the utility of AWAs for capital in these endeavours. Despite a disturbing level of opacity surrounding them, the government's own figures demonstrated incontrovertibly that AWAs systematically undermined employee rights and entitlements. A sample of 998 AWAs lodged between May and October 2006 found that:

- 76 per cent did not include shift loadings;
- 68 per cent did not include penalty rates;
- 59 per cent omitted annual leave loading;
- 30 per cent did not include rest breaks; and
- 23 per cent did not protect declared public holidays.[120]

These are conditions which were hard-won over a long period of time, cohering as part of the framework of protections and entitlements that were part and parcel of the antipodean Fordist wage-labour nexus. Although the AWA structure that permitted such flagrant conditions-stripping has since been dispensed with by the FWA, the very possibility of such an effort, together with its success, is demonstrative of the fact that the wage-labour nexus of liberal-productivism operates according to a very different logic to its Fordist predecessor.

Collectivism/Individualism and the Scale of Industrial Relations

Three key themes confront us when looking at the collectivism/individualism and scale of the labour law regime in the late 1990s and 2000s: the further degradation in the functions and powers of the federal Commission, the radically expanded scope for AWAs to be employed and the ever-increasing density of legal fetters placed upon the activities of trade unions.

The Commission's powers were attacked on a number of fronts. The ability of the Commission to compulsorily determine disputes was all but abolished, a function of the usurpation of the arbitral power. The award safety net for which it was responsible was further gutted by WorkChoices, which reduced the number of allowable matters from twenty to fourteen.[121] Furthermore, the removal of the NDT mentioned earlier severed the link between the skeletal award framework it oversaw and other instruments. Concerning the latter, the Commission lost even its role in approving collective agreements which, like AWAs, were now to be lodged with the OEA.

Perhaps most important was the diversification and empowerment of competitor institutions. As seen earlier, this began with the creation of the OEA in 1996 and was further evidenced by the establishment of the Fair Pay Commission, which was given the responsibility of determining the federal minimum wage hitherto exercised by the federal arbitral tribunal. Stripped even of its role in maintaining a meaningful basic safety net of award wages and conditions, the Commission became, in many respects, a voluntarist provider of conciliation services.[122] Gifted the opportunity, Prime Minister Howard made good his 1992 threat to the Commission: 'we will stab them in the stomach'.[123]

I have already noted that the rise of liberal-productivism involves a juridification of work relationships, whereby the law-administration continuum is pushed towards its former pole as administrative fixes to proletarian struggle give way to the purer legal form. The usurpation of the arbitration system was one manifestation of this process. I showed earlier how some employers in the mid-1980s achieved this through going behind the Commission's back, falling upon common law industrial torts and statutes like the Trade Practices Act 1974. After 1996, the process assumed a more direct and naked form, as the development of a more comprehensive statutory scheme of industrial regulation institutionalised channels outside the arbitration system.

In the Australian context, this involved an explicitly legalistic turn. Ludeke astutely noted in 1998 that 'another indicator of change is the growing tendency for parties to turn to the courts rather than the traditional tribunals . . . it has now been held that the structure of the present legislation itself "thrusts the parties towards the common law courts" '.[124] The 'structure of the present legislation' probably refers in part to the explicit enlargement of the Federal Court's jurisdiction under the Workplace Relations Act 1996 which, unlike its predecessor, granted the power for parties to *commence* actions in the court.[125] More broadly, the general devolution of bargaining to the enterprise and individual levels, and the emphasis this placed on the self-help of the parties, encouraged the pursuit of the full range of legal institutions and instruments to secure desired outcomes. In Victoria, for example, the Court of Appeal found that so long as employers had complied with their statutory obligations, there should be no barrier placed before them in accessing their common law rights,[126] a decision very much channelling the case of *Byrne v. Australian Airlines Ltd* discussed earlier.

The fact that the courts of ordinary standing were now competitors for the Commission's business was graphically demonstrated by the infamous 1998

Maritime Dispute, in which Patrick Stevedores attempted to expel the Maritime Union of Australia (MUA) from the waterfront. The case was notable for not directly involving the Commission. The flow of events involved Patricks seeking injunctions against picketing in the Supreme Courts of New South Wales, Victoria and Western Australia, before the MUA eventually won a High Court challenge based on the freedom of association provisions of the Workplace Relations Act 1996.[127] Although the MUA prevailed in this case, the observation made in chapter 3, that traditional forms of law tend to reassert themselves during periods of working-class weakness, holds.

Juridification was also apparent in the recasting of what had traditionally been collective rights into individual ones, as well as the generation of new institutions to enforce them. By severing the constitutional link between industrial legislation and the arbitral power, WorkChoices accorded a much greater role to the individual worker, building upon the developments of the early 1990s. The institutional expression of this was the expansion of the so-called Office of Workplace Services and, in the final months of the Howard government, its transformation into a 'Workplace Ombudsman' (a body subsequently maintained by the FWA). These were both bodies designed explicitly to address the complaints of employees *qua* individuals.[128] Something of their character can be discerned from the fact that the Office of Workplace Services deemed that a Cowra abattoir had not broken the law when it fired twenty-nine of its workers and attempted to rehire twenty of them on new contracts that cut their weekly pay by $180.[129]

The FWA has retained in many ways the fundamentally individualistic character of the rights and protections afforded by statute. Creighton notes that the individualistic element of the regime

> is also evidenced by the fact that all awards and enterprise agreements must contain provisions enabling the making of IFAs where the operation of the collective instrument can be modified in its application to individual employees, that individuals . . . have the capacity to enforce their entitlements under enterprise agreements and modern awards, and that the 'safety net' protections set out in Part 2–2 relate very much to the rights of the individual rather than the collectivity . . . *unions are increasingly treated as just another participant in the industrial process, rather than its driving force* (my emphasis).[130]

WorkChoices also radically intensified the individualism of the labour law regime through making AWAs more accessible to capital at the same time that the protections built in to them were wound back. Stung by the relatively slow take-up of AWAs, the Howard government increased their appeal in a number of ways. The abolition of the NDT severed the strings still binding it to the award system. Now, AWAs merely had to comply with a new statutory Fair Pay and Conditions Standards' scheme, prescribing only five basic conditions (basic rates of pay and casual loadings, maximum hours of work, annual leave, personal leave and parental leave). Moreover, they could be offered as a condition of employment for prospective workers.[131] For those employees already covered by collective agreements, employers proved willing to refuse to bargain when they came up for re-negotiation, instead waiting workers out (and in some cases firing them) in an attempt to force them onto AWAs.[132] In short, WorkChoices created 'a cascading hierarchy of instruments at the apex of which are AWAs, followed by collective agreements then awards. An instrument higher up the hierarchy operates to the complete exclusion of any instrument further down the list'.[133]

The generation of this hierarchy resulted in the rapid growth of the AWA stream. From the 2.4 per cent of employees calculated to be covered by AWAs in 2004, the rate rose to something between 5 per cent and 7 per cent in February 2008.[134] They were particularly concentrated in traditionally unionised industries, such as mining and transport, where they inflicted grievous damage to union strength.[135] Although never high in absolute terms, the disempowering impact of AWAs went far beyond their actual incidence. One AMWU official accurately grasped the case when they stated that 'employers now understand that a few AWAs here and there in key enterprises dent confidence in union bargaining, lower standards and diminish outcomes much more than the one or two per cent of workers that they cover'.[136] It is true that the FWA has subsequently dispensed with statutory individual contracts, but it has introduced 'Individual Flexibility Agreements' into modern awards and enterprise agreements, which permit variations of award conditions provided they satisfy the new 'Better Off Overall' test. Nevertheless, evidence demonstrating that they are open to abuse suggests that at least some of the managerial prerogative-enhancing quality of AWAs persists in them.[137]

The diffusion of AWAs was proceeding apace at the same time that the capacity of trade unions to resist them was weakening. WorkChoices struck at the heart of the ability of unions to organise and operate. Union rights of entry were even more severely limited than they had been, making it extremely difficult for organisers to access workplaces without any union members. The legislation played the dual trick of specifying a highly formalistic procedure by which union officials obtained 'permits' while at the same time preventing new workplace agreements from providing entry rights separate from the statutory regime.[138]

The list of 'prohibited content' in workplace agreements did not stop with rights of entry. Among the immense number of prohibited terms were any dealing with:

- deduction of union dues;
- paid trade union training and/or meeting;

- encouragement or discouragement of union membership;
- allowing industrial action; or
- restricting AWAs.[139]

These were clearly targeted directly at the ability of unions to obtain more favourable terms through enterprise bargaining.

The damage inflicted on trade unions by the increasingly hostile legislative framework from 1996 onwards is reflected in several key indicators, revealing a movement in a deep malaise. The end of the closed shop, tightened access to existing and potential members and the availability of instruments outside of union oversight combined with the broader secular decline of trade unions to hit membership hard. In 1997, there were still more than 2.1 million members, representing some 30.3 per cent of employees.[140] By 2009 there had been an absolute decline of more than 250,000 members, while union density had decreased to 19.7 per cent.[141] The FWA has proved to be of no help in arresting the decline; by August 2014, only 1.6 million people were trade unionists in their main job, with density standing at the historically low rate of 15 per cent.[142]

Levels of industrial disputation, which had been roughly steady for most of the 1980s before falling rapidly after the recession of the early 1990s,[143] proved remarkably sensitive to changes in the labour law regime. The ABS reported that 'there was a 42 per cent reduction in the number of working days lost between 1996 and 1997. The number of employees involved dropped by 45 per cent, and the number of disputes by 18 per cent'.[144] The fact that 1996 saw the introduction of the Howard government's anti-union programme is more than a little coincidental.

Disputation continued to decline throughout the Howard years, with the absolute nadir being reached in 2007. In that year, there were a paltry 135 disputes, involving a mere 36,000 employees.[145] Again, the FWA has proved of scant comfort to unionists, with historically low levels of industrial action, in terms of numbers of disputes, employees involved and working days lost remaining the order of the day.[146]

Legal Matrix

In the discussion of the Industrial Relations Reform Act 1993 and Workplace Relations Act 1996, I noted how the arbitral power was supplemented by both the corporations and external affairs powers. WorkChoices was a radical leap further down this road. After failing to get the states to 'refer' their industrial powers to the Commonwealth,[147] the government turned to the corporations power to found the bulk of the WorkChoices legislation. The prize for this effort, if successful, was twofold: the ability to bring many workers currently covered by the state system under the control of the Commonwealth and an ability to break the mould of conciliation and arbitration, with all its collectivist traditions, prescribed in the arbitral power.

Conservative parliamentarians made no bones about both objectives.[148] An ALP member incisively grasped the ramifications of the Coalition's scheme, stating:

> It is also important to note that this legislation shifts the most important principles in our legal constitution – the way we work and the way workplaces relations are run in this country – from the labour power to the corporations power. What does that mean? We are no longer talking about arbitration. We are no longer talking about two parties – the worker and the employer in their workplace – we are now talking about corporations power and about economic and employment costs. We are talking now about commodities and simple units of production.[149]

This expansive use of the corporations power would essentially usurp the arbitral power. Given the stakes, for both the union movement and state governments who were seeing an enormous disturbance in the balance of federalism, a High Court challenge was inevitable, despite the fact that its chances of success were seen by many experts as slim.[150]

In a massive 385-page decision, the High Court (by a five to two majority) held that the corporations power could be used to found the Howard government's industrial relations legislation.[151] Most significantly for my analysis, the majority held that the arbitral power did not contain positive prohibitions or restrictions on the ambit of the corporations power, nor did it imply that it alone was capable of grounding labour laws.[152] In other words, the High Court gave the government an enormous latitude in legislating for industrial relations, freeing the latter from the prescribed mode of industrial regulation established by the arbitral power.

In a strongly worded dissent, Justice Kirby hit upon one of the motive forces for this shift in terms supporting the theory of transition forwarded in this book:

> The feature of the independent determination of industrial disputes has the potential to encourage and promote collective agreements between parties and the protection of economic fairness to all those involved in industrial disputes, secured by the distinctive procedures of conciliation and arbitration. Such elements of fairness would not necessarily be assured by an unlimited focus of federal law on the activities of employers as constitutional corporations.[153]

The preceding chapters allow us to regard the claims for the arbitration system's historic fairness with the skepticism it deserves. Compulsory conciliation and arbitration was not a gift to ensure fairness to workers, but a structure sitting astride the competing demands of capital accumulation and a powerful labour movement. With that caveat in mind, however, I have demonstrated that part of arbitration's utility to Australian capitalism in its antipodean Fordist phase was precisely that it was more distributively 'fair' than the free labour market system which had preceded it. This ensured both the maintenance of adequate demand in the hands of the proletariat and the integration of organised labour into the fabric of the state. The survival of the system more or less intact for the majority of the twentieth century, together with the general acceptance of the federal state that its power to regulate industrial relations *was* contained within this power to the exclusion of others, attests to this fact. Liberal-productivism, however, is both premised upon and reproduces a different balance of forces and modalities of cohesion. What made arbitration 'fair' is precisely what made its destruction necessary in the new epoch of Australian capitalism.

The effective death of the arbitral power in 2006 was not reversed by the incoming ALP government, which instead exploited the constitutional shift in enacting their own industrial legislation. With that passed into history one of central foundation stones upon which the law-administration configuration unique to antipodean Fordism was erected.

CONCLUSIONS

In this chapter I have provided the second half of the concrete legal history needed to flesh out the abstract framework developed in chapter 4. From where the previous chapter left off, major developments across our four key themes have resulted in the destruction of the antipodean Fordist labour law regime and its replacement by a liberal-productivist successor.

The advent of the Accord between the ACTU and the ALP heralded a far more concerted effort at searching for ways out of crisis than had hitherto been the case, revolving initially upon intensifying the federal Commission and placing it as *the* lynchpin in aggregate wage fixation. However, the intractability of the crisis forced more drastic changes by 1989, as the state, labour and capital sought for a way to increase efficiency and competitiveness through a strategic decentralisation to the award and workplace level. The development of the restructuring and efficiency and structural efficiency principles was particularly important in this regard, especially to the extent that they built upon the emerging norm of precarity and enhanced managerial control over the organisation of the labour process. This movement towards new forms of the traditional award system co-existed with, and to a certain extent grated against, the development of new, more legalistic instruments of industrial control, such as secondary boycott prohibitions, and the recrudescence of industrial torts in set-piece battles between militant New Right employers and unions.

Juridification, this movement towards the 'purer' legal form, continued throughout the 1990s and 2000s, as collective rights gave way to individual ones and the Commission found itself competing for business with courts of ordinary standing. The emergence of enterprise bargaining further limited the tribunal's role and power, as ALP and Coalition governments sought to narrow the circumstances in which it could arbitrate disputes and/or refuse to certify enterprise agreements. In 1996, the Howard government took the next step, introducing statutory individual contracts that fundamentally threatened the collectivism of the labour law regime. In their war against pattern bargaining and secondary boycotts, they attacked this collectivism from another angle, finally severing the last remnants of the historical pattern of wage and conditions flow-on.

The activation of WorkChoices in 2006 marks the ascendency of the new liberal-productivist labour law regime. The remnants of the award system and the Commission were reduced to just that: institutions that, in the logic and effect of their action, shared little with their predecessors but the names. Unions were relegated to unwanted 'third parties', stifled by a wide array of legal fetters that largely survived the death of WorkChoices and remain integral to the FWA. The new regime was made complete when WorkChoices, building on exploratory moves in the 1990s, abandoned the arbitral power of the Constitution and sought the footing of the corporations power. This constitutional revolution, legitimated by the ALP in enacting the FWA, removed one of the keystones of the law-administration continuum unique to antipodean Fordism, and is perhaps the single most telling indication that liberal-productivism has remade labour law in its own image.

Chapter 7

The Metal Trades Sector and Antipodean Fordist Flow-On

This chapter marks the beginning of the case studies, where I isolate some of the most important changes identified in the previous two chapters and explore their application to specific industries/sectors in greater detail.

The focus in this particular segment is the rise and decline of the antipodean Fordist process of wage and conditions 'flow-on' centred on the articulation between the arbitration system and the leading metals sector. It has been established that the former performed the immensely important function of flowing-on gains won in the latter to the labour force at large through the award framework. Here, the mechanics of flow-on, the architecture of the award system and the role of metals within that structure will be examined in much greater detail. In particular, the analysis will focus upon the historical role of the Metal Trades and Metal Industry Awards as industrial pace-setters, an institutional expression *par excellence* of a Fordist lead sector. I will trace the ascension of these awards to the apex of the award hierarchy in the period of antipodean Fordist functionality, before witnessing the growing dissonance between their institutional entrenchment and the flagging dynamism of the metals, and broader manufacturing, sector. The enforced wage straitjacket of the Accord stopped the cycle of metal trade flow-on in its tracks, while the advent of enterprise bargaining and associated legislative change destroyed it once and for all.

The choice of this particular subject is informed by a variety of considerations. Firstly, the centrality of the flow-on process to the coherence of antipodean Fordism cannot be underestimated; indeed, in chapter 5 I stated that metal sector flow-on was 'the motive force by which the institutional structure turned'. Understanding the institutionalisation and usurpation of the metal trades as a lead sector is thus key to understanding one of the central pivots of antipodean Fordist functionality and crisis. Secondly, the bundle of legal changes investing the ascent and decline of the metals sector as an institutionalised pace-setter goes to the heart of several of the fundamental essences of the labour law regimes of antipodean Fordism and liberal-productivism, including:

- For the former: compulsory arbitration precociously institutionalising the Fordist wage-labour nexus, most particularly its linkage of the industrially strong and weak, the growth of administration fixes to worker power and broad occupational/industry-level bargaining;
- For the latter: the severing of the institutionalised links binding the labour force together, de-centralisation and intensified juridifcation.

Before the analysis can be constructed, however, it is necessary to briefly plot the early history of the relationship between the metal trades and the arbitration system.

EARLY HISTORY

By the time of Federation in 1901 there was already a small but growing manufacturing sector. The industrial impetus of World War I, the growth of the domestic market and the advent of a cogent system of substantial tariff protection combined in the 1920s and 1930s to provide a kick-start to manufacturing of a more industrial character, particularly basic metals, metal fabrication and machinery construction (referred to collectively here as the 'metal trades' and 'metal industry').

The metal trades unions (including at this time the Amalgamated Engineering Union, the Australasian Society of Engineers, the Federated Moulders Union of Australasia and the Blacksmiths' Society of Australasia) had pursued their own separate state awards until the 1920s, when the Amalgamated Engineering Union (AEU) sought and obtained its first federal award in 1921.[1] They were followed by the other craft unions and more general unions organising unskilled workers (such as the Federated Ironworkers Association), such that by the mid-1920s they all held awards in the federal jurisdiction,[2] representing the first concerted effort 'to standardise conditions of employment in the metal industries which were a key component of national industrial expansion'.[3]

A moment of critical importance for the analysis here was the creation of what would become the cornerstone of the post–World War II award structure, the consolidated Metal Trades Award in 1930.[4] Cockfield notes that, unlike the patchwork of awards which had characterised the sector up to this point, the award 'covered all occupational unions: both engineering unions, the blacksmiths', boilermakers', and moulders' unions, the Federated Ironworkers Association, and the Sheet Metal Workers Union'.[5] In an indication of how important the metals sector was even at this early stage, the tribunal stated of the case: 'The interests involved, all more or less related, constitute the most important group of secondary industries of the Commonwealth'.[6] In terms significant to my construction of the industrial paradigm according with antipodean Fordism, the award reflected the influence of the mass production techniques and semi-automatic machinery that were beginning to transform the sector and supplant the typical skilled 'jobbing' pattern which had characterised employment therein.[7]

From the mid-1930s onwards, the metal trades served a critical function as the base of recovery for organised labour in the aftermath of the Great Depression. A 1935 adjustment to the Metal Trades Award by Justice Beeby substantially increased margins for skilled workers and, more importantly, led to requisite movements in many other awards, in what was to be the first example of the award acting as an industrial pace-setter.[8] A concerted AEU campaign to extract over-award payments from metal employers throughout 1936–1937 proved extremely successful, triumphing despite the union being de-registered federally.[9] Upon being re-registered, Justice Beeby noted: 'It is obvious that this Union not being registered completely disorganises the Metal Trades Industry and the Metal Trades Award, *which is one of the most important ever made by the Court*' (my emphasis).[10]

This acknowledged significance of the metal trades industry only grew with the onset of World War II. Sheridan notes how 'the metal trades workforce practically doubled between 1938–1939 and 1943–1944 from 177,000 to 341,000'.[11] Technological innovations, such as tungsten carbide tipped tools, new steels and improved machinery, helped expand output vastly, while by 1943 domestic production of machine tools had increased seven times on the pre-war figure.[12] Just as significant was the increasing scale of production, with metal workers increasingly employed in large, more easily organised, workplaces.[13] Both developments combined were to provide the foundation of a post–War metals sector of a different qualitative magnitude to the one that existed before the conflict. With this industrial critical mass established, the metal unions, characterised by powerful and active industrial organisation and a pent-up worker desire to make good the privations incurred during the Depression and World War II, were placed to take a vanguard role in the post-War wave of militancy. In these struggles the Metal Trades Award would serve as a key institutional nexus.

ANTIPODEAN FORDISM AND THE METAL TRADES AWARD – RISE TO PARAMOUNTCY

With the end of hostilities in 1945, the path was finally cleared for the coherence of the antipodean Fordist model of development. Key to this process was moving the economy from a war footing through the reconversion of manufacturing capacity to peacetime production and the release of bottled-up consumer demand. The latter phenomenon, however, was stymied by the Chifley Australian Labor Party (ALP) government's maintenance of war-time wage and price controls. In particular, there was reluctance and hedging on the part of Chifley to relinquish the maximum wage ceiling and allow fresh applications for marginal rates variation.[14] His government's overwhelming desire to restrain inflation, and thus wages, placed it on a collision course with organised labour, whose hand was strengthened by the virtual elimination of pre-war unemployment. Unsurprisingly, the metal trades were the primary front along which the conflict was waged.

The freezing of margins cases during the War, along with the fact that the basic wage was varied in line with prices by automatic quarterly adjustments, meant that in nominal award terms the marginal relativity between skilled and unskilled employees had declined. In practice, however, metal unions had been generally successful in obtaining over-award payments (technically illegal under the government's wage-pegging scheme) from employers keen to profit from war production in a tight labour market.[15] Direct action at the point of production proved similarly propitious in the post-War environment. In the face of government and employer intransigence, a massive six-month dispute in the Victorian metal trades over the issue of over-awards and margins proved critical. Angered by the protracted bureaucratic wrangling over the basic wage and forty-hour week hearings, metal unions, most prominently the AEU, embarked on an over-award wage campaign. The employers responded with an ill-conceived lock-out, while the federal Commission (at this time still the Arbitration Court) appeared fundamentally confused, both as to the nature of wage-fixing regulations and how to control an industrial brawl that threatened to spill over state boundaries.[16] In the event, the employers and the Arbitration Court caved along the line, with a 1947 Full Bench Margins case granting substantial marginal increases.[17]

The *1947 Margins Case* was of critical importance to the institutionalisation of the role of the metal trades at the apex of the award structure. Although Hancock and Richardson note that 'the tendency for the overall wage structure to move in line with "metals" emerged as early as 1935',[18] this trend only really became consistent from the *1947 Margins Case* onwards. Although the Bench stated that the 1947 rulings were 'in settlement of a specific industrial dispute and . . . of little value as a precedent',[19] Hutson maintains that the proceedings 'took on the character of a national test case . . . because the increases eventually flowed to other awards'.[20] Despite their desire to prevent flow-on to other sectors, the Court was forced to acknowledge after the case that 'by consent and by adjudication, the metal trades marginal increases are beginning to percolate into other industries'.[21]

The case was something of a prototype for the pattern of margins determinations that would follow in the 1950s and 1960s. The participants in the hearing were still only the metal unions and metal employers, a situation that was to change drastically in future cases as their national significance was acknowledged. Moreover, the case represented a hybrid in terms of the grounds upon which marginal increases were granted. Whereas in a 1937 case evidence of a general economic recovery was regarded as inappropriate in the fixation of metal margins,[22] the 1947 hearings evinced a different methodology, whereby both the economic capacity of the metals sector *and* the capacity of industry generally were to be considered in the fixation of marginal rates in the Metal Trades Award.[23] This melding of the fortunes of the metals sector with industry at large was a key moment in the institutional entrenchment of the former as a lead-sector, a crystallisation that would be completed by the *1954 Margins Case*.[24]

The *1952 Margins Case* served as a mid-wife to the momentous 1954 case.[25] Although it did not yet formally unify the capacity of the metal trades sector with that of industry generally, Hancock notes that considerations of the macroeconomic impact of marginal adjustments were determining factors.[26] It was also conducted with the air of a national test case, with Hutson noting that 'there was a big increase in the participants to 16 metal unions, 4 white-collar unions, 8 employer organisations, 6 individual major employers, 3 State Governments, and 11 State Instrumentalities'.[27] Commissioner Galvin remarked of the nature of the proceedings:

> It has been said on numerous occasions . . . that, to an extent, the principles laid down in the Metal Trades Award, form the pattern for quite a large number of other awards. What transpired in the case of other awards subsequent to the then Full Court's decision of 1947 amply bears that out, and that being so it is evident that these proceedings do take on something in the nature of an economic inquiry in miniature.[28]

Galvin also traced the development of the fitter as the standard skilled employee when comparing inter-award marginal relativities, which was indicated in chapter 5. Again, it is worth quoting him at length:

> For many years past, first the members of the Court and later Conciliation Commissioners have adopted the practice of treating the rate of pay prescribed for the general engineering fitter as the focal point or yardstick upon which to measure the rates of other skilled tradesmen, and to relate thereto the services of the semi-skilled and unskilled class of workers. . . . That has been proved time and time again, and there is no more recent exemplification of it than what happened subsequent to the Full Court's 1947 Metal Trades decision, where notwithstanding the clear pronouncement that it was designed to cover the special

circumstances of the Metal Trades Industry, it was quickly imported into the awards of most other industries.[29]

This recognition that gains won in the Metal Trades Award tended to diffuse to industry generally underlay the momentous *1954 Margins Case*. The Arbitration Court (in what was to be its last major margins case before being reconstituted as the Arbitration Commission in 1956) understandably reasoned that if Metal Trades Award decisions were going to have macro-level significance, it followed that the capacity of the national economy should be the determining feature in the fixation of metal margins. It stated of the skilled employee: 'We cannot overlook the fact that any increase in his margin is likely to have some reflection in the marginal rates of other skilled employees not in this industry. It is particularly because of this fact that in making any increase for the skilled employee we have anxiously considered the state of the economy'.[30]

In determining whether or not the economy could bear the cost of increased marginal payments, the Court marshalled data on rural production and productivity, investment levels, employment and the state of secondary industry, little of which concerned the metals sector specifically. When requisite economic capacity had been ascertained, the principles of comparative wage-justice ensured that the margins thus determined flowed through the award structure at large.[31] The case, while building on the 1947 and 1952 decisions, represented a hitherto unprecedented entrenchment of the Metal Trades Award at the pinnacle of the award structure. From now on, the capacity of the metal trades and the capacity of the national economy were regarded as synonymous. The fact that this position of paramountcy was buttressed by powerful and generally militant metal unions ensured that the wage and conditions 'inputs' provided by their struggle found ready-made institutional channels through which to diffuse.

The pattern set by this critical 1954 case was followed with only minor variations until the *1967 Total Wage Case* and the 1967 *Metal Trades Work Value Inquiry*. The *1959 Margins Case* introduced a qualification into the use of general economic capacity as a guide for setting marginal rates in the Metal Trades Award, arguing that the economic position of particular industries *could* be a factor to be taken into account where capacity was greater or less than the economy generally.[32] However, the Commission proceeded to find that this was not the case with the metals industry, whose capacity (not by accident) was taken as analogous to the economy at large.[33] Another margins hearing in 1963, while affirming the 1959 qualification, essentially assumed the relationship between metal sector and general industrial capacity, with evidence of widespread overtime, over-award payments and a lack of employer dissent to the contrary taken as proof 'that by and large, the economic capacity of the Metal Trades industry is certainly not less than and probably more than that of industry generally'.[34]

The *1963 Margins Case* represents the institutional highpoint of the Metal Trades Award. Although conceptually distinct, the capacity of the metal trades and the economy generally were in practice unified. The industrial capacity of the nation was thus refracted through the prism of the Metal Trades Award; once so refracted, it could flow through the award structure, lubricated by the ideology of comparative wage justice. The Metal Trades Award was the nexus of this ideology, certainly for blue-collar workers and, in many instances, their white-collar brethren. Commissioner O'Reilly, in discussing the utility of the metal trades fitter as an industrial measuring rod, summed it up best: 'It seems elementary that some standard or measuring rod is indispensable in any measuring assignment. The adequacy of any wage or salary cannot be meaningfully assessed unless it is considered in relation to other wages or salaries. This seems just as fundamental *whether the jobs concerned have common features or not*' (my emphasis).[35]

Despite often repeating a stock-standard assertion that decisions concerning the metal trades were not meant to automatically apply to other industries, the award framework as it evolved in the 1950s and 1960s came to be dominated by the Metal Trades Award. Aside from the crucial role it played in margins determinations, it was also the vehicle for basic wage claims; that is, the Commission formally altered the basic wage in the Metal Trades Award, which was regarded as a decision of general application. Moreover, it was an important test award for the introduction of new standards of employment, such as provision for three weeks' annual leave.[36] From no more an authoritative source than the President of the Commission, Sir Richard Kirby, came the admission that the metal trades industry acted as a 'guide-liner or trend-setter for wages and working conditions'.[37] In short, it helped institutionalise the metals sector as an archetypal Fordist lead sector and facilitated the performance of its functions in this role; as I stated in chapter 5, flow-on exerted a strong homogenising impact on the wage structure at the same time that a 'standardized award structure' was produced.[38]

It is vital to note, however, that this position of industrial gravity was not achieved nor perpetuated by the institutions of arbitration alone. As seen in chapter 4, this period of institutional ascendency was based on the waxing of the manufacturing sector generally within Australian capitalism. In 1957–1958, there were some 1,073,807 people employed in what the-then Commonwealth Bureau of Census and Statistics dubbed 'industrial classes', of whom approximately 42.8 per cent (459,345) were classified as working in 'industrial metals, machines and conveyances' (in short, the metals sector).[39] Over the same period, manufacturing engaged on aggregate a massive 38.3 per cent of wage and salary earners in civilian employment.[40] We can thus say (somewhat crudely) that in this period, employees engaged in the metal trades accounted for 16.4 per cent of total civilian employment. It was also in the late 1950s and early 1960s that manufacturing as a contributor to gross domestic product (GDP) peaked, at just under 30 per cent.[41] Manufacturing in Australia was thus as large and significant, in relative terms, as it was ever to be, and within it the metals sector constituted the single largest industrial group. The Metal Trades Award was not simply important by dint of its institutional position; rather, this was premised on its critical importance within the fabric of Australian capitalism.

Moreover, the success of the union movement in achieving gains in the Metal Trades Award and then flowing them on was predicated on the strength of the metal unions themselves. Sheridan recounts at length the success the AEU and other metal unions achieved in basic wage and margins cases when backed by industrial campaigning and the application of plant by plant duress to individual employers.[42] The Commission itself rather lucidly described union strategy:

> The 'militant' approach . . . was based upon the view that the way to win a case before the Commission was, first to develop a major national propaganda campaign and make claims on every employer and seek to obtain over-award payments by demands backed by the threat of strikes, which should if necessary be carried into action. Application should then be made to the Commission to obtain recognition of the established fact.[43]

In the absence of such pressure, the Commission proved more hesitant to effect timely change. This reality would become of crucial importance as union power began to degrade through the 1980s.

TOTAL WAGE AND WORK VALUE – ATTEMPTED INSTITUTIONAL DISLOCATION AND INDUSTRIAL MILITANCY

As seen in chapter 5, capital came to lament the 'shunters law' set in motion by the metal trades, with employers feeling that unions were getting two bites at the wage cherry through using national capacity to buttress both basic wage *and* margins claims. Despite the functionality of the system for the overall coherence of antipodean Fordism, capital, governed by the corrosive laws of competition, often loses sight of the forest for the trees. A feeling that organised labour had the upper hand, along with the Commission supporting the trade union sponsored 'prices and productivity' method of adjusting the basic wage, convinced leading employer organisations that a change of tack towards the whole system of wage determination was necessary.[44]

The first attempts to disrupt the paramountcy of the Metal Trades Award were part of this broader effort to effect change in the methodology of the Commission. In chapter 5 I outlined the history of the employer's desire for a 'total wage', whereby the two-part basic wage and margins structure would be replaced by a single wage which would embrace both. After introducing the concept in 1964, it took only three years for the Commission to come around to the employer's point of view and jettison what had been the bedrock of wage fixation since 1907 in favour of the total wage. Although characterised by Justice Moore as 'no more than a procedural change',[45] the total wage concept bore within itself the ability to minimise the importance of metal trades decisions. Indeed, Hawke noted that 'while the present total wage system operates the only automatic flow to other awards of decisions made under the Metal Trades Award will be in respect of decisions in annual national wage cases'.[46] The formal abolition of margins, combined with the centrality of the Metal Trades Award in their determination, heightened this potential.

The primacy of the metal trades was also threatened by a huge work value inquiry over 1966–1967, the first in over thirty years.[47] It was a curious twist of fate that the structural basis of margins fixation in federal awards escaped work value analysis for such a long time, with Commissioner Winter noting that the award's comparative evaluation of the work processes 'has been allowed to remain perennially within the rigid time capsule of the decade of the 1920s'.[48] Over the objections of both employers and unions, the Commission initiated an inquiry on its own accord. After an exhaustive process of workplace inspections and hearings, it determined that the work value of employees (particularly tradesmen) in the metal trades had grown in a context of deep technological innovation and granted substantial marginal rises.[49]

In granting the increases, however, the Commission made two critical, interrelated qualifications which threatened the position of the Metal Trades Award as a pace-setter and upset the industrial relations of the sector generally. The first was the stated desire to avoid flow-on to other sectors. Although similar statements had been made in previous cases, they were largely token and undermined by the identification of metal trade capacity with the capacity of the national economy. This inquiry, however, was qualitatively distinct from the margins cases which had come before, in that the primary consideration was not abstract economic capacity, but the actual work value content of eleven pilot classifications *within* the Metal Trades Award. In this context, the following statement of the Commission assumed a new weight:

> We also emphasise that this is not a case in which increases in wage rates for the metal trades sets a pattern for wages in other industries. The increases which we would grant . . . relate solely to employees working under clause 4 of the Metal

> Trades Award and do not constitute a reason for awarding wage increases to employees covered by other awards or working in other industries.[50]

Second was the Commission's invitation to employers to 'absorb' the wage-rises granted out of existing over-award payments. In other words, an employer already paying a $6 over-award would only have to grant a $1.40 increment to tradesmen to fulfil the $7.40 increase ordered by the Commission. Given the comparatively generous nature of the wage-rises given, metal employers and their organisations needed no encouragement and, unlike previous margins cases, made a concerted effort to enforce absorption. As the prevailing level of over-award payments closely matched the work value increases, this effectively meant much of the metal trades workforce stood to gain next to nothing.[51]

The result was the monumental absorption struggle of early 1968. Metal unions embarked upon a series of rolling strikes, with the first six weeks of 1968 witnessing some 400 stoppages.[52] Judge Dunphy noted of the fracas: 'Never before, in my memory, have employers had more reason to fear industrial disruption of a grand scale than is now in evidence before us in New South Wales'.[53] Despite the levying of tens of thousands of dollars in fines for breaches of bans clauses and the imposition of what amounted to a blanket no-strike order, the union campaign was almost completely victorious, with the Commission stating, 'it appears to all of us that substantial absorption in over award payments of the wage increases recently granted has not in this industry been practicable in the existing circumstances'.[54]

The defeat of absorption paved the way for powerful currents of flow-on from the metal trades decision to other awards. Mills, writing in 1968, opined that the flow-on would be extensive.[55] A year later, Woodward noted that attempts to enforce flow-on had been a major factor in strikes in the building and railways industries, and observed that wage increases were being awarded on a comparative justice, rather than work value, basis.[56] He added that 'as more and more industries have fallen more or less into line, it has become increasingly difficult for any to be left aside'.[57]

The early efforts to disrupt the place of the metal trades sector and its all-important award in the wage structure were thus largely thwarted. Decisions which threatened to usurp the paramount position of the Metal Trades Award were rendered ineffective by the intense industrial militancy of metal unions and the continued inability of the Commission to match its rhetoric on flow-on with changed practice. This latter reality was best captured by Commissioner O'Reilly when he stated of the 1967–1968 work value increases: 'If I have paid insufficient heed to the strictures of the Metal Trades Bench I am not alone. The Metal Trades increases have by now been reflected substantially in other Federal and State awards'.[58]

EARLY 1970s–EARLY 1980s – INSTITUTIONAL EXHAUSTION AND ECONOMIC CRISIS

The first real signs of stress in the post-war award hierarchy began to manifest themselves in the early 1970s. Regarding the place of the Metal Trades Award at the apex of this structure, two of the biggest developments at this initial stage seem to have been the mounting contradictions between the award as a vehicle of general and specific interests (introduced in chapter 5) and a change in tactics on the part of employers.

Regarding the first point, Woodward opined in 1969: 'The developments of the last few years seem to have produced the result that award wages in the metal trades industry must now lag behind most others. If all increases in the metal trades are to flow elsewhere . . . and if other industries are to receive additional increases periodically, there must be a tendency for workers in those other industries to move ahead of the metal trades'.[59] In other words, the very ascendency of the Metal Trades Award as a tool of industrial regulation grated against its actual utility for workers employed in the metals sector, who sought to make good the shortfall through exacting greater over-award payments.[60]

Commissioner Winter, who was responsible for cases concerning the metals sector and had played a key role in the work value inquiry, made a very similar observation in 1971, noting that 'while large numbers of employees covered by other awards gained steadily and repeatedly by dint of applications for wage increases which did not "flow back" to any area of the Metal Trades Award, those covered by the latter award remained relatively static'.[61]

The intensified impulse to the traditional pattern of unions extracting over-award payments dovetailed with metal employers' desire to diminish the national significance attaching to the award and to avoid the pitched industrial battle they had lost so badly in 1968.[62] The result of this confluence of interests was a markedly different approach to the determination of what would become the new Metal Industry Award 1971.[63] Unlike previous cases, where respective claims were usually determined by the Commission after a protracted process of legal wrangling, both the unions and the Metal Trades Industry Association (MTIA)[64] agreed to a process of direct negotiation without going to arbitration. The parties received guidance in the form of conciliation hearings before Commissioner Hood, and he made some determinations as to wages and conditions, but the interim award handed down (the Metal Industry Interim Award *1971*) had largely been arrived at by consent.[65] It granted metal industry employees an extra $6 per week and was characterised by 'the speed and lack of acrimony' with which it was accepted by both sides.[66] The fact that the pay rises subsequently flowed-on to many other awards[67] and were not subject to the crucible of a national wage case hearing left many employers outside of the metal trades angry, with one commentator suggesting that the effect of Hood's decision 'was to retain the nexus between movements in the metal trades award and other industry awards without giving other employer organisations the benefit of being able to oppose the metal unions' claims as strongly as they might have if they had been the subject of a national wage case'.[68]

The reality of flow-on was evidence of the Metal Industry Award's entrenched institutional position at the peak of the award system. However, the shift towards negotiated outcomes between metal unions and employers took place in the context of the general upswing in *de facto* industry-level bargaining and wage rounds described in chapters 4 and 5.

In such an environment, the aforementioned tendency of the Metal Trades and Metal Industry Awards to fall behind wage movements in other industries *precisely because of* its lead sector role was intensified. Following the same pattern of direct negotiation employed in 1970–1971, metal unions and employers came to an agreement for a $15 per week pay rise in May 1974.[69] However, only six months later, Justice Moore felt compelled to increase rates by a further $9 due to large pay rises (usually of the order of $20 to $25 per week) granted in 118 awards since April 1974.[70] Most importantly for our purposes, he acknowledged that the judgement was recognition of the fact that pay rises in other industries were a threat to the stability of the metals sector. Crucially, he stated:

> I would emphasise that this is a 'catching up' by the Metal Industry Award because many other awards have already been varied in excess of $15.00. This is not a spring board from which all other awards should move, even awards which may in the past have followed the Metal Industry Award. The circumstances upon which I have acted demonstrate that *the significance of the Metal Industry Award as a leader has to some extent declined* (my emphasis).[71]

However, Justice Moore noted that the unions, employers and the state all desired some method of wage fixation more stable than that prevailing hitherto, with one possible answer being wage indexation. With that in mind, he declared, 'it is my view that a *firm base* must be established before an effective stability in wage fixation can be achieved . . . such stability can be achieved *only after there has been an increase in this award with any proper consequent flow*' (my emphasis).[72] In other words, despite his recognition of the fact that the current proceedings stemmed from wage pressures originating elsewhere in the economy, he nevertheless realised that the stability of the award framework still rested largely on the Metal Industry Award retaining its benchmarking function.

This confusing position, whereby an increasingly pluralistic industrial reality sat uneasily with the entrenched institutional position of metals atop the award pyramid, persisted throughout the 1970s and into the early 1980s. The pattern increasingly came to be that forward movements in other awards were used to buttress metal industry claims (which often took the form of consent awards), which then flowed through to other segments of the economy. This represented something of a hybrid system, whereby the actual economic steam of the metals sector was diminished but its institutionalised lead-sector role nevertheless remained profound. On the one hand, in 1975, the Commission was noting that the Metal Industry Award's influence had 'diminished' and that its status as a pace-setter had been tarnished by recent events, including the upswing in rates in other awards.[73] At a 1977 metal industry conference, both employers and unions 'agreed that the metal trades had not for some years been pace-setters in wage levels'.[74] This development was not necessarily seen as a bad one; indeed, Australian Council of Trade Unions (ACTU) President Bob Hawke had commented in 1974 that 'it might be of more benefit to the metal-trades unions if they were gradually phased out as the yardstick on awards'.[75]

On the other hand, however, was the continued industrial aggression of the metal unions[76] and the durability of comparative wage justice claims that took as their departure point the Metal Industry Award. An event demonstrating both forces in action was the granting of a catch-up wage increase to General Motors Holden employees to bring them in line with the Metal Industry Award standard. Although there was a historic nexus between metal awards and those governing the automobile industry, the claims for flow-on were strengthened by what Commissioner Clarkson dubbed 'guerilla tactics', such as the imposition of overtime bans.[77] In the context of general union strength, industrial militancy could force the hand of the Commission regarding flow-on even where it was reluctant to grant it.

Perhaps the best demonstration of the contradictory position of the metal trades as a lead sector in the increasingly dysfunctional antipodean Fordist model of development was the wage explosion of the early 1980s. In chapter 5 I noted how the rise of work value claims represented a return to the industry-level collective bargaining of the early to mid-1970s. In keeping with the pattern that had developed in that earlier period, the initial impulses towards higher wages appear to have largely arisen outside the metals sector. In particular, work value cases in the waterside, warehousing and transport industries had awarded large wage increases to workers employed therein.[78]

In the wake of the collapse of indexation, the ACTU pledged to an industry-by-industry campaign to lift wages.[79] In an affirmation of the continuing relevance of the industrial clout of the metal unions, they were the first off the block in following the ACTU Congress' determination and reached a consent award with the MTIA that was ratified by the Commission in

December 1981. It provided, among other things, $25 a week wage increase to the fitter (with proportionate rises to other classifications) and a reduction in the workweek from forty to thirty-eight hours.[80] The hours issue was particularly crucial, in that it represented a qualitative step forward for a general movement towards shorter hours, a movement which less than six months earlier had been in low waters after the Commission rejected a metal union claim for a thirty-five-hour week.[81]

Another sense in which the Commission's decision was critical was the reasoning behind it. Although the Commission was by this time increasingly being subsumed by the economistic logic surrounding its institutional intensification, it and the parties coming before it remained beholden to certain norms and understandings, among them the centrality of the Metal Industry Award. As was the case in late 1974, part of the justification for increases in the metal award was 'movements in wage rates and conditions of employment in other industries';[82] a reversal of the typical post–World War II chain of causality. On the other hand, the durability of the institutionalised channels linking the Metal Industry Award to others within the award framework was proven once again, in what was to be the last iteration of the typical antipodean Fordist process of flow-on. The Commission accepted that there would be some flow consequent upon their decision to ratify the consent award between metal unions and the MTIA.[83] Indeed, its continued *de facto* recognition of the legitimacy of the metal trades as a pace-setter was revealed by the reasoning underlying the ratification of a consent award between the Transport Workers' Union (TWU) and the Australian Road Transport Federation only a few days after the metal industry agreement. Multiple attempts by the TWU to have the Commission enforce the agreement were rejected on a number of grounds, including the fact that granting transport workers the wage increase would generate strong pressures for flow-on to other awards.[84] However, the approval of the metal industry consent award threw the TWU's claim in a new light, with the Commission noting the metal settlement and acknowledging that 'a $20 wage increase in the Transport Workers Award, 1972 could no longer be said to provide the basis for setting the pace for pay increases generally'.[85] In other words, despite the wage pressures emanating therefrom, the Commission was not prepared to make a determination that would establish the transport sector as an institutionalised pace-setter. Once the metal industry agreement had confirmed the metal trades in its historical position as the leader, however, the federal tribunal was open to granting the transport workers' claims.

The 1981 Metal Industry Award case would be the last turn of the traditional flow-on wheel, the final cycle of a process that, while once insuring the coherence of antipodean Fordism, had become dysfunctional. The flow-on was strong, with the 'metal industry standard' setting the parameters for a large number of awards in both the federal and state jurisdictions. Mulvey notes that within a mere two-month period after the December metals case, 'it was estimated by both the ACTU and the Commonwealth that around 20 per cent of all employees have received wage increases in line with those provided for in the Metal Industry Agreement'.[86] Moreover, by the end of 1982 the metal industry standard of the thirty-eight-hour week had flowed through to two-thirds of the workforce.[87] As was so often the case in the history of the federal tribunal, it too was forced to acknowledge the impact of the metal trades increases in the context of the 1983 national wage case, set against the backdrop of 'the worst economic recession since the 1930s'.[88] Among the factors the Commission deemed responsible for the crisis was 'the sharp increase in labour costs' which had 'resulted from general increases in pay and reductions in hours since the end of indexation flowing principally from the metal industry agreements of December 1981'.[89]

The downturn of 1982 signalled the end of the post-war award hierarchy dominated by the metal award. The fact that the Commission itself partially blamed the structure of flow-on for the crisis was significant in that it dovetailed with the demands of employers and the state to bring an end to the wage rounds centred on the Metal Industry Award. A 1983 South Australian decision refusing increases to shop assistants on the basis of the metal industry standard was prophetic in its trenchant attack on the system of comparative wage justice focused on the metal trades: 'The fact that some other, totally different, employees receive an increase does not mean that everyone else in the work force is similarly entitled. . . . The "me too" syndrome is the cancer in industrial relations which inevitably produces a leapfrogging effect which is detrimental to all and self defeating in the long term'.[90] Such a statement represents in essence an attack upon one of the central planks of antipodean Fordism's mode of regulation and its mechanisms of coherence.

1980s–1990s – THE ACCORD AND ENTERPRISE BARGAINING

As indicated in chapter 4, from the mid-1970s onwards the manufacturing sector entered a period of decline from which it has never since recovered. A similar development hit other Fordist societies, such as the US, the UK and France, but the Australian experience was especially pronounced. The metal industry was struck particularly hard. In just three years, from November 1973 to November 1976, nearly 100,000 jobs were lost in Australian factories.[91] In the 1980s this process of dissolution went critical. Plowman, drawing upon Metal Trades Federation of Unions (MTFU) figures, states that 'between 1981 and 1983 nearly 100,000 jobs were lost in the metal and engineering sector'.[92] The Australian Bureau of Statistics (ABS), although providing slightly different figures, traces a similarly dramatic decline. Whereas in 1979–1980 basic metals, fabricated metal products, transport and other machinery equipment sub-sectors employed some 499,404 people, by 1983–1984 this had declined to 415,364.[93] Of the four metal trade sub-sectors just mentioned, the first two experienced only a very modest growth in gross product (at average 1983–1984 prices) from 1981/1982 to 1990/1991, while the latter two declined absolutely.[94]

The increasing disintegration of the Australian metals sector exerted a profound influence on the developments in the award framework in the 1980s, most specifically through convincing the metal unions to sign on to the Accord, the history of which was traced in chapter 6. Given both the success and the historically entrenched character of post–World War II metal union tactics in securing over-award payments, the system of wage indexation represented by the Accord should *prima facie* have been repugnant to them. Earlier attempts to impose Accord-like measures, such as no-strike clauses and wage restraint, had been roundly rejected by metal workers;[95] indeed, the metal industry agreement of 1981 had proven the *coup de grâce* of the Fraser's government's failed experiment with wage indexation.

The severe economic crisis in the metal sector, the fundamentally nationalist character of the Australian left (which was strongly represented among the metal unions' leadership) and the opportunity the Accord provided the union officialdom to wrest control from more militant rank-and-file groups profoundly altered the attitude of the Amalgamated Metal Workers' and Shipwrights' Union (AMWSU)[96] and other metal unions to an incomes policy with an ALP government.[97] The wave of redundancies in the early 1980s meant that 'many former shopfloor militants were demoralised and became more open to the conservative argument that a continued wages push would simply exacerbate unemployment'.[98] Against this backdrop, the Accord's pledge to simultaneously control both wages and inflation in such a way as to hopefully restore full employment appeared attractive.[99] Moreover, as seen in chapter 6, the Accord, in its original 'Mark I' format, was a wide-ranging document in which a wages policy was buttressed by a variety of other initiatives attractive to manufacturing unions in particular, such as industry planning, new occupational health and safety institutions and the maintenance of industrial protection. The emphasis the Accord placed on tripartite institutions of macroeconomic standing was significant in buying the support of left-wing unions like the AMWSU, who got the impression (or, as it turned out, the illusion) that they would be involved in determining the future course of Australian capitalism in a meaningful way.[100]

Despite the seemingly logical reasons for which the ACTU struck an incomes policy, and bearing in mind the conviction seemingly shared by unions and metal employers that something had to be done to stem the crisis in the metals sector, the Accord inflicted enormous damage on organised labour generally, and on metal unions specifically. These had the most to gain from employing their industrial muscle to grab what they could from capital. By restricting wage-claims to the rate of inflation, the Accord applied a straitjacket to unions in the metals sector, disrupting their historical pattern of mobilisation, choking shop-floor organisation[101] and making them complicit in what amounted to large real-wage decreases for their members.[102] Most importantly for our purposes, the Accord almost completely destroyed the pattern of metal sector flow-on and the hierarchy of awards and, with them, one of the central planks in antipodean Fordism's mode of regulation.

That this development was not merely incidental, but rather was a central purpose of the Accord, can be gleaned easily enough from the text of the agreement itself. In speaking of the effort to maintain and improve living standards, the ACTU accepted that 'the achievement of this goal via an incomes and prices policy approach will require a suppression of sectional priorities and demands'.[103] The document further provided that 'both parties recognise that if the essential conditions of the centralised system are met that there shall be no extra claims except where special and extraordinary circumstances exist'.[104] 'Suppression of sectional priorities and demands' and 'no extra claims': these together represented a repudiation of the antipodean Fordist pattern of metal trade flow-on which, although sectional in origin, achieved general application.

The practical result of this commitment was that a generally militant rank-and-file movement, well-schooled in the application of industrial pressure to obtain over-award payments, had to be restrained by the leadership of metal unions. Bramble explores this in detail, with on-the-job action by militant workers often stymied by union leaders enforcing the 'no extra claims' provisions of the Accord.[105] In the following chapter, we will see that smaller unions with historical links to metal awards, such as the Food Preservers' Union and the Federated Confectioners' Association, were sold out by the AMWU (in its various incarnations) and the ACTU when they refused to sign onto the Accord or attempted to subvert its wage-fixing principles.

Not only did the Accord disrupt the historical relationship between the leading metal award and others within the framework, it also affected the structure and content of the Metal Industry Award itself. In chapter 6 I looked broadly at the unfolding of the 'Efficiency and Restructuring' and 'Structural Efficiency' principles in the late 1980s, the first attempts to decentralise wage fixation through granting access to 'second-tier' increases dependent upon industry and/or workplace-level negotiations. Given the desire of the AMWU[106] both to ensure the viability of the manufacturing sector and to retain some control over the decentralisation process, these principles took the form of national-level 'blueprint' agreements which were then tailored to the circumstances of individual enterprises/workplaces.[107] The following chapter on food processing will explore concrete examples of just how these efficiency principles changed the structure and content of awards. Suffice it to say here, the parent award was altered in a thoroughgoing fashion, with its 340-or-so classifications broad-banded into fourteen wage groups, important flexibilities in the use and deployment of labour introduced and restrictive practices removed.[108] Most important was the historical reversal of the metal trade motive chain; whereas before, the breakthrough in particularly militant 'hot shops' led to improvements for all metal workers (and from thence, many other employees), the movement towards award decentralisation promoted a more insular, inward-looking mentality, where, conceptually at least, the weak could be isolated from the gains of the strong.

This mentality became explicit with the movement to enterprise bargaining. We saw in chapter 6 that left-unions, most particularly the AMWU, were growing increasingly restive under the Accord straitjacket, and saw in enterprise bargaining a way to return to something resembling the old over-award system. Indeed, in rejecting the April 1991 application for enterprise bargaining, the Commission, agreeing with the MTIA (whose memory of the 1981–1982 wages explosion was still raw), stated that premature adoption of such a system 'would cause a reversion to the wide scale pattern of direct action and leap-frogging of wage levels existing prior to 1982'.[109] The Commission, along with the MTIA, thus feared that the old pattern of flow-on persisted below the surface and required only a change in the institutional environment to resurface. This was a view that appears to have been held by some metal union leaders. George Campbell, former Secretary of the AMWU, stated, 'We just couldn't control a centralised wage structure anymore. . . . Because of our delegate structure we've always had an ability to extract over-award payments'.[110] Even more tellingly, former AMWU Assistant National Secretary Laurie Carmichael regarded the movement to enterprise bargaining as simply one iteration of the historical flow-on cycle: 'In the past, we had gone enterprise bargaining-consolidation, enterprise bargaining-consolidation . . . *we'll run a campaign and then bring it back and make sure the whole class benefits*' (my emphasis).[111]

An over-award campaign by the metal unions in the early 1990s, dovetailing with the movement to enterprise bargaining, appeared to many to initially confirm the Commission's suspicions. In response to an MTIA proposal about pay, the Commission declared, 'Given the coverage of the metal industry award and the existence of counterpart state awards, how could flow-on of the increases agreed to in those awards be contained to employers working under those awards?'[112] As late as 1992, the MTIA was deeply concerned about the strength of metal unions and their ability to win large increases, a belief that underpinned their desire for the Commission to retain a central role in determining enterprise agreements through imposition of a public interest test. Employers in other sectors were still fearful of the spectre of pace-setting agreements in the metal trades flowing through industry at large, with Confederation of Australian Industry Chief Executive Ian Spicer opining of 4 per cent productivity gains being included in the metal award: 'It is the surest and quickest way for pay increases to flow throughout industry'.[113] In an interesting link to the later chapter on retail, Coles Myer general manager for employee relations Elise Callander was in 1991 complaining 'that the metal trades award is still the locomotive of change, setting the standard for other industries'.[114]

The views of all these participants, unions, employers and arms of the state, demonstrate a fundamental misunderstanding of the scale of the transformation of the economy throughout the 1980s and 1990s. Unemployment, declining union density, the atrophy of rank-and-file organisations and, perhaps most importantly, the increased corrosiveness of international competition had fundamentally weakened the hand of organised labour. The metal sector, and manufacturing more broadly, had continued to decline throughout the 1990s and 2000s. In 1989–1990, 411,700 people were employed in the four sub-sectors that mostly composed the metal trades.[115] In 2010–2011, this had declined absolutely to 354,100 in the context of a much larger labour force, a decrease of approximately 14 per cent.[116] This process intensified during the recession of the early 1990s, which hit basic metals, metal fabrication and transport equipment particularly hard, producing a crisis of profitability that helped determine the tenor of early enterprise bargaining.[117]

Moreover, the rush of the union movement to embrace enterprise bargaining was hasty and ill-conceived, premised upon an underestimation of 'their dependence on the existing arbitration system and legislation for their ability to run widespread over-award bargaining campaigns'.[118] Without this institutional buttress, enterprise bargaining would tend to promote the increasing intra- and inter-industry wage and conditions polarisation observed in the previous chapter and increase the tendency towards competition between union and non-union enterprises.

In the event, enterprise bargaining and associated legislative changes proved the death knell of the antipodean Fordist pattern of flow-on and the notion of comparative wage justice that lubricated it. After enforced stagnation under the Accord, the devolution of bargaining to the enterprise level, and the associated degradation of awards, ensured that the differences in wage and conditions outcomes between the industrially strong and the weak became more pronounced, while the general movement was towards 'a reduction in the power of workers and trade unions relative to employers singularly and collectively'.[119] Peter Tighe, National Secretary of the Communication, Electrical and Plumbing Union and a member of the MTFU, noted in 2000 the dramatic impact of enterprise bargaining on the conduct of wage cases in the metal industry:

> What we used to do in past . . . in the MTFU, we would have a national negotiating committee who would meet with the MTIA and the Australian Chamber of Manufactures . . . and negotiate about wages to try to get a consent variation to that award. We'd put to the MTIA that we want, say, $30 a week for trade labour, and maybe $25 for non-trades. They say, 'nope, you're not going to get it, get stuffed'. So we would go out and campaign directly nationally . . . we would have a rolling campaign in key companies, and once we have commitments from those companies, we'd go back to the MTIA . . . and sometimes the deal would be done. . . . It would be a consent award [so all workplaces in the industry would receive the increase gained directly in large workplaces] . . . *The difference is now that you don't do that. There are no industry negotiations. It is all enterprise by enterprise*. . . . They do not want to sit down and have negotiations for a State, or national negotiations, for an industry outcome. . . . The AiG[120] say, 'why should the non-unionised members of the MTIA get caught up in an industry outcome when they are quite happy to deal directly with their own employees?'. That's their view now (my emphasis).[121]

The system just described placed immense strain on all segments of organised labour. Whereas before the militancy of hot shops and a single national campaign could be used to force change in an award applying to the majority of metalworkers, now metal unions were faced with the necessity of organising and negotiating a myriad of separate agreements. Moreover, unlike awards, where unions were *prima facie* respondents to instruments covering workers within the ambit of their rules, the Commission determined that unions could only be parties to an enterprise agreement where they actually had members employed at the workplace concerned.[122] Given the fact that, like most industries, unionisation in the metals sector is most pronounced in large firms, this movement helped break the potential for flowing-on the gains won in better organised shops to non-union counterparts.

Changes in the legal framework surrounding enterprise bargaining also played their part in destroying the connective tissue binding the industrially strong and weak together. We have seen that enterprise bargaining in its formative years had the appeal of being all things to all people. In particular, organised labour perceived in it an addendum to what was still a fundamentally collectivist system, seeing union involvement in the bargaining process as a necessary prerequisite.[123] However, chapter 6 demonstrated that the actual evolution of the process was one of the enforced degradation of awards, the fragmentation of bargaining and union difficulties in ensuring some kind of uniformity of wage and conditions outcomes. The confluence of these factors ensured that those employees reliant only on awards increasingly fell behind those who struck enterprise agreements. As Briggs notes, 'Insulating awards from enterprise bargaining was considered essential to avoid another "wage breakout" and undoing the relationships established between minimum rate awards under award restructuring'.[124] Stung by its sidelining at the hands of the ACTU and the ALP government, the Commission came onside through the formulation of new wage principles governing the relationship between enterprise agreements and awards. On the one hand, it spoke of the necessity of equitable minimum standards implanted in awards; on the other, it noted that 'the stability and viability of those awards can be undermined if the disparate outcomes of enterprise bargaining *flow back into them*' (my emphasis).[125] The result has been described by Mylett: 'The transmission mechanism between successful over-award campaigns and award wage increases was broken'.[126]

Within the constraints of the early federal legislation, metal unions were more successful than most at initially securing better-than-average agreements. Given the role of the AMWU in the transition to enterprise bargaining in the first place, it came as no surprise that enterprise agreements in the metals sector were both more numerous and higher-paying than in industry at large.[127] As mentioned previously, a few high-profile cases where metal unions were successful in getting large wage increases sent shivers through the business community.[128] These came, however, in a context of increasing dispersion of wage and conditions outcomes, on both the intra- and inter-industry level. In 1996, for example, agreements in the metal manufacturing sector provided for wage increases ranging from 8.6 per cent to a miserly 0.7 per cent.[129] In 1997, it was found that non-union agreements in metals provided average annual wage increases nearly 2 per cent lower than union agreements.[130]

Perhaps even more disturbing was the usurpation of the notion of comparative wage justice. As I elucidated earlier, metal workers, through the vehicle of margins cases, had established wage relativities between classifications dependent upon skill. Although these often changed between margins hearings, they were broadly stable at any one point in time, a situation that persisted throughout the Accord period. Enterprise bargaining changed all this. The Australian Centre for Industrial Relations Research and Training observed:

> During the 1980s wage relativities remained almost constant. . . . In the 1990s, however, this situation began to change. . . . In the decade from 1986 to 1995, male trades workers improved their wages by about 56 per cent (in nominal terms), but this outcome favoured the more highly paid workers. . . . This suggests that as the wages system has decentralised, wages have not risen as quickly for the male unskilled as compared to the male skilled.[131]

THE WORKPLACE RELATIONS ACT AND PATTERN BARGAINING

Metal union apprehension of the danger posed by increasingly fragmented outcomes led to a reconsideration of tactics early on in the piece, with an emphasis on re-establishing *de facto* the industry-level negotiations which had been the norm prior to enterprise bargaining. The MTFU, and particularly the AMWU,[132] sought to do this through a canny campaign of striking similar enterprise agreements with common expiry dates, a strategy known as pattern bargaining. As early as 1994 this had been flagged as an option by the Automotive, Food, Metals and Engineering Union (predecessor to the modern AMWU), which cited the use of similar tactics by US auto unions.[133] Two business friendly commentators complained in September 1994 of a metal workers campaign: 'In a strategy similar to the old over-award campaigns before the accord, officials are using pattern bargaining – having a wages settlement secured at one plant adopted at every plant in the company, irrespective of the needs of each plant – to spread wage rises'.[134] Capital recognised the goal well enough, with Way noting of the attitude of the AMWU to enterprise bargaining: 'It wants the Metal Industry Award to be the core of any agreement, and then to build on this in specific agreements. This is why pattern bargaining is so crucial to the union – it allows it to spread the same basic conditions across an industry sector or within a diversified company'.[135] Of most concern to employers was that the example of the metal unions was being followed in other industries (particularly in the transport and building sectors), demonstrating the continued vanguard role played by the former.[136]

Pattern bargaining occupied a legal grey area in the early to mid-1990s, which gave trade unions the space to achieve some impressive wage outcomes. The success of pattern bargaining, in both metals and non-metals manufacturing,[137] is evidenced by the acceleration of wage rises provided for by enterprise agreements in the mid to late 1990s.[138] Employer associations, including the MTIA, protested bitterly, petitioning the government to amend the Workplace Relations Act 1996 and outlaw the practice.[139] The ACTU, however, which by this point had also come to realise the danger posed by the wage and conditions polarity inherent in enterprise bargaining, took heart, and in its biennial 1997 Congress endorsed a focus on industry-level bargaining.[140] Most significantly, Long notes that 'unions will also seek to channel pay rises won through bargaining back into the award system to arrest growing wage disparities'.[141] The ACTU was thus attempting, in a sense, to re-invent the wheel, recreating the 'transmission belt' whereby the gains of the industrially strong could be passed on the weak.

The Victorian AMWU's 'Campaign 2000' was the most ambitious exercise in pattern bargaining yet when swords were crossed in 1999–2000. The

Victorian branch of the AMWU, backed by seven other metal unions in the MTFU, sought to impose manufacturing sector-wide standards, including 6 per cent annual pay rises, bans on contracting out and greater controls over the use of casuals.[142] The MTFU had explicitly declared that one of the objectives of Campaign 2000 was to 'replace the current unfair, piecemeal system of enterprise bargaining with a single genuine industry-wide agreement'.[143] Although the AMWU was unsuccessful in the latter regard, it nevertheless achieved formidable success, due in no small part to the ascension of the militant 'Workers First' faction to leadership within the AMWU. Then-State Secretary of the Victorian Branch, Craig Johnston, declared of the wage and conditions improvements: 'We achieved those things with more than 1,000 agreements covering 40,000 workers. In about 85 per cent of cases we got the whole package [of demands]'.[144] The national campaign, although not as coherent, also experienced substantial success.[145]

It was at this moment, when the spectre of a return to industry-level bargaining appeared as a credible threat, that the Howard government showed its full hand. This government had always regarded the antipodean Fordist integration of trade unionism into the fabric of labour law and industrial relations as a pathology to be excised. It took immediate action upon the campaign's commencement in 1998–1999 to introduce legislation outlawing pattern bargaining.[146] Although the bill failed in the Senate, the AIG found a willing ally in the government, with whom it met several times to encourage the passage of the amendments.[147]

The Commission and Federal Court also revealed through their actions the tremendous change in the industrial relations landscape. Whereas the Clarrie O'Shea affair in 1969 had essentially rendered the prosecution of union officials politically untenable, the Federal Court had no qualms in levelling contempt charges against Craig Johnston, Electrical Trades Union Victorian Secretary Dean Mighell and Australian Workers' Union official Cesar Melhem when they defied Commission injunctions against mass meetings held in the course of Campaign 2000.[148] Fines of $20,000 were imposed on each of them[149] in a case reiterating the claim of increased juridification, the re-assertion of law's dominance over administration, made throughout this book.

Buoyed by the comparative success of Campaign 2000, the AMWU attempted to replicate its efforts with 'Campaign 2003', which again sought common wage and conditions improvements through renegotiating a host of enterprise bargains at once. This time, the employers and the state were better prepared. Once again, the Howard government came to the aid of the AIG with legislation, which this time successfully passed. The Workplace Relations Amendment (Genuine Bargaining) Act 2002 (Cth) gave the Commission enhanced powers to terminate bargaining periods where it deemed that genuine agreement was not being sought.[150] This meant industrial action taken was not deemed as protected and could be subject to fines and common law industrial torts. A government member made no bones about the object of the legislation: 'The unions claim that the bill will deny workers the right to strike. It will not do so, but it will put a serious dent in the side of irresponsible campaigns like the AMWU's so-called Campaign 2000 and Campaign 2003 . . . the unions, particularly the AMWU, advocate pattern bargaining because it gives them control over entire industries'.[151] Then-Minister for Employment and Workplace Relations Tony Abbott added: 'Elements within the union movement have attempted to orchestrate *a return to industry level bargaining* through the process known as pattern bargaining. . . . It represents an outdated, one-size-fits-all approach to workplace relations where union officials *utilised the centralised system* to dictate their agenda to both employers and employees (my emphasis)'.[152] Used in a number of cases, these new powers delighted the AIG.[153] For its part, the AIG held a tighter front, preparing early for the union campaign and supported wholeheartedly by the federal government.[154]

When combined with the internal machinations of the AMWU (the Victorian branch had been weakened through factional infighting that saw Craig Johnston removed in a coup orchestrated by the more moderate national leadership), Campaign 2003 was less successful than its predecessors. Employers and the state were able to ensure the AMWU's key common demands of shorter hours and a trust fund for employees in failed companies were not universalised throughout the industry.[155] The attempt by the AMWU and other unions to 'recentralise' bargaining to the sector-level, to ensure fairly common up-trending standards throughout manufacturing generally, had fallen foul of the changed circumstances of the Australian state and the instruments of industrial regulation.

The demise of pattern bargaining was made complete by the passage of the WorkChoices legislation. Section 431(1) of the amended act provided that the Commission *must* terminate a bargaining period if it was satisfied a party was engaged in pattern bargaining, while section 439 ensured that industrial action taken in support of it would not be protected. The repeal of WorkChoices and its replacement by the Fair Work Act 2009 (Cth) of the incoming ALP government did little to aid the union cause, with sections 409(4) and 422 maintaining the former's prohibitions against pattern bargaining *in toto*.

It may be argued that the fate of pattern bargaining is an example of law as reactive, being used instrumentally to achieve a pre-determined purpose. This is partially true. The fact that I identify law as a juridic form that helps constitute the capitalist mode of production does not mean that it cannot be used by the state in an instrumental way. However, the demise of pattern bargaining went deeper than this. Its outlawing was part of the broader logic of enterprise bargaining and individualisation, which I have demonstrated are key legal manifestations of liberal-productivism. Pattern bargaining was corrosive of the ability of these forces to serve their function within this model of development. The assault on pattern bargaining was more than just capitalists trying to augment their power and line their pockets; it was a vital moment in the liberal-productivist regime of labour law being purged of any revanchist tendencies on the part of organised labour.

CONCLUSIONS

This imposition of what amounts to an effective legislative ban on pattern bargaining is the perfect point on which to conclude the analysis of the destruction of the award hierarchy and the role of the metal trades within it. I have traced the institutionalisation of the metal industry as a lead sector through the immensely important Metal Trades and Metal Industry Awards. As antipodean Fordism came to cohere fully in the aftermath of World War II, the Metal Trades Award came to dominate the award framework, with successive margins cases in the 1940s and 1950s increasingly taking national economic capacity and that of the metal trades as synonymous. Based on the principle of comparative wage justice, pay and conditions improvements gained by metal unions flowed through the workforce readily, the 'connective bargaining' Boyer identifies as crucial to the architecture of Fordism.[156]

With the *Total Wage* and *Work Value Cases* of 1967 and 1968, the Commission and employers attempted to shape a new modality of industrial regulation, one in which opportunities for flow-on were reduced. Full employment and the industrial militancy of metal unions, however, put paid to these designs, resulting instead in an explosion of strikes that saw the defeat of absorption and powerful currents of flow-on.

The crisis of antipodean Fordism that took hold in the early to mid-1970s hit metal workers hard, with the result that the metal award began to lose steam in its pace-setting role, with the impetus shifting to other industries such as transport and warehousing. However, the durability of the institutionalised channels linking metal awards to others in the hierarchy ensured that large catch-up claims for metal workers, such as those granted in 1974 and 1981, were considered necessary for industrial stability and, once given, flowed through the wage structure.

It is only with the enforced wage stagnation of the Accord that a tipping point was reached, breaking the post-war pattern of metal trade flow-on. The deleterious effect the Accord had on the earnings of semi-skilled blue-collar workers eventually made the compact politically untenable, with the AMWU in particular advocating a movement to enterprise bargaining in the hope of being able to exploit its industrial strength and achieve better wage and conditions outcomes. In the minds of some AMWU officials, and certainly in the nightmares of elements of capital, the government, the Commission and the press, this was conceived as a return to the kind of collective over-award campaigns of post–World War II vintage.

Such a perspective failed to appreciate the fundamental transformation in Australian capitalism, in particular the reduced role of the manufacturing sector within it. Globalised production and the imperatives of international competition had led to profound job-shedding, reorganisation of the production process and an increasingly militant anti-union attitude on the part of employers. Combined with increasingly inhospitable governments (which became outright hostility with the election of the Liberal/National Party coalition in 1996) and chronic membership decline, unions found their bargaining power increasingly usurped. In this context, the essential destruction of the award system and the movement towards enterprise bargaining made it almost impossible for metal unions to employ their post-war tactics of relying on the award framework to universalise gains won by militant 'hot shops'. Not only was the ability of metal unions to win gains for the workforce disrupted; indeed, the metals sector itself, along with manufacturing as a whole, became increasingly polarised as the favourable agreements obtained by strategically placed, well-organised workers were successfully quarantined from non-union shops.

When the AMWU and its allies had realised the danger early in the history of enterprise bargaining, they attempted, with some initial success, to recentralise bargaining at the industry-level through pattern bargaining. However, the political, economic and, most importantly for our purposes, legal landscape had changed too much for these efforts to achieve durable success. When seriously threatened by the success of Campaign 2000, the government and employers closed ranks and enacted hostile new legislation designed to defeat pattern bargaining. These legal developments marked the destruction of the last elements of the antipodean Fordist modality of metal sector flow-on, substituting its tendency for universality with the liberal-productivist schema of decentralisation and polarity in the wage structure.

Chapter 8

Precarity, Intensification and Work Reorganisation in the Food Processing Sector

The previous chapter was focused on the role of awards, award restructuring and enterprise bargaining on the structure of the antipodean Fordist cycle of wage and condition flow-on. The purpose of this chapter is to better understand the implications of these same processes on the actual content of awards and enterprise bargains, particularly insofar as they bear upon the liberal-productivist industrial paradigm and wage-labour nexus outlined in chapter 4. By investigating when and how these came to be implanted in the labour law regime, it can be better understood how this regime fulfils the abstract functions according with it.

These forces will be elucidated in great detail here as they have applied to the food processing sector. This sector is most useful as a case study for a variety of reasons. Firstly, it has been one of the most deeply affected by the liberal-productivist norms of precarity and intensified real subordination of labour to capital. Being an industry which has retained something of a seasonal character, the presentation and profundity of these norms is especially sharp, and their manifestation through award restructuring and enterprise bargaining quite transparent. The relevance of these norms for industry generally is also bolstered by the fact that food processing has always been one of the largest industries constituting the manufacturing sector in Australia in terms of employment, trailing only the metals sector for the majority of the post–World War II years.[1] Indeed, in 2010–2011 'food product manufacturing' was the single largest sub-sector within manufacturing industry, both in terms of employment, industry value-added and capital expenditure.[2]

Secondly, it will be seen that food processing has been hit hard by the exposure to international competition that has been a defining trait of liberal-productivism in Australia. The incidence and depth of competition from lower-wage countries has been pronounced, enabling multinational corporations to play plants in different jurisdictions against each other (what has been dubbed 'whipsawing')[3] while forcing an ever leaner production system on those sites remaining in Australia. Food processing is thus an ideal sector for deeper study precisely because it has operated in the environment that has been reshaped most dramatically in the transition to liberal-productivism.

Lastly, the analysis of this particularly affected manufacturing industry provides a highly useful partner to the following chapter, which explores much the same processes except in the context of the retail sector. Indeed, the fact that very similar outcomes and patterns will be seen to emerge in two completely different industries strengthens the theory of transition forwarded in this book, demonstrating that liberal-productivist tendencies have taken hold of the workforce at large (even if they don't necessarily affect all workers to the same degree).

In order to demonstrate exactly what the formal and substantive impacts of award restructuring and enterprise bargaining have been on workers in food processing, it is necessary to briefly survey the nature of industrial relations and wage and conditions determination in the sector during the phase of antipodean Fordist functionality.

AWARD REGULATION IN FOOD PROCESSING – ANTIPODEAN FORDISM *EN RÉGULATION*

Broadly speaking, the industrial relations field was dominated until the late 1970s by then-generally docile unions such as the Food Preservers' Union (FPU), the Federated Confectioners' Association (FCA) and the Manufacturing Grocers' Employees' Federation of Australia. In line with the prevailing antipodean Fordist pattern of industrial regulation, these unions were respondents to a number of state and federal awards that were a comprehensive codification of the terms and conditions on which wage labour was to be exploited. These awards were very much in keeping with the general pattern: composed of a variety of finely gradated classifications, crystallising certain demarcation barriers and what in neo-liberal parlance would be considered 'restrictive practices', and establishing strict controls on the engagement of casual and part-time labour.[4] The position of the unions was often guaranteed by preference clauses, while industry-level logs of wage and conditions claims were common.[5] The pattern of flow-on identified in chapters 5 and 7 provided crucial inputs to the sector, with metal trades margins typically determining the parameters for food processing employees, who also benefited from comparative wage justice claims premised on the Metal Industry standard in the mid-1970s and early 1980s.[6] This conveyer belt served to compensate for the general lack of militancy among food processing unions into the 1970s.[7]

Antipodean Fordism's subsequent descent into crisis actually had a radicalising effect on key unions in the sector, namely the FPU and the FCA. Food processing was on the hard edge of the crisis, deeply affected by profound technological innovation, rationalisation of production consequent upon high and increasing foreign ownership, and, most importantly, the increased corrosiveness of international competition in the form of rapidly rising levels of food imports.[8] These developments dovetailed with the election of a more militant leadership in both unions, particularly in the Victorian branches. Indeed, the Victorian FCA had in 1976 and 1977 imposed overtime bans, limitations and had even engaged in strike action for over-award payments outside the indexation guidelines,[9] while it and the Victorian FPU had, in a solitary stand, defied the Australian Council of Trade Unions (ACTU) and refused to sign onto the Accord guidelines until late 1984.[10] As the Accord process deepened into the restructuring and efficiency and structural efficiency principles in the late 1980s, food manufacturers were thus faced with comparatively powerful unions who expected meaningful input to the process of reform. In this process, however, can be discerned the very norms of flexibility, precarity and work intensification which would be deepened by enterprise bargaining.

AWARD REFORM IN THE 1980s

Food processing industries proved particularly amenable to the species of change envisaged by the Commission when it laid down the restructuring and efficiency and structural efficiency principles. Profound labour process changes, in particular the deployment of more flexible and labour-displacing machinery,[11] along with the fact that casual labour had always played a significant role (particularly in the important Food Preservers Awards), ensured that the flexibilities desired by the Commission had a ready-made material basis in the sector.

In the initial stages of negotiations with the FPU over access to second-tier wage increases consequent upon structural efficiency agreements, the Australian Chamber of Manufactures (ACM), who represented employers subject to the Food Preservers Awards, made clear in a broad ambit claim the thoroughgoing changes it was after. Rejecting out of hand the FPU's claims, the ACM noted that for their offer to even be considered further, they must agree to:

- the introduction of stand-down provisions;
- the removal of restrictions on the employment of casuals outside the defined 'season';

- an increased spread of ordinary working hours;
- an increase in the length of a shift that could be worked without a break from five hours to six;
- the removal of penalty rates for shifts that fell partly on public holidays; and
- the introduction of part-time employment.[12]

Such changes represented a profound corrosion of the standard employment model central to the antipodean Fordist wage-labour nexus, as well as an intensification of labour through reducing the 'porosity' of the working day.[13]

Given the expected union opposition, the Commission was called upon to determine the dispute. It did so in a way that gave the ACM virtually everything that it wanted: the union application was dismissed out of hand for not fulfilling the goals of the structural efficiency exercise, particularly insofar as it did 'not ensure that working patterns and arrangements would enhance the flexibility of the industry'.[14] Among other things, the Commission granted the employers flexibility regarding employees and seasonal deployment, the extension of ordinary hours to the weekends and an increase in the minimum shift length without a break to 5.5 hours.[15] State awards followed suit.[16] At the macro-level, therefore, the initiative was in the hands of employers as they sought to effect the plant-level changes envisaged in the structural efficiency principle.

The nature of structural efficiency agreements at individual workplaces took their lead from the framework determined at the award level. A few representative agreements demonstrate the general trends of the increased spread of ordinary hours, relaxed restrictions on casual and part-time labour, increased flexibility in deploying labour and avoidance of disputes clauses. In one company, the offsets given for second-tier wage adjustments included the introduction of casual labour, the abolition of walking and washing-up times and adherence to a new disputes avoidance/settlement procedure.[17] An agreement for the Tasmanian Cadbury-Schweppes Drinks Division (struck with the Federated Liquor and Allied Industries Employees' Union of Australia) saw attempts to improve productivity and efficiency at peak times by rostering leisure days, extending ordinary hours, reducing lost time and new changeover procedures.[18] An enterprise award covering Nabisco Brands, a cereal and biscuit manufacturer, was varied to include an extension of the spread and flexibility of working hours and greater flexibility as to annual leave and meal breaks.[19]

Confectionary workers fared similarly. In much the same vein as the Food Preservers Awards, the federal Confectioners Award was varied primarily on the basis of the application put by the ACM and other confectionary manufacturer associations.[20] In particular, the Commission approved the employers' truncated, four-level classification structure, granted added flexibility in the deployment of part-time and casual labour and endorsed greater flexibility in working hours and annual leave provisions.[21] These changes framed developments at the plant level. At Allens Life Savers Lane Cove plant, off-sets included the voluntary substitution of Rostered Days Off (RDOs) to better match stock volumes, strict adherence to rest period times, an avoidance of disputes and settlement procedures and the reallocation of a labelling task previously done by fitters to confectioners.[22] In an agreement between Beatrice Foods and the FCA (by this time known as the Confectionary Workers Union), a disputes resolution clause accompanied greater flexibility in respect of RDOs and the implementation of a new computerised time clock costing system.[23]

The patently pro-employer decisions handed down by the Commission in both cases were, without doubt, a function of the inhospitable climate the FCA and FPU were operating within. Their stand against the Accord in 1983–1984 had won them few friends in the Commission, the ACTU and the broader labour movement.[24] This resulted in generally equivocal support from other unions during a series of showdowns with employers in the mid-1980s. As recounted in chapter 5, the FCA lost a bitter 1985 dispute with Dollar Sweets, a small confectionary manufacturer, which became a *cause célèbre* of the New Right. The FPU was also faced by increasingly militant employers from the mid-1980s onwards. The union won a major dispute at Rosella Lipton in 1984–1985 after a three-month strike, against the opposition of the Hawke ALP government who viewed it as an attack on the Accord.[25] Large employers such as Heinz and Nestle also mobilised, locking out workers in wrangles over pay and conditions in 1984.[26] Although initially successful in rebuffing management intransigence,[27] the employer effort continued throughout the 1980s and early 1990s, with an increasing focus on intensifying the use of casuals and expelling union militants.[28]

These specific attacks on food processing unions dovetailed with the broader disempowering impact of the Accord, which the FPU in particular identified as a major factor in 'weakening the structure of the trade union movement'.[29] This reality underlay the food employers' bold attitude in structural efficiency demands, which was described by the New South Wales branch of the FPU as a guise concealing an attempt to reduce conditions and over-awards while increasing the workweek.[30] A resolution passed by the same branch stated that members 'strongly protest against the employers expectations of continual trade-offs of hard won working conditions for wage increases'.[31]

Some workers at least thus realised the true nature of the restructuring and efficiency and structural efficiency exercises. As was outlined in chapter 6, both principles essentially revolved around the enhancement of managerial prerogative over the control and deployment of employees and the organisation of the labour process. In particular, they encouraged the intensification of labour while simultaneously corroding the standard employment model, compromising the trade-off which had sat at the heart of the antipodean Fordist wage-labour nexus. Unfortunately for food processing workers, the movement to enterprise bargaining in the early 1990s would only serve to sharpen these processes.

ENTERPRISE BARGAINING

The development of enterprise bargaining was not entirely without precedent in the food processing industry. Some of the larger enterprises within the sector, such as Darrell Lea, Cadbury-Schweppes and Kelloggs, had a history of enterprise and/or plant-level agreements, particularly when they fell within the jurisdiction of the states, while over-award bargains at individual workplaces were common.[32] However, the timing could not have been worse. It occurred in the context of a wave of union amalgamations: the FCA and FPU had amalgamated in 1992 to form the Confectionary Workers and Food Preservers Union of Australia (CWFPU), which then joined the Automotive, Metals and Engineering Union (AMEU) in 1994. After further amalgamations, the old CWFPU became the Food and Confectionary Division of the AMWU. Although ideally designed to bolster union strength, the amalgamations created considerable infighting and institutional friction, particularly regarding the financial autonomy of the division and the status of its officials.[33] This consumed time and resources that could have been better spent fighting for members' wages and conditions.

For both food preservers and confectioners, the situation was made worse by the fact that, nearly a decade after most other workers had won the thirty-eight-hour week, their awards had not been varied accordingly. Although the majority of employees covered by the awards were already working thirty-eight hours a week in practice, the Commission still demanded cost-offsets for the formal award variation.[34] Although in the event the CWFPU was able to tender the results of the structural efficiency exercise as evidence of such offsets,[35] the fact that the formal thirty-eight-hour week was achieved so late bespoke of a deeper problem: the fact that key federal awards, like the Food Preservers Award 1973, Food Preservers Interim Award 1986 and the Confectionary Award 1980 had been allowed to atrophy since the late 1980s, particularly concerning hours and various allowances.[36] This process of decay, although partially reversed by the mid-1990s,[37] underpinned the rush to enterprise bargaining in the food processing sector.

Broadly speaking, the enterprise agreements struck in the sector throughout the 1990s intensified the impulses towards flexibility, precarity and enhanced managerial power that had characterised the rolling-out of the structural efficiency principle. They tended to further polarise the workforce between an ever-decreasing 'core' of full-time employees and a growing population of casual and part-time workers, established new and more comprehensive performance indicators, increased the spread of ordinary working hours, removed restrictive practices and demarcation barriers and subordinated labour to a 'productivity culture'. The pattern was broadly similar to that which manifested itself in the retail sector, as will be demonstrated in the following chapter. However, given the greater relative power of unions like the AMWU compared to the docile retail union, the process acquired a harder edge in food processing, particularly as aggressive multinationals entered the industrial scene. We will see below that the experience of the 1990s and 2000s was that food processing capital made greater recourse to outsourcing, labour hire arrangements and open confrontation to sideline unions and undermine their bargaining position in the enterprise bargaining process.

A closer analysis of several representative agreements sharpens these general propositions. Less than a year after the federal Commission's adoption of enterprise bargaining principles in October 1991, a national-level enterprise agreement was signed with Edgell-Birds Eye, a major producer of canned vegetables and frozen foods, with a single-bargaining unit of concerned unions including the FPU. The objectives of the agreement betray the neoliberal logic that had infused labour relations in earnest after the passage of the Commission's new wage principles in the late 1980s. Key among them are a dedication to improve the efficiency and productivity of the enterprise, the creation of an environment conducive to flexible work organisation in response to new technologies and changing markets and an evinced desire to become 'a world competitive manufacturing enterprise'.[38] The 'productivity culture' being sought explicitly required workers and their unions to reduce demarcation barriers through 'the integration of all aspects of the production systems' and accept 'total flexibility of jobs and duties across the Company'.[39] Importantly, the agreement also stipulated that 'at all times terms and conditions of employment will be based upon the specific needs of the enterprise',[40] a refutation of the notion of comparative wage justice and metal trades flow-on discussed previously. Additionally, no quantitative limit was placed to the employment of casual labour.

Another enterprise agreement at canned fruit and juice producer Golden Circle synergised intensified flexibility with a profound review of work organisation.[41] Among the concessions being sought by the employer were flexible shift arrangements to match work patterns to enterprise needs, flexible starting and finishing times, increasing the daily maximum of work hours to 9.5 and staggering meal breaks and substituting public holidays to ensure continuity of production.[42] A much broader and deeper system of performance indicators was outlined, while employees had to be willing to 'accept total flexibility of jobs and duties across the Enterprise, subject only to individual skills or abilities to perform particular tasks'.[43] The desire to enforce flexibility and establish much more comprehensive performance indicators was equally apparent in a 1993 agreement at the Phoenix Biscuit Company, which also explicitly employed the language of 'Total Quality Management', 'Benchmarking' and 'Best Practice' which was becoming commonplace at this time.[44]

These trends, and the process of enterprise bargaining in the food processing sector generally, took on a harder edge as the 1990s drew on, a function of the entry/consolidation of aggressive multinational companies (such as Simplot, Nestle and the Campbell Soup Company) in an already foreign-dominated scene. These engaged in wage and conditions whipsawing between different jurisdictions and proved more than willing to exploit the union-diminishing potential of the Howard government's Workplace Relations Act 1996 (Cth), explored in chapter 6. American food giant Simplot acquired Edgell-Birds Eye in 1995 after it was divested by the Australian conglomerate Pacific Dunlop. The company brought with it the aggressive attitude to unionism characteristic of its homeland. The initial move to enterprise bargaining had helped divide workers at the sectoral level, but left individual work places more-or-less intact. Simplot, in common with many other manufacturers, intensified the process by fragmenting workers *within* the workplace. In a remarkable policy document, Simplot outlined a comprehensive strategy to wrest back the initiative from unions, who were perceived to be 'getting the upper hand'.[45] The scheme involved outsourcing key maintenance positions and the entire complement of casual workers to Manpower, an American-based labour hire and human resource consultancy multinational. A Manpower official had stated to Simplot that 'all the talk in the World has little affect [*sic*] on the Unions and at the end of the day actions speak louder and the Union tend to then get the message – Things must change'.[46] The end goal of the plan was to completely outsource work sites, reduce worker levels and use the new industrial relations legislation to further isolate individual workers and work groups[47] – in short, a paradigmatic liberal-productivist arrangement, combining precarity, enhanced managerial prerogative and juridical atomism.

The belligerent rhetoric was matched by action. As early as December 1996, just over a year after Simplot's acquisition of Edgell-Birds Eye's operations, the company had outsourced casual labour to Manpower at its Ulverstone plant.[48] In late 1997, all seasonal and casual work at Simplot's Devonport factory was similarly outsourced.[49] And in 1997/early 1998, a major industrial dispute erupted at the Echuca site, with Simplot locking-out employees after threatening to terminate all their employment contracts and completely outsource their positions.[50] This drastic action earned the rebuke of the federal tribunal, with Commissioner Tolley opining: 'I am also concerned that large multinational companies come into this country and try to foist, in my view, unacceptable human relations practices on people in this country. *I am severely limited by what I can do pursuant to the Workplace Relations Act* but I can under the Workplace Relations Act make it very clear there are to be no further threats of termination' (my emphasis).[51]

The limitations referred to by Commissioner Tolley were those that limited the tribunal's capacity to intervene in enterprise bargaining, a function of the Howard government's desire to reduce the role of the Commission, which was so graphically seen in chapter 6. Tolley here grasps the nub of the liberal-productivist labour law regime so far as the Commission is concerned. The recasting of the law-administration continuum saw the range of the Commission's responsibilities continually narrowed, while its discretion came to be increasingly fettered by statute. Law was re-asserting itself strongly, whittling away at the administrative fabric of arbitration to such a degree that, even in the case of the major stoppage at Echuca, the Commission found its ability to act severely constrained.

Although the workers affected eventually rebuffed management's attempts after the six week lock-out, the company succeeded in cutting the union's pay claim from 8 per cent to 3 per cent, while the new enterprise agreement went a long-way towards removing what Simplot regarded as 'restrictive practices', including new flexibility in the taking of RDOs, the introduction of twelve-hour shifts and the foisting of some maintenance responsibilities on production workers.[52]

In the meantime, the outsourcing of groups of workers to Manpower meant that the AMWU and other unions now had to devote resources to negotiations with that company. The well-observed tendency for the labour hire sector to have very low levels of unionisation,[53] together with the aforementioned fact that Manpower was party to a strategy of confronting unions, ensured that this was a task fraught with danger. The ACTU had successfully struck a 'heads of agreement' document with Manpower, which basically involved the former accepting the flexibility and efficiency demands of the company in exchange for recognition and the development of consultative arrangements with appropriate trade unions.[54] The AMWU came to a derivative agreement, which was broadly similar in tone.[55] This replicated the broader effort of the AMWU to come to agreements with labour hire companies to try and reduce pay and conditions differentials with the parent company (and so presumably reduce the incentive for the latter to outsource in the first place). Such efforts dovetailed with the movement to pattern bargaining in the mid to late 1990s, as unions sought to defend the standard employment model and re-establish some measure of uniformity at the sectoral level.

The results were inconsistent. Unsurprisingly, given its role in Campaign 2000 and Campaign 2003, the Victorian branch of the AMWU experienced more success than its brethren in other states.[56] The struggles over outsourcing and labour hire, however, informed the union effort to come to a national-level agreement with Simplot. In this it was aided by the fact that union density across its four processing plants was very high. Moreover, the Food & Confectionary Division of the AMWU had identified the threat posed by labour hire and resolved to either regulate its use or drive it entirely from the industry.[57] Although this was a very optimistic appraisal of union strength, particularly among smaller operators, the organisation of Simplot workers meant that the company's vision was not fully realised. Not only did the union achieve a national-level framework agreement (which set the parameters for agreements at the individual sites), but it also successfully retained some of the proportions clauses on part-time and casual labour which were being phased out of awards, including the Food Preservers Award 2000, generally. It remained the case, however, that the national framework agreement (which has, in various iterations, continued to this day) gave the company the ability to minimise demarcation barriers; deploy labour ever more flexibly across different jobs, duties and times; and use labour hire arrangements provided certain conditions of consultation were observed.[58]

The pressures facing unions involved in enterprise bargaining in the food sector became all the more difficult with the intensification of global competition. As indicated in chapter 4, whereas the crux of antipodean Fordist protectionist policy was to shield Australian manufacturers from the vicissitudes of the international market, within liberal-productivism these vicissitudes are welcomed, as competition is recast as a crucible producing vigorous and efficient firms. This newly open global space provided both the opportunity and the rationale for multinational companies to whipsaw between different jurisdictions in the hopes of encouraging a self-reinforcing cycle of wage and conditions undercutting.

The activities of the Australian branch of the American-owned Heinz Company provide an instructive example. Even under the award system, Heinz had demonstrated its commitment to enforcing flexibility in labour relations, using casual labour out of season and re-employing full-time workers who took voluntary redundancies as casuals.[59] The company, however, had in mind much greater changes. In a revealing 1993 policy document, it identified what it perceived as shortcomings and limitations to future growth, which included a poor industrial relations image, restrictive practices and a limited number of production days.[60] The vision anticipated for the company in 1996, although couched in the aspirational language of unitarist human resource management, clearly anticipated substantial rationalisation of production, the development of a low-cost, flexible and export-oriented manufacturing system, changed work practices, a predatory acquisition strategy and the potential relocation of factories;[61] a union, in short, of the precarious, lean production industrial paradigm and global production logic of liberal-productivism.

Heinz's 1992 acquisition of New Zealand–based food processor Wattie's armed management with the leverage to bargain towards these desired outcomes. A variety of reports had found cost advantages of doing business in New Zealand, with the immediate result being that certain operations in Australia (namely the plant at Dandenong) were threatened with closure.[62] AMEU National Organiser Neil Marshall noted of Heinz management, 'The Board will meet again in May to determine the future of the Dandenong plant, but the position has been made quite clear that if an Enterprise Agreement can't be finalised before this meeting the Dandenong operation will be transferred to New Zealand'.[63] In turn, Wattie's management encouraged a highly casualised production workforce, the integration of skilled workers into management, the removal of trade unions and the intensification of greater inter-Australasia competition, spurred by the fact that Heinz was internally comparing its Wattie's and Dandenong facilities at monthly performance reviews.[64]

The attempt by Heinz to play the two plants off against each other to strongarm the enterprise bargaining process was a complete success. The FPU, which until this point had been more reluctant than other unions to bargain with Heinz, was sidelined by the ACTU, which had taken over the negotiations.[65] The ACTU came to a radical agreement with Heinz in April 1993 over operations at the Dandenong factory, which provided, among other things, for:

- 130 immediate retrenchments, to be followed by another 90 over the following twelve months;
- the addition of a third shift, making for twenty-four-hour production; and
- the contracting out of some functions, including plumbing, boiler maintenance and electrical work.[66]

It also established the framework for further enterprise agreements that sought to reduce costs even further.[67] The historical irony was that these concessions wouldn't be enough for Heinz management, who would go on to ultimately close the Dandenong plant in 2000 and relocate its products to New Zealand and two other Australian sites after running the factory down through lack of investment.[68]

The story of Heinz is just the most instructive example of what was becoming a general trend in food-processing throughout the 1990s and 2000s, as multinational corporations whipsawed between different jurisdictions and plants, encouraging a competitive blood-letting of wages and conditions. Companies such as Arnott's, John West, Coca-Cola Amatil and Kerry Ingredients employed the tactic, on both intra-Australia and international scales, with factory closures and relocation of production cutting costs while serving as examples to other Australian food workers.[69] Although I explore throughout this book the characteristics and tendencies of liberal-productivism and its labour law regime in Australia, this process of whipsawing makes clear the inherently global configuration of this model of development. As argued in chapter 4, Australia has gained from this model more than many other countries, but it is important to remember here that this is due in no small part to the advantageous terms upon which Australian capitalism articulated with the world economy. The mass export of mining commodities to the growing Chinese economy coupled with capital whipsawing, union repression and precarisation at home: these were key elements in the coherence of Australian liberal-productivism made possible by the embrace of a global vista.

CONCLUSIONS

This case study has explored the unfolding of award restructuring and enterprise bargaining in the food processing sector, elucidating both the substantive content of agreements and the interaction of the bargaining process with broader political economic developments, such as the growing internationalisation of production and increasing foreign ownership. It has been demonstrated that the fundamental premises of enterprise bargaining within a liberal-productivist model of development, namely intensified precarity and flexibility, had their roots in the restructuring and efficiency and structural efficiency principles of the Accord years. Award reform under these heads involved, among other things, removing restrictions on the employment of casual and part-time labour, extending ordinary hours, increasing the flexibility of shift hours and RDOs and changing the payment of penalty rates. Importantly, at a time when the process was being painted as a progressive one leading to up-skilled, involved workers and career paths, food workers experienced, and acknowledged, that the principles were largely a cover for work intensification and the clawback of hard-won conditions.

Enterprise bargaining strengthened these developments, while also placing a premium upon the removal of demarcation barriers and the creation of a 'productivity' culture, a euphemism for employees being subordinated to the needs and requirements of their enterprise. This lattermost was a refutation of the unifying tendencies operative within the award system, and helped break the unification of the wage structure headed by the metal trades.

The general pattern of trade-offs required for enterprise bargaining-based wage increases was broadly similar to those in other sectors, as will be demonstrated when I come to the case of the retail sector. However, it acquired a harder edge in the food processing sector because of the historic militancy of key unions and a growing exposure to international competition. Whereas retailers, particularly food retailers, are often quite sheltered from global forces, Australian food workers increasingly had to compete against jurisdictions with lower wages and laxer regulations, such as New Zealand and Malaysia. Large multinationals such as Heinz proved exceedingly adept at exploiting this situation, whip-sawing between different locations to leverage the bargaining process in their favour and extract ever greater concessions from companies and communities.

This is the very stuff of the liberal-productivist model of development. Premised on a global production system and the easy movement of capital across national boundaries, capital is now more or less free to seek the greatest valourisation opportunities, with little regard for its 'home'. Whereas the labour law regime of antipodean Fordism obtained its logic and coherence in part from the synergy between high levels of industrial protection, the recycling of monopoly rents through the arbitration system and the standard employment model, the commensurate liberal-productivist regime relies instead upon the nexus between free trade, a polarised wage structure and employment precarity. For Australian workers generally, and food processing employees in particular, enterprise bargaining in such a context (a context it has helped constitute) is a font of union weakness rather than strength. While continued union organisation in the food manufacturing sector has at times frustrated the realisation of management's ideal vision, the overall trajectory has been one determined by capital.

Chapter 9

Precarity and Managerial Prerogative in the New South Wales Retail Sector

In the previous chapter, I studied how award restructuring and enterprise bargaining helped constitute a liberal-productivist labour law regime, particularly insofar as they crystallised the latter's industrial paradigm and wage-labour nexus. The current chapter explores much the same processes (with an additional focus on Australian Workplace Agreements) in the New South Wales (NSW) retail sector. Specifically, taking precarity and enhanced managerial prerogative as central to the transformed wage-labour nexus, I will focus on the ways in which awards and, more lately, enterprise agreements have evolved in the transition to liberal-productivism. Although the process has been protracted and uneven, these instruments of labour law have been denuded of virtually all restrictions, both quantitative and qualitative, on the use of casual and part-time labour. At the same time the model of a five-day, regular-hours workweek for full-time retail staff has been substantially displaced, particularly as normal trading hours have been continually extended while associated wage premiums have been reduced. In short, the standard employment model, central to the antipodean Fordist wage-labour nexus, has been largely destroyed. The result today is an industry which, more so than any other save hospitality, is characterised by a precarious employment structure, where management enjoy broad powers to engage workers across a fragmented 'time-regime' of working hours.[1]

There are a variety of reasons for selecting the NSW retail sector as a case study. In the previous chapter it was noted that this chapter should be read as a partner to it. By counter-posing a service industry to a manufacturing industry, I can trace similarities and differences in terms of the key processes identified. Indeed, I argue that the fundamental likeness of the food processing and retail stories immensely strengthens the thesis of transition made in this book. An equally important consideration, however, is the argument that sectors like retail can be thought of as new lead sectors in the fabric of liberal-productivism.[2] It will be recalled that in chapter 4 I defined lead sectors 'as those industries in which outcomes disproportionately affect industrial, economic and social outcomes in other industries'. Due to a combination of factors, including the flagging of the manufacturing sector and the increasing retailer domination of supply chains consequent upon a rapid concentration of retail capital, the retail sector can in a sense be regarded as a new lead sector.[3] Employment security, trade union militancy and workplace activism; these features of antipodean Fordism made the *least* impression on the retail sector. In the new world of liberal-productivism, precarity, a large, fragmented workforce and effete trade unionism became virtues with which the retail sector was liberally endowed. In particular, I will demonstrate in this chapter that the retail sector precociously enshrined the liberal-productivist wage-labour nexus of increased precarity and intensification of labour stripped of the *quid pro quo* of job security, rising remuneration and internal labour markets of antipodean Fordism.

The decision to focus largely on NSW is a function of a number of considerations. Firstly, a spotlight on a state jurisdiction counterbalances the largely federal focus of the analysis thus far. Secondly, in acknowledging the necessity of intimate analysis and the historically state-based character of retail awards, it makes sense to concentrate upon the concrete experience of one particular state. Given the fact that NSW is the most populous state, and a nexus existed between NSW retail awards and those in some other jurisdictions, such as Western Australia and the Australian Capital Territory,[4] it has been selected for this analysis. Where relevant, however, developments in other states will be described and integrated into the historical account. When I come to consider the changes effected by WorkChoices, the inquiry will have to be generalised, given the mortal blow this legislation dealt to state-based industrial systems.

To begin the analysis, an understanding of retail during the period of antipodean Fordist functionality must be reached. As shall be seen, insofar as the antipodean Fordist wage-labour nexus was concerned, this period in retail is notable for its brevity and belatedness.

NSW RETAIL AWARDS – THE BEGINNINGS

The retail sector proved a laggard in terms of the diffusion of the antipodean Fordist wage-labour nexus, particularly regarding the pattern of a regular five-day workweek central to the standard employment model. For much of the first half of the twentieth century, retail was characterised by regular Saturday and Sunday work.[5] Even after the advent of Sunday closing, full and, later, half-day trading on Saturday were considered normal working hours that could be worked as part of a six-day roster.[6] In NSW, it was only in 1971–1972 that the five-day week was introduced for retail workers.[7] By contrast, the majority of employees had won the five-day, forty-hour week in the wake of the historic federal Arbitration Commission's 8 September 1947 decision.

The belated granting of the standard workweek, which was introduced by consent between workers and retailers, came amid the intensifying class struggle of the late 1960s and early 1970s. Particularly concerning for retail capital was the fact that left-wing unions, such as the Miscellaneous Workers Union, were making ground against the right-wing Shop Assistants' and Warehouse Employees Union, today's Shop, Distributive and Allied Employees' Association (for simplicity, the union will be referred to as the SDA).[8] The peak retailers body, the Retail Traders' Association (RTA), believed 'that shop assistants were basically conservative in nature and tended to identify with the firm in which they were working',[9] a mindset the RTA wished to keep free from left-wing union leadership. The major retailers, such as Woolworths, Coles, Grace Bros, David Jones, Myer and Waltons, were especially vulnerable to disruption, given the fact that they were easier to organise and stoppages could wreak havoc given the perishability of many retail goods and the interdependent nature of supply chains.

In the event, both the union and the six major retailers aforementioned saw the benefit in a closed shop arrangement, whereby the SDA got 100 per cent coverage, while the employers entrenched the conservative union to the exclusion of more militant competitors.[10] The deal, struck in 1971, saw the membership of the NSW branch increase exponentially; whereas in 1968 its ranks numbered only 5,320, by 1973 it had swelled to 38,000 members.[11] The agreement was also of key importance to the unfolding of the five-day workweek for retail workers. Mortimer notes that part of the retail union strategy for winning this central feature of the antipodean Fordist wage-labour nexus was 'a long running and unsuccessful campaign to reduce shopping hours through Saturday closing'.[12] The necessity of bringing the SDA into the fold in an era of heightened class struggle brought with it the need for retailers to make certain concessions, among them the five-day week, but employer acquiescence was premised upon the union accepting the legitimacy of Saturday and late-night work. Union official Michael Johnston noted that 'the 5-day-week campaign was successfully concluded because the union changed its attitude from one of complete opposition to late night and Saturday trading to one of controlling the number of Saturdays and late nights our members had to work'.[13] Although such concessions were deemed necessary by the SDA, this method of accommodating employer demands, whereby every gain had to be offset by something relinquished, would increasingly undermine union bargaining power in the 1980s and 1990s and with it the ability of the union to shape the contours of the transformation in retail industrial relations.

It was thus only at the zenith of antipodean Fordism that the NSW retail sector exhibited the typical working-time arrangements that characterised the Fordist wage-labour nexus. The fact that this was achieved on the cusp of Fordist dysfunction ensured that this nexus found fallow soil.

THE 1970s AND 1980s – CRUCIAL TRANSITIONAL DECADES

I have elsewhere stated that 'the 1970s and 1980s were crucial transitional decades regarding the place of the retail sector within the fabric of Australian capitalism'.[14] In particular, the dominance of manufacturers over retailers within antipodean Fordism was usurped. In the period of antipodean Fordist functionality, oligopolistic manufacturers were able to exert control over comparatively homogenous markets that established clear demarcations between elements in the distribution network. Within these networks, the role of retailers 'was to buy goods from the range offered by the wholesaler or other intermediaries, and sell them on to the consumer . . . it was the manufacturers who decided what goods were available, and in most countries at what price they could be sold to the public'.[15] In Australia, this latter most point was expressed most clearly by the ability of manufacturers to control prices through resale price maintenance practices.[16]

As the manufacturing sector began to lose steam in the crisis of the 1970s, however, a number of developments changed the game. From the 1970 and 1980s onwards, Australian retailers, particularly grocery and liquor retailers, gained the apex position in supply chains through the combination of a growing monopoly over the sale of consumer goods,[17] the acquisition of direct interests in the manufacturing sector and the advent of retail 'house brand' products.[18]

This control was a key moment in the repositioning of retail as a lead sector, particularly insofar as it opened the channels by which its wage-labour nexus could be flowed up the supply chain to manufacturers.[19] Unfortunately for retail employees, this position of weightier industrial gravity coincided with the movement towards de-regulated trading hours. Large retailers sought to counteract stagnation in product markets, a product of antipodean Fordist crisis, by increasing consumption opportunities and squeezing out smaller retailers (who were generally granted exemptions from trading hours legislation).[20] Given the fact that, in the context of considerable union strength, work outside of normal hours attracted a penalty rate for full-time staff, the progressive extension of trading hours encouraged retailers to intensify their use of casual and part-time labour. This development required a transformation of retail awards, particularly to the effect of removing restrictions on the engagement of such workers, increasing the pool of potential labour and slowly undermining the privileged position of full-time employees. What was required, in short, was a degradation of the standard employment model as it applied to the retail sector.

In NSW, this process began in earnest in the 1980s. After gaining in the slew of work-value cases in the early 1980s,[21] retail workers soon found the retail awards controlling their terms and conditions of employment becoming a battle-ground between employers and the SDA which, with some notable exceptions, remained committed to pursuing outcomes through the arbitration system.[22]

The material premises of these debates were the accumulating symptoms of a changing industrial structure and employment relations in the 1970s. As early as 1977, Justice Macken of the NSW Industrial Commission (whom we shall come to know well in this chapter) noted in a case regarding the formulation of a single Shop Employees (State) Award that 'the evidence established a trend in the industry, from 1969 to the present date, by which casual juniors had come increasingly to be employed'.[23] He identified a variety of impulses tending towards this result, including filling employment gaps created by the five-day week and the impact of self-service technologies and new marketing procedures in allowing junior employees to perform the same duties as older workers.[24] In a 1980 work-value case, Justice Macken further observed the fundamental shift towards casualised retail labour, noting how it had effected profound labour process changes for *both* full-time and casual/part-time employees.[25] Convinced of the undesirability of retail casualisation, and under pressure from the union, Justice Macken had even taken some concrete steps in 1977 to combat the problem through requiring employers to pay casual employees penalty rates for work on public holidays, weekends and after 6.00 p.m. on weekdays.[26] This represented a marked departure from the historic attitude to casual employees, which was succinctly captured by Chief Industrial Magistrate Williams in a 1972 case denying casual retail workers Sunday penalty rates: 'Whatever entitlements a casual employee may have, they do not approach in extent, those of a part-time employee to the same degree as those of a part-time employee approach those of a full-time employee'.[27]

What was to be the first major institutional development in the reformulation of the retail wage-labour nexus, however, was the commencement of an inquiry in December 1982 into the desirability of extending retail trading hours, carried out by Justice Macken. Interestingly, the divide between large and small retailers was apparent immediately from the tenor of the submissions. As intimated earlier, many small retailers have long been in favour of prescribed opening and closing times given the fact they are usually excluded from their operation. The case was little different in NSW; most employers and the NSW RTA submitted to the Macken inquiry that no change to the trading hours regime was necessary.[28] Indeed, Lyons notes that 'the only submissions to fully embrace extended trading came from the major grocery supermarket chains', while the SDA 'submitted that extended trading would result in more casual staff and a decline in full-time and permanent employment'.[29]

In the event, Justice Macken recommended an additional evening's trading and the extension of trading hours until 4.00 p.m. on Saturdays,[30] while affirming the desirability of permanent employment over casual status. More significant than these comparatively modest developments was his recommendation that a specialist retail industry tribunal be created, a proposal given effect by the Industrial Arbitration (Retail Trade) Amendment Act 1983 (NSW). This move was key in securing union acceptance of the report; these had stated, 'We are of the opinion that the most appropriate manner in which the report can be implemented is through the establishment of an appropriate tribunal'.[31]

The result was the Retail Trade Industrial Tribunal ('the Tribunal'), a body composed of two members of the Industrial Commission (one as chair, the other as deputy chair) and two 'assessors' to provide advice, with one nominated by the Labor Council, the other by the RTA. Despite being born in crisis, it was a creature of the antipodean Fordist law-administration continuum, essentially combining the juridical structure of arbitration with a quasi-corporatist practice. It was very much in keeping with broader quasi-corporatist experiments to escape from the crisis of antipodean Fordism by intensifying its institutions. Of particular note in this regard is the Accord, which we have come to know well in this book. Although the form of the Tribunal and the Accord was very different, the similarities in their constitutive contexts are instructive. Both were developed in the same context of general economic crisis, yet were premised on the institutionalised power of the trade union movement and enhancing the authority of the arbitral tribunals. Both were supported by Australian Labor Party (ALP) governments and would attract the ire of intransigent employers.

This body was to prove a central site for the intensifying struggle over retail awards: its eventual failure was simultaneously part of the failure of antipodean Fordism to rescue itself from its contradictions.

THE 1980s – THE RETAIL TRADE INDUSTRIAL TRIBUNAL ERA

In 1984, the issue of newly de-regulated trading hours, and how to defuse the threat of retail employee resistance over them, was at the centre stage of a number of legal developments. Firstly, the SDA and major retailers struck two industrial agreements (arrived at by consent) to be certified by the NSW Industrial Commission.[32] These agreements were understood as the *quid pro quo* for union acceptance of de-regulated trading hours.[33] For workers engaged by major retailers, the most important gain was the establishment of a thirty-eight-hour week for full-time employees[34] and the provision of time-and-a-half penalty rates for Saturday work. Additionally, the agreements limited casual employment to 15 per cent of total hours worked, provided proportions clauses limiting the employment of part-time and junior staff[35] and sought to convert casual and part-time positions to full-time where possible.[36] In exchange, employers gained some of the flexibilities associated with the 'cost offsets' demanded by the arbitral tribunals in return for the thirty-eight-hour week. It is worth quoting the judgement at length in describing these changes:

> They include the enactment of radical changes to night-fill and non-selling staff employees' conditions, including a reduction in the loading for the working of ordinary hours from 27% to 17½%. The removal of tea money from employees who work ordinary hours past 6 p.m. on Thursday and Friday is in itself a saving of just on 1% in the case of Grace Bros and 1.68% in the case of Coles. . . . Other offsets include the introduction of premium hours, *a reduction in the minimum weekly hours of part-time employees from twenty to sixteen and an ability to roster permanent employees more flexibly* (my emphasis).[37]

It has always been the understanding in the retail industry that the levers of the sector are the bargains struck with the major retailers.[38] These consent arrangements were no different, with Lyons noting 'the lack of objectors to the certification of the agreements reflects the understanding between the government, major retailers, and RTA that the terms of the agreements would eventually apply to all employees in the industry'.[39] The increasing concentration of retail capital, and the competition consequent upon it, however, almost threw these arrangements into turmoil. The signing of the industrial agreements had split the RTA, with the President, Mr Tate, siding with the major retailers in their interpretation of the Macken report, ranged against the Secretary, Mr Lawrence, and other general shop operators.[40] Only after protracted discussion was a workable agreement reached. The Tribunal under Justice Macken thus made a new award to apply to all retail employees in shops employing fifteen or more employees, dubbed the Shop Employees (General Shops) Interim (State) Award. This was based in large part on the industrial agreements, recreating many of their key provisions. Of key significance for our purposes was the fact that the Tribunal found that extending Saturday penalty rates to casuals was a necessary step in the creation of this award. Justice Macken stated:

> If casual employees can be employed on Saturday afternoons at a lower hourly rate than that applicable to part-time and permanent employees then the award would provide an inducement to employers *to further causalise the industry* . . . in my view it is 'necessary' to ensure that permanents and part-time employees not be positively disadvantaged by the terms of the award (my emphasis).[41]

Macken here recognises the necessity of protecting the integrity of the standard employment model against the continued casualisation of the retail sector.

The cost-offsets established in the award (and agreed to by consent) are also revealing. Of particular importance was the radically recast status of part-time employment, which until that point had been restricted to women over the age of twenty-one and men over the age of sixty. Age and gender were removed as impediments to part-time worker status, as was the requirement that part-time employees only be engaged if no suitable full-time employee is available.[42]

In the 1984 industrial agreements and the first award of the Tribunal, therefore, we have a complex, dialectically evolving reality. Embryonic moves towards increased workplace flexibility, such as the greatly increased scope of part-time employment, the reduction of part-time employee minimum hours and increased employer latitude in rostering, co-exist with structures designed to buttress standard employment. This understanding dovetails neatly with the idea of institutional searching, the piecemeal and anarchic effort to escape economic crisis discussed in earlier chapters. The attempt to escape crisis through the generation of new institutions and norms is typically not an abrupt, once-for-all process; rather, it revolves around the dialectical relationship between the old and the new within a decaying model of development.

This process of institutional searching assumed a new form vis-à-vis retail awards with a major 1985 NSW Industrial Commission review of the retail industry in NSW, brought about in large part by RTA opposition to Justice Macken's ruling awarding all classes of employees penalty rates for Saturday work. In the first of many moves by which the Tribunal was marginalised by internally fractured employer groups, the RTA (90 per cent of whose membership was composed of small retailers employing fewer than twenty staff)[43] appealed to the Commission in Court Session regarding the overtime issue. Moreover, they argued before the Commission for the deletion of all penalty rates, no proportions clauses and the establishment of a new category of 'regular' employee (substantively a precarious form of part-time work) whose minimum shift per week was only eight hours.[44] The essence of these arguments was no less than a rejection of the antipodean Fordist wage-labour nexus, particularly insofar as it crystallised the standard employment model. The RTA appeal coincided with a union application to flow-on the provisions of the aforementioned industrial agreements to other retail awards, with the result being a combined hearing that essentially amounted to a complete review of Justice Macken's decision and the hierarchy of retail awards in NSW.

The result of the employer's forum shopping was considerably advantageous changes in the content and structure of retail awards, changes that represented the first unequivocal legal lubricants to retail precarity.

Structurally, the two existing retail awards, including the recently determined Employees (General Shops) Interim (State) Award, were collapsed into a single consolidated Shop Employees (State) Award.[45] From the perspective of retail employees, this could have been a progressive move if it had been on the basis sought by unions, that is, an extension of the industrial agreements throughout the retail award structure at large. In the event, however, the unification of the two awards represented a lowest common denominator arrangement given the substantive changes inserted by the NSW Industrial Commission.

The most significant development for the purposes of this book was the complete reversal of Justice Macken's efforts to minimise the potential for casual labour to supplant full and part-time workers. The lattermost lost out by seeing the Saturday afternoon penalty rate cut from the prevailing NSW standard of time-and-a-half to time-and-a-quarter.[46] Casuals, however, were denied the entitlement to penalty rates for Saturday afternoon work at all. The Commission maintained that, given the preference by full-time workers for weekly employment and statutory guarantees preventing employers coercing existing full-timers to work extended hours, the payment of Saturday afternoon penalty rates to casuals would not perform the standard employment-preserving function Justice Macken expected of it.[47]

While understandable in its own terms, this view of the Commission sits uneasily with another key development, namely the rejection of a union-supported proportions clause limiting casual employment to 15 per cent of total working hours in retail establishments. Despite claiming that both employers and unions were in agreement as to the preferability of full-time weekly employment, the Commission noted the increasing prevalence of casuals in the industry.[48] It noted of this tendency, 'Much of this has arisen from the necessity to staff shops through extended hours and as relief during peak or busy periods. *The need of employers to resort to causal employment has been exacerbated by seemingly inappropriate award limitations upon part-time employment*' (my emphasis).[49]

The significance of this statement is twofold. Firstly, it explicitly acknowledges the corrosive impact of trading hours de-regulation on the standard employment model, lately arrived as this was in the retail sector. Secondly, the Commission astutely observes the connection between employment patterns, employer strategy and the contours of retail awards. These do not operate in isolation from one another but together constitute a dialectically evolving regulatory space, in which the needs of crisis resolution and an emergent model of development come up against established institutions, norms and understandings.

Just as important as the material decision to remove restrictions on casual employment was the methodology by which the Commission arrived at it.

Noting the considerable variation in patterns of utilisation of casuals across the industry, it went on to say that 'in these circumstances we see some merit in the suggestion that the dynamics of the industry may assist in the resolving of the problem of the proper role of casual employment'.[50] In other words, the Commission endorsed a more de-centralised, self-regulatory method, in which the circumstances of individual retailers took precedence over the need to control and restrict casual employment in a collective way through the award system. The same attitude underlaid the decision to remove proportions clauses governing the ratio between adult and junior retail workers in general shops, with the Commission declaring 'we are prepared . . . to meet the employers' plea for flexibility. . . . We think that the issue of proportions is one which the industry, is[*sic*] so far as general shops are concerned, can meet *in a self-regulatory way*' (my emphasis).[51]

Aside from departing from the antipodean Fordist modality of award setting (namely, awards being used as tools to universalise gains won from individualised victories), the attitude of the Commission both presupposes and encourages a managerialist turn in the conception of labour law. The dressing of the casual and junior proportions issues in the language of flexibility and self-regulation is clearly derived from the emergent management concerns in the 1980s to promote efficiency, control and value maximisation through greater control over the engagement and disposal of labour.[52] That this was an explicit concern of retail capital in particular can be gleaned from a remarkable submission in 1982 by the Australian Retailers Association (ARA) (a national body to which the RTA was federated) to a federal committee reviewing Australian industrial relations law and systems. At a time when most employer groups feared the potential of a wages explosion stemming from a de-centralised industrial relations system, the ARA was submitting that compulsory arbitration was a failed system that should be replaced by a new modality of industrial regulation.[53] This system was to be premised on a rejection of the notion of comparative wage justice, instead endorsing an industry-centred arrangement guided by the principle 'that the establishment and variation of wages and conditions should be approached on an industry by industry basis with no reliance being possible on standards established in other industries'.[54] Against this backdrop, the ARA lambasted the importation of standards developed elsewhere in the industrial structure to the retail sector, particularly penalty rates for work outside hitherto ordinary business hours.[55] Full told, and aside from the fact that industrial tribunals are retained in the schema, the document represents nothing less than a complete rejection of the antipodean Fordist wage-labour nexus. The reproduction of elements of this industry-centred ideology, along with some substantive provisions to enact it, within the Commission's decision speaks of a new, intensified interpenetration of legal and managerialist norms in which the circumstances of concentrating and transforming retail capital infused the legal realm.

The decision of the Commission, although delighting employers,[56] sparked outrage among unions and retail workers, with the former declaring it 'one of the worst inflicted upon the union movement in this State'.[57] Justice Macken lamented that it was an 'almost certain fact that, whichever way a decision goes before the Retail Trade Industrial Tribunal, an appeal will be brought to the Commission in Court Session'.[58] In a timely demonstration of Jessop's assertion that the state is a complex amalgam of various institutional apparatuses, the coherence and functionality of which can never be assumed,[59] the SDA called upon the political capital it held with the NSW Labor government. The SDA has a long history on the right of the labour movement, heavily influenced by the post-War anti-communist Industrial Group movement and Catholic social doctrine. Bramble notes that NSW was a bastion of the traditional Catholic Right faction of the ALP, which controlled the party apparatus and the NSW Labor Council.[60] The SDA was thus in a position to wield its considerable influence over the legislative machinery to circumvent the decision of the Commission.[61]

Government anger at the apparent betrayal of the *quid pro quo* arrangement over extended trading hours was palpable, compounded by the actions of certain retailers flouting the liberalised arrangements and opening on Sundays.[62] Indeed, the notion of an agreement binding retailers, employees and the state was explicitly acknowledged by one government member, who stated:

> At a meeting of retail workers it was decided they would accept longer trading on the basis that the new working conditions would be fully applied. This conditional acceptance . . . of Saturday afternoon trading was put to the Government and accepted. What I am saying, in effect, is that the Government was part of that agreement and, further, that in this legislation they are honouring that agreement.[63]

The legislation referred to here was the Factories, Shops and Industries (Further Amendment) Act 1985 (NSW). Among other things, section 4 of the act empowered the government to decree regulations fixing the penalty rate for Saturday work at time-and-a-half. The act was panned by retail employers and the conservative opposition parties, who variously claimed that the ALP was beholden to SDA interests and that the government had usurped the authority and standing of the Industrial Commission.[64] The legislation passed, however, and in due course the government enacted regulations re-instating the Saturday penalty rate schema established by Justice Macken's original award.[65]

The response of the major retailers to these developments is indicative both of the increasing corrosiveness of the competition principle and the power of concentrated retail capital. Like most major employers, large retailers were generally happy to take wages out of competition, a desire that dovetailed with the relatively homogenous wage structure generated by the universalising tendencies of the arbitration system. This attitude certainly informed the willingness of major retailers to sign the industrial agreements with the SDA in the first instance, based on the understanding that the conditions they provided would be generalised in the industry. The 1985 Commission decision, however, directly assailed the stability of these arrangements by providing for lower wages and inferior conditions to those obtaining in the industrial agreements. The signatory employers claimed they had been conned by the government, the SDA and the Labor Council into providing higher Saturday pay, their anger intensified by perceived state and union laxity in prosecuting other retailers breaching penalty rate provisions.[66] Woolworths, Coles, Myer, Grace Brothers and Target demanded thoroughgoing changes in the terms of the industrial agreements, seeking in particular provisions that directly intensified the flexibility of labour and lubricated employee precarity, including:

- reducing the minimum hours of part-time employees from sixteen to eight hours a week;
- reducing minimum shifts for casuals from four hours to two hours;
- allowing school-aged children to be employed as casuals; and
- removing proportions clauses governing the employment of casuals and the ratio of junior to adult workers.[67]

The substance of these demands was in fact a rejection of the late-blooming antipodean Fordist wage-labour nexus and its substitution by one that placed a premium on flexibility, the breakdown of labour-power into increasingly fragmented units and increased access to transient pools of labour, including the young workers who were increasingly found in them (as seen in chapter 6). It contained, in short, several of the key planks of a cogent liberal-productivist wage-labour nexus.

If these changes were not forthcoming, the major retailers made repeated threats to cancel the agreements, which, according to Justice Macken, 'led to severe industrial instability in the industry'.[68] Macken attempted to provide something of a compromise solution, seeking to convert most of the terms of the original agreements into a new Shop Employees (Major General Shops) (State) Award while granting some concessions to employers, such as allowing the sought-after reduction in minimum casual shifts on an experimental basis.[69] The major retailers, however, could not be mollified. They challenged the award in the NSW Court of Appeal,[70] claiming that, having been made in the absence of one of the assessors, it was made without jurisdiction.[71] Incredibly, the Court agreed and duly voided the award, a demonstration *par excellence* of the distinction between administration and the purer legal form in the conduct of industrial relations.[72] While Macken was more concerned about industrial stability in the retail sector, for the Court of Appeal the case turned upon the minutiae of procedural rules.

As a result of the court's decision, Macken, who by this point was comparing the uncertainty surrounding the retail industry to the 'Sword of Damocles',[73] was forced to make an interim award which, although it rolled over the terms of the industrial agreements, was explicitly temporary and would be replaced after a period of negotiation/arbitration between the SDA and the increasingly militant employers.[74]

In light of these tensions, 1988 shaped up as a critical year. Firstly, the Tribunal was reconstituted, with Justice Macken, who had earned the ire of employers,[75] replaced by Deputy President Wells. While not wishing to overstate the importance of individuals to the transformations of Australian capitalism, it is nevertheless the case that the nature of state personnel can impact upon the speed and order of historical change.[76] This is particularly so in times of crisis when, as we have seen, emergent ideologies grate against established norms and understandings. Justice Macken, although hardly a radical, had throughout his tenure as chair of the Tribunal evinced a consistent view vis-à-vis the nature of the industrial arrangements entered into, the bargains underlying them and the role of the Tribunal broadly. Given the jurisdictional quarrels and the gulf between the respective awards of the Tribunal and the Commission, Macken's removal could not but help to change the terms of the debate. Given his apparent sympathies for retail employees and firm view of the binding nature of the deals the major retailers had struck, this was unlikely to be a change for the benefit of workers.

It was before this reconstituted Tribunal that a major case concerning the terms and conditions of retail employment, as well as ongoing confusion over contemporaneous but qualitatively different awards, was heard. Of key concern for both parties was the inconsistency borne by the fact that the majority of the retail industry fell under two awards, the aforementioned Shop Employees (State) Award and the Shop Employees (Major General Shops) Interim (State) Award. Both parties wanted to create a single award, but on very different bases: 'The unions wanted the new award to contain the same terms as the 1986 award whereas the RTA sought the provisions of the 1985 award adjusted to incorporate certain provisions re shift work'.[77] In essence, this distinction boiled down to an institutional clash; the unions wished to extend the decision of the Tribunal, while the employers looked to universalise the much less favourable conditions of the Commission's 1985 award.

The Tribunal responded by once again collapsing the awards into a consolidated Shop Employees (State) Award. Although the negotiations saw both parties come to consensus on certain issues, the key issues of Saturday overtime, penalty rates for casuals, junior rates and proportions clauses remained and had to be arbitrated. The case represented a definitive victory for the employers on the first of these matters. Time-and-a-quarter rates would now apply for full-time and part-time employees[78] and, unlike the case of the 1985

Commission decision, there was no longer a sympathetic ALP government willing to intervene (the Liberal/National Party Coalition had come to power in March 1988). More broadly, Deputy President Wells approved of the Commission's methodology in the 1985 case of *prima facie* rejecting a link between shop assistants and shift workers generally,[79] a move which certainly attacked the universalising wage-labour nexus of antipodean Fordism.

In the context of ever-increasing use of casual labour within the industry, several other elements of the decision were also highly significant. The union attempt to moderate the increasing resort of employers to casual labour by the elimination of fifteen-year-old junior rates was again rebuffed.[80] In light of the evidence of a deepening engagement of causal employees, the Tribunal surmised that the payment of penalty rates to causals for work outside ordinary hours, as provided in the industrial agreements, was ineffective in the deterrent role Justice Macken had intended and thus rejected them.[81] Admittedly, the Tribunal did give some substantive effect to the alleged 'mutually accepted concept that full-time employment was to be encouraged' by the reinstatement of a proportions clause placing a ceiling on the share casual labour could take in total hours worked in general stores employing thirteen or more employees.[82] However, this clause would now cap the casual share of total hours worked at 25 per cent, compared to the previous figure of 15 per cent.[83] Moreover, the Tribunal rejected the union claim for a quantitative restriction on part-time employees (namely, of no more than one part-timer for every full-time employee).[84] This decision thus presented retail employers with considerably enhanced opportunities to engage and exploit young, casualised labour at the same time it cut down remaining disincentives to employing it.

The year 1988 was most important, however, in an institutional sense. History overtook the experiment that was the Retail Trade Industrial Tribunal in late 1988, when the conservative Greiner government enacted the Industrial Arbitration (Retail Trade) Amendment Act 1988 (NSW), which abolished the Tribunal in its entirety and transferred its business back to the Industrial Commission. The government's stated rationale was that the jurisdictional nightmares that had beset the Tribunal imposed considerable costs of time and money on the parties, without real countervailing advantages to the industry.[85] In particular, the Minister of Industrial Relations and Employment, John Fahey, noted that both employers and unions complained of 'the drain on their resources in the dual supply of persons as assessors to the tribunal and as advocates before the tribunal'.[86] That this appears to have been a truthful representation of the parties' views is backed by the Labor Party's support for the passage of the bill, with ALP Councillor A. B. Manson stating that both the RTA and the SDA were 'unanimous in their view that the interests of all parties will be better served by abolishing the Retail Trade Industrial Tribunal'.[87]

There is no reason to doubt the sincerity of these claims. The strife between the Tribunal and the Commission had imposed real costs on the time and resources of participants. However, I have demonstrated that these burdens were essentially self-imposed on the part of retail employers and the RTA, given their desire to circumvent the more employee-friendly decisions emanating from the Tribunal. Indeed, benefits flowed for them upon the Tribunal's dissolution almost immediately, with the Commission granting employer claims for a reduction of the minimum weekly hours of part-time employees from sixteen to twelve hours.[88]

The SDA, on the other hand, saw the effort to realise the favourable outcomes achieved through the Tribunal continually frustrated as the Commission and superior court system undercut its standing. The SDA's change of attitude, from making the demand for an industry tribunal the *quid pro quo* for trading hours extension to advocating its abandonment, is thus understandable, but nevertheless ill-inspired. As explored in previous chapters, the 1980s was a period of institutional searching for ways out of the developing economic crisis. In the retail industry this process took on a form of juridified corporatism, with the role of worker and employer representatives (in the form of the assessors) woven into the specialist tribunal's institutional fabric. It was thus part of the effort to save antipodean Fordism from its crisis tendencies by intensifying its institutions. The end of the Tribunal represented the closure of an industry-specific form of crisis resolution, creating a vacuum into which unadulterated neo-liberal prescriptions would step.

THE 1990s – AWARD MODERNISATION, ENTERPRISE BARGAINING AND THE ASCENDENCY OF NEO-LIBERALISM

In NSW, as in other jurisdictions, the catch-cries of the late 1980s and early 1990s were structural efficiency and award modernisation (the latter being derivative of the former). As was discussed in chapters 6 and 8, these processes were designed with the stated purpose of removing institutional impediments to increased productivity and efficiency in the workplace. Although formulated at the federal level, the state commissions followed suit in implementing the principle, including NSW. Given the protracted disputes over rosters and working hours arrangements explored so far in this chapter, it is no surprise that the Shop Employees (State) Award proved a ripe target for the restructuring process, being overhauled in 1991. The main axis of change included a further commitment to the principle of enterprise arrangements and substantive changes to how work was organised and labour engaged. It is the latter that interests us here.

The 1991 restructuring process dedicated both employers and the SDA to the concept of award modernisation, with the renovated award stating explicitly: 'The parties are committed to examining this industry award to ensure it *reflects the needs of modern retailing* and to eliminating or amending provisions which restrict the ability of retailers and mixed enterprises with retail outlets *to adapt quickly and efficiently* to changes affecting their business and the provision of service to the consumer' (my emphasis).[89] It goes on to state that 'the unions are prepared to discuss with employers all matters raised by the unions and the employers for increased flexibility' and that 'the unions will not unreasonably oppose agreement'.[90] Although mitigated somewhat by assurances of union involvement in the process of change, the SDA and other unions involved in the retail sector were thus explicitly bound to lay open for negotiation long-standing practices around rostering, casual loadings and award classifications which had, for the employers, proved an impediment to the task of enforcing retail precarity.

The result of this agreed process of award modernisation essentially presaged the movement in enterprise agreements, except with fewer benefits and greater trade-offs, especially so far as causals were concerned. In general shops, the minimum shift engagement for a casual fell from four to three hours, while they could now work eleven hours on one day, and nine on every other, without attracting any overtime payment.[91] Part-time workers saw their minimum guaranteed daily and weekly hours drop, to three and twelve hours, respectively.[92] Ordinary trading hours were extended for all classes of shop, including up to 6.00 p.m. on Saturdays (thereby neutering the issue of Saturday penalty rates that had proved almost insoluble in the different political-economic climate of the 1980s).[93]

The flexibility of engagement was matched by a movement towards greater functional flexibility, with the modernised award providing that 'employees within each classification are to perform a wider range of duties including work which is incidental or peripheral to their main tasks or functions', while also preventing employees from imposing 'any restrictions or limitations on a reasonable review of work methods or standard work times'.[94] Although direct evidence is lacking, it seems highly likely that such a clause forestalled union opposition to the new technologies and Taylorist work forms that had increasingly taken hold in the industry.[95] In particular, a process of 'digital Taylorism'[96] had extended tendrils deeply into the organisation of work and deployment of labour in the 1980s, 1990s and 2000s, with scanning, electronic point-of-sale and computerised stock-keeping and warehousing technologies fundamentally altering the structure of the labour process in the retail industry.[97] Most significant for this book has been the development of a sophisticated nexus between point-of-sale scanning technologies and computerised rostering systems, allowing management to very closely align expected demand to labour supply.[98] The result has been an ability on the part of retailers, particularly large retailers, to produce a 'fragmented time-regime', whereby the working week can be broken into small, discontinuous components and reassembled, using the whole gamut of full-time, part-time and casual employees, to match the requirements of employers.[99] This development in particular facilitated and encouraged the retailer drive for the deeper precarity and flexibility they sought in award restructuring and enterprise bargaining. It is to the latter we now turn.

In chapter 6 I noted that in the early 1990s, under the pressure of recession, the Commonwealth and various state governments began to qualitatively change the modality of industrial relations by undermining the long-established institutions of compulsory conciliation and arbitration. In NSW, this process began in earnest with the Greiner government's legislative overhaul of 1990 and 1991, which included the Industrial Arbitration (Enterprise Agreements) Amendment Act 1990 (NSW) and the much more wide-ranging Industrial Relations Act 1991 (NSW). The latter act was a watershed moment in the history of NSW industrial relations, introducing sweeping changes that definitively challenged the arbitration model.

It is beyond the scope of this discussion to describe the legislation in detail, but broadly put it provided for 'the end of preference for unionists, the outlawing of closed shops, the creation of a new industrial court, a stronger enterprise focus and greater protection for awards and agreements'.[100] For our purposes, the most important elements of the new system were the encouragement of enterprise agreements and the provision of statutory part-time work contracts. Both served to intensify the development of employment precarity and undermine the bargaining power of retail workers.

As mentioned earlier, the retail industry has typically been characterised by state award regulation, overseen by semi-autonomous state branches of the SDA. Thus, although enterprise bargaining at the federal level did not really begin in earnest until the passage of the Industrial Relations Reform Act 1993 (Cth), the SDA state bodies were nevertheless compelled to confront the issue earlier than many other trade unions.[101]

The disempowering effect of this development cannot be overstated. The SDA is an archetypal example of the kind of bureaucratic and legalistic union which the arbitration system tended to produce. Lacking the kind of workplace organisation which allowed other unions to extract concessions from employers at the point of production, the SDA was heavily dependent upon formalised understandings with major retailers (usually bought at the price of industrial docility)[102] and the award system to secure gains for workers, often through the vehicle of National and State Wage Cases. The movement towards enterprise-level bargaining was thus one which the union regarded with foreboding, placing as it did a premium upon shop-floor organisation.[103]

Like the case in metals discussed in chapter 7, enterprise bargaining in retail encouraged increasing polarity in the sector, particularly between those who remained dependent on the increasingly inadequate award and workers able to strike enterprise deals. For the latter, enterprise bargains and enterprise awards[104] throughout the 1990s tended to intensify the trends towards retail precarity I have noted in exchange for headline wage increases. Generally speaking, agreements further increased the spread of normal hours, shrank the size of minimum part-time weekly work hours at the same time they increased potential maximum hours and reduced penalty rates and casual loadings, offering instead higher rates of ordinary pay and comfortable union-friendly clauses which entrenched the SDA to the exclusion of other unions.[105] The similarities to the food processing enterprise bargains discussed in the previous chapter are striking. Closer examination of a few of these agreements which I deem representative is warranted.

In early 1997, the SDA came to an agreement with Coles/Bi-Lo supermarkets, which, along with Woolworths (and to a lesser extent Franklins), had established a near-stranglehold on the Australian grocery retail scene.[106] The agreement, which operated for five years starting from 1 March 1997, provided for a series of staggered pay increases at six-month intervals which, over the life of the agreement, amounted to $93.30 for full-time adult service assistants (an effective pay rise of 21.65 per cent over the life of the agreement).[107] A range of allowances, such as those for freezer work and first aid skills, were also increased by 4 per cent per annum.[108] Against these headline improvements in pay, however, were counterposed a suite of developments harmful to retail workers, most particularly part-time and casual staff. The agreement reproduced the trends towards the de-regulation of trading hours playing out in the award system by further extending the spread of ordinary hours. Ordinary hours Monday to Friday were now stipulated as 5.00 a.m. until midnight (previously 5.00 a.m. to 10.00 p.m.) while the span of Sunday hours blew out to 7.00 a.m. until 8.00 p.m. (previously 8.00 a.m. to 6.00 p.m.).[109] This extension of hours was accompanied by a degradation in the conditions of those who would primarily work these unsocial hours, namely casual and part-time employees. For the former, the casual loading was decreased from 22 per cent to 20 per cent, done so with the explicit recognition that this was 'in line with many other agreements in retail and in industry generally'.[110] For the latter, the maximum number of hours that could be worked in a four-week cycle before the attraction of penalty rates rose from 128 to 144.[111] Both casuals and part-timers suffered from the continued reduction in penalty rates. Given the intensity of the issue of Saturday penalty rates we have explored in this chapter, it is a telling feature of this agreement that work from 5.00 a.m. until 10.00 p.m. on a Saturday attracted no penalty rate at all.[112]

The framework of change apparent in this agreement was very much the standard pattern of enterprise bargaining with major retailers. It was reproduced almost exactly in two major enterprise agreements struck in 1997 and 2000 between the SDA and discount department store Big W (a division of the Woolworths group). The 1 November 1997 agreement provided pay increases of between $41.35 and $47.85 for full-time adult employees (an effective rise of 9.9 per cent), depending upon their classification grade.[113] However, this headline pay increase for full-time employees was accompanied by a reduction in the loading for casual employees from 23 per cent to 20 per cent, while penalties for Saturday work were further eroded.[114] Importantly, the agreement institutionalised precarity by including a temporary employment clause that vested management with 'the right to engage employees on a temporary employment basis as either full-time or part-time employees', so long as the period of employment was not less than a month and not longer than a year.[115]

The 2000 agreement closely resembled its predecessor in terms of the contours of change. Full-time adult employees at the 'Retail Associate' grade saw their weekly pay packets increase by $48.90, or 10.12 per cent over the two year life-span of the agreement.[116] The usual trade-offs, however, applied with full force. The span of ordinary hours was widened, now encompassing 6.00 a.m. to midnight week days (previously 7.00 a.m. to midnight) and 6.00 a.m. to 10.00 p.m. on Saturday (a substantial increase on the preceding span of 8.00 a.m. to 6.00 p.m.).[117] The already scanty Saturday penalty rate existent in the previous agreement was further reduced; henceforth, the only rate that would apply would be a 25 per cent loading on work from 10.00 p.m. to midnight.[118] Perhaps most significant for my analysis were the new arrangements governing the deployment of part-time labour. In particular, it was stipulated that

> maximum weekly hours have been increased from 32 hours (128 over four weeks) to 36 hours (144 over four weeks).
>
> Minimum hours have reduced from 10 to 9 a week, or 36 hours over four weeks.
>
> The additional hours loading has decreased from 20 to 15 per cent.[119]

This clause came to the nub of changes in the retail sector in the transition from antipodean Fordism to liberal-productivism. It combined within itself substantial labour intensification and increased insecurity at work. Retail labour was forced to sell itself over a greater range of hours and with ever-decreasing benefits/premiums at exactly the same time that the *assurance* of this labour was eroded. Enterprise bargaining encodes, validates and facilitates the precarious wage-labour nexus of liberal-productivism, and forms an important plank in the latter's labour law regime. Given the fact that both of these representative agreements achieved at the stroke of a pen employer demands which had served as the basis of intense disputes in the 1980s, it is both a logical and a historical point that enterprise bargaining in the context of union decline is a central, as opposed to casual, structure in this transition phase.

It is also worth mentioning here the incidence of a new form of employment arrangement established by the 1991 act, namely statutory part-time work contracts that could formally derogate from the award. These agreements could be made prior to any pre-existing employment arrangement (in other words, they could be stipulated as a condition of employment) and operated outside any award provision otherwise restricting part-time employment, such as quotas, proportions clauses and minimum/maximum work hours provisions.[120]

The Minister for Industrial Relations tried to paint the availability of these arrangements as an outcome beneficial to both employers and workers, claiming the latter would be able to better balance their working and family/social life.[121] However, in elaborating the situation the part-time contracts were meant to address, he implicitly acknowledged that precarity is a central characteristic of a liberal-productivist model of development and that juridic fetters to its development must be removed. He stated, 'While there has been a strong growth in the incidence of part-time work in recent years, many awards either make no provision for part-time work or impose substantial restrictions on part-time work. . . . These restrictions not only limit the amount of part-time work available; they also mean that part-time work is often only available on a casual or temporary basis'.[122] An ALP parliamentarian succinctly grasped the elemental relationship between increased precarity and the changing labour law regime when he asked of the legislation: 'If common interests are so satisfactorily served by part-time work, why is it necessary to remove award protections?'[123]

Given the increasing incidence and insecurity of part-time retail work, it comes as no surprise that retail employers made numerous attempts to avail themselves of this new instrument. The SDA quickly appreciated the danger, with NSW State Secretary Joe de Bruyn stating that 'part-time contracts have emerged as the most serious threat to shop employees from the State Government's industrial legislation'.[124] In particular, the agreements threatened the increasingly scanty minimum and maximum limits of weekly part-time employment, the minimum daily engagement period of three hours, and opened the door for split-shift rostering on the part of retailers.[125]

In the event, the SDA appears to have been able to successfully hold the line against wide-scale deployment of part-time contracts. Attempts in this direction by major retailers such as David Jones resulted in court action, which served to clarify the rights of retail employees and made it incumbent upon employers to make known to workers the entitlements they were sacrificing. The true significance of the part-time contract provisions was institutional, in that they validated and extended spaces that existed largely outside the regulatory reach of the NSW Industrial Commission. For the first time, the principle was established that individual employees (as opposed to collective groups of workers engaged in enterprise bargaining) could have terms and conditions of employment that effectively derogated from the prevailing award: an award, I have demonstrated, that was itself being degraded under the impulses of structural efficiency and modernisation. Given the discussion throughout this book of the contrast between the collective subjects of administration and the individual subject of the abstract legal form, it is unsurprising that this early effort at individualisation was a statutory one, overseen by the ordinary court system as opposed to the traditional arbitral tribunal.

Instruments like the NSW part-time contracts were essentially precursor elements of a broader process of national labour law change, institutional experiments that presaged the development of the notorious federal scheme of Australian Workplace Agreements (AWAs). These had been in existence since 1996, but it was only with the passage of the WorkChoices legislation that their existence took on the parameters of an existential threat to the award system. For this and other reasons, WorkChoices and its successor, the Fair Work Act, mark the end point of my investigation into the evolution of precarity in the NSW retail sector.

2006 ONWARDS – WORKCHOICES AND AFTER

In chapter 6 I examined the WorkChoices legislation generally, noting how it was a watershed moment in the history of Australian industrial relations. Here I am concerned with the specific features of the regime that were of significance for the instruments and modality of labour law regulation of the NSW retail sector, particularly insofar as these developments further entrenched retail precarity. Of central importance in this regard was the recasting of the constitutional basis upon which federal industrial relations regulation was erected, a further undermining of the award system as the basis for enterprise bargaining, and a qualitative and quantitative intensification of AWAs. Combined, these forces did not so much amount to a revolution for retail as an extension and deepening of the structural changes elucidated in this chapter.

The first, and perhaps most important, impact of WorkChoices on the retail sector was its recasting of industrial regulation on the basis of the corporations power. Reliance on the corporations power meant that federal government legislation could now capture all employees of constitutional corporations, save that residue of employees directly employed by state governments and local councils. This development definitively foreclosed the long chapter of state-based regulation of the retail sector, as the vast majority of retail establishments now came within the purview of the Commonwealth. Although the reformulation of industrial relations in the NSW retail sector was deeply imbricated in the evolution of the mode of regulation at a national level, it had exhibited its own unique character, a product of the path-dependencies and cultural frames of the supporting institutional fabric, particularly the NSW Industrial Commission. WorkChoices radically swung the centre of industrial gravity to the federal level, and from this point on, the key determinants of industrial outcomes for the NSW retail sector were to be located there.

One of the principal impacts of WorkChoices was on the content of enterprise agreements in the retail sector. A major study of WorkChoices-era retail and hospitality collective agreements[126] from New South Wales, Victoria and Queensland revealed just how corrosive the majority of agreements were for employees' pay and conditions, with the majority discarding or reducing previously obtaining entitlements.[127] Of the 339 agreements analysed, 80 per cent removed annual leave loading, 76 per cent removed Saturday penalty rates, 71 per cent did away with Sunday penalty rates, 68 per cent disposed of overtime rates and 60 per cent removed public holiday penalty rates, all notionally 'protected award conditions'.[128] Certain other non-protected conditions suffered a similar fate, particularly those that fettered the deployment of casual and part-time labour and/or placed a premium upon its use. For example, a staggering 74 per cent of agreements decreased the loading paid to casuals, 62 per cent expunged limits on part-time hours, 62 per cent removed one- to four-week hours averaging[129] and 56 per cent removed minimum part-time daily hours.[130] The authors of the study pithily noted of the impacts on vulnerable part-time and casual employees, 'over time the award system has devised a number of basic standards designed to give such workers enforceable rights. Under *Work Choices*, none of these are guaranteed. Agreements in retail and hospitality have largely removed those protections'.[131]

The removal of these protections not only changed the terms upon which casual and part-time labour was deployed; it imposed a real cut to the earnings of retail workers. Modelling ten different scenarios based on commonly used rosters in the retail sector, falls in pay of between 1 per cent and 12 per cent occurred across the three categories of full-time, permanent part-time and casual employees.[132] When disaggregated on the basis of classification, the results are even starker, with 'part-time workers and casuals generally doing far worse than permanent full-time workers'.[133] The three casual scenarios saw a maximum percentage loss of earnings of 14.9 per cent, 37.4 per cent and 38.2 per cent, and embraced 75.3 per cent, 85.4 per cent and 84.6 per cent of agreements, respectively.[134] Although the percentage of agreements cutting earnings for permanent part-time workers was marginally lower than was the case for casuals (ranging between 64.9 per cent and 87.7 per cent), the average fall in earnings was even worse.[135]

Perhaps the most graphic demonstration of the continued significance of retail unionism, pliable as this had proven in the 1980s, 1990s and 2000s, was the gross disparity in the terms and conditions of enterprise agreements negotiated by a union compared to those that did not have union input. Evesson et al. note, ‘Union Collective agreements have overwhelming [*sic*] retained the protected award matters. About 90 percent of union agreements have kept most of these provisions’.[136] Moreover, the pay increases obtaining in union agreements, although generally modest, were still ‘consistently superior to that prevailing for those covered by non-union agreements’.[137] The SDA was even successful in retaining many of the clauses rendered unenforceable by WorkChoices (such as those surrounding dispute resolution and union rights), persuading some employers to sign memoranda of understanding (potentially enforceable in common law) preserving rights and entitlements.[138]

Perhaps it was the case that the major retailers, with whom the majority of the union-negotiated enterprise agreements were struck, had squeezed enough out of the SDA in the award modernisation and enterprise bargaining rounds of the 1990s and early 2000s to avoid risking the industrial relations troubles that could have resulted from large-scale efforts to sideline the union.[139] Given that the union density rate in food retailing in 2006 was approximately 32.4 per cent (much higher than the prevailing general rate in retail of 18.7 per cent), an outright confrontation with the SDA made little sense when so much had already been achieved with their active co-operation.[140]

Outside the sphere of collective bargaining, we are confronted by AWAs, the statutory individual contracts which were given a much wider and more flexible sphere of operation under the WorkChoices regime. The evidence of the wage and condition-degrading character of AWAs is abundant and damning, as was demonstrated in chapter 6. There is also a plethora of examples of retail employers attempting to avail themselves of the cost-cutting potential of AWAs, with NSW workplaces being well represented among them.[141] However, the quantitative incidence of AWAs in the retail sector, and the impact of WorkChoices upon it, is less than clear, thanks largely to the secrecy of the Office of the Employment Advocate. However, the federal Workplace Relations Minister, Kevin Andrews, noted in July 2005 (several months before WorkChoices was passed) that 16 per cent of AWAs approved in the previous three months had been in the retail sector.[142] Moreover, figures released demonstrated that the retail sector in 2007 had the highest number and concentration of AWAs of any industry.[143]

Despite the explosion of AWAs in the sector, however, aggregate ABS figures demonstrate the continued importance of awards and collective agreements. Although the secular pattern since figures were first collected in 2000 suggests a gradual diminution in award-only dependence, this level remains well above almost every other industry, while there has been a steady increase in the proportion of workers covered by collective agreements.[144] Given the fact that the latter included non-union agreements (which, as has been seen, produced poor wage and conditions outcomes for retail workers), it is not surprising that many retail employers appeared nonplussed in the dying days of WorkChoices, when renewed interest in non-union bargains appeared to forestall an anticipated rush on the part of retail employers to sign workers on to AWAs.[145]

Regarding the continued prevalence of awards in the sector, this result is actually quite easily explicable. Firstly, it has been demonstrated that retail capital had already achieved fundamental changes in the structure and content of industrial regulation through the vehicle of awards and collective agreements. Together with the broader degradation of the award system across state and federal jurisdictions, retail awards were thus rendered much less than what they had once been. Secondly, the structure of the industry itself ensures that individual agreements would have a very hard time displacing awards entirely. Although controlled by large retailers in terms of market share, the retail sector remains dominated quantitatively by small enterprises in a highly competitive environment, businesses with few resources to dedicate to a specialised understanding of the legal architecture within which workplace bargaining operates. Burgess, Sullivan and Strachan note that 'for such small businesses . . . awards are a convenient framework for determining pay and conditions'.[146]

The repeal of WorkChoices and its replacement by the Fair Work Act is the end point of the analysis here. In terms of the forces of retail precarity and enhanced managerial prerogative traced in this chapter, nothing was fundamentally changed by the passage of the legislation. Institutionally, the greatest innovation was the process of award modernisation, which saw the creation of approximately 120 modern awards, including the General Retail Industry Award and the Fast Food Industry Award. Based on the corporations power, these essentially had common rule effect, and definitively supplanted the state-based retail awards from 1 July 2010. Conspicuously absent were the proportions clauses governing juniors, part-timers and casuals, part-time minimum hours, Saturday penalty rates and official recognition of the SDA as the relevant union which had characterised the NSW Shop Employees (State) Award.

Perhaps the most graphic example of the changed fortunes of retail workers over the course of the study period is the continual degradation of minimum shift provisions. It has been seen that minimum shifts for part-time and casual retail workers were reduced from four hours to three in NSW, with the new modern awards reproducing the latter state of affairs. As if this were not enough, retailers have since at least 2010 been arguing for a decrease in the minimum shift duration, claiming 'the three-hour minimum did not accommodate young workers who could work for only two hours between the end of school and closing time'.[147] Although rebuffed by the Fair Work Commission in the first and second instance (much to employer chagrin),[148] three times proved a charm for the retailers, who were granted the right by the tribunal to schedule secondary-school students for mere ninety-minute shifts.[149] The case demonstrated just how thoroughly the language and ideology of neo-liberalism had colonised the fundamentally transformed federal tribunal, with Vice President Watson accepting the thoroughly neo-liberal prescription that the degradation of standards would encourage employers to increase employment, despite acknowledging that the strength of this change, and its impact on other workers, was 'unclear'.[150]

Few examples can better demonstrate the evolution of the wage-labour nexus in the retail sector, and its crystallisation in the mode of regulation. From the late-flowering of the standard employment model in retail in the early 1970s, we have arrived at a point where an institution which played a leading role in the fabric of antipodean Fordism has codified in the recast award system a particularly rabid form of precarity, whereby the most vulnerable (and cheapest) group of employees are accorded scant protection in terms of their working hours. Such a state of affairs would simply have been unthinkable in the 1970s and 1980s, bound as they were by the declining but still significant structures and understandings of the antipodean Fordist model of development.

CONCLUSIONS

In this chapter, I have traced the complex history of award and legislative regulation surrounding the wage-labour nexus in the NSW, and later national, retail sector. The most basal axis of change has been the substitution of a liberal-productivist wage-labour nexus for its antipodean Fordist predecessor. If the essence of this change could be distilled into one word, it is 'precarity': the degradation of the model of standard, full-time employment and the crisis tendencies it set in motion for capital through the dialectical evolution of antipodean Fordism. Associated with this development has been the enhancement of managerial prerogative over the control and engagement of workers in the organisation of the labour process.

In the NSW retail sector, this process has taken varying forms since the 1980s, but always moving, albeit unevenly and at times haltingly, towards the end of greater flexibility and insecurity for retail workers. By the late 1970s, it was becoming clear that the labour utilisation and employment portfolios of retailers was changing rapidly, with an increased reliance upon casual, and often junior, labour manifesting itself. It was only in the very late 1970s and

1980s, however, that the transformations of this industrial structure assumed a legal form. In a context of general union strength, a sympathetic ALP state government, divisions in the ranks of retail capital and an SDA somewhat more militant than it would later become, the flexibilisation of employment was partially handled by a unique institutional configuration, the Retail Trade Industrial Tribunal. This unique body, which combined the juridical structure of the arbitration system with a corporatist practice, was part of the broader intensification of antipodean Fordist institutions to negotiate an escape from crisis. The Tribunal attempted to reconcile new employment practices, such as extended trading hours and broadened part-time work, with a continued dedication to the basic pattern of standard, full-time work, confined within reasonably social hours.

In the event, the Tribunal proved to be one of Lipietz's 'crippled monstrosities',[151] actively subverted by retail employers who were dissatisfied with its awards. Any potential the Tribunal possessed of encouraging a new modality of retail industrial relations was frittered away in jurisdictional squabbles with the NSW Industrial Commission and the Court of Appeal, both of which tended to be forums more receptive to employer demands for lower penalty rates, reduced fetters on the employment of casual and junior workers and easier access to part-time labour. The vehicle of these changes, however, remained the traditional award system, even when employers sought to bypass the Tribunal through accessing courts of ordinary standing.

It was not until the early 1990s that a new modality of industrial relations for the retail sector started to cohere. The processes of structural efficiency reform and award modernisation substantially degraded the Shop Employees (State) Award, intensifying precarity through the spread of ordinary trading hours, reducing minimum shift lengths for casuals and cutting daily and weekly minimum hours for part-timers. This pattern was essentially reproduced, albeit usually with a wage premium, in the enterprise bargaining encouraged by the Industrial Relations Act, Industrial Relations Reform Act and Workplace Relations Act. Such agreements in the 1990s and 2000s were underpinned by a progressively stripped-down award and increasingly supplemented by forms of individual agreements, like the NSW part-time agreement contracts and AWAs.

WorkChoices and the Fair Work Act both marked the end of the state-based character of retail regulation, which had been progressively diluted from the early 1990s anyhow, as enterprise bargaining increasingly took place in the federal sphere. The apotheosis of this new modality is the modern retail and fast-food awards, which frame bargaining in the now-nationally regulated retail sector. Compared to the Shop Employees (State) Award's quantitative controls of junior and casual labour, guarantee of reasonable minimum and maximum hours for part-time workers, wide array of penalty rates for unsocial work, and institutionalised union role, the silence of modern awards on these matters is deafening. The antipodean Fordist wage-labour nexus, so lately implanted in the retail sector, was attacked before it had a chance to fully take root. It is the irony of history that it is this belatedness that has positioned an industry like retail as a new liberal-productivist lead sector. The pattern of precarity perfected in these sectors has ramifications far outside their boundaries, reflected in their new role as 'IR pace setters'.[152] As early as the late 1970s, retail carried within itself the essence of the liberal-productivist wage-labour nexus. The realisation of this essence through the patterns of labour law change is a central, organic plank in the transition to liberal-productivism, an understanding that reiterates the defining thread of this book: that the process of transition is an inherently legal phenomenon.

Chapter 10

Conclusion

I began this book with a quote from the renowned labour law scholar, Otto Kahn-Freund. He stated, 'The ever-changing forces of society incessantly mould and transform the law and yet it pretends to stand aloof and prides itself on its immutability in a tumultuous world. While it seems to be a spectator of the great social drama, serene and imperturbable, it suffers all the agonies and fights all the struggles of an actor in the play'.[1] Within this statement there are two central, dialectically related points. On the one hand, there is the notion that law, despite the pretence of its form, is moulded by its social context; on the other, that it is not just an observer of social change, but is instead one of its actors.

In this book, I have demonstrated the truth of both of these contentions so far as post–World War II Australian labour law is concerned. I have shown that a labour law regime is deeply imbricated in the model of development of which it is part. The specific ways in which the abstract function of labour law, the commodification of labour power, are exercised within different capitalist epochs is inexplicable without an understanding of the architecture of those epochs. In particular, it is very hard to elucidate the concrete roles of a labour law regime without grasping the mechanisms of coherence and trajectories of crisis opened by the model of development of which it is part. At the same time, an account of a model of development that does not include consideration of labour law is necessarily incomplete, precisely because law, as a juridic form of capital, has a central role in constituting it.

Having nearly come to the end of the analysis, it is necessary to reflect upon the implications of the approach taken and the utility of the theoretical model of labour law I have constructed.

THE UTILITY OF THE PARISIAN REGULATION APPROACH FOR PERIODISING AUSTRALIAN CAPITALISM

In chapter 2, I described the spiralling method of theory construction that lies at the heart of sophisticated regulationist work. This method demands a dialectical interaction between the abstract and the concrete, with theoretical concepts serving to elucidate key causal structures and relationships, while empirical study comments upon the adequacy of these concepts. This is an iterative process, whereby the initial theoretical departure point serves as a focusing device, justifying what to study and, more importantly, how to study it. In turn, the facts thus generated reflect on the soundness, and possible shortcomings, of the theoretical approach, which can then be modified if necessary.

This exercise has been a guiding thread of this book. Chapters 2 and 3 represented the most abstract departure point. In chapter 2, I explored the history, methodology and concepts of the Parisian Regulation Approach (PRA), emphasising how it could provide theoretically rigorous mid-range studies of particular capitalist epochs, cognisant of the longer-term crisis tendencies of capitalism yet accounting for stabilising forces in the short to medium term (a capacity, I noted, that could only be realised by restoring the regulation approach to its Marxist foundation). Just as significantly, I constructed law and the state as juridic forms of capitalist production and exchange relations, and as such part of the basket of invariant features characterising the capitalist mode of production. This understanding is perfectly commensurable with regulationist analysis and provides the tools to overcome what is perceived as an historic neglect of the law and the state.

Chapter 3 was dedicated to further expounding this theory of law as a juridic form. It was demonstrated that, although the rudimentary legal form is implicit in commodity exchange, its full development into an axiomatic system of abstract, universal and formal norms regulating juridically equal citizens is a specifically capitalist phenomenon. This abstract legal form, however, is constantly proven inadequate in the commodification of labour power as the law of ‘things’, contract and property law, attempts to subsume the living, breathing and thinking proletarian. Class struggle can tear holes in this abstract legal form, which can force the state to plug these gaps with administrative solutions, producing institutions and practices which take as their reference point collective subjects such as industrial organisations, and whose subject matter is often specific. I argued law and administration form two poles of a law-administration continuum, whose exact configuration is intimately tied to a model of development. In particular, the method by which the latter handles and orders the contradictions of capitalism, derives coherence and embeds or excludes working-class power fixes the nexus point of this continuum.

In chapter 4, I took key concepts, namely the Fordist and liberal-productivist ideal-typical models of development, and sensitised them to the Australian context, revealing two more concrete models: antipodean Fordism, stretching from 1945 to the early 1970s; and liberal-productivism, which had begun to cohere in the late 1980s and early 1990s and remains on foot today. I then illuminated the abstract roles and functions of labour law within these models of development.

Chapters 5 and 6 provided the concrete history of the general evolution of post–World War II Australian labour law. Utilising a 'slice' approach, the state of four key themes (wage fixation, forms of employment/flexibility, collectivism/individualism together with the scale of industrial relations, and the broader legal matrix) was investigated at key dates coinciding with the coherence and crisis of antipodean Fordism and the emergence and coherence of liberal-productivism. I demonstrated that both antipodean Fordism and liberal-productivism possessed their own regimes of labour law, which clearly executed the key functions of labour law within the ideal-types, yet did so in unique ways.

Chapters 7, 8 and 9 focused even closer on certain sectors as case studies to sharpen some of the more important claims. In chapter 7, I traced the ascent and decline of the antipodean Fordist cycle of wage and conditions flow-on centred on the metal trades, one of its central dynamics. The institutionalisation of this process between the end of World War II and the early 1960s, and its subsequent destruction from the 1980s onwards, were key moments in the constitution of antipodean Fordism and liberal-productivist labour law, respectively. Chapter 8 studied the emergence of the precarity, intensified managerial prerogative and work reorganisation central to the liberal-productivist wage-labour nexus and industrial paradigm in the food processing sector. After first accounting for the emergence of Fordist forms in the New South Wales retail sector, chapter 9 studies much the same processes as chapter 8. Taken together, chapters 8 and 9 demonstrated the similarity of outcomes and patterns of change in two completely different industries, strengthening my theory of transition by demonstrating that liberal-productivist tendencies have taken hold of the workforce at large.

The findings in chapters 5–9 demonstrate the soundness of the theoretical concepts forwarded in chapters 2–4, as well as indicating that the sensitisation process of chapter 4 accurately captured both the specificity of Australian capitalism and the fact it was bound by the general logic of the abstract Fordist and liberal-productivist models of development.

Below I will discuss the specific relevance of this theoretical soundness for legal theory. What is more significant here is the fact that the regulationist periodisation schema I have deployed has been validated, at least as far as this study has gone. The periods of antipodean Fordist and liberal-productivist functionality clearly accord with distinct labour law regimes, while the phase of most dramatic legal change closely matches the proposed timeline of institutional searching. To echo Treuren, empirical study has thus established the adequacy of the theory.[2]

This validation has far-reaching implications outside of the study of labour law. Antipodean Fordism and liberal-productivism depended for their coherence on a whole basket of legal, industrial, technological, political and cultural structures and practices. Having outlined in a rigorous and systematic manner the internal structure of these models of development, particularly regarding their underlying industrial paradigms, accumulation regimes and modes of regulation, the interrelationship of these structures and practices becomes much clearer. More broadly, the utility of the PRA for studying Australian capitalism has been affirmed. Given the generally limited impact the PRA has made in Australian scholarship, my work joins that of researchers like Lloyd, Chester, Broomhill and Treuren in clearly demonstrating the utility of the approach in studying Australian capitalism.[3] By firmly re-attaching the PRA to its Marxist roots, I can match the empirical richness and useful modelling of these authors with greater theoretical rigor.

In an even broader sense, I hope that the method of deploying regulationist concepts, and their placement within a rigorous hierarchy of abstraction, will contribute towards the reinvigoration of the approach. There is no doubt that, since its heyday in the 1980s and early 1990s, regulation theory has lost some of its shine (a development I attribute to the progressive abandonment of its Marxist foundations).[4] However, the approach is undergoing something of a renaissance, as critical scholars explicitly reposition it in-line with its Marxist heritage and seek to deepen and intensify its method.[5] Part of this effort has involved subjecting to regulationist analysis structures which have historically been under-explored and/or inadequately explained, such as the state and law. This book is a contribution towards this ongoing international project of regulationist revitalisation. This project is not one of mere academic interest. In this era of rapid political-economic change, an ability to grasp the continuities and ruptures in the fabric of capitalism, along with the political opportunities and dangers thus opened, is of the highest importance for progressive forces. This nuanced understanding is of special significance in our approach to labour law specifically, and law more generally.

THE UNION OF THE PRA AND A THEORY OF JURIDIC FORMS

The chief innovation of this book is the unification of this rejuvenated regulation approach with a theory of law as a juridic form of capital. I argued in chapters 2 and 3 that this fusion created a powerful theoretical synthesis that addressed shortcomings both approaches suffer from singularly. On the first score, the realisation that capital has a juridic, as well as economic, existence compelled us to acknowledge that the state and law were part of the basket of invariant features of the capitalist mode of production, in the absence of which it would be incorrect to speak of a capitalist society. This understanding should serve as a useful corrective to the relative historical neglect of law in PRA-inspired work. If a mode of regulation is a concrete arrangement of juridic forms, as I stated in chapter 2, then law must become a central focus of regulationist work. Moreover, this work cannot merely study law as a derivative institution regulating a broader capitalist economy. Rather, law must be studied as a form of capital's contradictions in and of itself, with its own capacity to impart disequilibria within a model of development. The result is a considerably deepened legal perspective within the PRA, particularly regarding the mode of regulation concept.[6]

On the other hand, much Marxist-inspired jurisprudence has tended to operate at a high level of abstraction, emphasising the abstract basis and functions of law within the capitalist mode of production. Such accounts have difficulty grasping *how* these abstract functions are exercised in concrete societies. It is at this point that the intermediate-level analysis of the PRA, best represented by the model of development concept, can be of immense value to the explanatory power of the notion of juridic forms. In particular, we have seen that different models of development do not deal with all of capitalism's crisis tendencies in the same way or to the same degree. Instead, they exhibit a hierarchised pattern of institutional forms, which focuses on some crisis tendencies more than others and achieves coherence in specific ways. An appreciation of this reality allows us to specify with much greater clarity the roles and functions of labour law within a particular capitalist epoch.

In chapters 4–9, I have demonstrated the value of this theoretical synthesis in the case of Australian labour law. Both antipodean Fordism and liberal-productivism in Australia had and have a unique regime of labour law corresponding with them, a regime that not only derives its dynamic from the model of development of which it is part, but helps constitute it. In both models of development, the most abstract function of labour law, the commodification of labour power, remains constant. This will ever be the case so long as the capitalist mode of production endures.

Every model of development, however, has its own mechanisms of coherence and trajectories of crisis. Antipodean Fordism had its roots in the ruination of the Great Depression, a worldwide crisis that was a function, in large part, of working-class underconsumption and disproportionality between large-scale capitalist production in Department I and the continued importance of petty bourgeois arrangements in Department II. It thus crystallised the wage-labour nexus as the site of primary contradiction and demanded for its coherence the placement of adequate purchasing power in the hands of the proletariat. In this fact is one of the keys to understanding the logic and structure of the Australian labour law regime during the antipodean Fordist phase. Chapter 4 demonstrated that for this nexus to both take shape and function, a series of legal conditions were necessary, namely those that allowed for the diffusion of wage increases from lead sectors, permitted collective and connective bargaining, encouraged the organisation of labour and developed a notion of a standard employment model.

These requirements undergirded the key features of this regime, namely a permissive attitude towards organised labour, bargaining between capital and labour at a broad occupational level, the diffusion of wage gains from leading sectors through the award framework and the growth of administrative fixes to heightened worker power. I demonstrated that the arbitration system was the central pivot of the whole regime, precociously institutionalising the antipodean Fordist wage-labour nexus, and was emblematic of a law-administration continuum where, so far as labour law was concerned, the latter was predominant. In particular, compulsory arbitration at this time facilitated the pattern of flow-on from the industrially strong to the industrially weak, further developed and diffused standard employment, and strongly integrated organised labour into the fabric of the law and the state, all essential planes of coherence in antipodean Fordism.

In the 1970s and early 1980s, however, these same features of compulsory arbitration had become deeply dysfunctional, setting in motion large, destabilising wage-rounds and entrenching trade union power at a time when it was pressing against and outside traditional arbitral channels. Liberal-productivism in Australia was thus born of a crisis rooted at least partially in the power of organised labour and its integration into the labour law regime, as well as the grating of national state boundaries against growing transnational capital. Within this model of development, the antipodean Fordist wage-labour nexus is displaced, reconstructed as a cost of international production and predicated on precarity. The liberal-productivist labour law regime, combining hostility to trade unions, a destruction of the conciliation and arbitration system in favour of individualisation, a severing of the institutional links homogenising the wage structure, erosion of the standard employment model and intensified juridification, helps constitute the fabric of the new model of development. The law-administration continuum is reconfigured, as the administrative structures of arbitration give way to the purer legal form, with the latter's focus on abstract, juridically equal citizen-subjects marginalising administration's collective subjects and practices.

It is the synthesis of these two bodies of theory that has allowed the generation of a theoretically rigorous yet empirically rich account of the evolution of Australian labour law. Counterposed to the traditionally abstract nature of Marxist jurisprudence is the theoretical impoverishment of most contemporary work on Australian labour law. This has generally not gone beyond the descriptive point that the rise of neo-liberalism has been associated with legal change that has disempowered organised labour, promoted individualism and generally intensified employment precarity and greater inequality in outcomes.[7] Accounts in this tradition generally rest upon a conspiratorial view of labour law change, whereby economic rationalists hijacked the state in the 1980s and 1990s and were able to pass laws (which are typically depicted as passive and reactive) reflecting their ideological world view. By uniting the PRA with a theory of law as a juridic form of capital, I have been able to integrate the economic, political and legal/state dimensions of Australia's evolving political economy in a deeper, more organic fashion. This, in turn, has elucidated actual causal relationships between labour law and models of development, far beyond the traditionally descriptive accounts of labour law and industrial relations scholarship.

Importantly, the union of the PRA and the theory of juridic forms has a much wider application than the study of Australian labour law. The process of sensitising ideal-typical models of development to particular contexts reveals a myriad of concrete instantiations, each with their own unique institutional path-dependencies, differing states of productive forces and histories of class struggle. Even within the framework of a common model of development, these idiosyncrasies act as a refractive layer, ensuring that no two societies experience the model in the same way. At the same time, the realisation that different societies are bound by the logic of an ideal-typical model of development focuses attention on similarities in evolution and outcomes.

Labour law is a particularly striking example of this reality. As outlined in chapter 4, the abstract Fordist wage-labour nexus required a number of legal preconditions to function. However, an appreciation of the diversity of labour law regimes of Fordist countries demonstrates that more than one concrete form was compatible with these functions. For example, although the Australian arbitration system and the traditional Swedish pattern of national-level wage and conditions negotiations fulfilled roughly the same functions of wage and conditions flow-on and homogenisation of the wage structure, they had very different modes of operation and institutional histories.[8] An even better example can be found closer to home. New Zealand was the only country in the world that shared with Australia an industrial relations system premised on compulsory arbitration, industrial tribunals and awards. Moreover, it explicitly turned to Australia as an exemplar of Fordist development.[9] Nevertheless, due to a host of institutional peculiarities and economic differences, the crisis of New Zealand Fordism's labour law regime and its replacement by a liberal-productivist successor assumed a far more rapid and violent character than was the case in Australia.[10] There, the destruction of awards, outlawing of the closed shop and the creation of a voluntary system of individual and collective agreements were achieved virtually at the stroke of a pen with the passage of the Employment Contracts Act 1991 (NZ). The same developments in Australia generally occurred in a more gradated fashion over a period of years. Even in the case of two countries that shared a unique institutional heritage, therefore, substantial differences in the tempo and degree of labour law change resulted.

However, the fact that broadly similar fundamental changes have been observed across Fordist countries indicates that there are common impulses at play. Despite the institutional differences and varying economic structures of Australia, the UK and the USA, for example, the overall pattern of increased precarity, marginalisation of trade unions, the erosion of administrative structures and worsening inequality and polarity in the wage structure is common to all three.[11] Collins' description of the emergence of business competitiveness as the dominant theme of labour law echoes throughout these countries, an indicator of the repositioning of competition as a site of dominant contradiction within liberal-productivism.[12]

This dual reality demonstrates two crucial points: the logic of a model of development encourages a degree of convergent evolution in labour law regimes; and, the latter nevertheless retain their own unique, historically conditioned character. The process of sensitising the ideal-typical models of Fordism and liberal-productivism to the Australian context reveals labour law regimes that clearly execute the key abstract functions of labour law in both models, yet do so in concretely unique ways. The same reality would hold for other countries subsumed by the logic of these models of development. Indeed, this must necessarily be the case, given the fact that in chapters 2 and 4 I noted that a model of development, when pitched at the ideal-typical level, does not grasp the concrete experience of any one society. The method of sensitisation I have adopted in this book to describe Australian labour law in a theoretically rigorous and empirically rich fashion is perfectly capable of application in other contexts and is demonstrative of one of the greatest virtues of the PRA – the ability to plot the relationship between broad capitalist epochs and specific instantiations. Such an ability both demands its middle-range analysis and presupposes the reconnection with a Marxist political economy I have argued for.

It is necessary at this point to reiterate a point made in the introduction, and particularly apparent in the early theoretical chapters. What I have generated here is a method of legal analysis, a way of looking at the labour law regimes of advanced capitalist countries from the close of World War II onwards. The logic of the Fordist and liberal-productivist models of development has governed countries as varied as the USA, UK, Canada, Germany and, of course,

Australia. In this book I have concentrated on operationalising my model of labour law change by deeply studying the Australian experience. However, the model of change itself, in particular the construction of a hierarchy of abstraction and the sensitisation of ideal-typical models to particular national contexts, is a tool that can be used in the study of the labour law regimes of the European and North America states that have experienced a Fordist and liberal-productivist phase. As stated in the introduction, this theoretical innovation makes this book more than a localised study of Australian capitalism; instead, it highlights the key role of labour law within the models of development that have characterised advanced capitalist states since World War II, and demonstrates the rich potential for legal analysis from within the regulationist project.

The union of the PRA and a theory of juridic forms could also be employed in describing the characteristics of law more broadly. I have focused on labour law as one of the most crucial subsets of law, the nexus point where the abstract legal form, pressed into service to commodify labour power, attempts to incorporate and regulate a living, breathing and thinking subject, the proletarian. However, as chapter 3 illuminated, the developed legal form itself is implanted in capitalist production and exchange relations. Law is an invariant feature of a capitalist society, yet I have determined, using the PRA, that some of its key predicates, such as the extent of the commodity form, the valency of market forces and, most importantly, the state and structuring of class struggle, vary between different capitalist epochs. Law generally will thus vary between these epochs. For example, the theoretical model of legal change I have developed in this book could quite easily take as its subject social security law, investigating how this body of law articulated with the broader antipodean Fordist/liberal-productivist dynamic. The same could be said of taxation law and occupational health and safety legislation.[13]

Most broadly, the synthesis of the PRA and the theory of juridic forms promises a sophisticated Marxist theory of law that overcomes the abstraction that has typically characterised even the best Marxist jurisprudence. This unified theory allows a dual movement, recognising the roots of the abstract legal form within capitalist social relations while at the same time accounting for the over-determination of its concrete manifestations. Schematically, this process begins, as I did in chapters 2 and 3, by tracing the most abstract features of the legal form within the capitalist mode of production. These features are to be considered the structural horizons of capitalist law, determining broadly what it *can and cannot be* while at the same time affording a wide space for the historical contingency consequent upon the interactions and over-determinations of capitalism's tendencies. Moving down the hierarchy of abstraction, the next step in the analysis involves ascertaining how concrete manifestations of these forms are ordered and hierarchised within distinct epochs of development, the subject matter of chapter 4. It is at this level that the PRA comes into its own, particularly through the model of development concept, which can grasp the place of law within this order of forms. Finally, at the most concrete level of investigation (as seen in chapters 5–9), an understanding must be gained as to how the concrete law of a model of development simultaneously crystallises its own unique configuration of capitalism's abstract tendencies, and relates to the trajectories of crisis it opens.

I have demonstrated the application of this theory in regards to Australian labour law, but with the appropriate sensitisation of the ideal-typical model, an understanding of the history of the particular area of law to be studied, and the specification of the means by which concrete laws articulate with the abstract goals and functions of the legal form, it can be used as an analytical tool of much broader legal compass.

POLITICAL IMPLICATIONS

Theory is necessarily and always political. For those of us working in the Marxist tradition, Marx's exhortation that the point of philosophy is not merely to describe the world, but to change it,[14] puts the political implications of our work at the centre stage. This book unashamedly holds to the view that the exploitation of the proletariat is the central dynamic of capitalism. Although it has been demonstrated that labour law can be made to register working-class power through recourse to administration, its most abstract and irreducible function, the commodification of labour-power is already, and always, a class measure, allowing the expropriation of surplus value from the worker. Even the most accommodative, administrative regime of labour law can never escape this central fact, that it is a vital moment in the process of capital arrogating to itself the fruits of the workers' labour. The concern I have for the political implications of my approach, therefore, is only the extent to which it could be used to the betterment of the working class.

Given the fact that this book is an historical study, it deals mainly with accomplished facts. However, the interpretation of the past is itself political, and the understanding of Australian labour law generated could be of value to the working class going forward. An understanding of the physiology of a labour law regime, and how it articulates with the broader dynamic of a model of development, can allow organised labour to better formulate strategies for navigating, negating and/or exploiting the limitations and opportunities presented by it. The dangers of lacking a clear vision, or sharing a vision that has been largely determined by capital, have been painfully exposed in this book. By committing itself to the Accord process and enterprise bargaining, the Australian Council of Trade Unions was buying into a conception of

Australian capitalism's crisis that saw the only solutions as wage restraint, halting of the antipodean Fordist cycle of wage and conditions flow-on, decentralisation, precarity and, perhaps most importantly, the restoration of profitability to capital. The vague conception of a Scandinavian-style social democracy envisaged by some elements of the union movement rapidly wilted in the face of governments and employers who saw with increasing clarity and focus the real thrust of the reforms they were implementing. Australian Manufacturing Workers' Union official Doug Cameron stated tellingly (in terms that, barring the discussion of award restructuring, could describe virtually any society in the transition between Fordism and liberal-productivism):

> We have sought real partnerships and been betrayed; we have promoted co-operation, not capitulation; we have benchmarked; we have introduced teams; we have talked endlessly about training and competency with almost no results for the bulk of our members; we have innovated; we have been flexible; we have restructured the Award; we have simplified the Award; we have strived for best practice in manufacturing workplaces; we have bargained and bargained and bargained. None of this has been enough for government or employers . . . the workers have been abandoned to market forces and the latest fads, such as downsizing, contracting out and re-engineering.[15]

A fuller understanding of the nature of the transformation under way could have helped organised labour perceive that the acts of flexibility, enterprise bargaining, benchmarking and workplace co-operation identified by Cameron were almost certainly going to result in the outcomes he observed, precisely because the overall vision of crisis resolution was one determined by employers and an increasingly neo-liberal state. If award restructuring, for example, had been perceived for what it was, an essential element of the roll-back of antipodean Fordist labour law and a precursor to the award system's marginalisation within liberal-productivism, unions might have been more willing to draw a line in the sand and fight harder for alternatives. The same could be said of the whole gamut of legal change in the 1980s and 1990s. Had unions and their members realised the overall direction and tenor of change, they may well have better foreseen the historic weakness they currently suffer from. Although some may argue that such a realisation is a counter-factual point of little current relevance, this is far from the truth. Appreciating the source and nature of past misapprehensions of legal development can help prevent future occurrences.

The mapping of models of development and their labour law regimes also has a more direct relationship to the future. Take liberal-productivism for instance. I have noted throughout this book that, although it is bound by the same basic tendencies and invariant features characterising all capitalist societies, it nevertheless has its own unique dynamic, range of institutions and trajectories of crisis. Given that antipodean Fordism imploded and liberal-productivism remains on foot today, it has been easier to trace the opportunities and limits the former posed to the working class. However, as noted in chapters 2 and 4, no model of development is capable of absolving capitalism of the contradictions inscribed in its DNA. Liberal-productivism is no exception. It is true that, both in Fordist countries generally and in Australia specifically, liberal-productivism was premised upon, and reproduces, an historic weakness in organised labour. The union movement in Australia is in crisis, beset by chronically dwindling density, the collapse of the standard employment model and a legal framework that constrains its ability to mobilise and engage in industrial action. However, this should not be taken to mean that class struggle is futile, or that it must be directed to the end of restoring antipodean Fordism.

Chapters 4 and 5 in particular demonstrated that the antipodean Fordist labour law regime was characterised by the degree to which trade unions were integrated into its fabric. Although this secured a privileged institutional position for organised labour, it also encouraged the growth of bureaucratic and moderate 'arbitral unionism'.[16] To gain access to the system through registration, unions had to make themselves subject to a profound level of state regulation over their industrial behaviour and internal workings. Moreover, arbitral unionism engendered an industrially lazy, dependent attitude on the part of many unions, who depended for their strength not on thorough, organic organisation of the rank and file, but instead on their standing before the Commission and closed-shop arrangements.

Liberal-productivism, by contrast, has transformed the tight embrace between labour law and trade unionism into a cool, often hostile, arms-length relationship. Although unions have not been *de jure* expelled from the system, they have been relegated to the role of unwanted third parties who are faced with the same (if not greater) imposts of registration without anything like the rewards that accrued in the antipodean Fordist era. Liberal-productivism would thus seem to be more vulnerable to a militant, community-centred trade unionism that deliberately chose to remain *outside* of the system.[17]

It has also been made clear that, despite some genuine instances where the links between the Australian Labor Party (ALP) and the union movement affected the form and degree of change, the relationship has become an increasingly fallow one for trade unions. The Hawke and Keating governments introduced many of the labour law changes that would inflict grievous damage to union strength. Moreover, the ALP's legislative baby, the Fair Work Act 2009 (Cth), has reproduced almost all of the key provisions of the draconian WorkChoices, such as its limitations on industrial action, bans on solidarity strikes, a tough right of entry code for union officials, a regime of largely individualistic rights and a reliance on the corporations power of the Constitution. Affiliation to the ALP thus seems no longer capable of effecting positive change, either in the labour law regime specifically or the broader course of Australian capitalism. In such a context, unions would be better served by disaffiliating from the ALP and using the money freed up for organising purposes.[18] European trade unions and their federations would similarly benefit by revising or repudiating their relationships with the social-democratic/labour parties, which have similarly reached their political limits in advancing the workers movement.

More broadly, the particular crisis tendencies of liberal-productivism render it far less stable than its Fordist predecessor. In Australia, the system is fuelled by debt, has tied the country's fortunes ever closer to the unstable currents of international production and competition, and has produced a potentially dangerous (to both itself and capital) underclass of precarious workers, what Standing has dubbed the 'precariat'.[19] The fragility of the whole edifice was revealed by the global financial crisis of 2008, while the continued slowdown of manufacturing in China has seen the hitherto high terms of trade, fuelled by mining commodity exports, decline precipitously. It may be that the boom time of liberal-productivism in Australia has come to an end; stagnation is creeping in, and crisis may be close to hand. Certainly, there is a strong case that in Europe and the USA a deep, multifaceted economic, political and social crisis is already under way, as liberal-productivism increasingly cracks up under the weight of its own contradictions. As with the decay of antipodean Fordism, such developments tend to open phases of institutional searching, periods in which competing institutions and ideologies grate against each other, and when attempts to change society's tack (short of a revolution) are most easily effected. If such a period is indeed upon us, a clear and informed conception of where we have come from is absolutely crucial to the working-class and social activist allies.

In the introduction I argued that the transition from Fordism to liberal-productivism has been characterised by a number of developments of deep concern to social justice advocates and organised labour, including escalating income inequality, the rise of a new working underclass, entrenched unemployment and the marginalisation of trade unions. Throughout this book I have let the facts speak for themselves; there can be doubt that these deeply troubling forces have increasingly taken a hold over the lives of Australian workers. An immense body of research built up over many years confirms the same for advanced capitalist countries generally. By elucidating the labour law regimes of antipodean Fordism and liberal-productivism, and the transition between them, I hope to have made one small contribution towards the clearer vision required to historically locate and combat these putrid forms of exploitation and disadvantage. The rise of liberal-productivism has been devastating for organised labour and the working class. They cannot afford a repeat in the tumultuous times to come.

Bibliography

The Age, selected dates.

Aglietta, Michel. *A Theory of Capitalist Regulation: The US Experience*. London: NLB, 1979.

Althusser, Louis. *For Marx*. Translated by Ben Brewster. London: NLB, 1977.

Althusser, Louis, and Étienne Balibar. *Reading Capital*. Translated by Ben Brewster. London: NLB, 1977.

Amalgamated Engineering Union v. Metal Trades Employers Association (1930) 28 CAR 923.

Amalgamated Society of Engineers v. Adelaide Steam-Ship Company Limited (1921) 15 CAR 297.

André, Christine. 'The Welfare State and Institutional Compromises: From Origins to Contemporary Crisis'. In *Régulation Theory: The State of the Art*, edited by Robert Boyer and Yves Saillard, 94–100. London: Routledge, 2002.

Ansett Transport Industries (Operations) Pty Ltd v. Australian Federation of Air Pilots (No 2) [1991] 2 VR 636.

Appeal re Morrison Knudsen Corp of Australia Ltd Certified Agreement 1993. In CCH, *Australian Industrial Law Review* 36(12) (16 June 1994): ¶204.

Application by Australian Chamber of Manufactures to vary the Food Preservers' Interim Award 1986. In CCH, *Australian Industrial Law Review* 33(18) (5 September 1991): ¶281.

Application by Food Preservers' (Interim) Award, 1986. In CCH, *Australian Industrial Law Review* 30(7) (8 April 1988): ¶127.

Application by Food Preservers' Union to vary Food Preservers Award. In CCH, *Australian Industrial Law Review* 22(16) (6 August 1980): ¶243.

Applications by Food Preservers' Union to vary Food Preservers' Award 1973. In CCH, *Australian Industrial Law Review* 26(7) (6 December 1984): ¶415.

Applications for variation of Shop Employees (State) Award. In CCH, *Australian Industrial Law Review* 26(18) (26 September 1984): ¶314.

Application to vary Metal Industry Award 1971. In CCH, *Australian Industrial Law Review* 24(1) (13 January 1982): ¶1.
Application to vary Metal Industry Award re hours of work. In CCH, *Australian Industrial Law Review* 23(9) (6 May 1981): ¶190.
Application to vary Nabisco Brands Pty Ltd (Cereal and Biscuit Processing etc) Award 1985. In CCH, *Australian Industrial Law Review* 32(25) (28 December 1990): ¶448.
Application to vary Transport Workers Award. In CCH, *Australian Industrial Law Review* 23(17) (26 August 1981): ¶378.
Application to vary Transport Workers Award, 1972. In CCH, *Australian Industrial Law Review* 24(3) (10 February 1982): ¶48.
Arup, Christopher, Peter Gahan, John Howe, Richard Johnstone, Richard Mitchell and Anthony O'Donnell, editors. *Labour Law and Labour Market Regulation*. Sydney, Australia: Federation Press, 2006.
Association v. Amalgamated Engineering Union (1935) 54 CLR 387.
The Australian, selected dates.
Australian Boot Trade Employees Federation v. Whybrow & Co (1910) 11 CLR 311.
Australian Bureau of Statistics. *Australian Labour Market Statistics*. 6105.0, July 2011.
Australian Bureau of Statistics. *Australian National Accounts: National Income, Expenditure and Product 1992–93*. 5204.0, 1994.
Australian Bureau of Statistics. *Australian National Accounts: National Income, Expenditure and Product*. 5206.0, March Quarter 2015, June Quarter 2015.
Australian Bureau of Statistics. *Australian Social Trends*. 4102.0, 2001, 2014.
Australian Bureau of Statistics. *Australian System of National Accounts*. 5204.0, 2008, 2012.
Australian Bureau of Statistics. *Characteristics of Employment, Australia*. 6333.0, 2014.
Australian Bureau of Statistics. *Employee Earnings and Hours*. 6306.0, 2000, 2006, 2008, 2012.
Australian Bureau of Statistics. *Employee Earnings, Benefits and Trade Union Membership*. 6310.0, 2006, 2009, 2013.
Australian Bureau of Statistics. *Forms of Employment*. 6359.0, 2011.
Australian Bureau of Statistics. *The Labour Force*. 6203.0, November 1975, December 1982, December 1989.
Australian Bureau of Statistics. *Labour Force Australia, Detailed, Quarterly*. 6291.0.55.003, May 2015.
Australian Bureau of Statistics. *Labour Statistics*. 6101.0, 1975, 1976, 1977, 1978, 1979, 1980.
Australian Bureau of Statistics. *Weekly Earnings of Employees (Distribution)*. 6310.0, 1997.
Australian Bureau of Statistics. *Year Book Australia*. 1301.0, 1973, 1974, 1976, 1980, 1982, 1984, 1986, 1988, 1992, 1994, 1996, 2001, 2005, 2010, 2012.
Australian Centre for Industrial Relations Research and Teaching. 'Agreements Database and Monitor'. No. 3, University of Sydney, 1994.

Australian Centre for Industrial Relations Research and Training. *Australia at Work: Just Managing?* Sydney, Australia: Prentice Hall, 1999.

Australian Constitution.

Australian Council of Trade Unions. 'Submission to Inquiry into independent contractors and labour hire arrangements'. House of Representatives Standing Committee on Employment, Workplace Relations and Workforce Participation, Submission No. 60, 2005.

Australian Financial Review, selected dates.

Australian Government Department of Employment. 'Trends in Federal Enterprise Bargaining – Trends Historical Table'. Accessed 14 October 2015. https://www.employment.gov.au/trends-federal-enterprise-bargaining.

Automotive, Food, Metals, Engineering, Printing and Kindred Industries Union and Simplot Australia. Transcript of proceedings, Australian Industrial Relations Commission, Case Nos. 20032 & 20072, 14 January 1998.

Balnave, Nikola, and Dennis Mortimer. 'Union Security in Retail: Legislative Intervention or Collective Agreement'. *International Journal of Employment Studies* 13(1) (2005): 81–105.

Balnave, Nikki, and Greg Patmore. 'The AMWU: Politics and Industrial Relations, 1852–2012'. In *Organise, Educate, Control: The AMWU in Australia 1852–2012*, edited by Andrew Reeves and Andrew Dettmer, 3–33. Clayton, Australia: Monash University Publishing, 2013.

Barnard, A., N. G. Butlin and J. J. Pincus. 'Public and Private Sector Employment in Australia, 1901–1974'. *Australian Economic Review* 19(1) (1977): 43–52.

Barry, Michael, and Nick Wailes. 'Revisiting the Australia-New Zealand Comparison'. *New Zealand Journal of Employment Relations* 30(3) (2005): 1–17.

Basic Wage Case (1961) 97 CAR 376.

Basic Wage Inquiry (1931) 30 CAR 2.

Basic Wage, Margins and Total Wage Cases of 1966 (1966) 115 CAR 93.

Bell, Stephen, and Brian Head. 'Australia's Political Economy: Critical Themes and Issues'. In *State, Economy and Public Policy in Australia*, edited by Stephen Bell and Brian Head, 1–24. Melbourne, Australia: Oxford University Press, 1994.

Bennett, Laura. *Making Labour Law in Australia: Industrial Relations, Politics and Law*. Sydney, Australia: The Law Book Company, 1994.

Bentley, Philip. 'Australian Trade Unionism 1970–71'. *Journal of Industrial Relations* 13(4) (1971): 405–18.

Bentley, Philip. 'Australian Trade Unionism 1973–74'. *Journal of Industrial Relations* 16(4) (1974): 374–87.

Binns, Peter. 'Law and Marxism'. *Capital & Class* 4(1) (1980): 100–113.

Blackledge, Paul. *Reflections on the Marxist Theory of History*. Manchester, UK: Manchester University Press, 2006.

Blanke, Bernhard, Ulrich Jürgens and Hans Kastendiek. 'On the Current Marxist Discussion on the Analysis of Form and Function of the Bourgeois State'. In *State and Capital: A Marxist Debate*, edited by John Holloway and Sol Picciotto, 108–47. London: Edward Arnold, 1978.

Boilermakers' Case (1924) 20 CAR 770.

Bonefeld, Werner. 'Reformulation of State Theory'. *Capital & Class* 11(3) (1987): 96–127.

Bosch, Gerhard. 'Towards a New Standard Employment Relationship in Western Europe'. *British Journal of Industrial Relations* 42(4) (2004): 617–36.

Boyer, Robert. 'How and Why Capitalisms Differ'. *Economy and Society* 34(4) (2005): 509–57.

Boyer, Robert. 'Perspectives on the Wage-Labour Nexus'. In *Régulation Theory: The State of the Art*, edited by Robert Boyer and Yves Saillard, 73–79. London: Routledge, 2002.

Boyer, Robert. 'The Political in the Era of Globalization and Finance: Focus on Some *Régulation* School Research'. *International Journal of Urban and Regional Research* 24(2) (2000): 274–322.

Boyer, Robert. *The Regulation School: A Critical Introduction*. Translated by Craig Charney. New York: Columbia University Press, 1990.

Boyer, Robert. 'Wage Formation in Historical Perspective: The French Experience'. *Cambridge Journal of Economics* 3(2) (1979): 99–118.

Boyer, Robert, and Yves Saillard. 'A Summary of Régulation Theory'. In *Régulation Theory: The State of the Art*, edited by Robert Boyer and Yves Saillard, 36–44. London: Routledge, 2002.

Bramble, Tom. 'Political Economy and the Management Strategy in the Metal and Engineering Industry'. *Journal of Industrial Relations* 31(1) (1989): 22–45.

Bramble, Tom. *Trade Unionism in Australia: A History from Flood to Ebb Tide*. Port Melbourne, Australia: Cambridge University Press, 2008.

Bramble, Tom, and Rick Kuhn. *Labor's Conflict: Big Business, Workers and the Politics of Class*. Port Melbourne, Australia: Cambridge University Press, 2011.

Braverman, Harry. *Labor and Monopoly Capital: The Degradation of Work in the Twentieth Century*. New York & London: Monthly Review Press, 1974.

Bray, Mark, and Andrew Stewart. 'From the Arbitration System to the *Fair Work Act*: The Changing Approach in Australia to Voice and Representation at Work'. *Adelaide Law Review* 34(1) (2013): 21–41.

Briggs, Chris. 'Australian Exceptionalism: The Role of Trade Unions in the Emergence of Enterprise Bargaining'. *Journal of Industrial Relations* 43(1) (2001): 27–43.

Briggs, Chris. 'The Rise and Fall of the ACTU: Maturation, Hegemony and Decline'. PhD diss., University of Sydney, 1999.

Brooks, Brian. 'Aspects of Casual and Part-Time Employment'. *Journal of Industrial Relations* 27(2) (1985): 158–71.

Broomhill, Ray. 'Australian Economic Booms in Historical Perspective'. *Journal of Australian Political Economy* 61 (2008): 12–29.

BRW, selected dates.

Buchanan, John, Gary Dymski, Julie Froud, Sukhdev Johal, Adam Leaver and Karel Williams. 'Unsustainable Employment Portfolios'. *Work, Employment and Society* 27(3) (2013): 396–413.

Bull, Sue. 'Victorian AMWU Plans Industrial Campaign'. *Green Left Weekly*, 12 June 2002. Accessed 28 January 2017. https://www.greenleft.org.au/content/victorian-amwu-plans-industrial-campaign.

Bureau of Industry Economics. *Reducing Standard Hours of Work: Analysis of Australia's Recent Experience*. Canberra, Australia: Australian Government Publishing Service, 1984.

Burgess, John, and Iain Campbell. 'Casual Employment in Australia: Growth, Characteristics, A Bridge or a Trap?'. *Economic and Labour Relations Review* 9(1) (1998): 31–54.

Burgess, John, and Iain Campbell. 'The Nature and Dimensions of Precarious Employment in Australia'. *Labour & Industry* 8(3) (1998): 5–21.

Burgess, John, Anne Sullivan and Glenda Strachan. 'Australian Workplace Agreements, EEO and Family Friendly Arrangements in the Retail Sector'. *Employment Relations Record* 4(2) (2004): 61–70.

Burwood Cinema Limited v. Australian Theatrical and Amusement Employees' Association (1925) 35 CLR 528.

Business Council of Australia Industrial Relations Study Commission. *Enterprise Based Bargaining Units: A Better Way of Working*. Melbourne, Australia: Business Council of Australia, 1989.

Byrne v. Australian Airlines Ltd (1995) 185 CLR 410.

Cadbury Schweppes Pty Ltd v. FLAIEU. In CCH, *Australian Industrial Law Review* 30(3) (11 February 1988): ¶52.

Cain, Maureen, and Alan Hunt, editors. *Marx and Engels on Law*. London: Academic Press, 1979.

Campbell, Iain. 'The Spreading Net: Age and Gender in the Process of Casualisation in Australia'. *Journal of Australian Political Economy* 45 (2000): 68–98.

Campbell, Iain, and Jenny Chalmers. 'Job Quality and Part-Time Work in the Retail Industry: An Australian Case Study'. *International Journal of Human Resource Management* 19(3) (2008): 487–500.

Canberra Times, selected dates.

Carpenters and Joiners Award, 1946 (1948) 59 CAR 957.

Carrick, Damien. 'Dandenong Crushed by Heinz Factory Closure'. Accessed 1 February 2017. http://www.abc.net.au/worldtoday/stories/s153786.htm.

Castles, Francis. 'The Wage Earners' Welfare State Revisited: Refurbishing the Established Model of Australian Social Protection, 1983–93'. *Australian Journal of Social Issues* 29(2) (1994): 120–45.

Castree, Noel, David Featherstone and Andrew Herod. 'Contrapuntal Geographies: The Politics of Organizing Across Sociospatial Difference'. In *The SAGE Handbook of Political Geography*, edited by Kevin Cox, Murray Low and Jennifer Robinson, 305–21. London: SAGE Publications, 2008.

Catanzariti, Joseph, and Shawn Wytenburg. 'Industrial Relations Legislation in 1991'. *Journal of Industrial Relations* 34(1) (1992): 128–52.

Chester, Lynne. 'Actually Existing Markets: The Case of Neoliberal Australia'. *Journal of Economic Issues* XLIV(2) (2010): 313–24.

Chester, Lynne. 'Another variety of capitalism?: The Australian mode of *regulation*'. Paper presented at the 13th Conference of the Association for Heterodox Economics, Nottingham, UK, 6–9 July, 2011.

Chester, Lynne. 'The Australian Variant of Neoliberal Capitalism'. In *Neoliberalism: Beyond the Free Market*, edited by Damien Cahill, Lindy Edwards and Frank Stilwell, 153–79. Cheltenham, UK: Edward Elgar, 2012.

Christophers, Brett. *The Great Leveler: Capitalism and Competition in the Court of Law*. Cambridge, MA: Harvard University Press, 2016.

Clark, Ian. *Governance, the State, Regulation and Industrial Relations*. London: Routledge, 2000.

Clarke, Simon. 'The Global Accumulation of Capital and the Periodisation of the Capitalist State Form'. In *Open Marxism Volume I: Dialectics and History*, edited by Werner Bonefeld, Richard Gunn and Kosmas Psychopedis, 133–50. London: Pluto Press, 1992.

Clyde Engineering Co. Ltd v. Cowburn (1926) 37 CLR 466.

Cochrane, Peter. 'Doing Time'. In *Making a Life: A People's History of Australia since 1788*, edited by Verity Burgmann and Jenny Lee, 177–93. Fitzroy, Australia: McPhee Gribble/Penguin, 1988.

Cockfield, Sandra. 'Arbitration, Mass Production and Workplace Relations: "Metal Industry" Developments in the 1920s'. *Journal of Industrial Relations* 35(1) (1993): 19–38.

Collins, Hugh. *Marxism and Law*. Oxford, UK: Clarendon Press, 1982.

Collins, Hugh. 'Regulating the Employment Relation for Competitiveness'. *Industrial Law Journal* 30(1) (2001): 17–48.

Commonwealth. *Parliamentary Debates*, House of Representatives, selected dates.

Commonwealth Bureau of Census and Statistics. *The Labour Force*. 6203.0, May 1969.

Commonwealth Bureau of Census and Statistics. *Year Book Australia*. 1301.0, 1960, 1962, 1964, 1965, 1970.

Commonwealth Conciliation and Arbitration Act 1904 (Cth).

Commonwealth Conciliation and Arbitration Act 1947 (Cth).

Confectionary Workers Union of Australia, Confectioners Award 1980 (6 December 1990) Print J5832.

Confectionary Workers Union of Australia v. Beatrice Foods. In CCH, *Australian Industrial Law Review* 30(7) (8 April 1988): ¶127.

Connolly, Ellis, and Christine Lewis. 'Structural Change in the Australian Economy'. *Reserve Bank of Australia Bulletin* (September Quarter 2010): 1–10.

Cooper, Rae. 'Australian unionism in a decollectivised environment'. Paper presented at the 19th Conference of the Association of Industrial Relations Academics of Australia and New Zealand, Sydney, Australia, 9–11 February 2005.

Cootamundra Daily Herald, selected dates.

Coulthard, Amanda. 'Non-Union Bargaining: Enterprise Flexibility Agreements'. *Journal of Industrial Relations* 38(3) (1996): 339–58.

Cowgill, Matt. 'A Shrinking Slice of the Pie'. ACTU Working Paper No. 1 (2013).

Creighton, Breen. 'One Hundred Years of the Conciliation and Arbitration Power: A Province Lost?'. *Melbourne University Law Review* 24(3) (2000): 839–65.

Creighton, Breen. 'A Retreat from Individualism? The Fair Work Act 2009 and the Re-collectivisation of Australian Labour Law'. *Industrial Law Journal* 40(2) (2011): 116–45.

Creighton, Breen, and Andrew Stewart. *Labour Law*. Annandale, Australia: The Federation Press, 2010.

Creighton, W. B., W. J. Ford and R. J. Mitchell. *Labour Law: Text and Materials*. Sydney, Australia: The Law Book Company, 1993.

Dabscheck, Braham. 'The 1975 National Wage Case: Now We Have an Incomes Policy'. *Journal of Industrial Relations* 17(3) (1975): 298–309.

Dabscheck, Braham. 'The Accord: Corporatism Visits Australia'. Accessed 2 January 2017. http://www.i-repository.net/contents/outemon/ir/501/501961207.pdf.

Dabscheck, Braham. 'The Arbitration System since 1967'. In *State, Economy and Public Policy in Australia*, edited by Stephen Bell and Brian Head, 142–68. Melbourne, Australia: Oxford University Press, 1994.

Danford, Andy. 'The "New Industrial Relations" and Class Struggle in the 1990s'. *Capital & Class* 21(1) (1997): 107–41.

Davis, Mark, with Misha Schubert. 'Workers' Rights Lost with AWAs'. *The Age*, 17 April 2007, 1.

de Rozairo, Stephen. 'Enterprise Bargaining: An ACTU Perspective'. ACTU Paper (1992). Accessed 19 December 2016. http://www.actu.org.au/actu-media/archives/1992/enterprise-bargaining-an-actu-perspective.

de Tuberville, Simon. 'Union Decline and Renewal in Australia and Britain: Lessons from Closed Shops'. *Economic and Industrial Democracy* 28(3) (2007): 374–400.

De Vroey, Michel. 'A Regulation Approach Interpretation of Contemporary Crisis'. *Capital & Class* 8(2) (1984): 45–66.

Delorme, Robert. 'A New View on the Economic Theory of the State: A Case Study of France'. *Journal of Economic Issues* XVIII(3) (1984): 715–44.

Delorme, Robert. 'The State as Relational, Integrated and Complex: l'etat relationnel integre complexe (ERIC)'. In *Régulation Theory: The State of the Art*, edited by Robert Boyer and Yves Saillard, 115–21. London: Routledge, 2002.

Department of Education, Employment and Workplace Relations. 'Submission to Inquiry into the Workplace Relations Amendment (Transition to Forward with Fairness) Bill 2008'. Canberra: 29 February 2008.

Department of Industrial Relations. *Report on the Operation of the Restructuring and Efficiency Principle*. Canberra, Australia: Australian Government Publishing Service, 1990.

Department of Industrial Relations. *Review of the Structural Efficiency Principle February–May 1989: Submission by the Commonwealth Government*. Canberra, Australia: Australian Government Publishing Service, 1989.

Department of the Treasury. 'Australia's Century since Federation at a Glance'. *Economic Roundup* 1 (2001): 53–63.

Dollar Sweets Pty Ltd v. Federated Confectioners Association of Australia [1985] AIRC 403.

Dollar Sweets Pty Ltd v. Federated Confectioners Association [1986] VR 383.

Dufty, Norman F. *Industrial Relations in the Australian Metal Industries*. Sydney, Australia: West Publishing Corporation, 1972.

Dunford, M. 'Theories of Regulation'. *Environment and Planning D* 8(3) (1990): 297–321.

Dunphy, E. A., and S.C.G. Wright. 'The Jubilee of Industrial Arbitration in the Federal Sphere'. *Australian Law Journal* 25 (1951): 360–78.

Dyster, Barrie, and David Meredith. *Australia in the Global Economy*. Port Melbourne, Australia: Cambridge University Press, 2012.

Edelman, Bernard. *Ownership of the Image: Elements for a Marxist Theory of Law*. Translated by Elizabeth Kingdom. London: Routledge & Kegan Paul, 1979.

Edelman, Lauren B., and Robin Stryker. 'A Sociological Approach to Law and the Economy'. In *The Handbook of Economic Sociology*, edited by Neil J. Smelser and Richard Swedberg, 527–51. Princeton, NJ: Princeton University Press, 2005.

Elam, Mark. 'Puzzling Out the Post-Fordist Debate: Technology, Markets and Institutions'. In *Post-Fordism: A Reader*, edited by Ash Amin, 43–70. Oxford, UK: Blackwell Publishers, 1994.

Ellem, Bradon. 'Trade Unionism in 2000'. *Journal of Industrial Relations* 43(2) (2001): 196–218.

Employee Relations Act 1992 (Vic).

Employers' Total Wage Case 1964 (1964) 106 CAR 683.

Employment Contracts Act 1991 (NZ).

Engels, Friedrich. *The Condition of the English Working Class in England*. London: Electronic Book Company, 1998.

Engels, Friedrich. 'Letter to Conrad Schmidt'. In *Essential Works of Socialism*, edited by Irving Howe, 70–72. New York: Holt, Rinehart and Winston, 1970.

Esser, Josef, and Joachim Hirsch. 'The Crisis of Fordism and the Dimensions of a "Post-Fordist" Regional and Urban Structure'. In *Post-Fordism: A Reader*, edited by Ash Amin, 71–98. Oxford, UK: Blackwell Publishers, 1994.

Evesson, Justine, John Buchanan, Larissa Bamberry, Betty Frino and Damian Oliver. ' "Lowering the standards": From Awards to *Work Choices* in Retail and Hospitality Collective Agreements'. Synthesis Report, Workplace Research Centre, 2007.

Ex parte H.V. McKay (1907) 2 CAR 1.

The Examiner, selected dates.

Factories, Shops and Industries (Further Amendment) Act 1985 (NSW).

Fair Work Act 2009 (Cth).

Faulkner, Neil. *A Marxist History of the World: From Neanderthals to Neoliberals*. London: Pluto Press, 2013.

Federated Clerks' Union of Australia v. Victorian Employers' Federation (1984) 154 CLR 472.

Fine, Ben, and Alfredo Saad-Filho. *Marx's 'Capital'*. London & New York: Pluto Press, 2004.

Fine, Bob. *Democracy and the Rule of Law: Marx's Critique of the Legal Form*. Caldwell, Australia: The Blackburn Press, 2002.

Fitzgerald, Scott, Al Rainnie and John Burgess. 'Rediscovering Braverman? Political Economy, Skill, and Skill Shortages'. *Australian Bulletin of Labour* 39(1) (2013): 2–18.

The Food Preserver, official journal of the Food Preservers' Union, Victorian Branch, selected dates.

Food Preservers Interim Award 1986. Transcript of proceedings, Australian Industrial Relations Commission, Case No. 30092, 7 June 1993.

Food Preservers Union of Australia, Australian Chamber of Manufactures, Food Preservers' Interim Award 1986 (1990) Print J3010.

Food Preservers Union of Australia and H.J. Heinz Co Australia Pty Ltd, Food Preservers Award, 1973 (1991) Print J7693.

Foodweek, selected dates.

Forsyth, Anthony. 'Arbitration Extinguished: The Impact of the Work Choices Legislation on the Australian Industrial Relations Commission'. *Australian Bulletin of Labour* 32(1) (2006): 27–44.

Frazer, Andrew. 'The Federal Conciliation and Arbitration Power: from Cradle to Grave'. Parliamentary Library Research Paper No. 15, 2002.

Frijters, Paul, and Robert Gregory. 'From Golden Age to Golden Age: Australia's "Great Leap Forward"?'. *Economic Record* 82(257) (2006): 207–24.

Furnishing Trades Award, 1964. In *Australian Industrial Law Review* 10(32) (23 November 1968): ¶461.

Giacché, Vladmiro. 'Marx, the Falling Rate of Profit, Financialization, and the Current Crisis'. *International Journal of Political Economy* 40(3) (2011): 18–32.

G J Coles & Co Ltd v. Retail Trade Industrial Tribunal (1986) 7 NSWLR 503.

Greenville, Jared, Clinton Pobke and Nikki Rogers. 'Trends in the Distribution of Income in Australia'. Productivity Commission Staff Working Paper, 2013.

Greig, Alastair. 'Australian Housing, Technological Change and the Fordist Regime of Accumulation'. *Housing Studies* 12(3) (1997): 321–35.

Hampson, Ian. 'Post-Fordism, The "French Regulation School", and the Work of John Mathews'. *Journal of Australian Political Economy* 28 (1991): 92–130.

Hancock, Keith. *Committee of Review into Australian Industrial Relations Law and Systems*. Canberra, Australia: Australian Government Publishing Service, 1985.

Hancock, Keith. 'The First Half-Century of Australian Wage Policy – Part II'. *Journal of Industrial Relations* 21(2) (1979): 129–60.

Hancock, Keith, and Sue Richardson. 'Economic and Social Effects'. In *The New Province for Law and Order: 100 Years of Australian Industrial Conciliation and Arbitration*, edited by Joe Isaac and Stuart Macintyre, 139–206. Port Melbourne, Australia: Cambridge University Press, 2001.

Harcourt, Tim. 'The ACTU's View – Accord Mark VI and Enterprise Bargaining'. Accessed 3 January 2017. http://www.actu.org.au/actu-media/archives/1993/the-actus-view-accord-mark-vi-and-enterprise-bargaining.

Harvey, David. *The Enigma of Capital and the Crises of Capitalism*. London: Profile Books, 2010.

Hawke, Bob. Speech delivered at *Metal Unions Seminar on the Future of Australian Manufacturing*, Sydney, 7–8 June 1977.

Hawke, R. J. 'Total Wage – An Analysis'. *Federal Law Review* 3(1) (1968): 86–115.

Heino, Brett. 'Award Regulation and the New South Wales Retail Sector, 1971–1988: Crisis and Experimentation amidst Changing Models of Development'. *Labour History* 109 (2015): 75–92.

Heino, Brett. 'Capitalism, Regulation Theory and Australian Labour Law: Exploring the Labour Law Regimes of Antipodean Fordism and Liberal-Productivism, 1964–2009'. PhD diss., University of Wollongong, 2016.

Heino, Brett. 'Capitalism, Regulation Theory and Australian Labour Law: Towards a New Theoretical Model'. *Capital & Class* 39(3) (2015): 453–72.

Heino, Brett. 'The State, Class and Occupational Health and Safety: Locating the Capitalist State's Role in the Regulation of OHS in NSW'. *Labour & Industry* 23(2) (2013): 150–67.

Heino, Brett, and James Dahlstrom. '*War Crimes* and the Parisian *Régulation* Approach: Representations of the Crisis of Antipodean Fordism'. *Journal of Australian Political Economy* 74 (2014/15): 95–117.

Higgins, H. B. 'A New Province for Law and Order: Industrial Peace through Minimum Wage and Arbitration'. *Harvard Law Review* 29(1) (1915): 13–39.

Holloway, John. 'The Great-Bear, Post-Fordism and Class Struggle: A Comment on Bonefeld and Jessop'. *Capital & Class* 12(3) (1988): 93–104.

Holloway, John, and Sol Picciotto, 'Introduction: Towards a Materialist Theory of the State'. In *State and Capital: A Marxist Debate*, edited by John Holloway and Sol Picciotto, 1–31. London: Edward Arnold, 1978.

Hooper, Narelle. 'Heinz Watties Defends Its Closure'. Accessed 1 February 2017. http://www.abc.net.au/worldtoday/stories/s153797.htm.

House of Representatives Standing Committee on Employment, Workplace Relations and Workforce Participation. *Making It Work: Inquiry into Independent Contracting and Labour Hire Arrangements*. Canberra: 2005.

Howard, W. A. 'Australian Trade Unions in the Context of Union Theory'. *Journal of Industrial Relations* 19(3) (1977): 255–73.

Howe, John. 'The Job Creation Function of the State: A New Subject for Labour Law'. *Australian Journal of Labour Law* 14(3) (2001): 1–27.

Howe, John, and Richard Mitchell. 'The Evolution of the Contract of Employment in Australia: A Discussion'. *Australian Journal of Labour Law* 12(2) (1999): 1–18.

Hughes, Alexandra. 'Forging New Cultures of Food Retailer-Manufacturer Relations?' In *Retailing, Consumption and Capital: Towards the New Retail Geography*, edited by Neil Wrigley and Michelle Lowe, 90–115. Essex, UK: Longman, 1996.

Hutson, J. *Six Wage Concepts*. Surry Hills, Australia: Amalgamated Engineering Union, 1971.

In re Shop Employees (State) Award (1984) AR 595.

In re Shop Employees (State) Award (No. 2) (July–September 1977, Pt 3) AR 555.

In re Shop Employees (State) Interim Award (July–September 1980, Pt 3) AR 555.

In Retail Shops (State) Award. In CCH, *Australian Industrial Law Review* 22(18) (3 September 1980): ¶282.

Independent Contractors Act 2006 (Cth).

Industrial Arbitration (Enterprise Agreements) Amendment Act 1990 (NSW).

Industrial Arbitration (Further Amendment) Act 1986 (NSW).

Industrial Arbitration (Retail Trade) Amendment Act 1983 (NSW).

Industrial Arbitration (Retail Trade) Amendment Act 1988 (NSW).

Industrial Enterprises Ltd v. Federated Storemen and Packers Union. In CCH, *Australian Industrial Law Review* 21(7) (4 April 1979): ¶106.

Industrial Relations Act 1988 (Cth).

Industrial Relations Act 1991 (NSW).

Industrial Relations Legislation Amendment Act 1992 (Cth).

Industrial Relations Reform Act 1993 (Cth).

Industry Commission, *Assessing Australia's Productivity Performance*. Canberra, Australia: Australian Government Publishing Service, 1997.

Interview with NSW SDA Official. Sydney, Australia, 22 November 2013.

Ivanova, Maria. 'Consumerism and the Crisis: Wither "the American Dream"?'. *Critical Sociology* 37(3) (2011): 329–50.

James, Toby S. 'Whatever Happened to Régulation Theory? The Régulation Approach and Local Government Revisited'. *Policy Studies* 30(2) (2009): 181–201.

Jamieson, Suzanne. 'Enterprise Bargaining – The Approach of the Business Council of Australia'. *Australian Journal of Labour Law* 3(1) (1990): 77–82.

Jessop, Bob. *The Capitalist State: Marxist Theories and Methods*. New York: New York University Press, 1982.

Jessop, Bob. 'Conservative Regimes and the Transition to Post-Fordism: The Cases of Britain and West Germany'. In *Capitalist Development and Crisis Theory: Accumulation, Regulation and Spatial Restructuring*, edited by Mark Gottdiener and Nicos Komninos, 261–99. Basingstoke, UK: Macmillan, 1989.

Jessop, Bob. 'Interpretive Sociology and the Dialectic of Structure and Agency'. *Theory, Culture & Society* 13(1) (1996): 119–28.

Jessop, Bob. 'Regulation Theory, Post Fordism and the State: More Than a Reply to Werner Bonefield'. *Capital & Class* 12(1) (1988): 147–68.

Jessop, Bob. 'Revisiting the Regulation Approach: Critical Reflections on the Contradictions, Dilemmas, Fixes and Crisis Dynamics of Growth Regimes'. *Capital & Class* 37(1) (2013): 5–24.

Jessop, Bob. *State Power*. Cambridge, UK: Polity Press, 2007.

Jessop, Bob. *State Theory: Putting the Capitalist State in Its Place*. Cambridge, UK: Polity Press, 1990.

Jessop, Bob. 'Survey Article: The Regulation Approach'. *Journal of Political Philosophy* 5(3) (1997): 287–326.

Jessop, Bob. 'Thatcherism and Flexibility: The White Heat of a Post-Fordist Revolution'. In *The Politics of Flexibility: Restructuring State and Industry in Britain, Germany and Scandinavia*, edited by Bob Jessop, Hans Kastendiek, Klaus Nielsen and Ove Kai Pedersen, 135–61. Aldershot: Edward Elgar, 1991.

Jessop, Bob, and Ngai-Ling Sum. *Beyond the Regulation Approach: Putting Capitalist Economies in Their Place*. Cheltenham, UK: Edward Elgar, 2006.

Jones, Sandra. 'Penalty Rates under Challenge'. *Journal of Industrial Relations* 23(4) (1981): 504–7.

Juillard, Michel. 'Accumulation Regimes'. In *Régulation Theory: The State of the Art*, edited by Robert Boyer and Yves Saillard, 153–60. London: Routledge, 2002.

Kahn-Freund, Otto. Introduction to *The Institutions of Private Law and Their Social Functions*, by Karl Renner, 1–44. London: Routledge & Kegan Paul, 1949.

Kalleberg, Arne L. *Good Jobs, Bad Jobs: The Rise of Polarized and Precarious Employment Systems in the United States, 1970s to 2000s*. New York: Russell Sage Foundation, 2011.

Katz, Harry C. 'The Decentralization of Collective Bargaining: A Literature Review and Comparative Analysis'. *Industrial and Labor Relations Review* 47(1) (1993): 3–22.

Kay, Geoffrey, and James Mott. *Political Order and the Law of Labour*. London: Macmillan Press, 1982.

Keating, Paul. 'Speech by the Prime Minister, The Hon. P.J. Keating MP'. Speech delivered at the Institute of Directors Luncheon, Melbourne, Australia, 21 April 1993.

Kelloggs (Australia) Pty Ltd v. Labor Council (NSW). In CCH, *Australian Industrial Law Review* 29(21) (21 October 1987): ¶402.

Kennedy, Peter. 'Beyond the Objective & the Subjective: Putting Value Back into the Social'. *Critique: Journal of Socialist Theory* 29(1) (2001): 227–44.

Kettell, Steven. 'Circuits of Capital and Overproduction: A Marxist Analysis of the Present World Economic Crisis'. *Review of Radical Political Economics* 38(1) (2006): 24–44.

Kingston, Beverley. *Basket, Bag and Trolley: A History of Shopping in Australia*. Melbourne, Australia: Oxford University Press, 1994.

Kirby, Richard. Foreword to *Industrial Relations in the Australian Metal Industries*, by Norman Dufty, v. Sydney, Australia: West Publishing Corporation, 1972.

Krinsky, John. 'Neoliberal Times: Intersecting Temporalities and the Neoliberalization of New York City's Public-Sector Labor Relations'. *Social Science History* 35(3) (2011): 381–422.

Kryger, Anthony. 'Casual employment in Australia: a quick guide'. Research Paper Series 2014–15, Parliamentary Library, 2015.

Kuhn, Rick. 'Militancy Uprooted: Labour Movement Economics 1974–1986'. *Socialist Action* (1986). Accessed 25 January 2017, http://www.anu.edu.au/polsci/rick/militancyuprooted.htm.

Lambert, Rob, Michael Gillan and Scott Fitzgerald. 'Electrolux in Australia: Reregulation, Industry Restructuring and the Dynamics of Bargaining'. *Journal of Industrial Relations* 47(3) (2005): 261–75.

Lansbury, Russell D. 'New Technology and Industrial Relations in the Retail Grocery Industry'. *Journal of Industrial Relations* 22(3) (1980): 275–92.

Lebowitz, Michael. *Beyond Capital*. Basingstoke & New York: Palgrave Macmillan, 2003.

Leigh, Andrew. 'Trade Liberalisation and the Australian Labor Party'. *Australian Journal of Politics and History* 48(4) (2002): 487–508.

Leon Laidley Pty Ltd v. Transport Workers Union of Australia (1980) 43 FLR 168.

Leyshon, A., and A. Tickell. 'Money Order? The Discursive Construction of Bretton Woods and the Making and Breaking of Regulatory Space'. *Environment and Planning A* 26(12) (1994): 1861–90.

Lipietz, Alain. 'Accumulation, Crises, and Ways Out: Some Methodological Reflections on the Concept of "Regulation"'. *International Journal of Political Economy* 18(2) (1988): 10–43.

Lipietz, Alain. *The Enchanted World: Inflation, Credit and the World Crisis*. Translated by Ian Patterson. London: Verso, 1985.

Lipietz, Alain. 'Fears and Hopes: The Crisis of the Liberal-Productivist Model and Its Green Alternative'. *Capital & Class* 37(1) (2013): 127–41.

Lipietz, Alain. 'From Althusserianism to "Regulation Theory"'. In *The Althusserian Legacy*, edited by E. Ann Kaplan and Michael Sprinkler, 99–138. London & New York: Verso, 1993.

Lipietz, Alain. *Mirages and Miracles: The Crisis of Global Fordism*. Translated by David Macey. London: Verso, 1987.

Lipietz, Alain. 'The Post-Fordist World: Labour Relations, International Hierarchy and Global Ecology'. *Review of International Political Economy* 4(1) (1997): 1–41.

Lipietz, Alain. 'Rebel Sons: the Regulation School – An Interview with Alain Lipietz, conducted by Jane Jenson'. *French Politics and Society* 5(4) (1987): 17–26.

Lipietz, Alain. 'Reflections on a Tale: The Marxist Foundations of the Concepts of Regulation and Accumulation'. *Studies in Political Economy* 26 (1988): 7–36.

Lipietz, Alain. *Towards a New Economic Order: Postfordism, Ecology and Democracy*. Translated by Malcolm Slater. Cambridge, UK: Polity Press, 1992.

Lipietz, Alain. 'Towards Global Fordism?'. *New Left Review* 132 (1982): 33–47.

Lloyd, Christopher. 'Australian Capitalism since 1992: A New Regime of Accumulation?'. *Journal of Australian Political Economy* 61 (2008): 30–55.

Lloyd, Christopher. 'The Lucky Country Syndrome in Australia: Resources, Social Democracy, and Regimes of Development in Historical Political Economy Perspective'. Paper presented at the Asia Pacific Economic and Business History Conference, Canberra, Australia, 16–18 February 2012.

Lloyd, Christopher. 'Regime Change in Australian Capitalism: Towards a Historical Political Economy of Regulation'. *Australian Economic History Review* 42(3) (2002): 238–66.

Lloyd, Peter. '100 Years of Tariff Protection in Australia'. *Australian Economic History Review* 48(2) (2008): 99–145.

Lowe, Philip. 'The Changing Structure of the Australian Economy and Monetary Policy'. Speech delivered at the 12th Annual Economic Forum of the Australian Industry Group, Sydney, Australia, 7 March 2012.

Ludeke, J. T. 'The Evolving Industrial Relations Regime: The Federal System – 1992–1998'. *Australian Law Journal* 72(11) (1998): 863–70.

Lukács, Georg. *History and Class Consciousness: Studies in Marxist Dialectics*. Translated by Rodney Livingstone. London: Merlin Press, 1971.

Lund, John, and Christopher Wright. 'State Regulation and the New Taylorism: The Case of Australian Grocery Warehousing'. *Relations Industrielles* 56(4) (2001): 747–69.

Lyons, Michael. 'An Appealing Outcome? Industrial Arbitration and Extended Retail Trading Hours in New South Wales in the 1980s'. *International Journal of Employment Studies* 13(1) (2005): 107–31.

Macintyre, Stuart. 'Arbitration in Action'. In *The New Province for Law and Order: 100 Years of Australian Industrial Conciliation and Arbitration*, edited by Joe Isaac and Stuart Macintyre, 55–97. Port Melbourne, Australia: Cambridge University Press, 2004.

Macintyre, Stuart. *Australia's Boldest Experiment: War and Reconstruction in the 1940s*. Sydney, Australia: NewSouth Publishing, 2015.

Mackinnon, Bruce Hearn. 'Employer Matters in 2003'. *Journal of Industrial Relations* 46(2) (2004): 226–41.

Mandel, Ernest. *An Introduction to Marxist Economic Theory*. Pathfinder Press, 1973.

Marsden, Richard. *The Nature of Capital: Marx after Foucault*. Abingdon, UK: Routledge, 1999.

Martain, Sandra. 'The Taylorisation of paid care work in aged care'. Paper presented at the 28th Conference of the Association of Industrial Relations Academics of Australia and New Zealand, Melbourne, Australia, 5–7 February 2014.

Marx, Karl. *Capital: A Critique of Political Economy Volume I*. Translated by Ben Fowkes. London: Penguin Classics, 1990.

Marx, Karl. *Capital: A Critique of Political Economy Volume II*. Translated by David Fernbach. London: Penguin Classics, 1992.

Marx, Karl. *Capital: A Critique of Political Economy Volume III*. Translated by David Fernbach. London: Penguin Classics, 1991.

Marx, Karl. *A Contribution to the Critique of Political Economy*. Translated by N. I. Stone. Chicago: Charles H. Kerr & Company, 1904.

Marx, Karl. *Grundrisse*. Translated by Martin Nicolaus. London: Allen Lane in association with New Left Review, 1973.

Marx, Karl. 'Inaugural Address of the Working Men's International Association'. In *Collected Works Volume XX*, edited by Karl Marx and Friedrich Engels, 5–13. London: Lawrence and Wishart, 2010.

Marx, Karl. 'Letter to Bolte'. In *Karl Marx: Selected Writings*, edited by David McLellan, 587–89. Oxford, UK: Oxford University Press, 1977.

Marx, Karl. 'On the Jewish Question'. In *The Marx-Engels Reader*, edited by Robert C. Tucker, 26–52. New York: W.W. Norton & Company, 1978.

Marx, Karl. 'Theses on Feuerbach'. In *The German Ideology*, edited by Karl Marx and Friedrich Engels, 121–23. New York: International Publishers, 1970.

Marx, Karl, and Friedrich Engels. *The Communist Manifesto*. Translated by Samuel Moore. London: Penguin Classics, 2002.

Marx, Karl. 'Debates on Freedom of the Press'. In *Collected Works Volume I*, edited by Karl Marx and Friedrich Engels, 132–81. Lawrence and Wishart, 2010. http://www.koorosh-modaresi.com/MarxEngels/V1.pdf.

Matthews, L. G. 'Drafting of Federal Awards'. *Journal of Industrial Relations* 12(3) (1970): 306–30.

Mavroudeas, Stavros. 'Regulation Theory: The Road from Creative Marxism to Postmodern Disintegration'. *Science & Society* 63(3) (1999): 310–37.

Mayhew, Claire, and Michael Quinlan. 'Fordism in the Fast Food Industry: Pervasive Management Control and Occupational Health and Safety Risks for Young Temporary Workers'. *Sociology of Health & Illness* 24(3) (2002): 261–84.

McCallum, Ronald C. 'The Internationalisation of Australian Industrial Law: The *Industrial Relations Reform Act* 1993'. *Sydney Law Review* 16(1) (1994): 122–35.

McGarvie, R. E. 'Principle and Practice in Commonwealth Industrial Arbitration after Sixty Years'. *Federal Law Review* 1(1) (1964): 47–94.

Meat Industry Case (1925) 22 CAR 794.

Metal Industry Award. In *Australian Industrial Law Review* 16(23) (13 September 1974): ¶565.

Metal Trades. In *Australian Industrial Law Review* 10(7) (23 March 1968): ¶80.

Metal Trades. In *Australian Industrial Law Review* 13(14) (28 May 1971): ¶278.

Metal Trades Annual Leave Case (1945) 55 CAR 595.

Metal Trades Award. In *Australian Industrial Law Review* 10(3) (17 February 1968): ¶28.

Metal Trades Employers Association v. Amalgamated Engineering Union (1937) 37 CAR 176.

Metal Trades Margins Case (1947) 58 CAR 1088.

Metal Trades Margins Case (1952) 73 CAR 324.

Metal Trades Margins Case (1954) 80 CAR 3.

Metal Trades Margins Case (1959) 92 CAR 793.

Metal Trades Margins Case (1963) 102 CAR 138.

Metal Trades Work Value Inquiry (1967) 121 CAR 587.

Miéville, China. *Between Equal Rights: A Marxist Theory of International Law*. Chicago: Haymarket Books, 2006.

Mills, C. P. 'Legislation and Decisions Affecting Industrial Relations'. *Journal of Industrial Relations* 10(2) (1968): 154–64.

Mitchell, Richard. 'Australian Industrial Relations and Labour Law Policy: A Post-War Review'. *The Australian Quarterly* 52(1) (1980): 40–59.

Mitchell, Richard. 'Industrial Relations under a Conservative Government: The Coalition's Labour Law Programme 1975 to 1978'. *Journal of Industrial Relations* 21(4) (1979): 435–65.

Mortimer, Dennis. 'Trade Union and Management Strategy: A Case Study of Compulsory Unionism'. *Employment Relations Record* 1(2) (2001): 81–97.

Mudginberri Station Pty Ltd v. Australasian Meat Industry Employees Union (1986) 15 IR 272.

Mulvey, Charles. 'Wage Policy and Wage Determination'. *Journal of Industrial Relations* 25(1) (1983): 68–74.

Mylett, Terri. 'The intensification of labour market polarisation in metals manufacturing in Australia in the 1900s'. PhD diss., University of Wollongong, 2003.

Nadel, Henri. '*Régulation* and Marx'. In *Régulation Theory: The State of the Art*, edited by Robert Boyer and Yves Saillard, 28–35. London: Routledge, 2002.

National Association of Retail Grocers of Australia. 'Submission to ACCC inquiry into the competitiveness of retail prices for standard groceries – Part B'. 13 March 2008.

National Retail Association [2011] FWA 3777. Accessed 7 February 2017. https://www.fwc.gov.au/documents/decisionssigned/html/2011fwa3777.htm.

National Wage Cases of 1965 (1965) 110 CAR 189.

National Wage Case 1970 (1970) CAR 135 244.

National Wage Case 1971–1972 (1972) 143 CAR 290.

National Wage Case 1974 (1974) 157 CAR 293.

National Wage Case April 1975 (1975) 167 CAR 18.

National Wage Case – June and September 1979 Quarters Decisions No. 1 (1980) 232 CAR 12.

National Wage Case – December 1979 and March 1980 Quarters (1980) 241 CAR 258.

National Wage Case, 23 December 1982. In CCH, *Australian Industrial Law Review* 25(2) (19 January 1983): ¶19.

National Wage Case April 1984. In CCH, *Australian Industrial Law Review* 26(7) (11 April 1984): ¶117.

National Wage Case March 1987 (1987) Print G6800.

National Wage Case August 1988 (1988) Print H4000.

National Wage Case August 1989 (1989) Print H9100.

National Wage Case April 1991 (1991) Print J7400.

National Wage Case October 1991 (1991) Print K0300.

National Workforce Pty Ltd v. Australian Manufacturing Workers' Union (1997) 76 IR 200.

Neilson, David. 'Formal and Real Subordination and the Contemporary Proletariat: Re-Coupling Marxist Class Theory and Labour-Process Analysis'. *Capital & Class* 31(1) (2007): 89–123.

Neilson, David. 'Remaking the Connections: Marxism and the French Regulation School'. *Review of Radical Political Economics* 44(2) (2012): 160–77.

Neilson, David, and Thomas H. Stubbs. 'Competition States in the Neoliberal Era: Towards Third-Generation Regulation Theory'. *Competition & Change* 20(2) (2016): 122–44.

Neocleous, Mark. *Administering Civil Society: Towards a Theory of State Power*. Basingstoke, UK: Macmillan Press, 1996.

New South Wales, *Parliamentary Debates,* Legislative Assembly, selected dates.

New South Wales, *Parliamentary Debates,* Legislative Council, selected dates.

New South Wales v. Commonwealth (2006) 229 CLR 1.

New Zealand Herald, selected dates.

Noël, Alain. 'Accumulation, Regulation, and Social Change: An Essay of French Political Economy'. *International Organization* 41(2) (1987): 303–33.

Noel Butlin Archives Centre, Australian National University: Australian Manufacturing Workers' Union, N628, selected documents.

Noel Butlin Archives Centre, Australian National University: Australian Retailers Association, Z441, selected documents.

Noel Butlin Archives Centre, Australian National University: Federated Confectioners Association, N194, selected documents.

O'Donnell, Anthony. ' "Non-Standard" Workers in Australia: Counts and Controversies'. *Australian Journal of Labour Law* 17(1) (2004): 1–28.

OECD. *Innovations in Labour Market Policies: The Australian Way*. Paris: OECD Publishing, 2001.

OECD. *OECD Employment Outlook 2014*. Paris: OECD Publishing, 2014.

O'Hara, Phillip Anthony. 'A Social Structure of Accumulation for Long Wave Upswing in Australia?'. *Journal of Australian Political Economy* 61 (2008): 88–111.

Oil Industry Case (1970) 134 CAR 159.

Pashukanis, Evgeny. 'The Marxist Theory of Law and the Construction of Socialism'. In *Pashukanis: Selected Writings on Marxism and Law*, edited by Piers Beirne and Robert Sharlet, 186–99. London & New York: Academic Press, 1980.

Pashukanis, Evgeny B. *Law and Marxism: A General Theory*. Translated by Barbara Einhorn. London: Ink Links, 1978.

Patrick Stevedores No 2 Pty Ltd v. Maritime Union of Australia (1998) 195 CLR 1.

Peck, Jamie. *Work-Place: The Social Regulation of Labour Markets*. New York: The Guilford Press, 1996.

Petit, Pascal. 'Structural Forms and Growth Regimes of the Post-Fordist Era'. *Review of Social Economy* 57(2) (1999): 220–43.

Peetz, David. *Brave New Work Place: How Individual Contracts Are Changing Our Jobs*. Crows Nest, Australia: Allen & Unwin, 2006.

Peetz, David. 'Trend Analysis of Union Membership'. *Australian Journal of Labour Economics* 8(1) (2005): 1–24.

Peetz, David, and Alison Preston. 'Individual Contracting, Collective Bargaining and Wages in Australia'. *Industrial Relations Journal* 40(5) (2009): 444–61.

Plowman, David. 'Administered Flexibility: Restructuring the Metal Industry Award'. *Economic and Labour Relations Review* 1(2) (1990): 48–70.

Plowman, David. 'Employer Associations: Challenges and Responses'. *Journal of Industrial Relations* 20(3) (1978): 237–262.

Political Research Group & Political Economy Movement (S.A.). 'Workers, Trade Unions & Industrial Democracy'. *Journal of Australian Political Economy* 3 (1978): 82–88.

Poulantzas, Nicos. *State, Power, Socialism*. Translated by Patrick Camiller. London: NLB, 1978.

Price, Robin. 'Down the aisle: the effects of technological change on retail workers skills'. Paper presented at the 27th International Labour Process Conference, Edinburgh, UK, 6–8 April 2009.

Price, Robin, Janis Bailey and Amanda Pyman. 'Varieties of Collaboration: The Case of an Australian Retail Union'. *International Journal of Human Resource Management* 25(6) (2014): 748–61.

Printing Industry Employees Union of Australia v. Balmoral Press (1942) 49 CAR 304.

Productivity Commission. 'Productivity Update'. July 2015.

Productivity Commission. 'The Role of Non-Traditional Work in the Australian Labour Market'. Productivity Commission Research Paper, 2006.

Provis, Chris. 'Comparative Wage Justice'. *Journal of Industrial Relations* 28(1) (1986): 24–39.

Queensland Government. 'Submission to Inquiry into independent contractors and labour hire arrangements'. House of Representatives Standing Committee on Employment, Workplace Relations and Workforce Participation, Submission No. 66, 2005.

R v. Holmes: Ex parte Public Service Association of New South Wales (1977) 140 CLR 63, 74.

R v. Kirby; Ex parte Boilermakers' Society of Australia (1956) 94 CLR 254.

R v. Portus; Ex parte A.N.Z. Banking Group Ltd (1972) 127 CLR 353, 371.

R. v. Wallis; Ex parte Employers' Association of Wool Selling Brokers (1949) 78 CLR 529.

Ramia, Gaby, and Nick Wailes. 'Putting Wage-Earners into Wage-Earners' Welfare States: The Relationship between Social Policy and Industrial Relations in Australia and New Zealand'. *Australian Journal of Social Issues* 41(1) (2006): 49–68.

Re Metal Trades Award; Re Annual Leave (1963) 103 CAR 637.

Re Shop and Warehouse (Wholesale Retail Establishments) Award No. 32 of 1976. In CCH, *Australian Industrial Law Review* 23(16) (12 August 1981): ¶377.

Re Shop Employees' (Major General Shops) (State) Award (1988) 17 Industrial Reports 155.

Re Shop Employees (State) Award. In CCH, *Australian Industrial Law Review* 27(17) (5 September 1985): ¶314.

Re Shop Employees (State) Award (1987) 15 Industrial Reports 26.

Re Vehicle Industry – Repair, Service and Retail – Award 1980. In CCH, *Australian Industrial Law Review* 25(10) (4 May 1983): ¶190.

Reid, Michael. 'Change at the Check-Out'. *The Economist* 334(7904) (1995): 3–5.

Retail Traders' Association. 'Submission of the Retail Traders' Association of NSW to the NSW Industrial Commission in respect to the Inquiry into Retail Trading Hours'. 1983.

Retail Traders' News Bulletin, official journal of the Retail Traders' Association of NSW, selected dates.

Review of Wage Fixing Principles (1993) Print K9700, 14.

Rimmer, Malcolm. 'Enterprise Bargaining, Wage Norms and Productivity'. *Journal of Industrial Relations* 40(4) (1998): 605–23.

Rimmer, Malcolm. 'The *Workplace Relations Act 1996*: An Historical Perspective'. *Australian Bulletin of Labour* 23(1) (1997): 69–81.

Rolfe, Mark. 'Antipodean Fordism: Postwar Americanisation Down Under'. In *Henry Ford: Critical Evaluations in Business and Management, Volume 2*, edited by John Wood and Michael Wood, 323–53. London & New York: Routledge, 2003.

Rosewarne, Stuart. 'The Political Economy of Retailing into the Eighties – Part 1'. *Journal of Australian Political Economy* 15 (1983): 18–38.

Rosewarne, Stuart. 'The Political Economy of Retailing into the Eighties – Part 2'. *Journal of Australian Political Economy* 16 (1984): 75–92.

Rowse, Tim. 'Elusive Middle Ground: A Political History'. In *The New Province for Law and Order: 100 Years of Australian Industrial Conciliation and Arbitration*, edited by Joe Isaac and Stuart Macintyre, 17–54. Port Melbourne, Australia: Cambridge University Press, 2001.

Rubber, Plastic and Cable Making Industry Award, 1972. In *Australian Industrial Law Review* 17(7) (14 March 1975): ¶151.

Saeger, Steven S. 'Globalization and Deindustrialization: Myth and Reality in the OECD'. *Weltwirtschaftliches Archiv* 133(4) (1997): 579–608.

Safety Net Review – Wages April 1997, accessed 3 January 2017, http://www.airc.gov.au/safetynet_review/decisions/P1997.htm.

Salvati, Michele. 'A Long Cycle in Industrial Relations, or: Regulation Theory and Political Economy'. *Labour* 3(1) (1989): 41–72.

SDA, New South Wales v. Woolworths Ltd. In CCH, *Australian Industrial Law Review* 26(18) (26 September 1984): ¶312.

SDA News, official journal of NSW SDA Branch, selected dates.

Sheridan, Tom. *Mindful Militants: The Amalgamated Engineering Union in Australia, 1920–1972*. Cambridge, UK: Cambridge University Press, 1975.

Shop and Distributive Worker, official journal of NSW SDA Branch, selected dates.

Shop, Distributive and Allied Employees Association v. Myer S.A. Stores Ltd. In CCH, *Australian Industrial Law Review* 25(18) (10 August 1983): ¶365.

Shop, Distributive and Allied Employees' Association v. Woolworths (Alice Springs) Ltd. In CCH, *Australian Industrial Law Review* 24(3) (10 February 1982): ¶53.

Shop Employees (State) Award. In *Australian Industrial Law Review* 14(11) (20 May 1972): ¶194.

Shop Employees (State) Award. In CCH, *Australian Industrial Law Review* 30(12) (16 June 1988): ¶232.

Shop Employees (State) Award (1991) 265 NSW Industrial Gazette 844.

Shop Employees (State) Award (1991) 266 NSW Industrial Gazette 612.

Shops (Premium Rates of Pay) Regulation 1985 (NSW).

Slattery v. Kentucky Fried Chicken Pty Ltd. In *Australian Industrial Law Review* 14(30) (10 November 1972): ¶628.

Sloan, Judith. 'The Economic Implications of Enterprise Bargaining'. *Economic and Labour Relations Review* 4(1) (1993): 27–49.

Smart Company, selected dates.

Standing, Guy. *The Precariat: The New Dangerous Class*. London and New York: Bloomsbury, 2014.

'Statement of Accord by the Australian Labor Party and the Australian Council of Trade Union regarding economic policy, February 1983'. In *The Accord . . . and Beyond: The Political Economy of the Labor Government*, edited by Frank Stilwell, 159–76. Sydney, Australia: Pluto Press, 1986.

Strickland v. Rocla Concrete Pipes Ltd (1971) 124 CLR 468.

Swanson, T. B., J. A. Davidson, A. G. Hartnell, A. Kerr and H. S. Schreiber. *Trade Practices Act Review Committee – Report to the Minister for Business and Consumer Affairs*. Canberra, Australia: Australian Government Publishing Service, 1976.

Sydney Morning Herald, selected dates.

Taiwo, Olufemi. *Legal Naturalism: A Marxist Theory of Law*. Ithaca, NY: Cornell University Press, 1996.

Taksa, Lucy. 'Scientific Management: Technique or Cultural Ideology?'. *Journal of Industrial Relations* 34(3) (1992): 365–95.

Taksa, Lucy. 'The Cultural Diffusion of Scientific Management: The United States and New South Wales'. *Journal of Industrial Relations* 37(3) (1995): 427–61.

Termination, Change and Redundancy Case (1984) 8 IR 34.

Théret, Bruno. 'To Have or to Be: On the Problem of the Interaction between State and Economy and Its "solidarist" Mode of Regulation'. *Economy and Society* 23(1) (1994): 1–46.

Thompson, E. P. *The Poverty of Theory and Other Essays*. London: Merlin, 1978.

Tickell, Adam, and Jamie A. Peck. 'Social Regulation *after* Fordism: Regulation Theory, Neoliberalism and the Global-Local Nexus'. *Economy and Society* 24(3) (1995): 357–86.

Tigar, Michael E., and Madeleine R. Levy. *Law and the Rise of Capitalism*. New York: Monthly Review Press, 2000.

Tillmans Butcheries Pty v. AMIEU. In CCH, *Australian Industrial Law Review* 22(1) (9 January 1980): ¶2.

Toner, Phil. 'The Crisis of Equipment Investment in Australia'. *Journal of Australian Political Economy* 22 (1988): 39–56.

Trade Practices Act 1974 (Cth).

Trading Economics. 'Gross fixed capital formation (% of GDP) in Australia'. Accessed 21 December 2016. http://www.tradingeconomics.com/australia/gross-fixed-capital-formation-percent-of-gdp-wb-data.html.

Treadgold, Alan. 'Food Retailing in Australia – Three Retailers, Three Strategies'. *International Journal of Retail & Distribution Management* 24(8) (1996): 6–16.

Treuren, Gerrit. 'Regulation Theory and Australian Theorising of Institutional Change in Industrial Regulation'. Paper presented at the 11th Conference of the Association of Industrial Relations Academics of Australia and New Zealand, Brisbane, Australia, 20 January–1 February 1997.

Treuren, Gerry. 'How and Why Do Institutions Change? A Four Phase Framework for the Description of Institutional Development'. *Journal of Economic and Social Policy* 7(2) (2003): 51–67.

Treuren, Gerry. 'State Theory and the Origins of Federal Arbitration Legislation in Australia'. *Policy, Organisation and Society* 13 (1997): 56–81.

Trotsky, Leon. *The History of the Russian Revolution*. New York: Monad Press, 1980.

van Barneveld, Kristin. 'Australian Workplace Agreements under *Work Choices*'. *Economic and Labour Relations Review* 16(2) (2006): 165–91.

Vehicle Builders Employees Federation of Australia v. General Motors-Holden Pty Ltd (1966) 115 CAR 931.

Victorian Chamber of Manufacturers v. Amalgamated Engineering Union (1947) 58 CAR 551.

Victorian Chamber of Manufactures v. Federated Confectioners' Association of Australia and also A.W. Allen Limited v. Federated Confectioners' Association of Australia. Transcript of proceedings, Australian Conciliation and Arbitration Commission, Case No. 3923 & 4578, 6 December 1976.

Vidal, Matt. 'Postfordism as a Dysfunctional Accumulation Regime: A Comparative Analysis of the USA, the UK and Germany'. *Work, Employment and Society* 27(3) (2013): 451–71.

Vidal, Matt. 'Reworking Postfordism: Labor Process versus Employment Relations'. *Sociology Compass* 5(4) (2011): 273–86.

Voice, official journal of the Shop Assistants and Warehouse Employees Federation of Australia, selected dates.

Von Arx, Susan. 'An Examination of E.B. Pashukanis's General Theory of Law and Marxism'. PhD diss., State University of New York, 1997.

Wage and Standard Hours Inquiry 1952–1953 (1953) 77 CAR 477.

Wage Rates – General Motors Holden's Pty Ltd. Employees. In *Australian Industrial Law Review* 17(22) (29 August 1975): ¶717.

Walsh, James. 'Mass Migration and the Mass Society: Fordism, Immigration Policy and the Post-War Long Boom in Canada and Australia, 1947–1970'. *Journal of Historical Sociology* 25(3) (2012): 352–85.

Warner, Kris. 'The Decline of Unionization in the United States: Some Lessons from Canada'. *Labor Studies Journal* 38(2) (2013): 110–38.

Warrington, Ronnie. 'Standing Pashukanis on His Head'. *Capital & Class* 4(3) (1980): 102–6.

Waters, Malcolm. *Strikes in Australia*. Sydney, Australia: George Allen & Unwin, 1982.

Wells, Jeane. 'Flexible Work in 2010 – The impact of the Fair Work Act 2009 on employer control of, and employee access to, flexible working hours'. Paper presented at the 3rd Our Work, Our Lives Conference, Darwin, Australia, 12–13 August 2010.

Whitwell, Greg. 'The Power of Economic Ideas? Keynesian Economic Policies in Post-War Australia'. In *State, Economy and Public Policy in Australia*, edited by Stephen Bell and Brian Head, 119–41. Melbourne, Australia: Oxford University Press, 1994.

Wood, Ellen Meiksins. *Empire of Capital*. London: Verso, 2003.

Woodward, A. E. 'Industrial Relations in the '70s'. *Journal of Industrial Relations* 12(2) (1970): 115–29.

Woodward, A. E. 'A Review of Industrial Relations 1968/9'. *Journal of Industrial Relations* 11(2) (1969): 89–98.

Workman, Thom. *If You're in My Way, I'm Walking: The Assault on Working People since 1970*. Black Point & Winnipeg, Canada: Fernwood Publishing, 2009.

Workplace Info, selected dates.

Workplace Relations Act 1996 (Cth).

Workplace Relations Amendment (Genuine Bargaining) Act 2002 (Cth).

Workplace Relations Amendment (Work Choices) Act 2005 (Cth).

Workplace Relations Legislation Amendment (More Jobs, Better Pay) Bill 1999 (Cth).

Workplace Relations Regulations 2006 (Cth).

Work Value Case (1967) 121 CAR 587.

Wright, Chris. 'Taylorism Reconsidered: The Impact of Scientific Management within the Australian Workplace'. *Labour History* 64 (1993): 34–53.

Wright, Christopher, and John Lund. 'Supply Chain Rationalization: Retailer Dominance and Labour Flexibility in the Australian Food and Grocery Industry'. *Work, Employment and Society* 17(1) (2003): 137–57.

Notes

CHAPTER 1

1. Otto Kahn-Freund, introduction to *The Institutions of Private Law and Their Social Functions*, by Karl Renner (London: Routledge & Kegan Paul, 1949), 43.

2. Kahn-Freund, introduction, 43.

CHAPTER 2

1. Michael Lebowitz, *Beyond Capital* (Basingstoke & New York: Palgrave Macmillan, 2003), 52.

2. George Lukács, *History and Class Consciousness: Studies in Marxist Dialectics*, trans. Rodney Livingstone (London: Merlin Press, 1971), 27.

3. David Neilson, 'Remaking the Connections: Marxism and the French Regulation School', *Review of Radical Political Economics* 44(2) (2012): 163.

4. Ellen Meiksins Wood, *Empire of Capital* (London: Verso, 2003), 9–25.

5. Ibid.

6. Karl Marx, *Capital: A Critique of Political Economy Volume I*, trans. Ben Fowkes (London: Penguin Classics, 1990), 251–52, 317.

7. Geoffrey Kay and James Mott, *Political Order and the Law of Labour* (London: Macmillan Press, 1982), 81–83.

8. Marx, *Capital Volume I*, 125–31.

9. Jamie Peck, *Work-Place: The Social Regulation of Labour Markets* (New York: The Guilford Press, 1996), 40.

10. Bob Jessop and Ngai-Ling Sum, *Beyond the Regulation Approach: Putting Capitalist Economies in Their Place* (Cheltenham: Edward Elgar, 2006), 329.

11. Ibid., 22.

12. Marx, *Capital Volume I*, 742.

13. Karl Marx, *Capital: A Critique of Political Economy Volume III*, trans. David Fernbach (London: Penguin Classics, 1991), 319; Ernest Mandel, *An Introduction to Marxist Economic Theory* (New York: Pathfinder Press, 1973), 63–65.

14. Marx, *Capital Volume III*, 339–48.

15. Lebowitz, *Beyond Capital*, 77–100.

16. Karl Marx and Friedrich Engels, *The Communist Manifesto*, trans. Samuel Moore (London: Penguin Classics, 2002), 225.

17. Robert Boyer, *The Regulation School: A Critical Introduction*, trans. Craig Charney (New York: Columbia University Press, 1990), 34.

18. Ibid., xxv–xxvi.

19. Alain Lipietz, *Mirages and Miracles: The Crisis of Global Fordism*, trans. David Macey (London: Verso, 1987), 15.

20. Alain Lipietz, 'Rebel Sons: the Regulation School – An Interview with Alain Lipietz, conducted by Jane Jenson', *French Politics and Society* 5(4) (1987): 17–26.

21. Jessop and Sum, *Beyond the Regulation Approach*, 23.

22. For a detailed overview, see Alain Lipietz, 'From Althusserianism to "Regulation Theory"', in *The Althusserian Legacy*, ed. E. Ann Kaplan and Michael Sprinkler (London & New York: Verso, 1993), 99–138.

23. Neilson, 'Remaking the Connections', 160.

24. Jessop and Sum, *Beyond the Regulation Approach*, 14–15.

25. Alain Noël, 'Accumulation, Regulation, and Social Change: An Essay of French Political Economy', *International Organization* 41(2) (1987): 306.

26. Boyer, *The Regulation School*, xxiii.

27. Michel Aglietta, *A Theory of Capitalist Regulation: The US Experience* (London: NLB, 1979), 13, 16.

28. Alain Lipietz, 'Reflections on a Tale: The Marxist Foundations of the Concepts of Regulation and Accumulation', *Studies in Political Economy* 26 (1988): 13–14.

29. Neilson, 'Remaking the Connections', 161.

30. Gerry Treuren, 'State Theory and the Origins of Federal Arbitration Legislation in Australia', *Policy, Organisation and Society* 13 (1997): 60–61.

31. Aglietta, *A Theory of Capitalist Regulation*, 15.

32. Lukács, *History and Class Consciousness*, 90.

33. M. Dunford, 'Theories of Regulation', *Environment and Planning D* 8(3) (1990): 306.

34. See, for example, Matt Vidal, 'Reworking Postfordism: Labor Process Versus Employment Relations', *Sociology Compass* 5(4) (2011): 273–86.

35. Harry Braverman, *Labor and Monopoly Capital: The Degradation of Work in the Twentieth Century* (New York & London: Monthly Review Press, 1974).

36. Aglietta, *A Theory of Capitalist Regulation*, 111.

37. Ibid., 116–22.

38. Bob Jessop, 'Thatcherism and Flexibility: The White Heat of a Post-Fordist Revolution', in *The Politics of Flexibility: Restructuring State and Industry in Britain, Germany and Scandinavia*, ed. Bob Jessop et al. (Aldershot: Edward Elgar, 1991), 136–37.

39. Boyer, *The Regulation School*, 35.

40. Ibid.

41. Ibid., 34.

42. Bob Jessop, 'Revisiting the Regulation Approach: Critical Reflections on the Contradictions, Dilemmas, Fixes and Crisis Dynamics of Growth Regimes', *Capital & Class* 37(1) (2013): 8.

43. Karl Marx, *Capital: A Critique of Political Economy Volume II*, trans. David Fernbach (London: Penguin Classics, 1992), 565–99.

44. Ibid.; Marx, *Capital Volume III*, 615.

45. Aglietta, *A Theory of Capitalist Regulation*, 71–72.

46. Ibid., 79–82.

47. Ian Clark, *Governance, the State, Regulation and Industrial Relations* (London: Routledge, 2000), 16.

48. Aglietta, *A Theory of Capitalist Regulation*, 79–82.

49. It is significant to note at this point that I use the term intensive accumulation to refer to a pattern of production and consumption which revolves around capitalist conditions of production in *both* Department I and Department II. There is another thread of regulationist scholarship which relies more explicitly on the balance between absolute and relative surplus value. The significance of this distinction will become apparent in chapter 4 when we come to define the accumulation regime of liberal-productivism.

50. Boyer, *The Regulation School*, 132–33.

51. Jessop and Sum, *Beyond the Regulation Approach*, 42.

52. Jessop has argued (correctly) that international relations are so closely tied to the other four structural forms that it is better to analyse it as it affects those forms, as opposed to treating it as a structural form in its own right; Jessop, 'Revisiting the Regulation Approach', 11, 14.

53. Adam Tickell and Jamie A. Peck, 'Social Regulation *after* Fordism: Regulation Theory, Neoliberalism and the Global-Local Nexus', *Economy and Society* 24(3) (1995): 360.

54. Ibid., 360.

55. Mark Elam, 'Puzzling Out the Post-Fordist Debate: Technology, Markets and Institutions', in *Post-Fordism: A Reader*, ed. Ash Amin (Oxford: Blackwell Publishers, 1994), 57.

56. Jessop has argued that whereas accumulation regimes are best seen as macro-level concepts, modes of regulation operate at the meso-level. Once the state and the law are recognised as forms of capitalist social relations in their own right, this conceptualisation loses traction. See Bob Jessop, 'Survey Article: The Regulation Approach', *Journal of Political Philosophy* 5(3) (1997): 291.

57. Neilson, 'Remaking the Connections', 162.

58. Robert Boyer and Yves Saillard, 'A Summary of Régulation Theory', in *Régulation Theory: The State of the Art*, ed. Robert Boyer and Yves Saillard (London: Routledge, 2002), 41.

59. Alain Lipietz, *Towards a New Economic Order: Postfordism, Ecology and Democracy*, trans. Malcolm Slater (Cambridge: Polity Press, 1992), 1–7.

60. Key texts in this tradition include Louis Althusser, *For Marx*, trans. Ben Brewster (London: NLB, 1977); Louis Althusser and Étienne Balibar, *Reading Capital*, trans. Ben Brewster (London: NLB, 1977).

61. Hugh Collins, *Marxism and Law* (Oxford: Clarendon Press, 1982), 9–16.

62. Boyer, *The Regulation School,* 23–24.

63. See, for example, Alain Lipietz, *The Enchanted World: Inflation, Credit and the World Crisis*, trans. Ian Patterson (London: Verso, 1985).

64. Henri Nadel, '*Régulation* and Marx', in *Régulation Theory: The State of the Art*, ed. Robert Boyer and Yves Saillard (London: Routledge, 2002), 28–35.

65. Neilson, 'Remaking the Connections', 161.

66. Ibid., 168–70. See also Robert Boyer, 'How and Why Capitalisms Differ', *Economy and Society* 34(4) (2005): 509–57.

67. Jessop and Sum, *Beyond the Regulation Approach*, 375.

68. Karl Marx, *Grundrisse*, trans. Martin Nicolaus (London: Allen Lane in association with New Left Review, 1973), 85–88.

69. Treuren, 'State Theory', 60–61.

70. Ibid., 61.

71. Boyer, 'How and Why Capitalisms Differ', 514. The three properties he identified were mechanisation-based intensive accumulation, a capital-labour compromise based on the sharing out of productivity gains and a circuit of capital operating largely within a national space.

72. Neilson, 'Remaking the Connections'; Matt Vidal, 'Postfordism as a Dysfunctional Accumulation Regime: A Comparative Analysis of the USA, the UK and Germany', *Work, Employment and Society* 27(3) (2013): 451–71; Brett Heino, 'Capitalism, Regulation Theory and Australian Labour Law: Towards a New Theoretical Model', *Capital & Class* 39(3) (2015): 453–72.

73. Werner Bonefeld, 'Reformulation of State Theory', *Capital & Class* 11(3) (1987): 105, 121.

74. Peter Kennedy, 'Beyond the Objective & the Subjective: Putting Value Back into the Social', *Critique: Journal of Socialist Theory* 29(1) (2001): 231.

75. Bonefeld, 'Reformulation of State Theory', 105.

76. John Holloway, 'The Great-Bear, Post-Fordism and Class Struggle: A Comment on Bonefeld and Jessop', *Capital & Class* 12(3) (1988): 101–3.

77. A point that has been made repeatedly by people working within the PRA. See, for example: Lipietz, 'Rebel Sons', 22; Boyer, *The Regulation School*, vii; Bob Jessop, 'Regulation Theory, Post Fordism and the State: More Than a Reply to Werner Bonefield', *Capital & Class* 12(1) (1988): 151.

78. Kennedy, 'Beyond the Objective & the Subjective', 231.

79. Bob Fine, *Democracy and the Rule of Law: Marx's Critique of the Legal Form* (Caldwell: The Blackburn Press, 2002), 134.

80. Marx, *Capital Volume I*, 138–39.

81. Fine, *Democracy and the Rule of Law*, 95.

82. Jessop and Sum, *Beyond the Regulation Approach*, 37.

83. See, for example: Robert Delorme, 'A New View on the Economic Theory of the State: A Case Study of France', *Journal of Economic Issues* XVIII(3) (1984): 715–44; Christine André, 'The Welfare State and Institutional Compromises: From Origins to Contemporary Crisis', in *Régulation Theory: The State of the Art*, ed. Robert Boyer and Yves Saillard (London: Routledge, 2002), 94–100.

84. Bob Jessop, 'Interpretive Sociology and the Dialectic of Structure and Agency', *Theory, Culture & Society* 13(1) (1996): 124.

85. Marx, *Grundrisse*, 85–88.

86. Vidal, 'Reworking Postfordism', 273.

87. Treuren, 'State Theory', 60–61.

88. Stavros Mavroudeas, 'Regulation Theory: The Road from Creative Marxism to Postmodern Disintegration', *Science & Society* 63(3) (1999): 321–22.

89. Michele Salvati, 'A Long Cycle in Industrial Relations, or: Regulation Theory and Political Economy', *Labour* 3(1) (1989): 41.

90. Boyer, *The Regulation School*, 92–94.

91. Simon Clarke, 'The Global Accumulation of Capital and the Periodisation of the Capitalist State Form', in *Open Marxism Volume I: Dialectics and History*, ed. Werner Bonefeld, Richard Gunn, and Kosmas Psychopedis (London: Pluto Press, 1992), 133–50.

92. Ian Hampson, 'Post-Fordism, The "French Regulation School", and the Work of John Mathews', *Journal of Australian Political Economy* 28 (1991): 115.

93. Jessop and Sum, *Beyond the Regulation Approach*, 43.

94. Karl Marx, *A Contribution to the Critique of Political Economy*, trans. N. I. Stone (Chicago: Charles H. Kerr & Company, 1904), 11–12.

95. Neilson, 'Remaking the Connections', 161.

96. Paul Blackledge, *Reflections on the Marxist Theory of History* (Manchester: Manchester University Press, 2006), 164–66.

97. Elam, 'Puzzling Out the Post-Fordist Debate', 57.

98. Fine, *Democracy and the Rule of Law*, 95.

99. Ibid., 96.

100. Richard Marsden, *The Nature of Capital: Marx after Foucault* (Abingdon: Routledge, 1999), 179.

101. Marx, *Capital Volume I*, 164–69.

102. Olufemi Taiwo, *Legal Naturalism: A Marxist Theory of Law* (Ithaca: Cornell University Press, 1996), 46–54.

103. Marx, *Capital Volume I*, 178.

104. Karl Marx, 'On the Jewish Question', in *The Marx-Engels Reader*, ed. Robert C. Tucker (New York: W.W. Norton & Company, 1978), 34.

105. Taiwo, *Legal Naturalism*, 59–65.

106. See, for example, John Holloway and Sol Picciotto, 'Introduction: Towards a Materialist Theory of the State', in *State and Capital: A Marxist Debate*, ed. John Holloway and Sol Picciotto (London: Edward Arnold, 1978), 5–10.

107. See, for example, Josef Esser and Joachim Hirsch, 'The Crisis of Fordism and the Dimensions of a "Post-Fordist" Regional and Urban Structure', in ed. Amin, *Post-Fordism: A Reader*, 71–98.

108. Jessop, 'Regulation Theory, Post Fordism and the State', 155.

109. See, for example, Bruno Théret, 'To Have or to Be: On the Problem of the Interaction between State and Economy and Its "Solidarist" Mode of Regulation', *Economy and Society* 23(1) (1994): 1–46; Robert Delorme, 'The State as Relational, Integrated and Complex: l'etat relationnel integre complexe (ERIC)', in *Régulation Theory: The State of the Art*, ed. Boyer and Saillard, 115–21; Bob Jessop, *State Power* (Cambridge: Polity Press, 2007).

CHAPTER 3

1. Michael Lebowitz, *Beyond Capital* (Basingstoke & New York: Palgrave Macmillan, 2003), 52.
2. Hugh Collins, *Marxism and Law* (Oxford: Clarendon Press, 1982), 10.
3. Maureen Cain and Alan Hunt, ed., *Marx and Engels on Law* (London: Academic Press, 1979), ix.
4. Bob Fine, *Democracy and the Rule of Law: Marx's Critique of the Legal Form* (Caldwell: The Blackburn Press, 2002), 66.
5. Karl Marx, 'Debates on Freedom of the Press', in *Collected Works Volume I*, ed. Karl Marx and Friedrich Engels (London: Lawrence and Wishart, 2010), 162, http://www.koorosh-modaresi.com/MarxEngels/V1.pdf.
6. Fine, *Democracy and the Rule of Law*, 5–8.
7. Karl Marx, *Capital: A Critique of Political Economy Volume I*, trans. Ben Fowkes (London: Penguin Classics, 1990), 178.
8. Ibid.
9. Susan Von Arx, 'An Examination of E.B. Pashukanis's General Theory of Law and Marxism' (PhD diss., State University of New York, 1997), 66.
10. Friedrich Engels, 'Letter to Conrad Schmidt', in *Essential Works of Socialism*, ed. Irving Howe (New York: Holt, Rinehart and Winston, 1970), 71.
11. See, for example: Marx, *Capital Volume I*, 389–416; Friedrich Engels, *The Condition of the English Working Class in England* (London: Electronic Book Company, 1998), 267–68, 330.
12. Karl Marx, 'Inaugural Address of the Working Men's International Association', in *Collected Works Volume XX,* ed. Karl Marx and Friedrich Engels (London: Lawrence and Wishart, 2010), 11.
13. Karl Marx, 'Letter to Bolte', in *Karl Marx: Selected Writings*, ed. David McLellan (Oxford: Oxford University Press, 1977), 589.
14. Marx, *Capital Volume I*, 344.
15. Marx studied 'the state, law and morality . . . only *in so far* as political economy professes to deal with these subjects'; Karl Marx, quoted in *The Poverty of Theory and Other Essays*, by E.P. Thompson (London: Merlin, 1978), 259.
16. Fine, *Democracy and the Rule of Law*, 95–96.
17. Ben Fine and Alfredo Saad-Filho, *Marx's 'Capital'* (London & New York: Pluto Press, 2004), 4.
18. Marx noted that 'all science would be superfluous if the form of appearance of things directly coincided with their essence': Karl Marx, *Capital: A Critique of Political Economy Volume III*, trans. David Fernbach (London: Penguin Classics, 1991), 956.
19. Geoffrey Kay and James Mott, *Political Order and the Law of Labour* (London: Macmillan Press, 1982), 94.
20. Nicos Poulantzas, *State, Power, Socialism*, trans. Patrick Camiller (London: NLB, 1978), 86.
21. Evgeny B. Pashukanis, *Law and Marxism: A General Theory*, trans. Barbara Einhorn (London: Ink Links, 1978), 55.
22. Marx, *Capital Volume I*, 178.
23. Ibid.

24. Pashukanis, *Law and Marxism*, 109–13.

25. Fine, *Democracy and the Rule of Law*, 160. Fine is correct in criticising Pashukanis when the latter placed the cell-form as the abstract legal subject, which is in fact a highly developed bourgeois form.

26. Peter Binns, 'Law and Marxism', *Capital & Class* 4(1) (1980): 102.

27. Fine, *Democracy and the Rule of Law*, 137–39.

28. Ibid.

29. Pashukanis, *Law and Marxism*, 71, 95.

30. Michael E. Tigar and Madeleine R. Levy, *Law and the Rise of Capitalism* (New York: Monthly Review Press, 2000), 74–77, 138–42.

31. Bernard Edelman, *Ownership of the Image: Elements for a Marxist Theory of Law*, trans. Elizabeth Kingdom (London: Routledge & Kegan Paul, 1979), 91–102.

32. A criticism that has been made of Pashukanis, despite the fact that he asserted otherwise. See, for example, Ronnie Warrington, 'Standing Pashukanis on His Head', *Capital & Class* 4(3) (1980): 105; Evgeny Pashukanis, 'The Marxist Theory of Law and the Construction of Socialism', in *Pashukanis: Selected Writings on Marxism and Law*, ed. Piers Beirne and Robert Sharlet (London & New York: Academic Press, 1980), 194–97.

33. Marx, *Capital Volume I*, 711.

34. Karl Marx, *Grundrisse*, trans. Martin Nicolaus (London: Allen Lane in association with New Left Review, 1973), 471–79.

35. Pashukanis, *Law and Marxism*, 135–36.

36. Ibid., 119–28.

37. Poulantzas, *State, Power, Socialism*, 86.

38. Ibid., 54–56.

39. Pashukanis, *Law and Marxism*, 94.

40. China Miéville, *Between Equal Rights: A Marxist Theory of International Law* (Chicago: Haymarket Books, 2006), 95, 105.

41. Burkhard Tuschling, cited in *The Capitalist State: Marxist Theories and Methods*, by Bob Jessop (New York: New York University Press, 1982), 85–86.

42. Kay and Mott, *Political Order and the Law of Labour*, 111.

43. Taiwo makes a similar argument when he claims that law is part of the constitutive essence of the capitalist mode of production: Olufemi Taiwo, *Legal Naturalism: A Marxist Theory of Law* (Ithaca: Cornell University Press, 1996), 64–75.

44. Brett Heino, 'Capitalism, Regulation Theory and Australian Labour Law: Towards a New Theoretical Model', *Capital & Class* 39(3) (2015): 461.

45. Ibid.

46. Lebowitz, *Beyond Capital*, 77–100.

47. Heino, 'Capitalism, Regulation Theory and Australian Labour Law', 461.

48. Bernhard Blanke, Ulrich Jürgens and Hans Kastendiek, 'On the Current Marxist Discussion on the Analysis of Form and Function of the Bourgeois State', in *State and Capital: A Marxist Debate*, ed. John Holloway and Sol Picciotto (London: Edward Arnold, 1978), 125–27.

49. Miéville, *Between Equal Rights*, 111–13.

50. Kay and Mott, *Political Order and the Law of Labour*, 131–35.

51. Ibid., 96.

52. Mark Neocleous, *Administering Civil Society: Towards a Theory of State Power* (Basingstoke: Macmillan Press, 1996), 107.

53. Pashukanis noted how the legal form has a capacity to subject other social relationships to its logic; Pashukanis, *Law and Marxism*, 109–33.

54. Poulantzas, *State, Power, Socialism*, 86–87.

55. Kay and Mott, *Political Order and the Law of Labour*, 133.

56. Ibid., 134.

57. Laura Bennett, *Making Labour Law in Australia: Industrial Relations, Politics and Law* (Sydney: The Law Book Company, 1994), 9–21.

58. Stuart Macintyre, 'Arbitration in Action', in *The New Province for Law and Order: 100 Years of Australian Industrial Conciliation and Arbitration*, ed. Joe Isaac and Stuart Macintyre (Port Melbourne: Cambridge University Press, 2004), 76–77.

59. Kay and Mott, *Political Order and the Law of Labour*, 133; Heino, 'Capitalism, Regulation Theory and Australian Labour Law', 465.

60. Ibid., 465–66.

61. Bob Jessop, 'Revisiting the Regulation Approach: Critical Reflections on the Contradictions, Dilemmas, Fixes and Crisis Dynamics of Growth Regimes', *Capital & Class* 37(1) (2013): 10–11; Louis Althusser, *For Marx*, trans. Ben Brewster (London: NLB, 1977), 87–128.

62. This is not to suggest that labour law does not affect the other institutional forms. Where these other forms are affected or effect change, they will be discussed in the coming chapters.

63. Robert Boyer, 'Perspectives on the Wage-Labour Nexus', in *Régulation Theory: The State of the Art*, ed. Robert Boyer and Yves Saillard (London: Routledge, 2002), 73–74.

64. Ibid., 74.

65. Gerry Treuren, 'How and Why Do Institutions Change? A Four Phase Framework for the Description of Institutional Development', *Journal of Economic and Social Policy* 7(2) (2003): 58–63; Brett Heino, 'The State, Class and Occupational Health and Safety: Locating the Capitalist State's Role in the Regulation of OHS in NSW', *Labour & Industry* 23(2) (2013): 160–61.

66. Robert Boyer, *The Regulation School: A Critical Introduction*, trans. Craig Charney (New York: Columbia University Press, 1990), 42.

67. Ibid., 44.

68. See, for example, Lynne Chester, 'Another Variety of Capitalism?: The Australian Mode of *Régulation*' (paper presented at the 13th Conference of the Association for Heterodox Economics, Nottingham, UK, 6–9 July 2011), 4–7.

69. Pashukanis, *Law and Marxism*, 55.

70. For a representative sample of such work, see Brett Heino, 'Capitalism, Regulation Theory and Australian Labour Law: Exploring the Labour Law Regimes of Antipodean Fordism and Liberal-Productivism, 1964–2009' (PhD diss., University of Wollongong, 2016), 66.

71. Lauren B. Edelman and Robin Stryker, 'A Sociological Approach to Law and the Economy', in *The Handbook of Economic Sociology*, ed. Neil J. Smelser and Richard Swedberg (Princeton: Princeton University Press, 2005), 527.

72. Heino, 'Capitalism, Regulation Theory and Australian Labour Law', 457.

CHAPTER 4

1. Bob Jessop, 'Regulation Theory, Post Fordism and the State: More Than a Reply to Werner Bonefield', *Capital & Class* 12(1) (1988): 155.

2. Bob Jessop and Ngai-Ling Sum, *Beyond the Regulation Approach: Putting Capitalist Economies in Their Place* (Cheltenham: Edward Elgar, 2006), 58–89.

3. Ian Hampson, 'Post-Fordism, The "French Regulation School", and the Work of John Mathews', *Journal of Australian Political Economy* 28 (1991): 115, 122–24.

4. Alain Lipietz, *Towards a New Economic Order: Postfordism, Ecology and Democracy*, trans. Malcolm Slater (Cambridge: Polity Press, 1992), 3–7.

5. Louis Althusser, *For Marx*, trans. Ben Brewster (London: NLB, 1977), 87–128.

6. Ibid.

7. Bob Jessop, 'Revisiting the Regulation Approach: Critical Reflections on the Contradictions, Dilemmas, Fixes and Crisis Dynamics of Growth Regimes', *Capital & Class* 37(1) (2013): 10.

8. See, respectively, Michel Aglietta, *A Theory of Capitalist Regulation: The US Experience* (London: NLB, 1979), 93–96; Steven Kettell, 'Circuits of Capital and Overproduction: A Marxist Analysis of the Present World Economic Crisis', *Review of Radical Political Economics* 38(1) (2006): 28–31.

9. Pascal Petit, 'Structural Forms and Growth Regimes of the Post-Fordist Era', *Review of Social Economy* 57(2) (1999): 221; Robert Boyer, 'The Political in the Era of Globalization and Finance: Focus on Some *Régulation* School Research', *International Journal of Urban and Regional Research* 24(2) (2000): 279–81.

10. See, respectively, Jessop, 'Revisiting the Regulation Approach', 14; David Neilson, 'Formal and Real Subordination and the Contemporary Proletariat: Re-coupling Marxist Class Theory and Labour-Process Analysis', *Capital & Class* 31(1) (2007): 102–3.

11. Maria Ivanova, 'Consumerism and the Crisis: Wither "the American Dream"?', *Critical Sociology* 37(3) (2011): 333.

12. Thom Workman, *If You're in My Way, I'm Walking: The Assault on Working People Since 1970* (Black Point & Winnipeg: Fernwood Publishing, 2009), 9–16.

13. Michel Juillard, 'Accumulation Regimes', in *Régulation Theory: The State of the Art*, ed. Robert Boyer and Yves Saillard (London: Routledge, 2002), 155.

14. Jessop and Sum, *Beyond the Regulation Approach*, 107.

15. Matt Vidal, 'Postfordism as a Dysfunctional Accumulation Regime: A Comparative Analysis of the USA, the UK and Germany', *Work, Employment and Society* 27(3) (2013): 458.

16. Kettell, 'Circuits of Capital and Overproduction', 32.

17. Neil Faulkner, *A Marxist History of the World: From Neanderthals to Neoliberals* (London: Pluto Press, 2013), 254.

18. See, for example, Aglietta, *A Theory of Capitalist Regulation*; Alain Lipietz, 'Accumulation, Crises, and Ways Out: Some Methodological Reflections on the Concept of "Regulation"', *International Journal of Political Economy* 18(2) (1988): 26–27; Bob Jessop, 'Conservative Regimes and the Transition to Post-Fordism: The Cases of Britain and West Germany', in *Capitalist Development and Crisis Theory:*

Accumulation, Regulation and Spatial Restructuring, ed. Mark Gottdiener and Nicos Komninos (Basingstoke: Macmillan, 1989), 261–99.

19. Barrie Dyster and David Meredith, *Australia in the Global Economy* (Port Melbourne: Cambridge University Press, 2012), 161.

20. Department of the Treasury, 'Australia's Century Since Federation at a Glance', *Economic Roundup* 1 (2001): 54.

21. Industry Commission, *Assessing Australia's Productivity Performance* (Canberra: Australian Government Publishing Service, 1997), 34–35.

22. Ibid.

23. Matt Cowgill, 'A Shrinking Slice of the Pie', ACTU Working Paper No. 1 (2013), 4–6; Paul Frijters and Robert Gregory, 'From Golden Age to Golden Age: Australia's "Great Leap Forward"?', *Economic Record* 82(257) (2006): 207–9.

24. A. Barnard, N. G. Butlin and J. J. Pincus, 'Public and Private Sector Employment in Australia, 1901–1974', *Australian Economic Review* 19(1) (1977): 50.

25. Phillip Anthony O'Hara, 'A Social Structure of Accumulation for Long Wave Upswing in Australia?', *Journal of Australian Political Economy* 61 (2008): 99.

26. O'Hara shows that the average rate of profit (after tax) from 1960–69 was 5.5% (compared, for example, to the 3.0% prevailing between 1980–89): Ibid., 100.

27. Ibid.

28. See, for example, Alastair Greig, 'Australian Housing, Technological Change and the Fordist Regime of Accumulation', *Housing Studies* 12(3) (1997): 321–35; Mark Rolfe, 'Antipodean Fordism: Postwar Americanisation Down Under', in *Henry Ford: Critical Evaluations in Business and Management Volume 2*, ed. John Wood and Michael Wood (London & New York: Routledge, 2003), 323–53; James Walsh, 'Mass Migration and the Mass Society: Fordism, Immigration Policy and the Post-War Long Boom in Canada and Australia, 1947–1970', *Journal of Historical Sociology* 25(3) (2012): 352–85; Lynne Chester, 'The Australian Variant of Neoliberal Capitalism', in *Neoliberalism: Beyond the Free Market*, ed. Damien Cahill, Lindy Edwards and Frank Stilwell (Cheltenham: Edward Elgar, 2012), 153–79.

29. Christopher Lloyd, 'Australian Capitalism Since 1992: A New Regime of Accumulation?', *Journal of Australian Political Economy* 61 (2008): 30–55; Ray Broomhill, 'Australian Economic Booms in Historical Perspective', *Journal of Australian Political Economy* 61 (2008): 12–29.

30. Gerrit Treuren, 'Regulation Theory and Australian Theorising of Institutional Change in Industrial Regulation' (paper presented at the 11th Conference of the Association of Industrial Relations Academics of Australia and New Zealand, Brisbane, Australia, 20 January–1 February 1997), 362.

31. Rolfe, 'Antipodean Fordism', 323–53.

32. Treuren, 'Regulation Theory', 366.

33. Alain Lipietz, 'The Post-Fordist World: Labour Relations, International Hierarchy and Global Ecology', *Review of International Political Economy* 4(1) (1997): 2.

34. Matt Vidal, 'Reworking Postfordism: Labor Process Versus Employment Relations', *Sociology Compass* 5(4) (2011): 279.

35. Bob Jessop, 'Thatcherism and Flexibility: The White Heat of a Post-Fordist Revolution', in *The Politics of Flexibility: Restructuring State and Industry in Britain, Germany and Scandinavia*, ed. Bob Jessop et al. (Aldershot: Edward Elgar,

1991), 136–37. For a discussion of the different meanings which can be attached to the term 'lead sector' see Brett Heino, 'Capitalism, Regulation Theory and Australian Labour Law: Exploring the Labour Law Regimes of Antipodean Fordism and Liberal-Productivism, 1964–2009' (PhD diss., University of Wollongong, 2016), 78.

36. Australian Bureau of Statistics, *Year Book Australia* (1301.0, No. 71, 1988), 673.

37. Chris Wright, 'Taylorism Reconsidered: The Impact of Scientific Management within the Australian Workplace', *Labour History* 64 (1993): 38.

38. Harry Braverman, *Labor and Monopoly Capital: The Degradation of Work in the Twentieth Century* (New York & London: Monthly Review Press, 1974), 124–26.

39. Lucy Taksa, 'Scientific Management: Technique or Cultural Ideology?', *Journal of Industrial Relations* 34(3) (1992): 383–87.

40. Wright, 'Taylorism Reconsidered', 40.

41. Rolfe, 'Antipodean Fordism', 335.

42. Lucy Taksa, 'The Cultural Diffusion of Scientific Management: The United States and New South Wales', *Journal of Industrial Relations* 37(3) (1995): 427–61.

43. Stephen de Rozairo, 'Enterprise Bargaining: An ACTU Perspective', ACTU Paper (1992), accessed 19 December 2016, http://www.actu.org.au/actu-media/archives/1992/enterprise-bargaining-an-actu-perspective.

44. Wright, 'Taylorism Reconsidered', 41.

45. Greig, 'Australian Housing', 322–27.

46. Wright, 'Taylorism Reconsidered', 43.

47. Tom Sheridan, *Mindful Militants: The Amalgamated Engineering Union in Australia, 1920–1972* (Cambridge: Cambridge University Press, 1975), 283–84.

48. Ibid., 40.

49. Aglietta, *A Theory of Capitalist Regulation*, 71–72.

50. Rolfe, 'Antipodean Fordism', 336.

51. Walsh, 'Mass Migration and the Mass Society', 364–65.

52. Nikki Balnave and Greg Patmore, 'The AMWU: Politics and Industrial Relations, 1852–2012', in *Organise, Educate, Control: The AMWU in Australia 1852–2012*, ed. Andrew Reeves and Andrew Dettmer (Clayton: Monash University Publishing, 2013), 19.

53. Australian Bureau of Statistics, *Year Book Australia* (1301.0, No. 83, 2001), 712.

54. Stephen Bell and Brian Head, 'Australia's Political Economy: Critical Themes and Issues', in *State, Economy and Public Policy in Australia*, ed. Stephen Bell and Brian Head (Melbourne: Oxford University Press, 1994), 10–13.

55. Commonwealth, *Parliamentary Debates*, House of Representatives, 12 March 1991, 1763 (Bob Hawke).

56. Christopher Lloyd, 'Australian Capitalism Since 1992', 35, 47–49.

57. Christopher Lloyd, 'Regime Change in Australian Capitalism: Towards a Historical Political Economy of Regulation', *Australian Economic History Review* 42(3) (2002): 239, 247.

58. Greig, 'Australian Housing', 329.

59. Ibid.

60. Greg Whitwell, 'The Power of Economic Ideas? Keynesian Economic Policies in Post-War Australia', in *State, Economy and Public Policy in Australia*, ed. Stephen Bell and Brian Head (Melbourne: Oxford University Press, 1994), 119–41.

61. Broomhill, 'Australian Economic Booms', 19–20.

62. For example, in the 1960s, just 9% of total export value was provided by the manufacturing sector, while agricultural exports accounted for 62%: Ellis Connolly and Christine Lewis, 'Structural Change in the Australian Economy', *Reserve Bank of Australia Bulletin* (September Quarter 2010): 2.

63. Lynne Chester, 'Actually Existing Markets: The Case of Neoliberal Australia', *Journal of Economic Issues* XLIV(2) (2010): 317.

64. *Ex parte H.V. McKay* (1907) 2 CAR 1, 4.

65. Gaby Ramia and Nick Wailes, 'Putting Wage-Earners into Wage-Earners' Welfare States: The Relationship Between Social Policy and Industrial Relations in Australia and New Zealand', *Australian Journal of Social Issues* 41(1) (2006): 53.

66. Francis Castles, 'The Wage Earners' Welfare State Revisited: Refurbishing the Established Model of Australian Social Protection, 1983–93', *Australian Journal of Social Issues* 29(2) (1994): 120–45.

67. Ibid., 124.

68. Robert Boyer, 'Wage Formation in Historical Perspective: The French Experience', *Cambridge Journal of Economics* 3(2) (1979): 115–16.

69. And reflected in the fact that the Australian wage structure in this epoch was notably compressed: Frijters and Gregory, 'From Golden Age to Golden Age', 207.

70. Peter Cochrane, 'Doing Time', in *Making a Life: A People's History of Australia Since 1788*, ed. Verity Burgmann and Jenny Lee (Fitzroy: McPhee Gribble/Penguin, 1988), 189.

71. Chris Provis, 'Comparative Wage Justice', *Journal of Industrial Relations* 28(1) (1986): 25.

72. Gerhard Bosch, 'Towards a New Standard Employment Relationship in Western Europe', *British Journal of Industrial Relations* 42(4) (2004): 618–19.

73. Ibid., 619–20.

74. John Howe, 'The Job Creation Function of the State: A New Subject for Labour Law', *Australian Journal of Labour Law* 14(3) (2001): 4.

75. Castles, 'The Wage Earners' Welfare State Revisited', 127–28.

76. H. B. Higgins, 'A New Province for Law and Order: Industrial Peace through Minimum Wage and Arbitration', *Harvard Law Review* 29(1) (1915): 23.

77. Michel De Vroey, 'A Regulation Approach Interpretation of Contemporary Crisis', *Capital & Class* 8(2) (1984): 55.

78. See, respectively, ibid., 55–56; Aglietta, *A Theory of Capitalist Regulation*, 119–22; Mark Elam, 'Puzzling Out the Post-Fordist Debate: Technology, Markets and Institutions', in *Post-Fordism: A Reader*, ed. Ash Amin (Oxford: Blackwell Publishers, 1994), 64; A. Leyshon and A. Tickell, 'Money Order? The Discursive Construction of Bretton Woods and the Making and Breaking of Regulatory Space', *Environment and Planning A* 26(12) (1994): 1875–84.

79. Department of the Treasury, 'Australia's Century Since Federation at a Glance', 55–56.

80. Ibid., 57.

81. Australian Bureau of Statistics, *Australian Social Trends* (4102.0, 2001), 137.

82. Frijters and Gregory, 'From Golden Age to Golden Age', 208.

83. Australian Bureau of Statistics, *Australian System of National Accounts* (5204.0, 2008), 7–8.

84. Industry Commission, 'Assessing Australia's Productivity Performance', 34–35.

85. Phil Toner, 'The Crisis of Equipment Investment in Australia', *Journal of Australian Political Economy* 22 (1988): 39–56; 'Gross Fixed Capital Formation (% of GDP) in Australia', Trading Economics, accessed 21 December 2016, http://www.tradingeconomics.com/australia/gross-fixed-capital-formation-percent-of-gdp-wb-data.html.

86. O'Hara, 'A Social Structure of Accumulation', 100.

87. For a discussion of the nature of these limits, see, Heino, 'Capitalism, Regulation Theory and Australian Labour Law', 96.

88. De Vroey, 'A Regulation Approach Interpretation of Contemporary Crisis', 55–56.

89. Broomhill, 'Australian Economic Booms', 21.

90. Tom Bramble, 'Political Economy and the Management Strategy in the Metal and Engineering Industry', *Journal of Industrial Relations* 31(1) (1989): 26–27.

91. Political Research Group & Political Economy Movement (S.A.), 'Workers, Trade Unions & Industrial Democracy', *Journal of Australian Political Economy* 3 (1978): 82.

92. Alain Lipietz, 'Towards Global Fordism?', *New Left Review* 132 (1982): 35.

93. Cowgill, 'A Shrinking Slice of the Pie', 4–5.

94. Australian Bureau of Statistics, *Australian System of National Accounts*, 7.

95. Australian Bureau of Statistics, *Australian National Accounts: National Income, Expenditure and Product 1992–93* (5204.0, 1994), 1.

96. Christopher Lloyd, 'The Lucky Country Syndrome in Australia: Resources, Social Democracy, and Regimes of Development in Historical Political Economy Perspective' (paper presented at the Asia Pacific Economic and Business History Conference, Canberra, Australia, February 16–18, 2012), 21.

97. Broomhill, 'Australian Economic Booms', 20–21.

98. For example, in 1960 approximately 50% of the workforce were engaged in the services sector. By 2011/12, this had increased to 75%: Philip Lowe, 'The Changing Structure of the Australian Economy and Monetary Policy' (speech delivered at the 12th Annual Economic Forum of the Australian Industry Group, Sydney, Australia, 7 March 2012).

99. Bramble, 'Political Economy and Management Strategy', 28–29.

100. John Lund and Christopher Wright, 'State Regulation and the New Taylorism: The Case of Australian Grocery Warehousing', *Relations Industrielles* 56(4) (2001): 747–69; Claire Mayhew and Michael Quinlan, 'Fordism in the Fast Food Industry: Pervasive Management Control and Occupational Health and Safety Risks for Young Temporary Workers', *Sociology of Health & Illness* 24(3) (2002): 261–84; Robin Price, 'Down the Aisle: The Effects of Technological Change on Retail Workers Skills' (paper presented at the 27th International Labour Process Conference, Edinburgh, UK, 6–8 April 2009); Sandra Martain, 'The Taylorisation of Paid Care Work in Aged Care' (paper presented at the 28th Conference of the Association of Industrial Relations Academics of Australia and New Zealand, Melbourne, Australia, 5–7 February 2014).

101. John Burgess and Iain Campbell, 'The Nature and Dimensions of Precarious Employment in Australia', *Labour & Industry* 8(3) (1998): 8.

102. While post–World War II strikes in Australia were frequent and often involved considerable numbers of workers, they also tended to be of very short duration compared to other countries: Malcolm Waters, *Strikes in Australia* (Sydney: George Allen & Unwin, 1982), 203–25.

103. Alain Lipietz, 'Fears and Hopes: The Crisis of the Liberal-Productivist Model and Its Green Alternative', *Capital & Class* 37(1) (2013): 129–30.

104. Steven S. Saeger, 'Globalization and Deindustrialization: Myth and Reality in the OECD', *Weltwirtschaftliches Archiv* 133(4) (1997): 579–608.

105. Petit, 'Structural Forms and Growth Regimes', 229–33.

106. Jessop, 'Revisiting the Regulation Approach', 18.

107. Vidal, 'Reworking Postfordism', 279–84.

108. Tom Bramble, *Trade Unionism in Australia: A History from Flood to Ebb Tide* (Port Melbourne: Cambridge University Press, 2008), 115.

109. Kettell, 'Circuits of Capital and Overproduction', 36–41.

110. David Harvey, *The Enigma of Capital and the Crises of Capitalism* (London: Profile Books, 2010), 17–18.

111. Jessop and Sum, *Beyond the Regulation Approach*, 109–11.

112. Ibid.

113. See, respectively, Bob Jessop, 'Survey Article: The Regulation Approach', *Journal of Political Philosophy* 5(3) (1997): 293; Ivanova, 'Consumerism and the Crisis', 342; Vladmiro Giacché, 'Marx, the Falling Rate of Profit, Financialization, and the Current Crisis', *International Journal of Political Economy* 40(3) (2011): 18–32.

114. Department of the Treasury, 'Australia's Century Since Federation at a Glance', 55–56.

115. See, respectively, Broomhill, 'Australian Economic Booms', 23; Australian Bureau of Statistics, *Year Book Australia* (1301.0, No. 92, 2012), 797.

116. Productivity Commission, 'Productivity Update' (July 2015), 9.

117. Frijters and Gregory, 'From Golden Age to Golden Age', 209; OECD, *Innovations in Labour Market Policies: The Australian Way* (Paris: OECD Publishing, 2001), 257–58; OECD, *OECD Employment Outlook 2014* (Paris: OECD Publishing, 2014), 77–78.

118. Cowgill, 'A Shrinking Slice of the Pie', 4–6. In 2011–12, the wages share of total factor income sat at 53.1%, much lower than the peak of 61.9% reached in 1974–75. The profit share had concomitantly skyrocketed, peaking at 29.9% in 2008–09: Australian Bureau of Statistics, *Australian System of National Accounts* (5204.0, 2012), 13–14.

119. Australian Bureau of Statistics, *Year Book Australia* (1301.0, No. 87, 2005), 430; Australian Bureau of Statistics, *Australian National Accounts: National Income, Expenditure and Product* (5206.0, March Quarter 2015), 35, 37.

120. Australian Bureau of Statistics, *Australian Social Trends 2014* (4102.0, 2014), accessed 22 December 2016, http://www.abs.gov.au/ausstats/abs@.nsf/lookup/4102.0main+features202014.

121. Vidal, 'Reworking Postfordism', 277–84.

122. Australian Bureau of Statistics, *Australian National Accounts: National Income, Expenditure and Product* (5206.0, June Quarter 2015), 12.

123. At no time during the mining boom did employment ever exceed 275,200 persons (reached in May 2012), representing only 2.4% of employed persons: Australian Bureau of Statistics, *Labour Force Australia, Detailed, Quarterly* (6291.0.55.003, May 2015), accessed 22 December 2016, http://www.abs.gov.au/AUSSTATS/abs@.nsf/DetailsPage/6291.0.55.003May%202015?OpenDocument.

124. Ibid.

125. A. E. Woodward, 'Industrial Relations in the '70s', *Journal of Industrial Relations* 12(2) (1970): 116.

126. Peter Lloyd, '100 Years of Tariff Protection in Australia', *Australian Economic History Review* 48(2) (2008): 124–25.

127. Andrew Leigh, 'Trade Liberalisation and the Australian Labor Party', *Australian Journal of Politics and History* 48(4) (2002): 487.

128. Burgess and Campbell, 'The Nature and Dimensions of Precarious Employment', 8.

129. Productivity Commission, 'The Role of Non-Traditional Work in the Australian Labour Market' (Productivity Commission Research Paper, 2006), 10.

130. Specifically, in August 2013, 24% of employees did not receive paid-leave entitlements, which is used as a proxy for casual employment: Australian Bureau of Statistics, *Employee Earnings, Benefits and Trade Union Membership* (6310.0, August 2013), 6

131. David Peetz, 'Trend Analysis of Union Membership', *Australian Journal of Labour Economics* 8(1) (2005): 18–19.

132. Australian Bureau of Statistics, *Characteristics of Employment, Australia* (6333.0, 2014), accessed 22 December 2016, http://www.abs.gov.au/AUSSTATS/abs@.nsf/allprimarymainfeatures/EF3BF9BDA5BF304ECA25801F00186541?opendocument.

133. Aglietta, *A Theory of Capitalist Regulation*, 121.

134. This process of the state confronting the most powerful segments of organised labour was replicated in other Fordist countries, such as the Thatcher government's showdown with the National Union of Mineworkers and the Reagan administration's conflict with the Professional Air Traffic Controllers Organization.

CHAPTER 5

1. E. A. Dunphy and S.C.G. Wright, 'The Jubilee of Industrial Arbitration in the Federal Sphere', *Australian Law Journal* 25 (1951): 365.

2. *Ex parte H.V. McKay* (1907) 2 CAR 1, 4, 7–16 (*Harvester* case).

3. Ibid., 4.

4. This expanded definition took into account the post–World War II reality that most work attracted a margin of some kind. See *Metal Trades Margins Case* (1954) 80 CAR 3, 24.

5. *Basic Wage Inquiry* (1931) 30 CAR 2.

6. *Wage and Standard Hours Inquiry 1952–1953* (1953) 77 CAR 477, 497.

7. *Oil Industry Case* (1970) 134 CAR 159, 165.

8. See, for example, *Boilermakers' Case* (1924) 20 CAR 770, 778; *Meat Industry Case* (1925) 22 CAR 794, 803–4.

9. Chris Provis, 'Comparative Wage Justice', *Journal of Industrial Relations* 28(1) (1986): 27–30.

10. J. Hutson, *Six Wage Concepts* (Surry Hills: Amalgamated Engineering Union, 1971), 144–45.

11. *Printing Industry Employees Union of Australia v. Balmoral Press* (1942) 49 CAR 304, 310.

12. Whereby price increases were taken into account in annual basic wage cases, while broader increases in productivity were to be factored in during reviews every three or four years: *Basic Wage Case* (1961) 97 CAR 376, 387.

13. Over-awards were payments typically made at the workplace/enterprise level, which were technically outside the formal arbitration system.

14. Tom Sheridan, *Mindful Militants: The Amalgamated Engineering Union in Australia, 1920–1972* (Cambridge: Cambridge University Press, 1975), 286–93.

15. Keith Stewart quoted in Hutson, *Six Wage Concepts*, 142–43.

16. Robert Boyer, *The Regulation School: A Critical Introduction*, trans. Craig Charney (New York: Columbia University Press, 1990), x.

17. *National Wage Cases of 1965* (1965) 110 CAR 189.

18. 'Employers Open Wage Case', *Canberra Times*, 22 April 1964, 3/16.

19. Indeed, by 1965 this was already occurring: Richard Mitchell, 'Australian Industrial Relations and Labour Law Policy: A Post-War Review', *The Australian Quarterly* 52(1) (1980): 46.

20. John Burgess and Iain Campbell, 'Casual Employment in Australia: Growth, Characteristics, A Bridge or a Trap?', *Economic and Labour Relations Review* 9(1) (1998): 33.

21. For a range of indicative sources, see, Brett Heino, 'Capitalism, Regulation Theory and Australian Labour Law: Exploring the Labour Law Regimes of Antipodean Fordism and Liberal-Productivism, 1964–2009' (PhD diss., University of Wollongong, 2016), 128.

22. *Standard Hours Inquiry, 1947* (1947) 59 CAR 581.

23. See, for example, '40-Hour Week', *Cootamundra Daily Herald*, 30 June 1947, 4; 'Unrest in N.S.W. Over 40-Hour Week', *The Examiner*, 2 July 1947, 1.

24. Sandra Jones, 'Penalty Rates Under Challenge', *Journal of Industrial Relations* 23(4) (1981): 505.

25. See, respectively, *Metal Trades Annual Leave Case* (1945) 55 CAR 595; *Re Metal Trades Award; Re Annual Leave* (1963) 103 CAR 637; Australian Bureau of Statistics, *Year Book Australia* (1301.1, No. 60, 1974), 301.

26. Commonwealth Bureau of Census and Statistics, *Year Book Australia* (1301.0, No. 51, 1965), 477–78.

27. Anthony O'Donnell, ' "Non-Standard" Workers in Australia: Counts and Controversies', *Australian Journal of Labour Law* 17(1) (2004): 13.

28. Particularly given the fact that full-time employees are more likely to be union members: David Peetz, 'Trend Analysis of Union Membership', *Australian Journal of Labour Economics* 8(1) (2005): 18–19.

29. *Commonwealth Conciliation and Arbitration Act 1904* (Cth), s 2(vi).

30. H. B. Higgins, 'A New Province for Law and Order: Industrial Peace through Minimum Wage and Arbitration', *Harvard Law Review* 29(1) (1915): 23.

31. W. B. Creighton, W. J. Ford and R. J. Mitchell, *Labour Law: Text and Materials* (Sydney: The Law Book Company, 1993), 931–32.

32. *Association v. Amalgamated Engineering Union* (1935) 54 CLR 387, 403–4.

33. Ibid., 405.

34. *Burwood Cinema Limited v. Australian Theatrical and Amusement Employees' Association* (1925) 35 CLR 528, 528–29.

35. Creighton, Ford, and Mitchell, *Labour Law*, 1002–04.

36. *Commonwealth Conciliation and Arbitration Act 1947* (Cth), sch 8.

37. *R. v. Wallis; Ex parte Employers' Association of Wool Selling Brokers* (1949) 78 CLR 529.

38. Unions were often able to enforce *de facto* closed shops through agreements with management at the workplace, enterprise or industry level.

39. Commonwealth, *Parliamentary Debates*, House of Representatives, 18 April 1947, 1434 (Hubert Lazzarini).

40. Andrew Frazer, 'The Federal Conciliation and Arbitration Power: from Cradle to Grave' (Parliamentary Library Research Paper No. 15, 2002), 29.

41. Ibid., 2; Malcolm Rimmer, 'The *Workplace Relations Act 1996*: An Historical Perspective', *Australian Bulletin of Labour* 23(1) (1997): 74.

42. David Peetz, *Brave New Work Place: How Individual Contracts Are Changing Our Jobs* (Crows Nest: Allen & Unwin, 2006), 161–62.

43. Higgins, 'A New Province for Law and Order', 14.

44. *R v. Kirby; Ex parte Boilermakers' Society of Australia* (1956) 94 CLR 254.

45. Laura Bennett, *Making Labour Law in Australia: Industrial Relations, Politics and Law* (Sydney: The Law Book Company, 1994), 78–84.

46. Norman F. Dufty, *Industrial Relations in the Australian Metal Industries* (Sydney: West Publishing Corporation, 1972), 199.

47. *Conciliation and Arbitration Act 1904* (Cth), s 4.

48. *R v. Portus; Ex parte A.N.Z. Banking Group Ltd* (1972) 127 CLR 353, 371.

49. *Australian Constitution*, s 51(xxxv).

50. *Australian Boot Trade Employees Federation v. Whybrow & Co* (1910) 11 CLR 311.

51. See, for example, *Burwood Cinema Limited v. Australian Theatrical and Amusement Employees' Association* (1925) 35 CLR 528.

52. *Clyde Engineering Co. Ltd v. Cowburn* (1926) 37 CLR 466, 489–90.

53. L. G. Matthews, 'Drafting of Federal Awards', *Journal of Industrial Relations* 12(3) (1970): 306.

54. Keith Hancock, *Committee of Review into Australian Industrial Relations Law and Systems* (Canberra: Australian Government Publishing Service, 1985), 29–30.

55. Creighton, Ford, and Mitchell, *Labour Law*, 443.

56. *Employers' Total Wage Case 1964* (1964) 106 CAR 683, 689, 695.

57. *Basic Wage, Margins and Total Wage Cases of 1966* (1966) 115 CAR 93, 116–20.

58. *Employers' Total Wage Case 1964* (1964) 106 CAR 683, 694–95.

59. Dufty, *Industrial Relations*, 151–94.

60. Harold W. Fry, 'Metal-Trades Unions Conference – In Search of Consensus Instead of a Polarised Society', *Canberra Times*, 17 June 1977, 2.

61. Tom Bramble, *Trade Unionism in Australia: A History from Flood to Ebb Tide* (Port Melbourne: Cambridge University Press, 2008), 41–77.

62. *Metal Trades Margins Case* (1963) 102 CAR 138, 141.

63. *Metal Trades Work Value Inquiry* (1967) 121 CAR 587, 680.

64. The strike was in response to the gaoling of union leader Clarrie O'Shea for contempt of court, revolving broadly around the refusal of his union to pay outstanding fines for breaches of bans clauses.

65. Hancock, *Committee of Review*, 61–62.

66. These were essentially agreements negotiated between employers and unions which were presented to the Commission for ratification.

67. W. A. Howard, 'Australian Trade Unions in the Context of Union Theory', *Journal of Industrial Relations* 19(3) (1977): 271.

68. *National Wage Case 1970* (1970) CAR 135 244, 247.

69. Philip Bentley, 'Australian Trade Unionism 1970–71', *Journal of Industrial Relations* 13(4) (1971): 410, 418.

70. *Vehicle Builders Employees Federation of Australia v. General Motors-Holden Pty Ltd* (1966) 115 CAR 931, 944, 946.

71. Hancock, *Committee of Review*, 81.

72. Philip Bentley, 'Australian Trade Unionism 1973–74', *Journal of Industrial Relations* 16(4) (1974): 377.

73. See, for example, Bramble, *Trade Unionism in Australia*, 80.

74. Commonwealth, *Parliamentary Debates*, House of Representatives, 20 November 1974, 3748 (Clyde Cameron).

75. Braham Dabscheck, 'The 1975 National Wage Case: Now We Have an Incomes Policy', *Journal of Industrial Relations* 17(3) (1975): 306.

76. Keith Hancock and Sue Richardson, 'Economic and Social Effects', in *The New Province for Law and Order: 100 Years of Australian Industrial Conciliation and Arbitration*, ed. Joe Isaac and Stuart Macintyre (Port Melbourne: Cambridge University Press, 2001), 182.

77. See, for example, 'Metal Employers Support Wage Indexation', *Canberra Times*, 30 August 1975, 3.

78. *National Wage Case 1974* (1974) 157 CAR 293.

79. *National Wage Case April 1975* (1975) 167 CAR 18, 32.

80. See, respectively, Commonwealth Bureau of Census and Statistics, *The Labour Force* (6203.0, May 1969), 4; Australian Bureau of Statistics, *The Labour Force* (6203.0, November 1975), 6.

81. Hancock, *Committee of Review*, 74. The figures Hancock uses do not distinguish between part-time and casual labour.

82. Union density increased from 50% of total wage and salary earners in 1970 to 58% in 1975, representing an influx of nearly 500,000 new members: Australian Bureau of Statistics, *Year Book Australia* (1301.0, No. 59, 1973), 278; Australian Bureau of Statistics, *Year Book Australia* (1301.0, No. 61, 1976), 309–10.

83. See, respectively, Commonwealth Bureau of Census and Statistics, *Year Book Australia* (1301.0, No. 50, 1964), 501; Commonwealth Bureau of Census and Statistics, *Year Book Australia* (1301.0, No. 56, 1970), 271; Australian Bureau of Statistics, *Year Book Australia* (1976), 305.

84. Bentley, 'Australian Trade Unionism 1970–71', 414.

85. Howard, 'Australian Trade Unions', 269.

86. Commonwealth, *Parliamentary Debates*, House of Representatives, 12 April 1973, 1424 (Clyde Cameron).

87. Commonwealth, *Parliamentary Debates*, House of Representatives, 15 April 1970, 1117 (Billy Snedden).

88. 'Unions Defy Laws and Aarbitration', *Canberra Times*, 1 October 1970, 3.

89. *Strickland v. Rocla Concrete Pipes Ltd* (1971) 124 CLR 468. The corporations power provides that the Commonwealth can make laws with respect to 'foreign corporations, and trading or financial corporations formed within the limits of the Commonwealth': *Australian Constitution*, s 51(xx).

90. Braham Dabscheck, 'The Arbitration System Since 1967', in *State, Economy and Public Policy in Australia*, ed. Stephen Bell and Brian Head (Melbourne: Oxford University Press, 1994), 150.

91. Ibid., 151.

92. *National Wage Case – December 1979 and March 1980 Quarters* (1980) 241 CAR 258, 272.

93. Ibid., 266.

94. *National Wage Case – June and September 1979 Quarters Decisions No. 1* (1980) 232 CAR 12, 14–15.

95. Ibid., 15, 26.

96. *Inquiry into Wage Fixation Principles* (1981) 254 CAR 341, 356.

97. Ibid., 365.

98. Bramble, *Trade Unionism in Australia*, 110–14.

99. Hancock, *Committee of Review*, 74. These figures are subject to the same caveat made in endnote 81.

100. Brian Brooks, 'Aspects of Casual and Part-Time Employment', *Journal of Industrial Relations* 27(2) (1985): 159.

101. Hancock, *Committee of Review*, 75.

102. *Re Vehicle Industry – Repair, Service and Retail – Award 1980*, in CCH, *Australian Industrial Law Review* 25(10) (May 4, 1983): ¶190.

103. Ibid.

104. See, respectively, Australian Bureau of Statistics, *Year Book Australia* (1301.0, No. 64, 1980), 184; Australian Bureau of Statistics, *Year Book Australia* (1301.0, No. 68, 1984), 156.

105. Richard Mitchell, 'Industrial Relations Under a Conservative Government: The Coalition's Labour Law Programme 1975 to 1978', *Journal of Industrial Relations* 21(4) (1979): 444.

106. Commonwealth, *Parliamentary Debates*, House of Representatives, 20 October 1977, 2231 (John Martyr).

107. Mitchell, 'Industrial Relations Under a Conservative Government', 446.

108. Ibid., 446–47.

109. 'Tram-Strike Girl Accepts New Job', *Canberra Times*, 8 September 1978, 1.

110. Bramble, *Trade Unionism in Australia*, 105.

111. Commonwealth, *Parliamentary Debates*, House of Representatives, 4 December 1980, 376 (Bob Hawke); 'IRB Federal Court Appeal Dismissed', *Canberra Times*, 7 August 1979, 8.

112. Commonwealth, *Parliamentary Debates*, House of Representatives, 10 May 1979, 2063 (Bill Hayden).

113. Tim Rowse, 'Elusive Middle Ground: A Political History', in *The New Province for Law and Order: 100 Years of Australian Industrial Conciliation and Arbitration*, ed. Joe Isaac and Stuart Macintyre (Port Melbourne: Cambridge University Press, 2001), 43.

114. 'Wage-Freeze Agreement Historic: Anthony', *Canberra Times*, 9 December 1982, 15.

115. Hancock, *Committee of Review*, 30.

116. Dabscheck, 'The Arbitration System Since 1967', 152.

117. *R v. Holmes: Ex parte Public Service Association of New South Wales* (1977) 140 CLR 63, 74, 79, 88–90.

118. T. B. Swanson et al., *Trade Practices Act Review Committee-Report to the Minister for Business and Consumer Affairs* (Canberra: Australian Government Publishing Service, 1976), 1.

119. Ibid., 85.

120. Commonwealth, *Parliamentary Debates*, House of Representatives, 26 May 1977, 1981–82 (Mick Young).

121. 'Union Loses in Secondary Boycott Case', *Canberra Times*, 18 December 1979, 3.

122. *Industrial Enterprises Ltd v. Federated Storemen and Packers Union*, in CCH, *Australian Industrial Law Review* 21(7) (4 April 1979): ¶106; *Tillmans Butcheries Pty v. AMIEU*, in CCH, *Australian Industrial Law Review* 22(1) (9 January 1980): ¶2; *Leon Laidley Pty Ltd v. Transport Workers Union of Australia* (1980) 43 FLR 168.

CHAPTER 6

1. Braham Dabscheck, 'The Accord: Corporatism Visits Australia', accessed 2 January 2017, http://www.i-repository.net/contents/outemon/ir/501/501961207.pdf.

2. 'Statement of Accord by the Australian Labor Party and the Australian Council of Trade Union Regarding Economic Policy, February 1983', in *The Accord . . . and Beyond: The Political Economy of the Labor Government*, ed. Frank Stilwell (Sydney: Pluto Press, 1986), 162.

3. Commonwealth, *Parliamentary Debates*, House of Representatives, 3 May 1983, 94 (Bob Hawke).

4. *National Wage Case April 1984*, in CCH, *Australian Industrial Law Review* 26(7) (11 April 1984): ¶117.

5. Braham Dabscheck, 'The Arbitration System Since 1967', in *State, Economy and Public Policy in Australia*, ed. Stephen Bell and Brian Head (Melbourne: Oxford University Press, 1994), 155.

6. *National Wage Case March 1987* (1987) Print G6800, 35.

7. *National Wage Case August 1988* (1988) Print H4000, 6–8; *National Wage Case August 1989* (1989) Print H9100, 13, 20–21.

8. Australian Bureau of Statistics, *The Labour Force Australia* (6203.0, December 1982), 18; Australian Bureau of Statistics, *The Labour Force Australia* (6203.0, December 1989), 21.

9. John Burgess and Iain Campbell, 'Casual Employment in Australia: Growth, Characteristics, A Bridge or a Trap?', *Economic and Labour Relations Review* 9(1) (1998): 35.

10. Bureau of Industry Economics, *Reducing Standard Hours of Work: Analysis of Australia's Recent Experience* (Canberra: Australian Government Publishing Service, 1984), 59.

11. Stilwell, *The Accord*, 54.

12. *National Wage Case March 1987*, 12–14.

13. Ibid., 16.

14. Department of Industrial Relations, *Report on the Operation of the Restructuring and Efficiency Principle* (Canberra: Australian Government Publishing Service, 1990), 17–18.

15. Ibid., 14–16.

16. Ibid., 20, 24–30.

17. Karl Marx, *Capital: A Critique of Political Economy Volume I*, trans. Ben Fowkes (London: Penguin Classics, 1990), 534.

18. Department of Industrial Relations, *Report on the Operation*, 25–26.

19. *National Wage Case August 1988*, 6.

20. *National Wage Case August 1989* (1989) Print H9100, 10.

21. Department of Industrial Relations, *Review of the Structural Efficiency Principle February–May 1989: Submission by the Commonwealth Government* (Canberra: Australian Government Publishing Service, 1989), 68.

22. Keith Hancock, *Committee of Review into Australian Industrial Relations Law and Systems* (Canberra: Australian Government Publishing Service, 1985).

23. Ibid., 678.

24. *Industrial Relations Act 1988* (Cth), s 116(1)(a).

25. Ibid., s 115(4)(7).

26. Ibid., s 95.

27. *National Wage Case April 1991* (1991) Print J7400, 30–31.

28. Business Council of Australia Industrial Relations Study Commission, *Enterprise Based Bargaining Units: A Better Way of Working* (Melbourne: Business Council of Australia, 1989).

29. John Howe and Richard Mitchell, 'The Evolution of the Contract of Employment in Australia: A Discussion', *Australian Journal of Labour Law* 12(2) (1999): 15.

30. 'Statement of Accord', 167.

31. Ibid.

32. W. B. Creighton, W. J. Ford and R. J. Mitchell, *Labour Law: Text and Materials* (Sydney: The Law Book Company, 1993), 537, 732.

33. *Federated Clerks' Union of Australia v. Victorian Employers' Federation* (1984) 154 CLR 472.

34. *Termination, Change and Redundancy Case* (1984) 8 IR 34.
35. *Mudginberri Station Pty Ltd v. Australasian Meat Industry Employees Union* (1986) 15 IR 272, 312.
36. 'Compromise Reached in Abattoir Dispute', *Canberra Times*, 29 March 1986, 8.
37. *Dollar Sweets Pty Ltd v. Federated Confectioners Association* [1986] VR 383.
38. Pamela Williams, 'Union Pays Up in Milestone Dispute', *Australian Financial Review*, 12 April 1988, 1/2.
39. *Dollar Sweets Pty Ltd v. Federated Confectioners Association of Australia* [1985] AIRC 403.
40. *Ansett Transport Industries (Operations) Pty Ltd v. Australian Federation of Air Pilots (No 2)* [1991] 2 VR 636.
41. Mike Taylor, 'How Hawke and Co Fixed the Pilots', *Canberra Times*, 28 May 1992, 1.
42. Bob Fine, *Democracy and the Rule of Law: Marx's Critique of the Legal Form* (Caldwell: The Blackburn Press, 2002), 142.
43. Evgeny B. Pashukanis, *Law and Marxism: A General Theory*, trans. Barbara Einhorn (London: Ink Links, 1978).
44. A reality acknowledged by the Commission: *National Wage Case April 1991*, 11.
45. Suzanne Jamieson, 'Enterprise Bargaining – The Approach of the Business Council of Australia', *Australian Journal of Labour Law* 3(1) (1990): 77–82.
46. Ibid., 80.
47. *National Wage Case April 1991*, 24.
48. Ibid.
49. Leon Trotsky, *The History of the Russian Revolution* (New York: Monad Press, 1980), 77.
50. *National Wage Case April 1991*, 34.
51. Ibid., 36.
52. Ibid., 38.
53. 'A Wage Decision for the Times', *The Age*, 17 April 1991, 13.
54. Bill Kelty quoted in Judith Sloan, 'Enterprise Bargaining's Quest for Maturity', *The Australian*, 8 November 1996, 15.
55. Ross Peake, 'Keating Unhappy at Missed Chance to Change', *The Age*, 17 April 1991, 4; Nicholas Way, 'Commission Rejects Enterprise Deals', *BRW*, 19 April 1991, 36; Tim Harcourt, 'The ACTU's View – Accord Mark VI and Enterprise Bargaining', accessed 3 January 2017, http://www.actu.org.au/actu-media/archives/1993/the-actus-view-accord-mark-vi-and-enterprise-bargaining.
56. John Howard quoted in Lynne Cossar and Tim Colebatch, 'Wage Ruling Shows Need for Change, Says ACTU', *The Age*, 18 April 1991, 5.
57. *National Wage Case October 1991* (1991) Print K0300, 12.
58. Ibid., 16.
59. *Industrial Relations Act 1988* (Cth), s 115.
60. Ibid., ss 96, 115(7).
61. 'Wage Bargaining in the Spotlight', *Canberra Times*, 29 August 1991, 3.
62. J. T. Ludeke, 'The Evolving Industrial Relations Regime: The Federal System – 1992–1998', *Australian Law Journal* 72(11) (1998): 864.

63. Breen Creighton, 'One Hundred Years of the Conciliation and Arbitration Power: A Province Lost?', *Melbourne University Law Review* 24(3) (2000): 860.

64. Paul Keating, 'Speech by the Prime Minister, The Hon. P.J. Keating MP' (speech delivered at the Institute of Directors Luncheon, Melbourne, Australia, 21 April 1993), 10–11.

65. Australian Centre for Industrial Relations Research and Training, *Australia at Work: Just Managing?* (Sydney: Prentice Hall, 1999), 77.

66. Ibid.

67. In 1992–93, award rates of pay increased 1.3%, constituting a large segment of the 1.7% in average weekly ordinary time earnings. By 1995–96, the equivalent figures were 1.2% and 3.8%. Thus, award adjustments went from constituting more than two-thirds of the increase in average earnings in 1992–93 to less than a third in 1995–96: Malcolm Rimmer, 'Enterprise Bargaining, Wage Norms and Productivity', *Journal of Industrial Relations* 40(4) (1998): 616.

68. *Safety Net Review-Wages April 1997*, accessed 3 January 2017, http://www.airc.gov.au/safetynet_review/decisions/P1997.htm.

69. Ed Shann, 'Why Work Is Spread Unevenly', *BRW*, 4 December 1992, 58.

70. Burgess and Campbell, 'Casual Employment in Australia', 35.

71. Iain Campbell, 'The Spreading Net: Age and Gender in the Process of Casualisation in Australia', *Journal of Australian Political Economy* 45 (2000): 85.

72. Ibid., 85.

73. Burgess and Campbell, 'Casual Employment in Australia', 40.

74. Australian Centre for Industrial Relations Research and Training, *Australia at Work*, 51.

75. *Workplace Relations Act 1996* (Cth), ss 89A(2), 89A(4).

76. I say 'substantial' because, despite its central place in the development of a liberal-productivist labour law regime, the *Workplace Relations Act 1996* was a political compromise. Difficulties in the Senate led to the dilution of the original Bill, and meant that the original vision of the government would not be realised until the passage of WorkChoices in 2005.

77. Commonwealth, *Parliamentary Debates*, House of Representatives, 28 October 1993, 2781 (Laurie Brereton).

78. Tim Pallas quoted in Nicholas Way, 'Employers, Unions Warm to Flexibility', *BRW*, 10 July 1995, 20.

79. Steve Lewis and Mark Davis, 'Optus Staff in Non-Union Deal', *Australian Financial Review*, 22 August 1994, 3; 'Attempt to Bypass Bank Union Stymied', *The Age*, 12 May 1995, 4.

80. The establishment process was complex, while unions retained rights to be involved in negotiations or challenge agreements: Amanda Coulthard, 'Non-Union Bargaining: Enterprise Flexibility Agreements', *Journal of Industrial Relations* 38(3) (1996): 357–58.

81. *Workplace Relations Act 1996* (Cth), s 170LK.

82. Ibid., s 298A(a).

83. Commonwealth, *Parliamentary Debates*, House of Representatives, 26 June 1996, 2748 (Mark Vaile).

84. Malcolm Rimmer, 'The *Workplace Relations Act 1996*: An Historical Perspective', *Australian Bulletin of Labour* 23(1) (1997): 72–73.

85. *Workplace Relations Act 1996* (Cth), s 94. For the success of the government's efforts, see Simon de Tuberville, 'Union Decline and Renewal in Australia and Britain: Lessons from Closed Shops', *Economic and Industrial Democracy* 28(3) (2007): 374–400.

86. David Peetz, *Brave New Work Place: How Individual Contracts Are Changing Our Jobs* (Crows Nest: Allen & Unwin, 2006), 102–7.

87. Mark Bray and Andrew Stewart, 'From the Arbitration System to the *Fair Work Act*: The Changing Approach in Australia to Voice and Representation at Work', *Adelaide Law Review* 34(1) (2013): 26.

88. *Industrial Relations Reform Act 1993* (Cth), s 38.

89. Ibid., s 170PM.

90. Commonwealth, *Parliamentary Debates*, House of Representatives, 28 October 1993, 2782–83 (Laurie Brereton).

91. Commonwealth, *Parliamentary Debates*, House of Representatives, 19 June 1996, 2225 (Michael Cobb).

92. Breen Creighton and Andrew Stewart, *Labour Law* (Annandale: The Federation Press, 2010), 719–20.

93. *Australian Constitution*, s 51(xxix).

94. Ronald C. McCallum, 'The Internationalisation of Australian Industrial Law: The *Industrial Relations Reform Act* 1993', *Sydney Law Review* 16(1) (1994): 127.

95. Andrew Frazer, 'The Federal Conciliation and Arbitration Power: From Cradle to Grave' (Parliamentary Library Research Paper No. 15, 2002), 41.

96. *Byrne v. Australian Airlines Ltd* (1995) 185 CLR 410, 412.

97. Ibid., 410–11.

98. Ibid., 421.

99. Australian Bureau of Statistics, *Australian Labour Market Statistics* (6105.0, July 2011), accessed 4 January 2017, http://www.abs.gov.au/AUSSTATS/abs@.nsf/Previousproducts/6105.0Feature%20Article1July%202011?opendocument&tabname=Summary&prodno=6105.0&issue=July%202011&num=&view.

100. Ibid.

101. Australian Bureau of Statistics, *Employee Earnings and Hours* (6306.0, May 2000), 52.

102. Australian Bureau of Statistics, *Employee Earnings and Hours* (6306.0, August 2008), 34.

103. Commonwealth, *Parliamentary Debates*, House of Representatives, 3 November 2005, 12–13 (Andrew Robb).

104. David Peetz and Alison Preston, 'Individual Contracting, Collective Bargaining and Wages in Australia', *Industrial Relations Journal* 40(5) (2009): 450–51.

105. Ibid., 454.

106. Patricia Karvelas, 'One in Seven Deals Fails Fairness Test', *The Australian*, 6 September 2007, 1/4.

107. Australian Bureau of Statistics, *Employee Earnings and Hours* (6306.0, May 2012), accessed 4 January 2017, http://www.abs.gov.au/AUSSTATS/abs@.nsf/DetailsPage/6306.0May%202012?OpenDocument.

108. Ibid.

109. Jared Greenville, Clinton Pobke and Nikki Rogers, 'Trends in the Distribution of Income in Australia' (Productivity Commission Staff Working Paper, 2013), 32–33, 36–37, 40.

110. *Workplace Relations Act 1996* (Cth), s 89A(4)(a).

111. This may have been a factor in the stabilisation of the rate of casual employment throughout the late 1990s and 2000s: Anthony Kryger, 'Casual Employment in Australia: A Quick Guide' (Research Paper Series 2014–15, Parliamentary Library, 2015), 1–2.

112. House of Representatives Standing Committee on Employment, Workplace Relations and Workforce Participation, *Making It Work: Inquiry into Independent Contracting and Labour Hire Arrangements* (Canberra: 2005), 7, 15.

113. Australian Bureau of Statistics, *Forms of Employment* (6359.0, 2011), 3.

114. House of Representatives Standing Committee on Employment, Workplace Relations and Workforce Participation, *Making It Work*, 42.

115. Australian Council of Trade Unions, 'Submission to Inquiry into independent contractors and labour hire arrangements' (House of Representatives Standing Committee on Employment, Workplace Relations and Workforce Participation, Submission No. 60, 2005), 12–20.

116. *Industrial Relations Act 1988* (Cth), s 127A–B; *Workplace Relations Act 1996* (Cth), s 127A–B.

117. House of Representatives Standing Committee on Employment, Workplace Relations and Workforce Participation, *Making It Work*, 28.

118. *Workplace Relations Regulations 2006* (Cth), ch 2 reg 8.5(1)(h)(i).

119. Tom Bramble, *Trade Unionism in Australia: A History from Flood to Ebb Tide* (Port Melbourne: Cambridge University Press, 2008), 218.

120. Mark Davis with Misha Schubert, 'Workers' Rights Lost with AWAs', *The Age*, 17 April 2007, 1.

121. The matters dispensed with included wages and salaries, superannuation, long-service leave, jury service and notice of termination: Creighton and Stewart, *Labour Law*, 258.

122. Anthony Forsyth, 'Arbitration Extinguished: The Impact of the Work Choices Legislation on the Australian Industrial Relations Commission', *Australian Bulletin of Labour* 32(1) (2006): 27.

123. Commonwealth, *Parliamentary Debates*, House of Representatives, 24 June 1992, 3811 (John Howard).

124. Ludeke, 'The Evolving Industrial Relations Regime', 869.

125. *Workplace Relations Act 1996* (Cth), s 412(1)(b).

126. *National Workforce Pty Ltd v. Australian Manufacturing Workers' Union* (1997) 76 IR 200, 213.

127. *Patrick Stevedores No 2 Pty Ltd v. Maritime Union of Australia* (1998) 195 CLR 1.

128. Commonwealth, *Parliamentary Debates*, House of Representatives, 30 May 2007, 60–61 (Phillip Barresi); Commonwealth, *Parliamentary Debates*, House of Representatives, 7 August 2007, 38 (Joe Hockey).

129. David Humphries, 'Battle Resumes as Sackings Confirmed Legal', *Sydney Morning Herald*, 8–9 July 2006, 4.

130. Breen Creighton, ‘A Retreat from Individualism? The Fair Work Act 2009 and the Re-collectivisation of Australian Labour Law’, *Industrial Law Journal* 40(2) (2011): 143–44.

131. Commonwealth, *Parliamentary Debates*, House of Representatives, 8 November 2005, 56 (Julie Owens).

132. Bramble, *Trade Unionism in Australia*, 214.

133. Mark Gibian quoted in Kristin van Barneveld, ‘Australian Workplace Agreements Under *Work Choices*’, *Economic and Labour Relations Review* 16(2) (2006): 167–68.

134. See, respectively, Creighton and Stewart, *Labour Law*, 296; Department of Education, Employment and Workplace Relations, ‘Submission to Inquiry into the Workplace Relations Amendment (Transition to Forward with Fairness) Bill 2008’ (Canberra: 29 February 2008), 8.

135. Peetz, *Brave New Work Place*, 116–56.

136. AMWU official quoted in Rae Cooper, ‘Australian Unionism in a Decollectivised Environment’ (paper presented at the 19th Conference of the Association of Industrial Relations Academics of Australia and New Zealand, Sydney, Australia, 9–11 February 2005), 162.

137. Jeane Wells, ‘Flexible Work in 2010 – The Impact of the Fair Work Act 2009 on Employer Control of, and Employee Access to, Flexible Working Hours’ (paper presented at the 3rd Our Work, Our Lives Conference, Darwin, Australia, 12–13 August 2010).

138. *Workplace Relations Regulations 2006* (Cth), ch 2 reg 8.5(1)(g).

139. Ibid., ch 2 reg 8.5(1),(2),(3),(8). It is significant to note here that many of these items are no longer regarded as prohibited content under the FWA.

140. Australian Bureau of Statistics, *Weekly Earnings of Employees (Distribution)* (6310.0, 1997), 40.

141. Australian Bureau of Statistics, *Employee Earnings, Benefits and Trade Union Membership* (6310.0, 2009), 34.

142. Australian Bureau of Statistics, *Characteristics of Employment, Australia* (6333.0, 2014), accessed 22 December 2016, http://www.abs.gov.au/AUSSTATS/abs@.nsf/allprimarymainfeatures/EF3BF9BDA5BF304ECA25801F00186541?opendocument.

143. Australian Bureau of Statistics, *Year Book Australia* (1301.0, No. 78, 1996), 169–70.

144. Australian Bureau of Statistics, *Year Book Australia* (1301.0, No. 81, 1999), 151.

145. Australian Bureau of Statistics, *Year Book Australia* (1301.0, No. 91, 2010), 269.

146. Australian Bureau of Statistics, *Year Book Australia* (1301.0, No. 92, 2012), 311–12.

147. Aside from Victoria, which had referred its powers to the Commonwealth in 1996.

148. Commonwealth, *Parliamentary Debates*, House of Representatives, 8 November 2005, 62–63 (Margaret May); Commonwealth, *Parliamentary Debates*, House of Representatives, 30 November, 69 (Kevin Andrews).

149. Commonwealth, *Parliamentary Debates*, House of Representatives, 9 November 2005, 154 (Sharon Grierson).

150. Marcus Priest, 'Insiders' Verdict: IR Challenge Doomed', *Australian Financial Review*, 28 April 2006, 1.

151. *New South Wales v. Commonwealth* (2006) 229 CLR 1.

152. Ibid., 4.

153. Ibid., 190.

CHAPTER 7

1. *Amalgamated Society of Engineers v. Adelaide Steam-Ship Company Limited* (1921) 15 CAR 297.

2. For a list of the relevant awards, see Brett Heino, 'Capitalism, Regulation Theory and Australian Labour Law: Exploring the Labour Law Regimes of Antipodean Fordism and Liberal-Productivism, 1964–2009' (PhD diss., University of Wollongong, 2016), 211.

3. Tom Sheridan, *Mindful Militants: The Amalgamated Engineering Union in Australia, 1920–1972* (Cambridge: Cambridge University Press, 1975), 64.

4. *Amalgamated Engineering Union v. Metal Trades Employers Association* (1930) 28 CAR 923.

5. Sandra Cockfield, 'Arbitration, Mass Production and Workplace Relations: "Metal Industry" Developments in the 1920s', *Journal of Industrial Relations* 35(1) (1993): 25.

6. *Amalgamated Engineering Union v. Metal Trades Employers Association* (1930), 927.

7. Cockfield, 'Arbitration, Mass Production and Workplace Relations', 23–24, 28.

8. Keith Hancock, 'The First Half-Century of Australian Wage Policy – Part II', *Journal of Industrial Relations* 21(2) (1979): 145.

9. Sheridan, *Mindful Militants*, 130–43.

10. Justice Beeby quoted in ibid., 143.

11. Ibid., 145.

12. Ibid.

13. Ibid., 146.

14. Stuart Macintyre, *Australia's Boldest Experiment: War and Reconstruction in the 1940s* (Sydney: NewSouth Publishing, 2015), 346–52.

15. Sheridan, *Mindful Militants*, 151–53.

16. The Court was forced to sacrifice principle for pragmatism, with moves to settle the dispute occurring despite the fact that the unions were still on strike, a break with established industrial precedent. Such a development demonstrates almost perfectly the recourse to administrative practice in times of waxing working-class militancy. See *Victorian Chamber of Manufacturers v. Amalgamated Engineering Union* (1947) 58 CAR 551, 552.

17. *Metal Trades Margins Case* (1947) 58 CAR 1088 ('*1947 Margins Case*').

18. Keith Hancock and Sue Richardson, 'Economic and Social Effects', in *The New Province for Law and Order: 100 Years of Australian Industrial Conciliation*

and Arbitration, ed. Joe Isaac and Stuart Macintyre (Port Melbourne: Cambridge University Press, 2001), 183.

19. *1947 Margins Case*, 1092.

20. J. Hutson, *Six Wage Concepts* (Surry Hills: Amalgamated Engineering Union, 1971), 157.

21. *Carpenters and Joiners Award, 1946* (1948) 59 CAR 957, 959.

22. *Metal Trades Employers Association v. Amalgamated Engineering Union* (1937) 37 CAR 176, 182.

23. *1947 Margins Case*, 1090.

24. *Metal Trades Margins Case* (1954) 80 CAR 3 ('*1954 Margins Case*').

25. *Metal Trades Margins Case* (1952) 73 CAR 324, 345 ('*1952 Margins Case*').

26. Hancock, 'The First Half-Century', 154.

27. Hutson, *Six Wage Concepts*, 157.

28. *1952 Margins Case*, 340.

29. Ibid., 345.

30. *1954 Margins Case*, 32.

31. Ibid., 53.

32. *Metal Trades Margins Case* (1959) 92 CAR 793, 803–4.

33. Ibid.

34. *Metal Trades Margins Case* (1963) 102 CAR 138, 146 ('*1963 Margins Case*').

35. *Furnishing Trades Award, 1964*, in *Australian Industrial Law Review* 10(32) (23 November 1968): ¶461.

36. R. E. McGarvie, 'Principle and Practice in Commonwealth Industrial Arbitration After Sixty Years', *Federal Law Review* 1(1) (1964): 66–67.

37. Richard Kirby, foreword to *Industrial Relations in the Australian Metal Industries*, by Norman Dufty (Sydney: West Publishing Corporation, 1972), v.

38. E. A. Dunphy and S.C.G. Wright, 'The Jubilee of Industrial Arbitration in the Federal Sphere', *Australian Law Journal* 25 (1951): 365.

39. Commonwealth Bureau of Census and Statistics, *Year Book Australia* (1301.0, No. 46, 1960), 161.

40. Ibid., 453–54.

41. Australian Bureau of Statistics, *Year Book Australia* (1301.0, No. 92, 2012), 510.

42. Sheridan, *Mindful Militants*, 282–91.

43. *National Wage Cases of 1965* (1965) 110 CAR 189, 261.

44. Hutson, *Six Wage Concepts*, 256–60.

45. *Basic Wage, Margins and Total Wage Cases of 1966* (1966) 115 CAR 93, 188.

46. R. J. Hawke, 'Total Wage – An Analysis', *Federal Law Review* 3(1) (1968): 114.

47. *Work Value Case* (1967) 121 CAR 587.

48. *Metal Trades Award, 1952* (1966) 114 CAR 39, 66.

49. Despite the different tenor of employer and union submissions (depending upon the implications they wished to draw regarding the real value of labour and the magnitude of wage increases), both appeared agreed on the intensification of labour and the link between the diffusion of new technologies and mass production techniques, the essence of the antipodean Fordist labour process.

50. *Work Value Case*, 594.

51. Tom Bramble, *Trade Unionism in Australia: A History from Flood to Ebb Tide* (Port Melbourne: Cambridge University Press, 2008), 41.

52. Ibid., 42.

53. *Metal Trades Award*, in *Australian Industrial Law Review* 10(3) (17 February 1968): ¶28.

54. *Metal Trades*, in *Australian Industrial Law Review* 10(7) (23 March 1968): ¶80.

55. C. P. Mills, 'Legislation and Decisions Affecting Industrial Relations', *Journal of Industrial Relations* 10(2) (1968): 157.

56. A. E. Woodward, 'A Review of Industrial Relations 1968/9', *Journal of Industrial Relations* 11(2) (1969): 93.

57. Ibid.

58. *Furnishing Trades Award, 1964*, ¶461.

59. Woodward, 'A Review of Industrial Relations', 94.

60. Dufty, *Industrial Relations*, 151–94.

61. *Metal Trades*, in *Australian Industrial Law Review* 13(14) (28 May 1971): ¶278.

62. David Plowman, 'Employer Associations: Challenges and Responses', *Journal of Industrial Relations* 20(3) (1978): 253–54.

63. Unlike its predecessor, which covered both public and private employers, this award applied primarily to the latter.

64. Which had come into being in 1970 after an amalgamation of the largely NSW-based Metal Trades Employers' Association and the Metal Industries Association of Victoria. This concentration of employer associations matched similar movements among union ranks, particularly the formation of the giant Amalgamated Metal Workers' Union in 1973 from a merger of the AEU, Sheet Metal Workers' Union and the Boilermakers' and Blacksmiths' Society.

65. Hutson, *Six Wage Concepts*, 254.

66. Warwick Bracken, 'Doubts on Future of National Wage Case', *Canberra Times*, 10 May 1972, 25.

67. *National Wage Case 1971–1972* (1972) 143 CAR 290, 298, 302.

68. Bracken, 'Doubts on Future', 25.

69. *Metal Industry Award*, in *Australian Industrial Law Review* 16(23) (13 September 1974): ¶565.

70. Ibid.

71. Ibid.

72. Ibid.

73. *Rubber, Plastic and Cable Making Industry Award, 1972*, in *Australian Industrial Law Review* 17(7) (14 March 1975): ¶151.

74. Harold W. Fry, 'Metal-Trades Unions Conference – In Search of Consensus Instead of a Polarised Society', *Canberra Times*, 17 June 1977, 2.

75. 'Metal Workers Get $9-a-Week Rise', *Canberra Times*, 12 September 1974, 1.

76. In 1975, for example, of the approximate 1.74 million working days lost in manufacturing industry strike action, nearly 1.28 million were lost in the metal, machinery and equipment sector: Australian Bureau of Statistics, *Year Book Australia* (1301.0, No. 61, 1976), 302.

77. *Wage rates – General Motors Holden's Pty Ltd. Employees*, in *Australian Industrial Law Review* 17(22) (29 August 1975): ¶717.

78. David Plowman, 'Administered Flexibility: Restructuring the Metal Industry Award', *Economic and Labour Relations Review* 1(2) (1990): 49.

79. 'Metal Unions Ready to Launch Campaign', *Canberra Times*, 16 September 1981, 7.

80. *Application to vary Metal Industry Award 1971*, in CCH, *Australian Industrial Law Review* 24(1) (13 January 1982): ¶1.

81. *Application to vary Metal Industry Award re hours of work*, in CCH, *Australian Industrial Law Review* 23(9) (6 May 1981): ¶190.

82. *Application to vary Metal Industry Award 1971*, ¶1.

83. Ibid.

84. *Application to vary Transport Workers Award*, in CCH, *Australian Industrial Law Review* 23(17) (26 August 1981): ¶378.

85. *Application to vary Transport Workers Award, 1972*, in CCH, *Australian Industrial Law Review* 24(3) (10 February 1982): ¶48.

86. Charles Mulvey, 'Wage Policy and Wage Determination', *Journal of Industrial Relations* 25(1) (1983): 69.

87. Ibid., 68.

88. *National Wage Case, 23 December 1982*, in CCH, *Australian Industrial Law Review* 25(2) (19 January 1983): ¶19.

89. Ibid.

90. *Shop, Distributive and Allied Employees Association v. Myer S.A. Stores Ltd*, in CCH, *Australian Industrial Law Review* 25(18) (10 August 1983): ¶365.

91. Bob Hawke (speech delivered at *Metal Unions Seminar on the Future of Australian Manufacturing*, Sydney, 7–8 June, 1977), 6.

92. Plowman, 'Administered Flexibility', 51.

93. Australian Bureau of Statistics, *Year Book Australia* (1301.0 No. 66, 1982), 413; Australian Bureau of Statistics, *Year Book Australia* (1301.0 No. 70, 1986), 394.

94. Australian Bureau of Statistics, *Year Book Australia* (1301.0 No. 75, 1992), 502.

95. Bramble, *Trade Unionism in Australia*, 69–70, 116.

96. The AMWU had amalgamated with the Federated Shipwrights' and Ship Constructors' Association in 1976.

97. Chris Briggs, 'The Rise and Fall of the ACTU: Maturation, Hegemony and Decline' (PhD diss., University of Sydney, 1999), 176–78.

98. Tom Bramble and Rick Kuhn, *Labor's Conflict: Big Business, Workers and the Politics of Class* (Port Melbourne: Cambridge University Press, 2011), 102.

99. 'Statement of Accord by the Australian Labor Party and the Australian Council of Trade Union Regarding Economic Policy, February 1983', in *The Accord . . . and Beyond: The Political Economy of the Labor Government*, ed. Frank Stilwell (Sydney: Pluto Press, 1986), 159–62.

100. Rick Kuhn, 'Militancy Uprooted: Labour Movement Economics 1974–1986', *Socialist Action* (1986), accessed 25 January 2017, http://www.anu.edu.au/polsci/rick/militancyuprooted.htm.

101. Bramble, *Trade Unionism in Australia*, 130, 155.

102. The ACTU itself was forced to acknowledge that the fitter, the traditional heart of metal awards, had undergone a 9.6% reduction in award rates between 1983 and 1991, a figure that increased to 12.4% when market wages were considered: Chris Briggs, 'Australian Exceptionalism: The Role of Trade Unions in the Emergence of Enterprise Bargaining', *Journal of Industrial Relations* 43(1) (2001): 32.

103. 'Statement of Accord', 162.

104. Ibid., 164.

105. Bramble, *Trade Unionism in Australia*, 131.

106. Which had reverted to its old name in 1985.

107. Plowman, 'Administered Flexibility', 61–63.

108. Ibid., 53–65.

109. *National Wage Case April 1991* (1991) Print J7400, 35.

110. George Campbell quoted in Briggs, 'Australian Exceptionalism', 34.

111. Laurie Carmichael quoted in Briggs, 'Australian Exceptionalism', 36.

112. Nicholas Way, 'The IRC Asks Some Awkward Questions', *BRW*, 15 February 1991, 24.

113. Ian Spicer quoted in Nicholas Way, 'Bitter Debate Will Have Big Impact', *BRW*, 9 November 1990, 30.

114. Elise Callander quoted in Nicholas Way, 'Reassembling the Work Practices Jigsaw', *BRW*, 1 February 1991, 30.

115. *Year Book Australia 1992*, 503.

116. *Year Book Australia 2012*, 616.

117. Australian Bureau of Statistics, *Year Book Australia* (1301.0 No. 76, 1994), 560.

118. Terri Mylett, 'The intensification of labour market polarisation in metals manufacturing in Australia in the 1900s' (PhD diss., University of Wollongong, 2003), 141.

119. Ibid., 137.

120. The Australian Industry Group (AIG), formed by a merger of the MTIA and the Australian Chamber of Manufactures in 1998.

121. Peter Tighe quoted in Mylett, 'The Intensification of Labour Market Polarisation', 154.

122. *Appeal re Morrison Knudsen Corp of Australia Ltd Certified Agreement 1993*, in CCH, *Australian Industrial Law Review* 36(12) (16 June 1994): ¶204.

123. Judith Sloan, 'The Economic Implications of Enterprise Bargaining', *Economic and Labour Relations Review* 4(1) (1993): 27–49.

124. Briggs, 'The Rise and Fall of the ACTU', 313.

125. *Review of Wage Fixing Principles* (1993) Print K9700, 14.

126. Mylett, 'The Intensification of Labour Market Polarisation', 142.

127. Australian Centre for Industrial Relations Research and Teaching, 'Agreements Database and Monitor' (No. 3, University of Sydney, 1994), 6–7.

128. Perhaps the best example is the early success metal unions had in obtaining comparatively large wage increases through bargaining with Email, the Australian-based whitegoods manufacturer: Rob Lambert, Michael Gillan and Scott Fitzgerald, 'Electrolux in Australia: Reregulation, Industry Restructuring and the Dynamics of Bargaining', *Journal of Industrial Relations* 47(3) (2005): 266–67.

129. Briggs, 'The Rise and Fall of the ACTU', 321.

130. Australian Centre for Industrial Relations Research and Training, *Australia at Work: Just Managing?* (Sydney: Prentice Hall, 1999), 50.

131. Ibid., 79.

132. Which by now was going through a series of name changes reflecting the wave of amalgamations in the 1980s and early 1990s. In 1995 it came to its current title, the Australian Manufacturing Workers Union.

133. David Clark, 'Challenge of New Industrial Relations', *Australian Financial Review*, 20 April 1994, 30.

134. Amanda Gome and Nicholas Way, 'Wage Fixing's New Deals', *BRW*, 26 September 1994, 48.

135. Nicholas Way, 'Metal Bid Follows a Familiar Pattern', *BRW*, 7 November 1994, 32.

136. Nicholas Way, 'Why the TWU Is Going for the Jugular', *BRW*, 14 November 1994, 34; Mark David, 'Construction Wage Talks Fail', *Australian Financial Review*, 6 September 1995, 5.

137. By 1995, the AMWU in its modern form had come about, covering workers from a great many manufacturing industries, including metals, vehicle construction, food processing, ship-building and white goods. At this stage, therefore, it becomes more difficult to talk about metals in isolation and the story of pattern bargaining must include other sectors covered by the AMWU.

138. 'Trends in Federal Enterprise Bargaining – Trends Historical Table', Australian Government Department of Employment, accessed 14 October 2015, https://www.employment.gov.au/trends-federal-enterprise-bargaining.

139. Stephen Long, 'Metals Group Urges Changes', *Australian Financial Review*, 30 May 1997, 3.

140. Stephen Long, 'Wage Claims: ACTU Goes Industry-Wide', *Australian Financial Review*, 3 September 1997, 1.

141. Ibid.

142. Nina Field, 'Look Who Is Trying to Set the IR Agenda – It's the Men from the Manufacturing Unions', *Australian Financial Review*, 17 June 2000, 24.

143. MTFU quoted in Michael Bachelard, 'Unions Strike Out – Campaign 2000 Is Having Some Unexpected Outcomes', *The Australian*, 7 September 2000, 28.

144. Sue Bull, 'Victorian AMWU Plans Industrial Campaign', *Green Left Weekly*, 12 June 2002, accessed 28 January 2017, https://www.greenleft.org.au/content/victorian-amwu-plans-industrial-campaign.

145. Ibid.

146. *Workplace Relations Legislation Amendment (More Jobs, Better Pay) Bill 1999* (Cth).

147. Nina Field, 'AIG Fights Metal Union Plan', *Australian Financial Review*, 3 May 2000, 3.

148. Bradon Ellem, 'Trade Unionism in 2000', *Journal of Industrial Relations* 43(2) (2001): 210.

149. Ibid.

150. The irony of these powers being granted in a period when the broader powers and purview of the Commission were being whittled away will not be lost on the reader.

151. Commonwealth, *Parliamentary Debates,* House of Representatives, 24 June 2002, 4246–47 (Don Randall).

152. Commonwealth, *Parliamentary Debates,* House of Representatives, 20 February 2002, 504–5 (Tony Abbott).

153. Bruce Hearn Mackinnon, 'Employer Matters in 2003', *Journal of Industrial Relations* 46(2) (2004): 228.

154. Ibid., 229; Commonwealth, *Parliamentary Debates*, House of Representatives, 13 February 2003, 11841 (Tony Abbott).

155. Mackinnon, 'Employer Matters', 228.

156. Robert Boyer, *The Regulation School: A Critical Introduction*, trans. Craig Charney (New York: Columbia University Press, 1990), x.

CHAPTER 8

1. Commonwealth Census of Bureau and Statistics, *Year Book Australia* (1301.0, No. 48, 1962), 168; Australian Bureau of Statistics, *Year Book Australia* (1301.0, No. 60, 1974), 732.

2. In 2010–2011, it employed some 203,900 people, accounting for approximately 20.1% of total manufacturing employment. In 2009–2010, its contribution to the total value added by the manufacturing sector was 17.4%, while its share of capital expenditure was 17.4%: Australian Bureau of Statistics, *Year Book Australia* (1301.0, No. 92, 2012), 614, 616.

3. Noel Castree, David Featherstone and Andrew Herod, 'Contrapuntal Geographies: The Politics of Organizing Across Sociospatial Difference', in *The SAGE Handbook of Political Geography*, ed. Kevin Cox, Murray Low and Jennifer Robinson (London: SAGE Publications, 2008), 313.

4. For example, clause 8 of the Food Preservers Interim Award 1986 provided that casuals were only to be employed in situations of genuine need occasioned by absenteeism or special production demand and must only account for 15% of the total number of full-time employees. Part-time employment was limited to 10% of total weekly employees, after not being a feature of the award at all in the 1980s: Noel Butlin Archives Centre, Australian National University: Australian Manufacturing Workers' Union, N628 Box 64, 'Letter to Tom Ryan, General Secretary of the FPU, from the Australian Chamber of Manufacturers', 20 April 1988. Part-time employment in the various confectioners awards was typically dependent upon the employer seeking the written approval of the FCA. See, for example: Confectioners (State) Award (NSW), cl 3A.

5. See, for example: Noel Butlin Archives Centre, Australian National University: Federated Confectioners Association, N194/30, Box 4, 'Report on Federal Wage Claim Put Before Employers on 11th of April 1973'.

6. Noel Butlin Archives Centre, Australian National University: Federated Confectioners Association, N194/29 Box 4, 'FCA General-Secretary's Report', March 1968; *Application by Food Preservers' Union to vary Food Preservers Award*, in CCH, *Australian Industrial Law Review* 22(16) (6 August 1980): ¶243.

7. Indeed, the FPU had been regarded as a 'tame cat' union by employers, while FCA members in Victoria and Tasmania had last struck in 1910 before the upheavals

in the 1970s and 1980s. See Tom Ryan, 'Editorial', *The Food Preserver* 13(4) (1985): 3; Noel Butlin Archives Centre, Australian National University: Federated Confectioners Association, N194/71 Box 8, John Soreli, 'Lolly Leader Sells a Gentle Line'.

8. For detailed examples of union recognition of these developments, see Brett Heino, 'Capitalism, Regulation Theory and Australian Labour Law: Exploring the Labour Law Regimes of Antipodean Fordism and Liberal-Productivism, 1964–2009' (PhD diss., University of Wollongong, 2016), 254–55.

9. Indeed, Commissioner Clarkson had accused the FCA of being 'prepared to throw indexation to the wind': *Victorian Chamber of Manufactures v. Federated Confectioners' Association of Australia and also A.W. Allen Limited v. Federated Confectioners' Association of Australia* (transcript of proceedings, Australian Conciliation and Arbitration Commission, Case No. 3923 & 4578, 6 December 1976), 10.

10. *Applications by Food Preservers Union to vary Food Preservers' Award 1973*, in CCH, *Australian Industrial Law Review* 26(7) (6 December 1984): ¶415.

11. See, for example, the massive technological change documented by the Commission at cereal manufacturer Kelloggs over the course of several years in the mid-1980s: *Kelloggs (Australia) Pty Ltd v. Labor Council (NSW)*, in CCH, *Australian Industrial Law Review* 29(21) (21 October 1987): ¶402.

12. Letter to Tom Ryan from the Australian Chamber of Manufacturers.

13. Karl Marx, *Capital: A Critique of Political Economy Volume I*, trans. Ben Fowkes (London: Penguin Classics, 1990), 534.

14. *Food Preservers Union of Australia, Australian Chamber of Manufactures, Food Preservers' Interim Award 1986* (1990) Print J3010, 1.

15. Ibid., 204.

16. See, for example, Noel Butlin Archives Centre, Australian National University: Australian Manufacturing Workers' Union, N628 Box 64, *NSW Food Preservers (State) Award*, 26 June 1990.

17. *Application by Food Preservers' (Interim) Award, 1986*, in CCH, *Australian Industrial Law Review* 30(7) (8 April 1988): ¶127.

18. *Cadbury Schweppes Pty Ltd v. FLAIEU*, in CCH, *Australian Industrial Law Review* 30(3) (11 February 1988): ¶52.

19. *Application to vary Nabisco Brands Pty Ltd (Cereal and Biscuit Processing etc) Award 1985*, in CCH, *Australian Industrial Law Review* 32(25) (28 December 1990): ¶448.

20. It is important to note at this point that the construction of arbitration as an administrative structure taking collectives of labour and capital as its subject should not be taken as a suggestion that it was destined to provide decisions friendly to workers. As these cases graphically demonstrate, the arbitral tribunals were perfectly capable of delivering openly pro-capital decisions.

21. *Confectionary Workers Union of Australia, Confectioners Award 1980* (6 December 1990) Print J5832, 2–3.

22. Noel Butlin Archives Centre, Australian National University: Federated Confectioners Association, N194/169 Box 19, 'Allens Life Savers Limited Confectioners-Lane Cove List of Agreed Offsets for 4% Second Tier Wage Increase'.

23. *Confectionary Workers Union of Australia v. Beatrice Foods*, in CCH, *Australian Industrial Law Review* 30(7) (8 April 1988): ¶127.

24. In a demonstration of how the Accord demanded unions become industrial policemen, the Commission declared during the April 1984 National Wage Case that 'it is regrettable that the unions concerned did not see fit to give their members award protection by declaring their commitment to the Principles as required in the spirit of the Accord to which they are party': *National Wage Case – April 1984*, in CCH, *Australian Industrial Law Review* 26(7) (11 April 1984): ¶117.

25. Gail Cotton, 'The Rosella Dispute', *The Food Preserver* 13(3) (1985): 20.

26. Gail Cotton, 'Gail's Report', *The Food Preserver* 12(3) (1984): 10.

27. Ibid.

28. See, respectively, *Application by Australian Chamber of Manufactures to vary the Food Preservers' Interim Award 1986,* in CCH, *Australian Industrial Law Review* 33(18) (5 September 1991): ¶281; Noel Butlin Archives Centre, Australian National University: Australian Manufacturing Workers' Union, N628 Box 64, Tom Ryan, 'Report of General Secretary and Federal Council to Meeting of Federal Conference', 7 December 1988.

29. Noel Butlin Archives Centre, Australian National University: Australian Manufacturing Workers' Union, N628 Box 28, letter from P. Decker on behalf of FPU Secretary Tom Ryan, 23 September 1991.

30. Noel Butlin Archives Centre, Australian National University: Australian Manufacturing Workers' Union, N628 Box 64, undated article from the NSW Branch in *The Food Preserver.*

31. Noel Butlin Archives Centre, Australian National University: Australian Manufacturing Workers' Union, N628 Box 64, letter from NSW FPU Secretary Ray Warn to Tom Ryan, FPU General Secretary, 15 November 1989.

32. For examples, see Heino, 'Capitalism, Regulation Theory and Australian Labour Law', 260.

33. See, for example, Noel Butlin Archives Centre, Australian National University: Australian Manufacturing Workers' Union, N628 Box 2, Freda Bogar, *AMWU Food and Confectionary Division Bulletin*, 31 May 1995.

34. See, for example, *Food Preservers Interim Award 1986* (transcript of proceedings, Australian Industrial Relations Commission, Case No. 30092, 7 June 1993), 3–4, 7.

35. Ibid., 3–5.

36. Bogar, *AMWU Food and Confectionary Division Bulletin.*

37. Noel Butlin Archives Centre, Australian National University: Australian Manufacturing Workers' Union, N628 Box 2, Freda Bogar, 'Report to the AMWU National Conference', 3–4.

38. Noel Butlin Archives Centre, Australian National University: Australian Manufacturing Workers' Union, N628 Box 3, 'Edgell-Birds Eye (Enterprise Bargaining) Agreement', September 1992.

39. Ibid.

40. Ibid.

41. Noel Butlin Archives Centre, Australian National University: Australian Manufacturing Workers' Union, N628 Box 111, 'Golden Circle Enterprise Agreement'.

42. Ibid., 2.

43. Ibid., 3–5.

44. Noel Butlin Archives Centre, Australian National University: Australian Manufacturing Workers' Union, N628 Box 111, 'The Phoenix Biscuit Company Enterprise Agreement 1993', 3–5.

45. Noel Butlin Archives Centre, Australian National University: Australian Manufacturing Workers' Union, N628 Box 5, letter from Peter Tighe, National Secretary of the Communications, Electrical and Plumbing Union of Australia, to Tim Pallas, Australian Council of Trade Unions Assistant Secretary, 25 March 1997.

46. Noel Butlin Archives Centre, Australian National University: Australian Manufacturing Workers' Union, N628 Box 5, letter from Chris McKay, Manpower official, to Ron Howell, General Manager (Human Resources) Simplot Australia, 9 October 1996.

47. Letter from Peter Tighe to Tim Pallas.

48. Noel Butlin Archives Centre, Australian National University: Australian Manufacturing Workers' Union, N628 Box 2, letter from Freda Bogar, National Secretary of the AMWU Food and Confectionary Division, to Noel Treharne, Regional Secretary AMWU Food & Confectionary Division, 19 December 1996.

49. Noel Butlin Archives Centre, Australian National University: Australian Manufacturing Workers' Union, N628 Box 26, letter from Anne Urquhart, AMWU Tasmania State Organiser, to C. McKay, Manpower Services, 21 November 1997.

50. Noel Butlin Archives Centre, Australian National University: Australian Manufacturing Workers' Union, N628 Box 26, 'Simplot Lock-Out Fact Sheet'.

51. *Automotive, Food, Metals, Engineering, Printing and Kindred Industries Union and Simplot Australia* (transcript of proceedings, Australian Industrial Relations Commission, Case Nos. 20032 & 20072, 14 January 1998), 9.

52. Noel Butlin Archives Centre, Australian National University: Australian Manufacturing Workers' Union, N628 Box 5, 'Simplot Echuca Enterprise Bargaining Agreement 1998'.

53. Queensland Government, 'Submission to Inquiry into independent contractors and labour hire arrangements' (House of Representatives Standing Committee on Employment, Workplace Relations and Workforce Participation, Submission No. 66, 2005), 16.

54. Noel Butlin Archives Centre, Australian National University: Australian Manufacturing Workers' Union, N628 Box 26, 'Heads of Agreement Between Manpower and the ACTU', 26 November 1997.

55. Noel Butlin Archives Centre, Australian National University: Australian Manufacturing Workers' Union, N628 Box 26, 'AMWU/Manpower Agreement'.

56. Terri Mylett, 'The intensification of labour market polarisation in metals manufacturing in Australia in the 1900s' (PhD diss., University of Wollongong, 2003), 266–72.

57. Noel Butlin Archives Centre, Australian National University: Australian Manufacturing Workers' Union, N628 Box 24, 'Labour Hire and Casual Employment in the Food and Confectionary Industry'.

58. Noel Butlin Archives Centre, Australian National University: Australian Manufacturing Workers' Union, N628 Box 26, 'Simplot Australia Pty Limited (National Framework) Agreement 1999'.

59. *Food Preservers Union of Australia and H.J. Heinz Co Australia Pty Ltd, Food Preservers Award, 1973* (1991) Print J7693.

60. Noel Butlin Archives Centre, Australian National University: Australian Manufacturing Workers' Union, N628 Box 111, 'H.J. Heinz Australia-Now and the Future', 12 January 1993, 3–4.

61. Ibid., 7–9.

62. Kevin Hart, 'Heinz Will Switch Some Aust Activity to NZ', *New Zealand Herald*, 13 February 1993.

63. Noel Butlin Archives Centre, Australian National University: Australian Manufacturing Workers' Union, N628 Box 111, letter to George Campbell, AMEU National Secretary, and Doug Cameron, AMEU Assistant National Secretary, from Neil Marshall, AMEU National Organiser, 25 February 1993.

64. Noel Butlin Archives Centre, Australian National University: Australian Manufacturing Workers' Union, N628 Box 111, 'Watties Briefing Paper', 2–3.

65. 'Heinz Job Cuts Sound A Warning', *The Age*, 2 April 1993, 13.

66. Cathy Bolt, 'Heinz and ACTU in Watershed Pact to Secure Future', *Australian Financial Review*, 27 April 1993, 7.

67. Ibid.

68. Damien Carrick, 'Dandenong Crushed by Heinz Factory Closure', accessed 1 February 2017, http://www.abc.net.au/worldtoday/stories/s153786.htm; Narelle Hooper, 'Heinz Watties Defends Its Closure', accessed 1 February 2017, http://www.abc.net.au/worldtoday/stories/s153797.htm.

69. For specific examples, see Heino, 'Capitalism, Regulation Theory and Australian Labour Law', 269.

CHAPTER 9

1. Iain Campbell and Jenny Chalmers, 'Job Quality and Part-Time Work in the Retail Industry: An Australian Case Study', *International Journal of Human Resource Management* 19(3) (2008): 488.

2. 'IR pace-setters', in the words of Justine Evesson et al., "Lowering the standards": From Awards to *Work Choices* in Retail and Hospitality Collective Agreements' (Synthesis Report, Workplace Research Centre, 2007), 49.

3. I say 'in a sense' due to the fact that it has certainly not assumed the economic role of the metals and broader manufacturing sectors during the period of antipodean Fordist functionality. Sectors such as retail and hospitality account for a higher proportion of total employment than their contribution to GDP. Moreover, unlike the positive feedback loop of lead sector manufacturing within antipodean Fordism, the pattern within liberal-productivism appears to be largely negative, with retail employers being at the forefront of poor pay, precarious positions and award stripping.

4. *Re Shop and Warehouse (Wholesale Retail Establishments) Award No. 32 of 1976*, in CCH, *Australian Industrial Law Review* 23(16) (12 August 1981): ¶377; *Shop, Distributive and Allied Employees' Association v. Woolworths (Alice Springs) Ltd*, in CCH, *Australian Industrial Law Review* 24(3) (10 February 1982): ¶53.

5. Beverley Kingston, *Basket, Bag and Trolley: A History of Shopping in Australia* (Melbourne: Oxford University Press, 1994), 111–15.

6. Saturday morning work did, in some circumstances, attract an allowance: *Re Shop Employees (State) Award*, in CCH, *Australian Industrial Law Review* 27(17) (5 September 1985): ¶314.

7. The requisite awards were varied in 1971 and 1972. See: *Shop Employees (State) Award*, in *Australian Industrial Law Review* 14(11) (20 May 1972): ¶194; *Re Shop Employees (State) Award* (5 September 1985), ¶314.

8. Dennis Mortimer, 'Trade Union and Management Strategy: A Case Study of Compulsory Unionism', *Employment Relations Record* 1(2) (2001): 86.

9. Ibid.

10. Nikola Balnave and Dennis Mortimer, 'Union Security in Retail: Legislative Intervention or Collective Agreement', *International Journal of Employment Studies* 13(1) (2005): 98–102.

11. *Voice* 5(1) (1973): 3.

12. Mortimer, 'Trade Union and Management Strategy', 81.

13. Michael Johnston, 'Industrial Notes', *Voice* 5(2) (1973): 8.

14. Brett Heino, 'Award Regulation and the New South Wales Retail Sector, 1971–1988: Crisis and Experimentation Amidst Changing Models of Development', *Labour History* 109 (2015): 81.

15. Michael Reid, 'Change at the Check-Out', *The Economist* 334(7904) (1995): 3–4.

16. Stuart Rosewarne, 'The Political Economy of Retailing into the Eighties – Part 2', *Journal of Australian Political Economy* 16 (1984): 86.

17. In the mid-1980s, some of the largest mergers seen in the Australian retail sector were taking place, namely the Coles/Myer and Woolworths/Safeway combinations. The market share of both Coles and Woolworths increased by more than 15% between 1975 and 1987: National Association of Retail Grocers of Australia, 'Submission to ACCC inquiry into the competitiveness of retail prices for standard groceries – Part B' (March 13, 2008), 6.

18. Stuart Rosewarne, 'The Political Economy of Retailing into the Eighties – Part 1', *Journal of Australian Political Economy* 15 (1983): 33–34. The existence of a similar transformation in other Fordist countries (albeit usually to a less extreme degree) demonstrates that the roots of these processes lay in the crisis of Fordism. See, for example, Alexandra Hughes, 'Forging New Cultures of Food Retailer-Manufacturer Relations?', in *Retailing, Consumption and Capital: Towards the New Retail Geography*, ed. Neil Wrigley and Michelle Lowe (Essex: Longman, 1996), 90–115.

19. Christopher Wright and John Lund, 'Supply Chain Rationalization: Retailer Dominance and Labour Flexibility in the Australian Food and Grocery Industry', *Work, Employment and Society* 17(1) (2003): 140.

20. Rosewarne, 'The Political Economy of Retailing into the Eighties – Part 1', 25.

21. *In Retail Shops (State) Award*, in CCH, *Australian Industrial Law Review* 22(18) (3 September 1980): ¶282; Brian O'Neill, 'A New Minimum Wage of $225', *Shop and Distributive Worker* (Summer 1981): 3.

22. For examples of strike action in NSW, see 'Wollongong Strike', *Voice* 7(4) (1975): 7; Damon Frith, 'Business as Usual as Workers Protest', *Australian Financial Review*, 10 November 1988, 6. Generally speaking, retail strikes were small

in number and usually drew in relatively few employees. See Australian Bureau of Statistics, *Labour Statistics 1975–1980* (6101.0).

23. *In re Shop Employees (State) Award (No. 2)* (July–September 1977, Pt 3) AR 555, 569.

24. Ibid., 568–70. Although Justice Macken does not phrase it in these terms, his implicit observation of the impact of self-service technology on the skill content of retail jobs is thoroughly consistent with the thesis of Taylorism in the tertiary sector advanced in chapter 4.

25. *In re Shop Employees (State) Interim Award* (July–September 1980, Pt 3) AR 555, 556.

26. *In re Shop Employees (State) Award (No. 2)*, 575–84.

27. *Slattery v. Kentucky Fried Chicken Pty Ltd*, in *Australian Industrial Law Review* 14(30) (10 November 1972): ¶628.

28. The RTA noted that only 10% of their membership supported de-regulated trading hours, the same 10% who supported Sunday trading, namely, large retailers: 'Shopping Hours Inquiry', *Retail Traders' News Bulletin* (March 1983): 3.

29. Michael Lyons, 'An Appealing Outcome? Industrial Arbitration and Extended Retail Trading Hours in New South Wales in the 1980s', *International Journal of Employment Studies* 13(1) (2005): 113.

30. A move supported by NSW Labor premier Neville Wran: 'Wran Supports Extended Hours', *Canberra Times*, 29 August 1983, 3.

31. 'Shop-Hours Proposals Accepted by Unions', *Canberra Times*, 22 October 1983, 8.

32. Industrial Agreement no. 7249, Matter No. 1529 of 1984 bound Coles, Grace Brothers, Target, Safeway, Woolworths and Jack Butler. Industrial Agreement no. 7258, Matter No. 1564 of 1984 bound Myer.

33. J. Taylor, 'Extended Shopping Hours Have Been Delayed Again', *Sydney Morning Herald*, 3 August 1984, 3.

34. As seen in chapter 5, the thirty-eight-hour week was at this time becoming commonplace throughout Australian workplaces, thanks to the pace-setting December 1981 consent award in the metal trades. Indeed, the RTA noted rather sheepishly in early 1984 that 'the retail industry is the last major employing industry maintaining a 40 hour week': '38 Hour Week', *Retail Traders' News Bulletin* (March–April 1984): 5.

35. Proportions clauses had a long history in NSW retail awards. For a detailed overview, see: *In re Shop Employees (State) Award (No. 2)*, 561–68.

36. New South Wales, *Parliamentary Debates*, Legislative Assembly, 1 October 1985, 7374 (Robert Debus).

37. *SDA, New South Wales v. Woolworths Ltd*, in CCH, *Australian Industrial Law Review* 26(18) (26 September 1984): ¶312.

38. Interview with NSW SDA Official (Sydney, Australia, 22 November 2013).

39. Lyons, 'An Appealing Outcome?', 114.

40. New South Wales, *Parliamentary Debates*, Legislative Assembly, 14 August 1984, 66 (Pat Hills). One of the key issues seems to have been the spread of penalty rates for Saturday work. The agreements with the six major retailers provided

for time-and-a-half rates for all Saturday work, a scheme unpalatable to other general stores. The split was solved through adopting a differential rate in the award, with Saturday morning work recompensed at time-and-a-quarter while Saturday afternoon attracted time-and-a-half: New South Wales, *Parliamentary Debates*, Legislative Assembly, 20 November 1985, 10101 (Pat Hills).

41. *Applications for variation of Shop Employees (State) Award*, in CCH, *Australian Industrial Law Review* 26(18) (26 September 1984): ¶314.

42. *In re Shop Employees (State) Award* (1984) AR 595, 586.

43. RTA, 'Submission of the Retail Traders' Association of NSW to the NSW Industrial Commission in respect to the Inquiry into Retail Trading Hours' (1983), 14.

44. 'RTA Action to Free Shop Award', *Retail Traders' News Bulletin* (March–April 1985): 3.

45. *Re Shop Employees (State) Award* (5 September 1985), ¶314.

46. Ibid. Various reasons were forwarded, including the need to protect the public interest in the amenity of Saturday afternoon shopping and the industrial interest in further employment opportunities free from undue cost burdens.

47. Ibid.

48. Ibid.

49. Ibid.

50. Ibid.

51. Ibid.

52. Indeed, the RTA stated that a necessary outcome of the case was heightened efficiency and flexibility: 'Shop Award Proceeding Smoothly', *Retail Traders' News Bulletin* (May–June 1985), 5.

53. Noel Butlin Archives Centre, Australian National University: Australian Retailers Association, Z441 Box 30, 'Submission to the Committee of Review into Australian Industrial Relations Law and Systems', 1982.

54. Ibid., 25. The document is extraordinary in the way it presages the system that was eventually to arise, a reality which in itself strengthens the claim that the retail industry operates as a new lead sector, particularly insofar as the wage-labour nexus that holds there has come to characterise the working arrangements and experiences of a great many Australian workers.

55. Ibid., 15–16.

56. Lyons, 'An Appealing Outcome?', 115.

57. E. Campbell, 'Unions to Fight Pay Cut Flow-On', *Sydney Morning Herald*, 19 August 1985, 2. Harking back to the previous chapter, the 1985 decision reiterates the fact that, despite the collectivist understandings inscribed in their administrative fabric, the arbitral tribunals were perfectly capable of delivering very pro-capital decisions.

58. *Re Shop Employees (State) Award* (1987) 15 Industrial Reports 26, 27.

59. Bob Jessop, *State Theory: Putting the Capitalist State in Its Place* (Cambridge: Polity Press, 1990), 261.

60. Tom Bramble, *Trade Unionism in Australia: A History from Flood to Ebb Tide* (Port Melbourne: Cambridge University Press, 2008), 55.

61. Influence oiled by substantial financial contributions to the ALP: New South Wales, *Parliamentary Debates*, Legislative Assembly, 20 November 1985, 10089–91 (Peter Collins).

62. See, respectively, New South Wales, *Parliamentary Debates*, Legislative Council, 26 November 1985, 10518 (P. F. Watkins); New South Wales, *Parliamentary Debates*, Legislative Assembly, 19 November 1985, 9843 (Pat Hills).

63. Watkins, *Parliamentary Debates*, 10515.

64. See, for example, 'Removal of Appeal Rights', *Retail Traders' News Bulletin* (June 1986): 1; Collins, *Parliamentary Debates*, 10089–91; New South Wales, *Parliamentary Debates*, Legislative Council, 20 November 1985, 10536–37 (Elisabeth Kirkby).

65. *Shops (Premium Rates of Pay) Regulation 1985* (NSW).

66. Helen Grant, '"Conned" Retailers Seek Redress Over Weekend Wage Bill', *Australian Financial Review*, 22 April 1986, 36.

67. Helen Grant, 'SDA Appeals to Wran as Big Five Stand Firm', *Australian Financial Review*, 23 April 1986, 37.

68. *Re Shop Employees' (Major General Shops) (State) Award* (1988) 17 Industrial Reports 155.

69. Brad Norington and Keith Martin, 'Shops Face New Threat as Stocks Run Out', *Sydney Morning Herald*, 13 November 1986, 3.

70. A direct appeal from the Tribunal to the Commission was ruled out by the *Industrial Arbitration (Further Amendment) Act 1986* (NSW). In particular, this inserted a privative clause which provided that 'no appeal lies to the commission from any order, award, ruling or decision of the Tribunal'. The peculiarity of this legislation, abolishing the right of appeal for a specific industry, goes someway to demonstrating the influence of the SDA on the Labor Government.

71. The absent assessor was ironically the employer's nominee, the aforementioned Mr Lawrence. Even more ironically, Lyons notes that Lawrence 'made no objection at the time to his absence, as this had been a common practice with the Tribunal's proceedings since 1984': Lyons, 'An Appealing Outcome?', 117.

72. *G J Coles & Co Ltd v. Retail Trade Industrial Tribunal* (1986) 7 NSWLR 503.

73. *Re Shop Employees' (Major General Shops) (State) Award*, 155.

74. Ibid., 157.

75. 'Monthly Update', *Retail Trader' News Bulletin* (June 1986): 1.

76. Leon Trotsky, *The History of the Russian Revolution* (New York: Monad Press, 1980), 95, 100.

77. *Shop Employees (State) Award*, in CCH, *Australian Industrial Law Review* 30(12) (16 June 1988): ¶232.

78. Ibid.

79. Ibid.

80. Ibid.

81. Ibid.

82. Ibid.

83. Ibid.

84. 'Success for R.T.A', *Retail Traders' News Bulletin* (Special Edition, 1988): 1.

85. New South Wales, *Parliamentary Debates*, Legislative Assembly, 13 October 1988, 2270 (John Fahey).

86. Ibid.

87. New South Wales, *Parliamentary Debates*, Legislative Council, 7 December 1988, 4508 (A. B. Manson).

88. 'Industrial Commission Increases Wages', *Retail Traders' News Bulletin* (Special Edition, 1988): 1.

89. *Shop Employees (State) Award* (1991) 266 NSW Industrial Gazette 612.

90. Ibid., 613.

91. 'Landmark Agreement Structural Efficiency', *Retail Traders' News Bulletin* (September 1990): 1–2.

92. *Shop Employees (State) Award* (1991) 265 NSW Industrial Gazette 844, 845.

93. 'Landmark Agreement Structural Efficiency', 2.

94. *Shop Employees (State) Award* (1991) 266 NSW Industrial Gazette 612, 613–14.

95. For the generally ambivalent attitudes of the SDA towards technological change, particularly since the 1990s, see Brett Heino, 'Capitalism, Regulation Theory and Australian Labour Law: Exploring the Labour Law Regimes of Antipodean Fordism and Liberal-Productivism, 1964–2009' (PhD diss., University of Wollongong, 2016), 298.

96. Scott Fitzgerald, Al Rainnie and John Burgess, 'Rediscovering Braverman? Political Economy, Skill, and Skill Shortages', *Australian Bulletin of Labour* 39(1) (2013): 11.

97. See, for example, Russell D. Lansbury, 'New Technology and Industrial Relations in the Retail Grocery Industry', *Journal of Industrial Relations* 22(3) (1980): 275–92; John Lund and Christopher Wright, 'State Regulation and the New Taylorism: The Case of Australian Grocery Warehousing', *Relations Industrielles* 56(4) (2001): 747–69; Wright and Lund, 'Supply Chain Rationalization', 137–57; Robin Price, 'Down the Aisle: The Effects of Technological Change on Retail Workers Skills' (paper presented at the 27th International Labour Process Conference, Edinburgh, UK, 6–8 April 2009).

98. Price, 'Down the Aisle', 8–9.

99. Campbell and Chalmers, 'Job Quality and Part-Time Work in the Retail Industry', 492.

100. Joseph Catanzariti and Shawn Wytenburg, 'Industrial Relations Legislation in 1991', *Journal of Industrial Relations* 34(1) (1992): 135–41.

101. However, once the federal scheme of bargaining was on foot, enterprise agreements were increasingly located there: Joe de Bruyn, 'SDA on a Winner', *Shop and Distributive Worker* (Winter 1994): 1.

102. Robin Price, Janis Bailey and Amanda Pyman, 'Varieties of Collaboration: The Case of an Australian Retail Union', *International Journal of Human Resource Management* 25(6) (2014): 753–54.

103. See, for example, Greg Donnelly, 'Another Pay Rise At Coles', *Shop and Distributive Worker* (Winter 1993): 6.

104. Enterprise agreements sometimes took the form of company-specific awards, particularly in the early years of enterprise bargaining.

105. For specific examples, see Heino, 'Capitalism, Regulation Theory and Australian Labour Law', 301–2.

106. Alan Treadgold, 'Food Retailing in Australia – Three Retailers, Three Strategies', *International Journal of Retail & Distribution Management* 24(8) (1996): 6.

107. Greg Donnelly, 'SDA Wins $93.30 at Coles/Bi-Lo Supermarkets', *Shop and Distributive Worker* (Autumn 1997): 5.

108. Ibid., 6.

109. Ibid., 7.

110. Ibid., 6.

111. Ibid.

112. Ibid., 7.

113. Greg Donnelly, 'SDA Wins New Big W Agreement', *SDA News* (Summer 1997): 3.

114. Ibid., 5–6.

115. Ibid., 6.

116. Greg Donnelly, 'SDA Wins 10.12% at Big W', *SDA News* (Summer 2000): 2.

117. Ibid.

118. Ibid.

119. Ibid.

120. *Industrial Relations Act 1991* (NSW), s 82.

121. New South Wales, *Parliamentary Debates*, Legislative Assembly, 28 August 1991, 724 (John Fahey).

122. Ibid., 725.

123. New South Wales, *Parliamentary Debates*, Legislative Assembly, 10 September 1991, 940 (David Bowman).

124. Joe de Bruyn, 'Part-Time Contracts Winning the Fight', *Shop and Distributive Worker* (Summer 1992): 6.

125. Joe de Bruyn, 'Don't Be Fooled! Say NO! to Part-Time Contracts', *Shop and Distributive Worker* (Spring 1992): 6.

126. The decision to consider retail and hospitality together stemmed from the fact both were formerly heavily award dependent and share very similar employment structures: Evesson et al., 'Lowering the Standards', 15.

127. Ibid., v.

128. Ibid., 33.

129. Although normal full-time working hours remained thirty-eight hours a week, these could now be averaged over fifty-two weeks. Employees could thus conceivably work any number of hours per week, provided the average over the year was thirty-eight.

130. Evesson et al., 'Lowering the Standards', 34.

131. Ibid., 35.

132. Ibid., viii, 38.

133. Ibid., 42.

134. Ibid., 40.

135. Ibid., 39–40, 42.

136. Ibid., 36. The exception was clauses related to Saturday penalties; only a quarter of union agreements were able to retain a loading.

137. Ibid., 42.

138. Price, Bailey and Pyman, 'Varieties of Collaboration', 754.

139. Indeed, the SDA proved more than willing to trade conditions in exchange for coverage. In several cases, the enterprise bargains reached failed to meet the

No-Disadvantage or the later Better-Off-Overall Tests, and were struck down by the Australian Industrial Relations Commission/Fair Work Australia. See, for example, Marcus Priest, 'It's Not All Right, Jack', *Australian Financial Review*, 12 March 2003, 7; Ben Schneiders, Nick Toscano and Royce Millar, 'Sold Out: Quarter of a Million Workers Underpaid in Union Deals', *Sydney Morning Herald*, accessed 8 February 2017, http://www.smh.com.au/business/workplace-relations/sold-out-quarter-of-a-million-workers-underpaid-in-union-deals-20160830-gr4f68.html.

140. Australian Bureau of Statistics, *Employee Earnings, Benefits and Trade Union Membership* (6310.0, 2006), 38–39.

141. For concrete cases, see Heino, 'Capitalism, Regulation Theory and Australian Labour Law', 311.

142. 'Andrews Urges Retailers to Take on AWAs', *Workplace Info*, accessed 8 February 2017, https://workplaceinfo.com.au/awards/agreements/news/andrews-urges-retailers-to-take-on-awas#.VEjj1PmUd8E.

143. 'Retailers Lead on AWA Implementation', *Foodweek*, 1 June 2007. Factiva (FOOWEE0020070601e3610000a).

144. Australian Bureau of Statistics, *Employee Earnings and Hours* (6306.0, 2000), 46; Australian Bureau of Statistics, *Employee Earnings and Hours* (6306.0, 2006), 28.

145. Sid Marris, 'No Rush to AWAs', *The Australian*, 1 May 2008, 2.

146. John Burgess, Anne Sullivan and Glenda Strachan, 'Australian Workplace Agreements, EEO and Family Friendly Arrangements in the Retail Sector', *Employment Relations Record* 4(2) (2004): 66.

147. Paul Bibby, 'Casuals Face Two-Hour Shifts', *Sydney Morning Herald*, 7 May 2010, 10.

148. 'Retailers Association slams Fair Work for upholding minimum three hour shift requirement', *SmartCompany*, 12 July 2010. Factiva (SMACOM0020100712e67c00006).

149. *National Retail Association* [2011] FWA 3777, accessed 7 February, 2017, https://www.fwc.gov.au/documents/decisionssigned/html/2011fwa3777.htm.

150. Ibid.

151. Alain Lipietz, *Mirages and Miracles: The Crisis of Global Fordism*, trans. David Macey (London: Verso, 1987), 15.

152. Evesson et al., 'Lowering the Standards', 49.

CHAPTER 10

1. Otto Kahn-Freund, introduction to *The Institutions of Private Law and Their Social Functions*, by Karl Renner (London: Routledge & Kegan Paul, 1949), 43.

2. Gerry Treuren, 'State Theory and the Origins of Federal Arbitration Legislation in Australia', *Policy, Organisation and Society* 13 (1997): 60–61.

3. See, for example, Christopher Lloyd, 'Australian Capitalism Since 1992: A New Regime of Accumulation?', *Journal of Australian Political Economy* 61 (2008): 30–55; Lynne Chester, 'The Australian Variant of Neoliberal Capitalism', in *Neoliberalism: Beyond the Free Market*, ed. Damien Cahill, Lindy Edwards and Frank Stilwell (Cheltenham: Edward Elgar, 2012), 153–79; Ray Broomhill,

'Australian Economic Booms in Historical Perspective', *Journal of Australian Political Economy* 61 (2008): 12–29; Gerrit Treuren, 'Regulation Theory and Australian Theorising of Institutional Change in Industrial Regulation' (paper presented at the 11th Conference of the Association of Industrial Relations Academics of Australia and New Zealand, Brisbane, Australia, 20 January–1 February 1997).

4. Toby S. James, 'Whatever Happened to Régulation Theory? The Régulation Approach and Local Government Revisited', *Policy Studies* 30(2) (2009): 183–84.

5. See, for example: Matt Vidal, 'Reworking Postfordism: Labor Process Versus Employment Relations', *Sociology Compass* 5(4) (2011): 273–86; Matt Vidal, 'Postfordism as a Dysfunctional Accumulation Regime: A Comparative Analysis of the USA, the UK and Germany', *Work, Employment and Society* 27(3) (2013): 451–71; David Neilson and Thomas H. Stubbs, 'Competition States in the Neoliberal Era: Towards Third-Generation Regulation Theory', *Competition & Change* 20(2) (2016): 122–44; Brett Christophers, *The Great Leveler: Capitalism and Competition in the Court of Law* (Cambridge: Harvard University Press, 2016).

6. For another very significant contribution to this process of legal deepening within the PRA, see Christophers, *The Great Leveler*.

7. For a useful compendium of such work, see Christopher Arup et al., *Labour Law and Labour Market Regulation* (Sydney: Federation Press, 2006).

8. Harry C. Katz, 'The Decentralization of Collective Bargaining: A Literature Review and Comparative Analysis', *Industrial and Labor Relations Review* 47(1) (1993): 4–5.

9. Mark Rolfe, 'Antipodean Fordism: Postwar Americanisation Down Under', in *Henry Ford: Critical Evaluations in Business and Management Volume 2*, ed. John Wood and Michael Wood (London & New York: Routledge, 2003), 323–53.

10. Michael Barry and Nick Wailes, 'Revisiting the Australia-New Zealand Comparison', *New Zealand Journal of Employment Relations* 30(3) (2005): 4.

11. See, for example, Jamie Peck, *Work-Place: The Social Regulation of Labour Markets* (New York: The Guilford Press, 1996), 119–52, 185–231; Andy Danford, 'The "New Industrial Relations" and Class Struggle in the 1990s', *Capital & Class* 21(1) (1997): 107–41; Arne L. Kalleberg, *Good Jobs, Bad Jobs: The Rise of Polarized and Precarious Employment Systems in the United States, 1970s to 2000s* (New York: Russell Sage Foundation, 2011); John Krinsky, 'Neoliberal Times: Intersecting Temporalities and the Neoliberalization of New York City's Public-Sector Labor Relations', *Social Science History* 35(3) (2011): 381–422; Kris Warner, 'The Decline of Unionization in the United States: Some Lessons from Canada', *Labor Studies Journal* 38(2) (2013): 110–38; John Buchanan et al., 'Unsustainable Employment Portfolios', *Work, Employment and Society* 27(3) (2013): 396–413.

12. Hugh Collins, 'Regulating the Employment Relation for Competitiveness', *Industrial Law Journal* 30(1) (2001): 17.

13. See, for example, Brett Heino, 'The State, Class and Occupational Health and Safety: Locating the Capitalist State's Role in the Regulation of OHS in NSW', *Labour & Industry* 23(2) (2013): 150–67.

14. Karl Marx, 'Theses on Feuerbach', in *The German Ideology*, ed. Karl Marx and Friedrich Engels (New York: International Publishers, 1970), 123.

15. Doug Cameron quoted in Stephen Long, 'The New Australian Militancy', *Australian Financial Review*, 18 March 2000, 22.

16. David Peetz, *Brave New Work Place: How Individual Contracts Are Changing Our Jobs* (Crows Nest: Allen & Unwin, 2006), 161–62.

17. The best example of this globally is the explosion of minimum wage campaigns in the United States, where activist unions like the Service Employees International Union have managed to create broader community coalitions to spearhead legislative change.

18. As the Victorian branch of the Electrical Trades Union voted to do in 2010.

19. Guy Standing, *The Precariat: The New Dangerous Class* (London & New York: Bloomsbury, 2014).

Index

About the Author

Brett Heino is a Lecturer in the School of Law at the University of Wollongong. He has published research articles in *Capital & Class*, *Labour History*, *Journal of Australian Political Economy*, *Labour & Industry* and *Social Alternatives*. His research interests include the political economy of law (with a focus on labour law), the structure of post–World War II Australian capitalism and regulation theory.

www.ingramcontent.com/pod-product-compliance
Lightning Source LLC
LaVergne TN
LVHW101445200926
848483LV00001B/53
* 9 7 8 1 7 8 6 6 0 3 5 5 5 *